D0916486

DEACONESSES

An Historical Study

Aimé Georges Martimort

DEACONESSES
An Historical Study

Translated by K. D. Whitehead

Ignatius Press   San Francisco

Title of the French original
Les Diaconesses: Essai historique
© 1982 C.L.V. Edizioni Liturgiche, Rome

Cover by Darlene Lawless

© 1986 Ignatius Press, San Francisco
All rights reserved
ISBN 0–89870–114–7
Library of Congress catalogue number 86–81423
Printed in the United States of America

Contents

PART TWO

Deaconesses in the Latin Church

Centuries); Deaconesses-Abbesses in Rome and Elsewhere (Tenth Century); The Silence of the Carolingian Legislation; The Pontifical of Saint Alban of Mainz (950) and its Utilization in Rome

Introduction

Since the seventeenth century the history of deaconesses in the Church has been the subject of numerous monographs. There are two modern works, however, that outclass everything written before them. The first of these is Adolf Kalsbach's *Die Altkirchliche Einrichtung der Diakonisse bis zu ihrem Erlöschen*, published in 1926.[1] In 1957 the author provided a very complete summary of this work in the dictionary *Reallexikon für Antike und Christentum* under the entry *"Diakonisse"*.[2] The second of these works is that of Roger Gryson, *Le Ministère des femmes dans l'Eglise ancienne*, which came out in 1972.[3] The introduction to each of these works provides a complete bibliography of earlier works on the subject.

Given the existence of these two excellent works, is there room for yet another study? It seems to me that there is, in part because the caution wisely recommended by Roger Gryson has not always been observed of late. He wrote that "the conscientious historian, who is accustomed not to affirm anything except on the basis of careful and sustained research, is surely obliged to question the naïve assurance of those for whom everything is simple and clear at first glance."[4] What is most evident about the history of deaconesses, however, is the complexity of the whole subject. Even the Latin and Greek names, *diacona* and διακόνισσα, designated institutions that, in the history of the Church, were very different depending upon the era as well as upon the region concerned. The great scholar Du Cange was already well aware of this fact as early as the seventeenth century.[5]

Another reason for an additional study, I believe, is the amount of light that can be thrown on the subject by looking at the liturgical formulas of both East and West, and also by extending the inquiry into the Middle Ages and even beyond by studying the documents of theology and canon law of the period. We cannot, of course, do more than sample the latter,

---

[1] *Römische Quartalschrift*, 22 Supplementheft (Freiburg: Herder, 1926).

[2] Vol. 3 (Stuttgart: Hiersemann, 1957), col. 917–28.

[3] Gembloux, Duculot, *Recherches et synthèses*, Section d'histoire, IV (1972).

[4] Op. cit., p. 17.

[5] C. du Fresne du Cange, *In . . . Annae Comnenae Alexiadem . . . notae*, in the edition of Ioannes Cinnami, *Historiarum libri sex* (Parisiis: ex typ. Regia, 1670), pp. 416–21, Διακονισσῶν. And, by the same author, *Glossarium ad scriptores mediae et infimae Graecitatis*, Lugduni, Annisson, etc., 1688, Διακόνισσα; *Glossarium ad scriptores mediae et infimae Latinitatis* (Lutetiae Parisiorum, L. Billaine, 1678), *Diacona, Diaconissa*.

since many of the applicable documents remain unpublished. Nevertheless, we must corroborate—or correct—the testimony provided by purely liturgical books by looking also at other documentary sources. As is well known, liturgical books were often copied from earlier liturgical models, and they frequently preserved rites that had long since fallen into disuse. Thus it was that the Roman Pontifical of 1888 continued to include medieval *ordines* which had not been used for centuries: for example, the rite for the degradation of clerics. A similarly careful study must be made of compilations and collections of canon law, which often include texts from many sources and are of uneven value and sometimes uncertain authenticity.

Two methodical principles are required today for the type of inquiry I propose to conduct. First, in writing the history of any ecclesiastical institution, one must respect the particular geographical localities where the inscriptions and documents attesting to the existence of that ecclesiastical institution were produced. The churches of antiquity, like those of the Middle Ages, permitted and preserved great diversity in their ecclesiastical discipline, and there were numerous reciprocal influences at work. We must therefore examine a whole series of monographs relating to particular localities before ever venturing to construct a synthesis—if indeed it is possible to construct such a synthesis even then.

Second, regarding the specific question of deaconesses, it is not enough that texts are available that attest to their existence. We must also attempt in each instance to understand who and what these deaconesses and their functions were, for the historical reality about them was constantly shifting and unstable: sometimes they were recruited from the ranks of widows, other times from the ranks of virgins. Often ecclesiastical legislation about them was conflicting or confused, as have been also both ancient and modern authors. Typically, they have simply been assimilated into the deaconesses mentioned in the Pastoral Epistles. One of the merits of the work of Roger Gryson is that it tries so patiently to unravel the tangled skein of evidence for the period of the early Church.[6]

Having presented in as complete and objective a fashion as possible the history of deaconesses in their various concrete manifestations in history, I think it necessary to confront, at least in a modest way, the theological

---

[6] Roger Gryson provides a very complete modern bibliography on the subject of deaconesses, op. cit., pp. 197–200. To his bibliography must be added only a few articles that have appeared since 1972: C. Vagaggini, *L'ordinazione delle diaconesse nella tradizione greca e bizantina*, OCP 40 (1974): 146–89; G. Ferrari, *Le diaconesse nella tradizione orientale*, in *Oriente cristiano* (Palermo) 14 (1974): 28–50; Ph. Delhaye, *Rétrospective et prospective des ministères féminins dans l'Eglise*, in *Revue théologique de Louvain* 3 (1972): 55–75. Cf. also Chapter 3, n. 66 below.

controversies that the institution of deaconesses in the Church has inspired in our own day. I will content myself with the reflections suggested to me by this inquiry, which extended over several years, and also, especially, with those reflections suggested to me by the history of the liturgy in general.

Rome, September 28, 1980

Abbreviations of the Works and Collections Consulted

AASS = *Acta sanctorum quotquot toto orbe coluntur* . . . Antuerpiae, apud Ioannem Meursium (now: Brussels, Society of Bollandists), from 1643.

Andrieu OR = M. Andrieu, *Les Ordines Romani du haut moyen âge*, Louvain, 1931–61. 5 vols. (*Spicilegium sacrum Lovaniense* . . . 11, 23, 24, 28, 29). Vol. of tables in preparation.

Andrieu PR = M. Andrieu, *Le Pontifical romain au moyen âge*, Vatican City, Biblioteca Apostolica Vaticana, 1938–41. (*Studi e testi*, 86, 87, 88, 99). 4 vols.

BAC = *Biblioteca de autores cristianos*, Madrid, from 1944.

Baumstark, *Geschichte der syrischen Literatur* = A. Baumstark, *Geschichte der syrischen Literatur, mit Ausschluss der christlich-palästinensichen Texte*, Bonn, Marcus and Weber, 1922 (reprinted Berlin, 1968).

CCL = *Corpus christianorum, Series Latina*, Turnhout, Brepols, from 1954.

CCLCM = *Corpus christianorum, Continuatio mediaevalis*, Turnhout, Brepols, from 1971.

CCOF = S. Congregatio pro Ecclesia Orientali, *Codificazione canonica orientale, Fonti*, Tipografia Poliglotta Vaticana, from 1930.

CSCO = *Corpus scriptorum christianorum orientalium*, curantibus I. B. Chabot, I. Guidi, H. Hyvernat, B. Carra de Vaux (now: editum consilio Universitatis catholicae Americae et Universitatis catholicae Lovaniensis), Parisiis, e typographia Regia, etc. (now: Louvain, Secrétariat du Corpus SCO), from 1904.

CSEL = *Corpus scriptorum ecclesiasticorum Latinorum*, editum consiliis et impensis Academiae litterarum Caesareae Vindobonensis, Vindobonae, C. Gerold (now: Hoelder-Pichler-Tempsky), from 1866.

Denzinger = H. Denzinger, *Ritus orientalium, Coptorum, Syrorum et Armenorum in administrandis sacramentis*, Wirceburgi, Stahel, 1863–64 (reprinted).

DTC = *Dictionnaire de théologie catholique* . . . begun under the editorship of A. Vacant . . . , continued under that of E. Mangenot . . . , Paris, Letouzey (and Ané), 1908–72, 15 vols. and 3 vols. of tables.

EL = *Ephemerides liturgicae, Commentarium de re liturgica*, Roma, Edizioni liturgiche, from 1887.

GCS = *Die griechischen christlichen Schriftsteller der ersten drei Jahrhunderten*, Leipzig, Hinrichs (now: Berlin, Akademie Verlag), from 1897.

Gryson, *Ministère des femmes* = R. Gryson, *Le Ministère des femmes dans l'Eglise ancienne*, Gembloux, Duculot, 1972 (*Recherches et synthèses*, Section d'histoire, 4).

Joannou = P. P. Joannou, *Discipline générale antique* (IIᵉ–Xᵉ siècle). Grottaferrata, Tip. S. Nilo, 1962–64 (CCOF 9). 4 vols.

JTS = *The Journal of Theological Studies*, London-Oxford, from 1900.

Kalsbach, *Altkirchliche Enrichtung* = A. Kalsbach, *Die Altkirchliche Einrichtung der Diakonissen bis zu ihrem Erlöschen*, Freiburg, B. Herder, 1926 (*Römische Quartalschrift*, 22 Supplementheft).

Kalsbach, *Diakonisse* = A. Kalsbach, *Diakonisse*, in *Reallexikon für Antike und Christentum*, vol. 3, Stuttgart, Heirsemann, 1957, 917–28.

Leroquais, *Pontificaux* = V. Leroquais, *Les pontificaux manuscrits des bibliothèques publiques de France*, Mâcon, Protat, 1937, 4 vols.

LQF = *Liturgiegeschichtliche* (later: *Liturgiewissenschaftliche*) *Quellen und Forschungen* . . . Münster, W. Aschendorff, from 1918.

MAMA = *Monumenta Asiae Minoris antiqua*, Manchester University Press, 1928–62 (*Publications of the American Society for Archeological Research in Asia Minor*). 8 vols.

Mansi = I. D. Mansi, *Sacrorum Conciliorum nova et amplissima collectio* . . . Florentiae, A. Zatta, 1759–98, 31 vols. *Continuata* . . . curantibus Ioanne Baptista Martin et Ludovico Petit, Parisiis (etc.), H. Welter, 1900–1927, vols. 32–53.

OC = *Oriens christianus* . . . from 1901.

OCA = *Orientalia christiana analecta* . . . Roma, P. Institutum orientalium studiorum, from 1923.

OCP = *Orientalia christiana periodica, Commentarii de re orientali* . . . , Roma, P. Institutum orientalium studiorum, from 1935.

OS = *L'Orient syrien, Revue trimestrielle d'études et de recherches sur les Eglises de langue syriaque*, Paris, 1956–67. 12 vols.

PG = J. P. Migne, *Patrologiae cursus completus* . . . , *Series graeca* . . . , Lutetia Parisiorum, apud J. P. Migne, 1857–86. 161 bks. in 165 vols.

PL = J. P. Migne, *Patrologiae cursus completus* . . . , *Series latina* . . . , Lutetia, Parisiorum, apud J. P. Migne, 1844–64. 221 vols.

PO = *Patrologia orientalis* (ed. R. Graffin, F. Nau, then F. Graffin), Paris, Firmin-Didot, from 1907.

RAC = *Reallexikon für Antike und Christentum* . . . , Stuttgart, Hiersemann, from 1950.

RechSR = *Recherches de science religieuse*, Paris, from 1910.

REDF = *Rerum ecclesiasticarum documenta, cura P. Athenaei Sancti Anselmi de Urbe edita* . . . , Series maior, Fontes, Roma, Herder, from 1956.

RevBén = *Revue bénédictine*, Abbaye de Maredsous, from 1884.

RevSR = *Revue des sciences religieuses*, published under the direction of the professors of the Faculty of Catholic Theology of the University of Strasbourg, from 1921.

RHE = *Revue d'histoire ecclésiastique*, Louvain, from 1900.

SC = *Sources chrétiennes*, founders-directors, H. de Lubac and J. Daniélou; director C. Mondésert, Paris, Editions du Cerf, from 1943.

ST = *Studi e testi*, Roma, Tipografia Vaticana (later: Vatican City, Biblioteca Apostolica Vaticana), from 1900.

TS = *Texts and Studies, Contributions to Biblical and Patristic Literature*, edited by J. A. Robinson, Cambridge University Press, from 1891.

TU = *Texte und Untersuchungen zur Geschichte der altchristlichen Literatur* . . . , Leipzig, Hinrich, 1883–1941; from vol. 56 on; Berlin, Akademie Verlag, from 1951.

CHAPTER ONE

Were There Deaconesses in
The Church of the First Two Centuries?

A considerable number of exegetes and historians have attempted to supply an answer to this question, whether by citing texts from the New Testament or by scrutinizing authors of the second and early part of the third centuries. The sheer number of commentaries that these documents have inspired, however, demonstrates conclusively that their proper interpretation is anything but simple; in no way can simple recourse to citations from them settle a controversy that was already being heatedly debated among the Fathers of the Church.

1. THE NEW TESTAMENT TEXTS

Let us pass over Luke 8:2–3, a passage in which the Evangelist, describing the group accompanying Jesus on his itinerant ministry, indicates that several women were present along with the Twelve: Mary Magdalen, Joanna, the wife of Chuza, Susanna and "many others", who "provided [διηκόνουν] for them out of their means". Luke must have wanted to include this detail in order to emphasize the role that women would play in the work of the Kingdom, no matter how unusual the inclusion of women in this fashion might have appeared to the Palestinian mentality of the time. But can we suppose that Luke was thinking of deaconesses as such?[1] That hypothesis must surely appear to be gratuitous.[2]

[1] H. Conzelmann, *Die Mitte der Zeit* (Tübingen, 1960), no. 41, n. 1; E. E. Ellis, *The Gospel of Luke*, *The Century Bible* (London: Nelson, 1960), p. 127. Cf. the parallel text Mt 27:55–56 (διακονοῦσαι), which is used in the *Didascalia*, Chapter 2 below.

[2] A. George, *Le Ministère et les Ministères selon le Nouveau Testament*, *Parole de Dieu* (Paris: Le Seuil, 1974), p. 238, n. 83.

A. The Case of Phoebe (Rom 16:1–2)

As is well known, there are critical problems surrounding this passage
from Romans 16.[3] In it St. Paul commends to the Romans "our sister
Phoebe, a deaconess of the church at Cenchreae" (Φοίβην τὴν ἀδελφὴν
ἡμῶν, οὖσαν διάκονον τῆς ἐκκλησίας τῆς ἐν Κεγχρεαῖς). According to St.
Paul, Phoebe deserved to be received and assisted "for she has been a
helper of many and of myself as well" (καὶ γὰρ αὐτὴ προστάτις πολλῶν
ἐγενήθη καὶ ἐμοῦ αὐτοῦ). How must we understand the expression that
appears here: οὖσαν διάκονον τῆς ἐκκλησίας τῆς ἐν Κεγχρεαῖς (a deaconess of
the church at Cenchreae)? The adjective διάκονος, which did not have a
feminine ending, appears frequently in the New Testament.[4] There are at
least two instances of this where the word must be understood in a
technical, hierarchical sense. The first of these is found in the salutation of
the Epistle to the Philippians (1:1): "To all the saints in Christ Jesus who
are at Philippi, with the bishops and deacons" (πᾶσιν τοῖς ἁγίοις ἐν Χριστῷ
Ἰησοῦ τοῖς οὖσιν ἐν Φιλίπποις σὺν ἐπισκόποις καὶ διακόνοις). The second
instance is found in the First Epistle to Timothy (3:8, 12). In both of these
cases the technical, hierarchical sense of the term is justified by the
parallelism of its appearance with the word ἐπίσκοποι. Latin versions of
these passages, grasping the parallelism, preserve the Latinized Greek
word *diaconi*, as they do also in the case of the Latinized Greek word
episcopi. In other New Testament passages where the term *diakonos* is
encountered, it has often been translated as "minister" or an equivalent
word because it was not perceived in a technical, hierarchical sense. In fact,
the verb διακονεῖν, which appears often in the Gospels, usually refers to
the activity of a servant, especially at table; it also signifies more generally
an attitude of being available to serve, and even a spiritual orientation (Jn
12:26). In apostolic times, the word was employed to describe every type
of service to the community. The same was true of *diakonos*. St. Paul
employs the word often but qualifies it in various ways; he speaks of a
diakonos, or servant, of God, of Christ, of the gospel, of the new Covenant,
of justice—but also of Satan, of sin and of the circumcision. The Prince
himself is a servant of God for the good. All of these Pauline senses of the
word certainly go beyond the simple profane notion of "servant"; they

---

[3] J. Cambier, in *Introduction à la Bible, éd. nouvelle, Nouveau Testament, Les Lettres
apostoliques* (Tournai: Desclée, 1977), 3: 138–39, lays out the arguments presented by various
exegetes for the continued inclusion of Rom 16:1–20 in Romans, and those presented by
others for moving this passage to Ephesians—in any case, it is the work of Paul himself. We
may leave this controversy aside for our purposes in the present study. Cf. A. Wikenhauser
and J. Schmid, *Einleitung in das Neue Testament* (Freiburg: Herder, 1973), pp. 460–61.

[4] H. W. Beyer, in *Theologisches Wörterbuch des Neuen Testaments* (1935), 2:81–93; C.
Spicq, *Saint Paul, Les Epîtres pastorales*, 4th ed., *Etudes bibliques* (Paris: Gabalda, 1969), 1:74.

suggest in each case some sort of mission, some sort of effective action that transcends the person who is acting. None of these correspond to the diaconate as such, however.

For Phoebe also the word *diakonos* is qualified: she is "διάκονος of the church at Cenchreae". One is tempted to understand this usage in the same way as Colossians 1:25, where Paul speaks of "the Church . . . of which I became a minister" (τῆς ἐκκλησίας . . . ἧς ἐγενόμην ἐγὼ διάκονος). Nevertheless, there is a difference here in spite of appearances, because Paul is not tied to any particular church; his service, like that of Apollos (1 Cor 3:5), is primarily a missionary service. In the case of Phoebe, the ancient Latin versions of the Scriptures, with the exception of the version utilized by Ambrosiaster, unanimously translated this passage as "*quae est in ministerio*".[5] In the version employed by Ambrosiaster, however, we read *ministra*.[6]

There seems to have been a certain evolution in interpretation as far as modern exegesis is concerned. Fr. Lagrange, for example, did not even raise the issue and simply translated "Phoebe, a deaconess of the church at Cenchreae".[7] He was followed in this in 1953 by S. Lyonnet, in 1956 by the *Jerusalem Bible* and in 1975 by the French Ecumenical Translation of the Bible. Nevertheless, this last work, in the notes to its complete edition, recognizes that the title of deaconess is "unknown to the New Testament" and that other exegetes have translated the word as she "who serves the church at Cenchreae".[8] More and more, scholars are emphasizing that there is an anachronism involved in giving this word a precise meaning corresponding to an ecclesiastical institution[9] to which the first

---

[5] While waiting to have available the *Vetus latina* version of Beuron on this passage, I consulted P. Sabatier, *Bibliorum sacrorum latinae versiones antiquae* . . . (Parisiis: F. Didot, 1751) 3:651. I also consulted separate editions of several manuscripts.

[6] Ambrosiaster, *In Epistulam ad Romanos* 16:1, ed. H. I. Vogels, CSEL 81 (1966): 476–77. However, it is possible to argue that many of the old Latin versions hesitated to introduce the Latin neologism *diacona* because the Greek *diachonos* had no feminine form.

[7] M. J. Lagrange, *Saint Paul, Epître aux Romains, Etudes bibliques* (reprinted) (Paris: Gabalda, 1950), p. 362. In his commentary, however, Lagrange notes, pp. 362–63, that "it is the only instance where the New Testament speaks of a woman as exercising an office. . . . In the Vulgate the version '*quae est in ministerio*' vindicates those who understand the word '*diakonos*' in a broad sense."

[8] *Traduction oecuménique de la Bible, Nouveau Testament* (Paris: Le Cerf, 1973), p. 487.

[9] A. Kalsbach, *Altkirchliche Einrichtung*, p. 10; *Diakonisse*, in RAC, vol. 3 (1957), col. 917; J. G. Davies, "Deacons, Deaconesses and Minor Orders in the Patristic Period", in *Journal of Ecclesiastical History* 14 (1963): 1; A. Lemaire, *Les ministères aux origines de l'Eglise, Lectio divina* 68 (Paris: Le Cerf, 1971), p. 94; R. Gryson, *Ministère des femmes*, p. 22; P. Grelot, in *Le ministère et les ministères . . .* , p. 65; L. De Lorenzi, in *Paul de Tarse, apôtre de notre temps* (Rome: Saint Paul outside the Walls, 1979), p. 439. H. W. Beyer, op. cit., p. 93, says: "Whether it was supposed to express a characteristic of the services rendered to the

real references, as we shall see, date from much later—from some time after the year 200 A.D. Even more than that, it is possible to argue that what follows in the text provides the best clue to the nature of the service rendered by Phoebe. St. Paul specifies that for him, as for many others, she has been a helper, or protectress (προστάτις).[10] This term suggests activities pertaining to the established and accepted practices, recognized by all, of providing hospitality and assistance. This interpretation is especially plausible when we remember that Cenchreae was the port of Corinth facing east; it was there that the Christian brethren from Syria or Asia Minor would normally have debarked in Greece.[11]

B. The Prescriptions of 1 Tim 3:11

The desired qualities of bishops and deacons are described in 1 Timothy. A phrase referring to women is found in the passages that deal with deacons (1 Tim 3:8–13):

> Deacons likewise must be serious, not double-tongued, not addicted to much wine, not greedy for gain; they must hold the mystery of the faith with a clear conscience. And let them also be tested first; then if they prove themselves blameless let them serve as deacons. The women likewise must be serious, no slanderers, but temperate, faithful in all things [γυναῖκας ὡσαύτως σεμνάς μὴ διαβόλους, νηφαλίους, πιστὰς ἐν πᾶσιν].
>
> Let deacons be husbands of one wife, and let them manage their children and their households well, for those who serve well as deacons gain a good standing for themselves and also great confidence in the faith which is in Christ Jesus.[12]

Occurring as it does in the middle of a passage concerned with the desirable qualities of deacons, the sudden reference to "the women" has suggested to some commentators that we are here dealing with an interpolation.[13] If so, it must be a very early one, since no extant manuscript or version provides any variant to the text as we have it. Other critics have

community is uncertain." It is to be noted, however, that A. Lemaire is personally favorable to the hypothesis that there existed deaconesses in apostolic times . . . , p. 114.

[10] With good reason, the French Ecumenical Translation of the Bible comments that "this term, in the legal sense, designated someone who represented foreigners who did not possess juridical safeguards; but this meaning would have to be excluded where women were concerned" (n. r). Cf. M. J. Lagrange, op. cit., p. 363.

[11] A. Kalsbach, *Altkirchliche Einrichtung*, p. 10, quoting C. Weizsäcker, *Das apostolische Zeitalter der christlichen Kirche*, 2nd ed. (1892), p. 609; R. Gryson, *Ministère des femmes*, pp. 23–24.

[12] The French text uses the French Ecumenical Translation of the Bible here; in the English the Catholic Edition of the Revised Standard Version is used here, as throughout [Tr.].

[13] C. Spicq, *Saint Paul, Epîtres pastorales*, 4th ed., *Etudes bibliques* (Paris: Gabalda, 1969), p. 456: "It is possible that this is a marginal note introduced very early into the text. Nevertheless there is nothing to prevent us from attributing to Paul himself this hasty allusion to 'deaconesses'. But it cannot be considered a title properly speaking."

remarked that this Epistle is "badly written", with the logical development of the chain of ideas in the text interrupted in this fashion in more than one place.[14] But who are "the women" referred to here? Exegetes of antiquity provided very different answers to this question. They tended to read into the text the particular discipline of their own various local churches; we shall have occasion to encounter citations from some of them. The exegetes of the twentieth century are no more agreed on the question, however, than were those of antiquity.

According to J. G. Davies,[15] the reference is to women in general. A nearly identical enumeration of requisite virtues is to be found in the letter of Titus 2:3–5 apropos of πρεσβύτιδες (older women). As R. Gryson has correctly remarked, this "is a word denoting age, not function, as is clear from the context". The same passage mentions in succession πρεσβῦται (older men), verse 2; πρεσβύτιδες (older women), verse 3; νεαί (young women), verse 4; and νεώτεροι (young men), verse 6.[16] But the context of 1 Timothy 3 is very different from this: it is entirely concerned with hierarchical ministries. A reference to women in the middle of a passage concerned with deacons makes it seem likely that the women in question did have some relationship to the deacons being discussed; this would presumably have been the intention of the redactor or interpolator who included the reference to women at that particular point.

Were these women, then, the wives of the deacons? This hypothesis, although presenting several difficulties, should not be excluded.[17] If the author had really intended to specify the wives of deacons, why did he not write τὰς γυναῖκας αὐτῶν, instead of just γυναῖκας? Moreover, the author then goes on to discuss the families of deacons, specifying that a deacon must be "the husband of one wife", without relating this specification to what has just been said before about the women, as would have seemed normal. And why would he have spoken about the things required of wives of deacons in particular without also saying anything about what was required of the wives of the bishops?[18]

It is because of these questions that a certain number of commentators[19]

---

[14] Op. cit., pp. 549, 575.

[15] Op. cit., p. 2.

[16] R. Gryson, *Ministère des femmes*, p. 33, no. 4.

[17] *Traduction oecuménique de la Bible*, loc. cit., n. d: "The wives of deacons (called to assist their husbands) or deaconesses [cf. Rom 16:1]." For the list of authors in favor of this opinion, see: C. Spicq, op. cit., p. 460; cf. St. Thomas Aquinas, *Comm. in Epist. I ad Tim* 3, lectio 2, Parma edition, 13 (1862): 600.

[18] A. Kalsbach, *Altkirchliche Einrichtung*, p. 11; R. Gryson, *Ministère des femmes*, pp. 30–31; R. M. Lewis, "The 'Women' of 1 Tim 3:11", in *Bibliotheca Sacra* 136 (1979): 167–69.

[19] Among recent commentators who have adopted this view: A. Kalsbach, *Altkirchliche Einrichtung*, pp. 10–11; *Diakonisse*, col. 917, who says, "*wahrscheinlich*", "probably"; *Bible de Jérusalem*, 1951, fasc. *Les Epîtres de saint Paul à Timothée et à Tite* (P. Dornier), p. 31, n. b; 1955

believe that the reference to women here is to a specific category of feminine ministry bearing some relationship to the ministry of deacons. But is it a legitimate reading of the author's intention to assert that these women are simply "deacons" themselves? It is possible to hold that the name itself was not included along with the mention of women because *diakonos*, as we have seen, does not have a feminine form. Therefore the author did not think it necessary to repeat the word; the context was sufficient to make clear what he meant by the reference to γυναῖκας.[20] There is also the parallelism of verses 8 and 11, where "deacons likewise must be serious" (διακόνους ὡσαύτως σεμνούς) corresponds to "the women likewise must be serious" (γυναῖκας ὡσαύτως σεμνάς). The qualities required in deacons thus turn out to be the same as those required in "the women".[21] This parallelism, however, is so conspicuous as to arouse some suspicion of artifice, and indeed this is another argument in favor of considering the sentence to be a later interpolation into the text. Nevertheless, no specific function is mentioned in connection with "the women", nor are they given any special name. Whatever ministry they may have carried out was thus in no way as definite as the ministry of deacons.[22] And in contrast to the references to the families of both bishops and deacons, nothing at all is said about the family situation of the women. In the eyes of both ancient and modern commentators, therefore, this text from the third chapter of 1 Timothy contains serious unresolved difficulties; it cannot be read in just a single sense that compels absolute conviction about its meaning.[23]

---

edition, p. 1566, n. d; C. Spicq, op. cit., pp. 76–77, 460–61; R. Gryson, *Ministère des femmes*, pp. 29–31; A. Lemaire, in *Le ministère et les ministères*, p. 114: "These 'women' are very probably 'female deacons', and, like deacons, they were probably available to carry out a variety of tasks, especially liaison missions among the churches . . . even though the pastoral letters do not permit us to paint a complete and detailed picture of all the activities of deacons, both men and women. . . ."

[20] A. Kalsbach, *Altkirchliche Einrichtung*, p. 11.

[21] I would never dare to push the parallelism as far as R. Gryson has in *Ministère des femmes*, p. 31, n. 1. The requirement for deacons that "they must hold the mystery of the faith with a clear conscience", (ἔχοντας τὸ μυστήριον τῆς πίσεως ἐν χαθαρᾷ συνειδήσει) (verse 9) clearly suggests something very different from merely being "faithful in all things", (πιστάς 'εν πᾶσιν) (verse 11).

[22] It is more than a question of not having a very definite ministry: certain exegetes believe that "it was not a question of a fixed, already established ministry of women, but rather one rendered to deacons requesting it", according to the formula of J. Belser in *Die Briefe des Apostel Paulus an Timotheus und Titus* (Freiburg, 1907), p. 82. This formula was approved by A. Kalsbach in *Altkirchliche Einrichtung*, p. 11.

[23] R. M. Lewis, art. cit., pp. 171–75, has suggested yet another interpretation: these women were unmarried women who assisted the deacons in their work of service to the Church.

C. The Widows of 1 Tim 5:9–10

It is owing to these unresolved difficulties of 1 Tim 3:11 that the prescriptions concerning widows set forth in 1 Timothy 5:9–10 (below) very early came to be considered as extending to deaconesses; indeed some have preferred to ground the origin of deaconesses in this later passage rather than in the earlier one:

> Let a widow be enrolled χήρα καταλεγέσθω if she is not less than sixty years of age, having been the wife of one husband; and she must be well attested for her good deeds, as one who has brought up children, shown hospitality, washed the feet of the saints, relieved the afflicted and devoted herself to doing good in every way.[24]

Here we are clearly dealing with a group of women who enjoyed official recognition in the Church. Entry into membership in this group was not merely the result of some spontaneous personal decision to join it; rather, one had to be designated, "enrolled" in the group. No doubt the decision for this enrollment emanated from the authority presiding over the community. A widow who was chosen to be enrolled thereby had conferred upon her a distinct honor. It was for this reason that she had to have given an exceptional example by "doing good in every way" (ἐν ἔργοις καλοῖς μαρτυρουμένη) in her family life and in other spheres of charitable activity. She had to be no less than sixty years of age and the wife of only one husband. This latter condition made the group of widows comparable to groups of both bishops and deacons. We must not, however, read into this passage any disapproval of second marriages—second marriages are expressly approved, in fact, a few lines later (verse 14). Rather, this condition fulfilled an important demand of ecclesial symbolism: those in the Church who occupied a place that distinguished them from the simple faithful were obliged to embody a sign of the Covenant in their own lives; they were obliged to live the nuptial mystery of the Church united to Christ, her unique Spouse.[25] But did this mean that they were invested with a clerical ministry? A certain number of commentators have certainly believed this to be the case.[26] Most often, however, as A. Kalsbach has remarked,[27] they only reach this conclusion

---

[24] See n. 12 to this chapter.

[25] I. de la Potterie, "Mari d'une seule femme", le sens théologique d'une formule paulinienne, in Paul de Tarse, apôtre de notre temps (Rome: Saint Paul outside the Walls, 1979), pp. 619–38.

[26] The ancient commentators will be reviewed in the course of this book. As for the modern commentators, see R. Gryson, Ministère des femmes, p. 31, no. 4. I take note of the typical inattention of A. George in Le ministère et les ministères, p. 238, n. 83, who refers back to 1 Tim 5:9–16 as a source of knowledge regarding deaconesses.

[27] A. Kalsbach, Altkirchliche Einrichtung, p. 15.

as a result of their more or less conscious desire to carry all the way back to the apostolic age feminine ministries in the Church whose evolution actually occurred later. In fact, nothing in the context of 1 Timothy provides support for linking "the women" of chapter 3 with "the widows" of chapter 5.

The complete passage of 1 Timothy 5:3–16, in fact, covers the whole range of pastoral problems connected with widows. For widows who are still young, it is deemed desirable that they should "marry, bear children, rule their households and give the enemy no reason to revile us" (verse 14). Nothing is worse than idleness for them (verse 13). Widowhood always created difficult material problems, of course. Normally it was the children, grandchildren or near relatives who had the duty to provide for the needs of widows (verses 4, 8 and 16); the Church took responsibility only for those widows who were "real widows" (τὰς ὄντως χήρας) (verses 3 and 16). For these "real widows", the Church provided a service of assistance, but their very aloneness and lack of immediate family would help to orient them toward a more spiritual life: "She who is a real widow and is left all alone has set her hope on God and continues in supplications and prayers night and day" (verse 5). This ideal, of course, had already been sketched out by St. Paul in 1 Corinthians 7:8–9. With regard to the widows mentioned in 1 Timothy 3:9–10 as being "enrolled", must we understand them to have all been widows assisted by the Church or was only a more restricted group of those assisted actually "enrolled"? The fact is that these two verses describe an ideal state of perfection; implied in them is both recognition by the Church and commitment on the part of the individual widow herself; this is why widows were not enrolled before the age of sixty—to guarantee the fidelity of their commitment. There can be no question, therefore, of responsibilities that were exercised within the community, at least directly, unless they were perhaps a continuation of the widow's earlier charitable activities, described in verse 10 ("having shown hospitality, washed the feet of the saints, relieved the afflicted and . . . doing good in every way"). The apostle certainly seems to want to discourage widows from going visiting house to house (verse 13).[28]

In the final analysis, the texts of the New Testament that we have examined here derive their principal interest from the retrospective value placed upon them by later commentators.[29] These texts could never be

---

[28] Ibid., pp. 11–16; A. Oepke, Γυνή, in *Theologisches Wörterbuch des Neuen Testaments* I (1949): 788–89; A. Kalsbach, *Diakonisse*, col. 918; C. Spicq, op. cit., pp. 77–81, 524–40; R. Gryson, *Ministère des femmes*, pp. 31–33.

[29] R. M. Lewis, art. cit., p. 171, n. 18, aptly remarks: "One must also not confuse Church history with Bible exegesis, regardless of the practice followed in the Church of the third and fourth centuries."

accepted as proving the existence of deaconesses—female deacons—in apostolic times unless the documents of the second century were to confirm this finding by demonstrating the continuity of this supposed apostolic institution of deaconesses. The role of women in evangelization and catechesis, described in the Acts of the Apostles, represents an undisputed reality, one highly important in many ways. It is a reality, however, that risks causing us to neglect the search for the true origins of a feminine ministry that in fact developed later. This ministry appeared only toward the second decade of the third century—and when it did appear, it did so only in a limited number of churches.

2. DOCUMENTS OF THE SECOND AND EARLY THIRD CENTURIES

There is an observation of some significance to be made at the outset regarding the period to be covered here: the *Biblia Patristica* does not contain any reference to either Romans 16:1 or 1 Timothy 3:11 as having been cited in the Christian literature of the second century.[30] Moreover, with the exception of one passage from Pliny the Younger, all of the texts usually employed in the effort to prove that the institution of deaconesses existed uniformly during this period refer to widows, not deaconesses.

A. *The Letter from Pliny the Younger To the Emperor Trajan*

In his famous letter on the subject of Christians sent to the emperor Trajan some time during 111–113 A.D., Pliny the Younger, then governor of Bithynia, pointed out that in order to obtain exact information on what he regarded as the sect of Christians, "*quo magis necessarium credidi ex duabus ancillis, quae ministrae dicebantur, quid esset veri et per tormenta quaerere.*"[31] The word *ministrae*, of course, is certainly not a synonym for *ancillae*. R. Gryson aptly notes in this regard: "In this passage, *ancilla* is a term designating the social condition of the women in question, while *ministra* is the title given to them among their fellow Christians.[32] Marcel Durry does not hesitate to translate Pliny's supposed meaning as follows: "I believed it all the more necessary to worm the truth out of two servants

---

[30] *Biblia patristica* . . . vol. 1, *Des origines à Clément d'Alexandrie et Tertullien* (Paris, Ed. du C.N.R.S., 1975), pp. 444, 507. In point of fact, however, Clement of Alexandria, as we shall see, makes an unmistakable allusion to 1 Tim 3, although it is not a citation as such.

[31] *Epist. Lib.* 10, 96, no. 8; 2nd edition, M. Schuster (Leipzig: Teubner, 1952), p. 356.

[32] R. Gryson, *Ministère des femmes*, p. 39.

who were called deaconesses."[33] Now Bithynia was a Greek-speaking region, and Pliny's *"quae ministrae dicebantur"* could be a Latin version of the Greek formula αἱ καλούμεναι διάκονοι. This phrase is very close to the manner in which St. Justin the Martyr, writing in 150 A.D., speaks about deacons: "οἱ καλούμενοι παρ' ἡμῖν διάκονοι".[34] The similarity here is striking, but it refers only to the words themselves. Justin expressly attributes to deacons a liturgical role in the distribution of the Eucharist, but we know absolutely nothing, from Pliny or any other witnesses, about what the role or function might have been of these *ministrae* in the community of Bithynia. [Thus, to translate this word simply as "deaconess" is certainly to force the sense of the text unduly and to get caught in a plain anachronism.] R. Gryson reaches the following conclusion about this particular point: "We are permitted on the basis of the title given to these *ministrae* to associate them with 'the women' who are themselves associated with deacons in 1 Timothy 3:11, but in so doing we must not lose sight of the fact that this association remains a very fragile and contingent one."[35]

B. St. Ignatius of Antioch and St. Polycarp of Smyrna

The epistles of St. Ignatius of Antioch date from approximately the same period as the letter of Pliny the Younger. It is true, of course, that the ecclesiastical institutions found in Syria's great capital of Antioch did not necessarily correspond to those in Bithynia, but the epistles of St. Ignatius of Antioch bear witness to the existence there of a well-established local church hierarchy composed of bishops, presbyters and deacons. At the same time, these epistles do not contain even the faintest trace of the existence of any feminine ministry. It is in vain that some have looked to one curious expression in the Epistle to the Smyrnaeans as possibly providing that trace: "I greet the families of my brothers", St. Ignatius wrote, "with their wives and children and the virgins called widows" (καὶ τὰς παρθένους τὰς λεγομένας χήρας).[36] We shall shortly find Tertullian

---

[33] *Pline Le Jeune*, vol. 4, *Belles Lettres* (Coll. des Universités de France . . . Assoc. Guillaume Budé) (Paris: Belles Lettres, 1947), p. 74.

[34] St. Justin, *Première Apologie*, 65, edition of L. Pautigny (*Textes et documents* 1) (Paris: Picard, 1904), pp. 140–41 (PG 6, col. 428).

[35] R. Gryson, ibid. Cf. A. Kalsbach, *Altkirchliche Einrichtung*, p. 16: "The remark [of Pliny] is just as insufficient and indeterminant as is Rom 16:1–2; still, it reveals that Christian titles were already familiar [*dicebantur*] and no longer had merely subjective meanings, as was the case with Paul." J. G. Davies, op. cit., pp. 2–3, believes that no conclusion can be based on the text of Pliny as it stands.

[36] *Lettre aux Smyrniotes* 13:1, trans. by P. T. Camelot, SC 10, p. 167. In a note, this translation comments: "We think of these virgins as having been assimilated into the group

complaining loudly about virgins in the assembly taking a place among the widows; but here it does indeed seem that young virgins were given the title of widows on the model of 1 Timothy 5. This term seems to refer above all to a state of perfection recognized by the community at Smyrna and characterized by a commitment to continence. St. Ignatius, however, included these "virgins called widows" among the laity. A few lines earlier, he had rendered his greetings separately to the bishops, presbyters and deacons—that is to say, to the clergy. To imagine that these women were invested with any specific ministry or function is a supposition that finds no support in the text.[37]

The bishop of Smyrna, St. Polycarp, writing during roughly the same period to the Christians of Philippi, was lavish in the advice he offered to widows, following the advice about their duties he had offered to married couples:

> Widows ought to be wise in the faith that they owe to the Lord. They should intercede tirelessly for all; they should shun all calumny, slander, false witness, love of money and every other evil. They should realize that they are the altar of God.[38]

St. Polycarp went on in his epistle to exhort deacons, young men, virgins and presbyters. The lack of any rhyme or reason to this listing prevents us from basing any argument upon the fact that deacons come right after widows. Nor is it possible to assimilate the qualities that St. Polycarp wants to see embodied in widows to "the women" of 1 Timothy 3:11. On the contrary, they correspond naturally with "the widows" of 1 Timothy 5. They are supposed to "intercede tirelessly for all", just as those described by St. Paul were supposed to continue "in supplications and prayers night and day" (1 Tim 5:5). The expression of St. Polycarp, "they are the altar of God", is a most striking one, but, as we shall see, it is one that was taken up by other Christian writers.[39] These other writers did so, no doubt, because it was by means of these widows that the uninterrupted prayer of the Church rose up to God; but it was also because, living as they

---

of 'widows' and we understand the reference to them in a technical and ecclesiastical sense as describing the order of widows that was already becoming organized, as in 1 Tim 5:3–16, and was distinct from that of deaconesses."

[37] A. Kalsbach, *Altkirchliche Einrichtung*, pp. 18–19, who observes that the word χήρα can have a broader meaning: "χήρα is the broader meaning [empty, bare, denuded] for the unmarried, especially widows, but also for maidens whom no man has had or wanted." Also Gryson, *Ministère des femmes*, pp. 36–37.

[38] *Lettre aux Philippians* 4:3, trans. P. T. Camelot, SC 10, p. 209.

[39] Tertullian, *Ad uxorem* 1:7:4, CCL 1, p. 381, line 24; cf. *Didascalie des Apôtres* 9, edition of R. H. Connolly, pp. 88–89; translation of A. Vööbus, p. 100; *Constitutions apostoliques*, 2:26:8, edition of F. X. Funk, 1:105, lines 26–29.

did on the offerings of the faithful, they resembled in a literal sense the altar on which offerings were customarily presented to God.[40] There is no indication, however, that would permit us to conclude that they exercised any of the functions of a minister.

C. Tertullian

With Tertullian we have already reached the end of the second century and the beginning of the third. The first Christian writer in Latin, Tertullian engaged abundantly in polemics in both his Catholic period and the period after he became a Montanist. His works permit us to observe in a very precise way the organization of the churches of his time in the face of the disorders of various splinter sects. Nowhere in any of his works do we encounter the words *diacona*, *ministra* or their equivalents; nor does he make the slightest allusion to either Phoebe or 1 Timothy 3:11.[41] There are, however, certain authors who have imagined that when he spoke about widows he was really speaking about deaconesses.[42]

It is true that the language Tertullian employed indicates that he believed the "widows" described in 1 Timothy belonged to an *ordo*, or order: "*Disciplina ecclesiae et praescriptio apostoli . . . cum viduam adlegi in ordinem nisi univiram non concedat.*"[43] Thus, even within the assembly, widows constituted a group with a special place. After he became a Montanist, Tertullian complained bitterly about a bishop who had associated a young virgin with the group of widows (*in viduatu collocatam*), allowing her to be seen seated (*sedet*) in their midst, although she did not fulfill any of the conditions St. Paul had specified: she was not yet twenty years old, for example, and she did not wear the customary veil that consecrated virgins wore.[44]

But of what, then, did this *ordo* of widows consist? It was a group of widows who had specially consecrated themselves, who lived at the

---

[40] A. Kalsbach, *Altkirchliche Einrichtung*, pp. 17–18; P. T. Camelot, op. cit., p. 208, n. 3; R. Gryson, *Ministère des femmes*, p. 36.

[41] G. Claesson, *Index Tertullianeus*, 3 vols. (Paris, *Etudes augustiniennes*, 1974–75). The words *diacona*, *diaconissa* or Phoebe are not mentioned. I myself checked all the references to the words *diaconus* (in) *ministerio*, *ministra*, *ministrare*, *vidua*, *viduatus*, *viduitas*; also CCL 2, *Index locorum sacrae*, *Scripturae*, pp. 1457–93, *Index nominum*, pp. 1497–1507, *Index rerum et locutionum*, pp. 1509–1626.

[42] Several of them are mentioned by R. Gryson, *Ministère des femmes*, p. 48, n. 4; this opinion was rather widespread around the end of the nineteenth century.

[43] *Ad uxorem* 1:7, CCL 1, p. 381. Nor can one draw any particular conclusions from the passage in *De praescriptione haereticorum* 3:5, CCL 1, p. 198, "*Quid ergo, si episcopus, si diaconus, si vidua, si virgo, si doctor, si etiam martyr lapsus a regula fuerit?*"

[44] *De virginibus velandis* 9:2–3, CCL 2, p. 1219.

expense of the Church, and who had been married no more than once. They thus bore witness to the institution of monogamy, as did the bishops, priests and deacons; theirs was an example that was bound to put to shame those who might otherwise have contemplated a second marriage. Would a widow be able to present herself for a second marriage before the bishop, the priests, the deacons and the other widows—before, in other words, all those who were themselves committed to monogamy?[45] How could a remarried widower have the courage to recite prayers in the assembly for two wives and bring up his offerings for both of them to a bishop who was either monogamous or celibate (*per sacerdotem de monogamia ordinatum aut etiam de virginitate sancitum*) or surrounded by monogamous widows (*circumdatum viduis univiris*)?[46] Would it be possible to admit an adulterer, dressed in a hair shirt and covered with ashes, into the assembly as a penitent, asking him to prostrate himself before chaste priests and widows?[47]

The connection becomes clear: the only thing linking the widows with the priests is the law of monogamy imposed upon both. It was Tertullian's aim to see it imposed upon all the faithful; but, as things stood, the fact that widows shared this discipline with priests in no way implied that they were also members of the clergy.[48] In fact, this would contradict the evidence. Evidently widows played no active role in the assembly. Certainly, during his Catholic period Tertullian never accepted that women could exercise any ministerial function, teach in the Church or baptize; he stigmatized roundly these errors of the sects in this regard, notably those to be found in the apocryphal "Acts of Paul".[49] During his Montanist phase, he exhibited the same rigor; it was only outside the assembly that he recognized charisms belonging to women.[50] Thus the idea of a female diaconate under any form was an idea totally alien to Tertullian.[51]

[45] *De monogamia* 11:1, CCL 2, p. 1244: "*Ut igitur in Domino nubas secundum legem et apostolum (si tamen vel hoc curas), qualis es id matrimonium postulans, quod eis a quibus postulas non licet habere, ab episcopo monogamo, a presbyteris et diaconis eiusdem sacramenti, a viduis quarum sectam in te recusasti?*"

[46] *De exhortatione castitatis* 11:2, CCL 2, p. 1031.

[47] *De pudicitia* 13:7, CCL 2, p. 1304: "*Et tu quidem paenitentiam moechi ad exorandam fraternitatem in ecclesiam inducens, conciliciatum et concineratum cum dedecore et horrore compositum prosternens in medium ante viduas, ante presbyteros. . . .*"

[48] A. Kalsbach, *Altkirchliche Einrichtung*, p. 73: "Because this *Ordo* was without any doubt clerical. . . ."

[49] *De baptismo* 17:4, CCL 1, pp. 291–92; SC 35, pp. 90–91. On this text see the commentary of R. Gryson, *Ministère des femmes*, pp. 42–43.

[50] R. Gryson, *Ministère des femmes*, pp. 44–45.

[51] Ibid., pp. 48–49.

D. *The Apostolic Tradition of St. Hippolytus of Rome*

Both the work called the *Apostolic Tradition* and the identity of its author, St. Hippolytus of Rome, continue to inspire many controversies. For one thing, the authentic text of the work itself is not easy to establish: of the original Greek we have only the consecratory prayer of the bishop; the Latin version has come down to us containing numerous gaps that were caused by scraping the parchment on which it was written for the purpose of reuse. Ultimately we know the work of St. Hippolytus through the Egyptian tradition; the Sahidic version, in particular, preserves all the Greek technical terms. This allows us to be quite sure of the original, at least with respect to all of the passages that concern us here.[52] Moreover, in spite of the various hypotheses about the true identity of St. Hippolytus of Rome, there is a general consensus regarding the date of the *Apostolic Tradition*, which is that it was written in Rome around 215–220 A.D. Also, there is a striking convergence between the prescriptions contained in the work and what we know of the discipline of the church in Rome in that period; this may be either because St. Hippolytus faithfully reflected the Roman tradition, or because his work actually influenced the development of the Roman discipline.[53] Be that as it may, the work, in its various versions and adaptations, has exercised a decisive influence in many regions of the Christian world. No doubt the liturgy described in the work is somewhat idealized because St. Hippolytus was much more respectful toward what he believed to be the liturgical heritage handed down from the past than he was toward the rites as they were practiced in his own time. "On the whole, however", Botte concludes, "it is correct to hold that the *Apostolic Tradition* represents very well the Roman discipline of the first part of the third century."[54]

Among other things, St. Hippolytus enumerated the various categories of membership in the Church of his day; he both described the nature of these categories of membership and made clear distinctions about how Christians were invested with various Church functions. First, there were the three clerical degrees for which the Holy Spirit was invoked, along with a laying on of hands: bishops, priests and deacons. Second,

---

[52] The best edition remains that of B. Botte, *La Tradition apostolique de Saint Hippolyte*, LQF 39 (Münster: W. Aschendorff, 1963), reprinted several times. This is the edition used here. B. Botte also prepared a less technical edition, SC 11b. Each of the different versions has its own separate edition; a list of these editions will be found in Botte's Introductions.

[53] On this subject, see the Introduction of B. Botte to his edition of 1963. Also, J. M. Hanssens, *La liturgie d'Hippolyte*, vol. 1, OCA 155 (Rome: P. Institutum Orientalium Studiorum, 1959); vol. 2 (Rome: Universita Gregoriana, 1970); B. Botte, *A propos de la "Tradition apostolique"*, in *Recherches de théologie ancienne et médiévale*, 33 (1966): 177–86.

[54] B. Botte, *La Tradition . . .* , p. XIV.

Hippolytus examined the case of confessors eligible to receive one of these three clerical degrees. Third, he described other groups in the Church (widows, lectors, virgins, subdeacons and those who possessed the power of healing), and to these he expressly forbade the laying on of hands. Out of these various groupings, there were only two composed of women, and they are the same two groupings we have already identified: widows and virgins. No rite at all was involved as far as virgins were concerned, nor were they distinguished in any special way: "Hands are not imposed upon a virgin [παρθένος]; her decision [προαίρεσις] alone is what makes her a virgin."[55] As for widows, in addition to those assisted by the Church,[56] there were others who were initiated into the group of widows and who occupied a special place, at least in the assembly:

> When a widow is installed [καθιστάναι] as a widow [χήρα] she is not ordained [χειροτονεῖν]; rather she is designated by her title. If her husband has been dead for a long time, she may be installed. If her husband has not been dead long, then it is not possible to have confidence in her automatically; even if she is advanced in age, she should be tested [δοκιμάζειν] for a certain period of time. For often the passions continue into old age in those who have earlier allowed them to rule them.
>
> The widow should be installed by the recitation of words only, and she should then join the other widows. She should not receive the laying on of hands because she does not offer the sacrifice [προσφορά], and she does not have a liturgical [λειτουργία] function. Ordination [χειροτονία] is for clerics [κλῆρος] destined for liturgical service. Widows, however, are installed for the purpose of prayer, which is actually for everybody.[57]

These prescriptions are entirely consistent with what is found in 1 Timothy 5. The official designation of widows is accomplished by "the recitation of words"—that is to say, doubtlessly, recited in the course of a special liturgical rite. "She should then join the other widows." This suggests the distinction accorded to widows that resulted in the special place they occupied in the assembly and that Tertullian also described. Perhaps widows even had a life in common. At the very least, official installation as a widow meant an entry into a state of life; it involved a consecration that required a guarantee of perseverance on the part of the woman entering therein. Yet this state of life is always perfectly consistent with St. Paul's description of widows vowed to a life of prayer.[58] St. Hippolytus is

[55] No. 12, pp. 32–33.
[56] Nos. 20, 24, 30, pp. 42–43, 62–63, 74–75.
[57] No. 10, transmitted by the Sahidic versions, both Arabic and Ethiopian; Greek terms were transcribed with Coptic prefixes in the Sahidic versions: W. Till and J. Leipoldt, *Der koptische Text der Kirchenordnung Hippolyts*, TU 58 (Berlin: Akademie Verlag, 1954), pp. 8–9.
[58] In addition to what has been said in n. 10 to this chapter above, see also Chapter 3, n. 23. "Widows and virgins fast often and pray for the Church."

also consistent with St. Polycarp; he insists that there is no liturgical role whatsoever for widows and actually gives this as the reason why they receive no laying on of hands. The laying on of hands is tied to an ordination which is related to the *leitourgia* and the *prosphora*. Did Hippolytus perhaps insist upon this so strongly because he was reacting to abuses in this area? This is certainly a possibility. Like Tertullian, he was no doubt acquainted with various sects that tried to base their practices in this area upon apocryphal scriptures.

In the Arabic and Ethiopian translations of St. Hippolytus, his prescriptions regarding widows immediately follow those concerning confessors and precede those concerning lectors, virgins, subdeacons and those possessing the power of healing.[59] Botte has followed the same order of enumeration in his edition of the *Apostolic Tradition*, even though he recognized that "it is hardly possible to determine what the original order was".[60] This order varies considerably depending upon the source.[61] We therefore cannot even conjecture about what the actual order was, although we can undoubtedly assume that the newly created ministries of lector and subdeacon did not yet have a clearly defined status.

A conclusion imposes itself upon us at this point: the ecclesiology of St. Hippolytus of Rome simply excluded the possibility of deaconesses, as did the ecclesiology proclaimed by Tertullian all his life as well.[62] The most we might ask in this connection is whether, at the time he composed his *Apostolic Tradition*, perhaps St. Hippolytus had already heard about the initiative that the *Didascalia of the Apostles* was soon going to be making better known and was determined, in what he wrote concerning widows, to resist the innovation.

---

[59] J. and A. Perier, *Les 127 canons des Apôtres*, PO 8, fasc. 4 (Paris: Firmin-Didot, 1912), pp. 593–95; H. Duensing, *Der äthiopische Text der Kirchenordnung des Hippolyt.* (Göttingen: Vandenhoeck and Ruprecht, 1946) (*Abhandl der Akad. der Wissenschaften in Göttingen*, Phil. hist. Klasse, 3 Folge, Nr. 32), pp. 36–41.

[60] B. Botte, *La Tradition apostolique* . . . , p. 31, n. 1; cf. p. 33, n. 1.

[61] In the Coptic translation, this is the order: confessor, lector, subdeacon, widow, virgin, healer (Till-Leipoldt, op. cit., pp. 4–9); in the "Canons of Hippolytus": confessor, lector, subdeacon, healer, widow (R. G. Coquin, *Les Canons d'Hippolyte*, PO 31, fasc. 2 (1966), pp. 358–63); in the *Testamentum Domini*: confessor, widow, subdeacon, lector, virgin, healer (F. Nau-P. Ciprotti, *La version syriaque de l'Octateuque de Clément* [Paris: Lethielleux, 1967], pp. 52–56); in the *Apostolic Constitutions*: deaconess, subdeacon, lector, confessor, virgin, widow, exorcist (F. X. Funk, *Didascalia et Constitutiones apostolorum* [Paderborn: Schoeningh, 1905], 1:524–29); in the *Epitome*: deaconess, subdeacon, lector, confessor, virgin, widow (F. X. Funk, op. cit., 2:81–82).

[62] We shall defer examination of the texts of Clement of Alexandria until Chapter 4, in order to be able to present a complete view of the Egyptian tradition.

PART ONE

Deaconesses in the Greek-Speaking Churches
And the Churches of Oriental Languages

CHAPTER TWO

Deaconesses in the Churches
In the East of the Roman Empire
(Third to Seventh Centuries)

It is on the eastern *limes* of the Roman Empire that we finally see deaconesses emerging. The first document that specifically mentions deaconesses, one that, in a sense, constitutes their birth certificate as an ecclesial institution, is the document called the *Didascalia of the Apostles*.

I. THE DIDASCALIA OF THE APOSTLES

The *Didascalia of the Apostles* has only been known since 1854, when Paul de Lagarde published its Syriac text from a manuscript found in the Bibliothèque Nationale in Paris. In ancient times, however, the document enjoyed a rather wide diffusion; it figures in a number of collections of canons in Syriac, of those translated into Arabic or Ethiopic and even into Latin. A Coptic version once existed but is no longer extant. The original *Didascalia* was, however, reworked and, with many revisions and additions, completely incorporated into the great compilation known as the *Apostolic Constitutions*. On the basis of the available testimony from antiquity, we can readily conclude that the work was originally written in Greek; indeed, a fragment of the Greek version has been discovered.[1] More than

---

[1] On the subject of the manuscripts of the *Didascalia*, the reader is referred to the following listed works. I have utilized to some degree all of the available translations into modern languages: F. Nau, *La Didascalie des douze Apôtres* . . . , 2nd edition (*Ancienne littérature canonique syriaque* 2) (Paris: Lethielleux, 1912); R. H. Connolly, *Didascalia Apostolorum, the Syriac Version Translated and Accompanied by the Verona Latin Fragments* (Oxford: Clarendon, 1929); A. Vööbus, *The Didascalia Apostolorum in Syriac* . . . (Louvain, 1979), 2 vols. of text (CSCO 41 and 407) and 2 vols. of translations (CSCO 402 and 408). The Greek fragment of the *Didascalia* has been edited by J. V. Bartlet, *Fragment of the Didascalia Apostolorum in Greek*, JTS 8 (1917): 301–9; this has been reproduced by E. Tidner in the work indicated below, n. 4, on its pp. 50–51. See also J. M. Hanssens, *La liturgie d'Hippolyte*, vol. 1, OCA 155 (Rome, 1959), pp. 13–30 (on the Greek text that the various versions assume).

that, the very ancient date of the non-Greek versions obliges us to date the original work from the first half of the third century, some time before the persecution of Decius.[2]

The *Didascalia* discusses deaconesses—female deacons—in two places. The first of these is the ninth chapter of the document, which deals with the honor owed to the bishop by all the people. Instead of the sacrifices of the Old Testament, the text specifies:

<table>
<tr><td>Syriac Version</td><td>Latin Version</td></tr>
</table>

Instead of the sacrifices of that time are offered prayers and supplications and thanksgiving. In that time there were first fruits, tithes, sacrifices and gifts; now there are the offerings presented to the Lord God by the bishops. They are your high priests. The priests and Levites of this present time are the priests and deacons and the orphans and widows— but the high priest and Levite is the bishop. He is the minister of the word and the mediator; and for you he is a doctor as well as your father in God: he gave you birth through water. He is your leader and guide and a powerful king. He guides you in the place of the All-Powerful. He is to be honored by you as is God himself, because, for you, the bishop stands in the place of the All-Powerful God. The deacon stands in the place of Christ and you should love him. The deaconess should

Quae tunc era(n)t sacrificia, modo sunt orationes et praecationes et gratiarum actiones: quae tunc fuerunt primitiae et decumae et delibationes et dona, nunc sunt prosforae q(uae) per episcopos offeruntur domino deo in remissione peccatorum. Isti (sunt) enim primi sacerdotes uestri. Qui tunc erant Leuitae, modo sunt diacones, praesbyteri, uiduae et orfani. Primus uero sacerdos uobis est leuita, episcopus. Hic est qui uerbum uobis ministrat et mediator uester est: hic est rex uester potens: hic est magister et post deum, per aquam regenerans, pater uester. Hic locum dei sequens sicuti deus honoretur a uobis, quoniam episcopus in typum dei praesedet uobis. Diaconus autem in typum Christi adstat: ergo diligatur a uobis. Diaconissa uero in typum sancti spiritus honoretur a uobis. Praesbyteri etiam in typum apostolorum sperentur [*sic*] a uobis: uiduae

---

[2] A. Harnack, after having first dated the *Didascalia* from the last half of the third century, later decided that it had been written in the first half: *Geschichte der altchristlichen Literatur*, Part I (Leipzig: Hinrich, 1893), pp. 515–16; Part 2, vol. 2 (1904), pp. 488–501 (especially p. 492). F. Nau, op. cit., p. xxi: "If we admit some interpolations . . . , internal evidence permits us to date this composition to the beginning of the third century." A. Baumstark, *Geschichte der syrischen Literatur* (Bonn, 1922, repr. Berlin, 1968), p. 263: "A product of the third century"; R. H. Connolly, op. cit., p. xci: "My own inclination is to place the *Didascalia* earlier rather than later; or, if that is too vague, before the Decian persecution rather than after the grant of toleration by Gallienus"; J. Quasten, *Patrologia*, ed. española preparada por I. Oñatibia, vol. I, BAC 206 (Madrid, 1961), p. 438: "Composed according to the most recent studies in the first half and perhaps in the first decades of the third century". P. Galtier, in *La date de la Didascalie des Apôtres*, RHE 42 (1947), pp. 315–51, also opts for the first half of the third century.

be honored by you as the Holy Spirit is honored. Priests ought to be considered by you as the apostles would be considered and widows and orphans should be esteemed by you as you would esteem the altar of God.[3]

et orfani in typum altaris putentur autem a uobis. . . .[4]

It is immediately apparent from this passage that, except, to be sure, for the reference to deaconesses, the other elements of this passage are well known. For example, St. Ignatius of Antioch had written to the Magnesians: "Have a care to accomplish all things with a divine concord, under the leadership of the bishop, who stands in the place of God for you [εἰς τόπον Θεοῦ]; under the priests who stand in the place of the college of the apostles [εἰς τόπον συνεδρίου τῶν ἀποστόλων]; and under the deacons who are so dear to me and to whom has been confided the service of Jesus Christ [πεπιστευμένων διακονίαν Ἰησοῦ Χριστοῦ]."[5] There was St. Polycarp, who, as we have seen above, wanted widows to be conscious of the fact that they were "the altar of God" (γινωσκούσας ὅτι εἰσὶ θυσιαστήριον Θεοῦ).[6] The author of the *Didascalia* quite naturally associated orphans with widows; this was, after all, a biblical tradition. But was it because of the influence of the letter of St. Polycarp that he placed deacons ahead of priests in his listing? It appears that he accorded much more importance to deacons than he did to priests. Moreover, since he was making mention also of deaconesses (who were not included in his first enumeration), he placed them immediately after deacons. There are two reasons why he then went on to compare deaconesses to the Holy Spirit. The first is the logical progression involved in enumerating the three Divine Persons (the bishop takes the place of the Father, the deacon that of Christ, etc.). The second reason is that in the Semitic languages, spirit is a feminine noun—we must always remember this fact in trying to place the *Didascalia* geographically.

In chapter sixteen of the document, of which unfortunately we possess only a few lines in the Latin version, it is no longer a question of a simple mention of deaconesses; rather, we have a description of their role alongside that of the deacons:

[3] I have made corrections in the French translation of F. Nau, op. cit., pp. 81–82, following the English translation of A. Vööbus, *Didascalia . . .* , CSCO 402, pp. 99–100.

[4] Text of the palimpsest of Verona, Biblioteca Capitolare, LV (53), ff., 67r–67v (= xxv-xxvi), ed. R. H. Connolly, op. cit., pp. 87, 89, and E. Tidner, *Didascaliae Apostolorum, Canonum ecclesiasticorum, Traditionis apostolicae versiones latinae*, TU 75 (Berlin: Akademie Verlag, 1963), pp. 41–42.

[5] Ignace d'Antioch, *Aux Magnésiens* 6, ed. P. T. Camelot (SC 10), pp. 98–99. Cf. R. H. Connolly, p. lxxix.

[6] Polycarpe de Smyrne, *Aux Philippiens* 4, ed. P. T. Camelot, SC 10, pp. 208–9.

On the Institution of Deacons and Deaconesses[7]

This is why, O bishop, you must take to yourself workers for justice, helpers who will cooperate with you in guiding others toward life. Those among the people who most please you in this respect should be chosen and instituted as deacons: on the one hand, a man for the administration of the many necessary tasks; on the other hand, a woman for ministry among the women. For there are houses where you may not send deacons, on account of the pagans, but to which you may send deaconesses. And also because the service of a deaconess is required in many other domains.

In the first place, when women go down into the water, it is necessary that those going down into the water be anointed with the oil of unction by a deaconess. Where no other woman is present, especially where no deaconess is present, it will then be necessary that the one who is conducting the baptism must anoint the woman being baptized, but they should then be anointed only on their heads. But where another woman is present, especially a deaconess, it is not good for women to be viewed by men. Just as in ancient times the priests and kings in Israel were anointed, so must you anoint the heads of those receiving baptism—this applies to both men and women. Afterward, whether you yourself are carrying out the baptisms, or whether you have charged the deacons and priests with that responsibility, a female deacon should anoint the women, as we have already indicated. But a man should recite the invocation [ἐπίκλησιν] over them in the water.[8]

When the woman who has been baptized comes up out of the water, the deaconess should receive her and instruct and educate her so that the unbreakable seal of baptism will be preserved in holiness and purity.

For these reasons, we assert that the ministry of a female deacon is especially required and urgent. For our Lord and Savior was himself served by deaconesses, such as Mary Magdalen,

Mary, daughter of James and mother of Joseph[9] and the mother of the sons of Zebedee, along with still other women.[10]	et Maria Iacobi et Ioseph mater et mater filiorum Zebedei.[10]
The ministry of deaconesses is necessary	Tu ergo in aliis rebus diaconissam neces-

---

[7] F. Nau, op. cit., p. 134, translates "ordination" instead of "installation" or "institution" here. R. H. Connolly, op. cit., p. 146, prefers "appointment"; A. Vööbus, CSCO 408, p. 156, gives "institution". This last term must be preferred, everything considered. The Syriac retained the Greek word κατάστασις, which, in St. Hippolytus of Rome, is employed for ministries and states of life not requiring the laying on of hands. As for the phrase in the next line, "take to yourself workers for justice", the *Apostolic Constitutions* attest to the term προχείριζου. The latter is a word that implies no connection whatsoever with a laying on of hands and cannot be considered a technical term, contrary to the insinuation of C. Vagaggini, op. cit., p. 149, n. 1.

[8] This term *epiklēsin* is verified by the *Apostolic Constitutions*, 3:16:4 (ed. Funk, p. 211), as A. Vööbus has pointed out, CSCO 408, p. 157, n. 13.

[9] On this mistake in the Gospel quotation from Mt 27:56, see A. Vööbus, CSCO 402, p. 53.

[10] Cf. Mt 27:55–56. On the parallel text, Lk 8:2–3, see Chapter 1, above.

for you for many reasons. The fact is that deaconesses are necessary for those houses of pagans where Christian women are also living. Deaconesses can go there and visit those who are ill, serve them in whatever their needs might be and bathe those who have begun to recover from their illness.

Deacons should take bishops as models for the kind of conduct they must follow. But they should work even harder than the bishop works. And they should not desire dishonest gains[11] but should be diligent in their ministry.

The number of deacons should be proportioned to the number of the people of the Church in the assembly. There should be enough so that everyone is known and everyone succored. Thus, old women whose strength has declined and brothers and sisters who are ill should be able to enjoy from the deacons the service they properly need.

The women especially should be diligent in their service to other women and the men, deacons, in their service to other men. The deacon should be ready to obey and submit to the commands of the bishop. The deacon should work and spend himself wherever he may be sent to serve or bear a message to someone.[12]

It is truly necessary that everyone should understand his proper place (charge) and be diligent in carrying it out. You should have but one aim, one thought, one soul, even though they exist in two bodies.[13]

sariam habebis, et ut eas gentilium domos ingredia(n)tur, ubi uos accedere non potestis, propter fideles mulieres, et ut eis quae infirmantur ministret quae necessantur, et in balneis iterum eas quae meliorant ut labe(n)t.

Qualis debet esse diaconus.

Diacones sint in actib(us) similes episcopis suis, sed exercitatiores, et *non malum adpetentes lucrum*,[11] ut bene ministrent.

Secundum multitudinem ecclesiae sufficientes erunt, ut et senioribus mulieribus, quae iam non pussunt, fratrib(us) et sororib(us) quae in infirmitate ditinentur, possint placere, in celeritate ministeria sua complentes.

Ex mulier circa mulieres festinabit, diaconus vero, quoniam vir est, (et) circa viros: et ad peregrinationem et ministerium et seruitium ad iussionem episcopi paratissimus et mobilis sit.

Ita ergo unusquisq(ue) proprium agnoscat locum (et) in festinatione impleto; et unum sentiendo, unu(m) spirantes et duo corpora in una anima portantes, cognoscite quantum sit ministerium

[11] Cf. 1 Tim 3:8.

[12] Although this passage about carrying messages is not to be found in the Latin version, it is considered to be authentic. See R. H. Connolly, op. cit., p. 148.

[13] This sentence is without a subject but this is interpreted to be "O bishop and deacon", since the bulk of the chapter is addressed to the bishop. See R. H. Connolly, op. cit., p. 148, and A. Vööbus, CSCO 408, p. 158.

You should understand what your ministry is, in conformity with what was
said by our Master and Savior in the
Gospel:[14] "Whoever would be great
among you must be your servant."[15]

diaconiae, sicut dicit dominus Deus in
euangelio:[14] *Qui uult esse inter uos maior
sit uester diaconus. . . .*[16]

Let us interrupt here our direct quotation from the text. The author goes
on, of course. He writes that the Savior is the model for the deacon, since
the Savior made himself into a servant, and so on. It should not be
surprising that this important text attracted the attention of many commentators.[17]

Achelis wonders if the passages concerned with deaconesses were part
of the original text of the *Didascalia*.[18] In fact, deaconesses are mentioned
nowhere else in the document apart from the passages just quoted. As for
deacons, however, they are frequently and regularly mentioned.[19] The
author also enumerates both the diverse functions and the diverse groups
to be found among the laity.[20] We have already mentioned one of his
anomalies. But in reality, it is the very existence of the Latin version that
guarantees the primitive character of the two passages we have seen
concerning deaconesses, although it also seems reasonably clear that the

[14] Mt 20:26–28.

[15] As in the preceding text, I have corrected the French translation of F. Nau, op. cit., pp.
134–36, by means of the English translation of A. Vööbus, CSCO 408, pp. 156–59.

[16] Text of the palimpsest of Verona, folio 76r (= xxxv), in R. H. Connolly, op. cit., p.
149, and in E. Tidner, op. cit., pp. 59–60.

[17] I refer especially to F. Nau, op. cit., p. xix; A. Kalsbach, *Altkirchliche Einrichtung*, pp.
25–28; idem., *Diakonisse*, col. 919, R. H. Connolly, op. cit., p. xlii; R. Gryson, *Ministère des
femmes*, pp. 75–79; C. Vagaggini, *L'ordinazione delle diaconesse nella tradizione greca e bizantina*,
OCP 40, 174, pp. 147–54; A. Vööbus, CSCO 402, pp. 59–60, 62–63; 408, pp. 155–60 (notes
at the bottom of the pages).

[18] H. Achelis and J. Fleming, *Die syrische Didaskalia, übersetzt und erklärt*, TU, n. F. X, 2
(Leipzig, 1904), p. 265.

[19] But deacons, of course, were inseparably linked with the bishops, whose principal
collaborators they were in the administration of the Church, chaps. 6, 9, 11, 15. Along with
the bishop, deacons were required to persevere in the service of the altar, chap. 18 (Vööbus,
CSC 408, p. 163); they visited the sick (ibid., p. 166); they played a definite role in the
liturgy, chap. 12 (ibid., pp. 131–34), cf. chap. 11 (ibid., pp. 127–28); they were intermediaries
between the bishop and the faithful, chap. 9 (CSCO 402, p. 100).

[20] Bishop, priests, Levites, deacons, chap. 8 (ibid., p. 94); portions to be offered to the
bishop or to widows, deacons, priests and lectors, chap. 9 (ibid., p. 101); below the bishop,
priests, deacons and subdeacons, chap. 9 again (ibid., pp. 106–7); neither the bishop, the
priest, the deacon nor the widow will ever stoop to cursing, chap. 15 (CSCO 408, p. 155); St.
James of Jerusalem, along with his priests, his deacons and, indeed, the whole Church, chap.
24 (ibid., p. 215). We may safely pass over the additions subsequent to the original
establishment of the Syriac text, e.g., the preamble (CSCO 402, p. 8) and chap. 3 (ibid., pp.
29, 37, 41).

installation of deaconesses was both a new and a rather unstable institution in the Church.[21]

In the original Greek *Didascalia*, the term employed for a deaconess must have been ἡ διάκονος or, when the absence of the article meant that gender was not indicated, γυνὴ διάκονος (woman deacon). This usage would have been consistent with the parallel passages found in the *Apostolic Constitutions*.[22] In Syriac there was not the same ambiguity as in Greek, since the Syriac word for servant in general, *m'shamshonitho*, has a feminine form. Sometimes we find simply "woman" (γυνή). The institution of deaconesses recommended to the bishop was not obligatory; if there was no deaconess available, her functions at baptism could be fulfilled by a man. Such a case is specifically foreseen in the text where no woman is available to assist the one baptizing. Only the evident additions to the Syriac version imply any necessity of having deaconesses present at baptisms.[23] Moreover, the author seems strongly constrained to justify the existence of deaconesses at all, whereas the existence of deacons is taken for granted. It is rather surprising in this connection that, in the justification he makes for the existence of deaconesses, the author makes no mention either of Phoebe in the Epistle to the Romans or of "the women" in 1 Timothy 3. Instead, he mentions as examples of deaconesses in the New Testament the women who followed after Jesus and the apostles and "served him" (διακονοῦσαι αὐτῷ) or "ministered to him", as we read in Matthew 27:55.

Only a hasty and superficial reading of the *Didascalia* could ever have prompted anyone to confuse what the *Didascalia* says about deaconesses with what it says elsewhere in its pages about widows. In fact, the two chapters that precede chapter 16, where the description of deaconesses appears, contain a long description of widows as a separate group, along with abundant advice and counsel for them.[24] Along with those widows who were simply helped and supported by the Church, there were also widows who had been officially instituted or installed in an official ecclesial role—the *Apostolic Constitutions* confirm the use of the Greek verb καθίστημι for this institution. To these widows belonging to the estab-

[21] These facts are correctly stressed by R. Gryson, *Ministère des femmes*, p. 78.

[22] In the passages taken from the *Didascalia*, the *Apostolic Constitutions* consistently employs these two terms, whereas elsewhere in the same document, almost without exception, the neologism διακόνισσα is used. This neologism appeared for the first time in Canon 19 of the Council of Nicaea; see Gryson, *Ministère des femmes*, p. 77, n. 2. The word lists for both the *Didascalia* and the *Apostolic Constitutions* are to be found in the *Index vocabulorum* of the edition of F. X. Funk, vol. 1 (Paderborn, Schoeningh, 1905), p. 655.

[23] A. Vööbus, CSCO 402, pp. 59–60.

[24] F. Nau, op. cit., pp. 121–33, cf. p. xix; R. H. Connolly, op. cit., pp. 130–45, cf. pp. xlii–xlv; A. Vööbus, CSCO 408, pp. 141–55; cf. Gryson, *Ministère des femmes*, pp. 65–75.

lished group of that name, the author of the *Didascalia* applies the criteria
we have already reviewed in 1 Timothy 5:9–10, developing these criteria
even further. However, the author lowered to fifty the age at which
otherwise eligible widows could officially be instituted. These widows
were to live a secluded life apart; their role was strictly contemplative.
Teaching activities and, even more strongly, participation in the administration of baptism were forbidden to them.[25] At each mention of their
being forbidden to administer baptism, the same reason was given: Jesus
Christ accorded no such mission to the women who followed him. It is, of
course, quite possible that the bishop could recruit deaconesses from the
ranks of the widows. However, nowhere does the *Didascalia* say this.[26] In
any case, deaconesses were clearly distinguished from widows by the
double activity assigned to them.

The first task of the deaconess was to visit the homes of those Christian
women who lived in pagan households and were immobilized by illness
or could not otherwise go out. The deaconesses were supposed to "serve
them in whatever their needs might be", a spiritual work of mercy, but
they were also supposed to perform corporal works of mercy and "bathe
those who [had] begun to recover from their illness."[27] The same
kinds of acts were performed by deacons for men.

The second task of the deaconess involved the baptism of women.
Certainly the deaconess, like the widow, was herself forbidden to baptize.
The bishop alone administered baptism, or, at his command, the priests
and deacons could administer it: "But a man should recite the epiclesis
over them in the water." For the Church of the author of the *Didascalia*,
however, the baptismal immersion was accompanied by an anointment
with holy oils over the whole body, and it was not considered "good for
women to be viewed by men". Thus, when a deaconess was present, the
celebrant limited himself to anointing women candidates for baptism on
the head only; the deaconess would then go on to apply the oil over the
whole body. In fact, in the absence of a deaconess, this function could be
carried out by another woman. But the participation of a deaconess meant
that she assumed a responsibility vis-à-vis the neophyte similar to that of a
godmother: "When the woman who has been baptized comes up out of
the water, the deaconess should receive her and instruct and educate
her. . . ."

The ministry performed by deaconesses was thus an important one. In

---

[25] Here, again, the Syriac text gathered a few additions in the course of time: A. Vööbus,
CSCO 402, pp. 62–63.

[26] R. H. Connolly, op. cit., p. xlii.

[27] The Latin version of the text confirms that it is not baptism that is being referred to here
but definitely "baths": ". . . *in balneis . . . ut lavet*".

chapter 16 of the *Didascalia*, it is presented as parallel with that of the deacon, so much so that Fr. Cipriano Vagaggini was moved to describe it as one of the two branches of the Church's total ministry subsumed under the diaconate: "The diaconal ministry of the Church had two branches: a masculine ministry and a feminine one for ministering to women specifically."[28] This is to forget, however, as we saw earlier in chapter 9 of the *Didascalia*, that deaconesses were placed in a separate category from deacons. Moreover, throughout the document as a whole, except for the passages we have quoted, deaconesses are not mentioned at all while deacons are mentioned constantly. The roles were thus not exactly parallel. Deaconesses took no part in the liturgy. Indeed, their part in the rite of baptism itself was very restricted; they simply completed the anointing begun by the celebrant. Nor did they pronounce the invocation, or epiclesis. In no way could they be considered on the same level as deacons: they were their auxiliaries.[29]

The *Didascalia* indicates that it was the pressure of social conditions that brought about the creation of deaconesses in the Church; social conditions made their creation necessary at least in a relative sense. This necessity came to be perceived as more absolute in the course of the development of the Syriac text. There were households to which the bishop could never have sent a deacon to minister to the Christian women living therein, because the households were headed by pagans. A female deacon, however, could gain admittance without difficulty.

But it was the rite of baptism, in that era as common for adults as for children, that created the greatest practical difficulties. Contrary to what certain historians of the liturgy may have supposed based on the model of later practice, baptism required total nudity. The author of the *Didascalia* in effect points out, however, that the customs of his country did not accept that naked women should be viewed by men; certainly they could not be anointed over their entire bodies by men. Thus the celebrant anointed them on the head only and held out his hands to pronounce over them the baptismal invocation. We shall see further on how the later discipline of some of the Eastern churches made sure that he would be able to do this without beholding the nudity of the baptismal candidate. Deaconesses emerged in the Church in a region of the East where the strict

[28] C. Vagaggini, art. cit., p. 151.

[29] Cf. J. G. Davies, "Deacons, Deaconesses and the Minor Orders in the Patristic Period", in *Journal of Ecclesiastical History* 14 (1963): 4: "The initial identity of nomenclature would suggest that [the order of deaconesses] derived from the male diaconate for the special purposes outlined above. . . . Several of the minor orders developed from the diaconate in this same period due to the increase in congregations, and it is at least reasonable that the same cause was operative in the foundation of the order of deaconesses."

separation of women required a specific feminine ministry to serve other women.[30]

What church was it, then, in which deaconesses first appeared? It was not one of the churches of a great urban center. The clergy were not numerous; perhaps there were no more than one or two deacons. Sub-deacons are mentioned in the *Didascalia* only fleetingly. The way of proceeding with the liturgy when no lector was available is covered.[31] Priests had no independent role to speak of.[32] As for the region in which this church was located, various elements in the document allow us to place it approximately. First, it is evident that the original author, although he wrote in Greek, was himself a Semite.[33] He was probably a Jewish-Christian who was acquainted with the apocryphal literature related to the Old Testament—in particular, the Prayer of Manasseh. This author opposed the Judaizers in δευτερῶσις (the Church); he actively opposed Deuteronomy and the *Mishna*.[34] He knew the so-called "Gospel of Peter", to which he alludes[35] and which is, of course, a Jewish-Christian work.[36]

Considering all these facts, it would not be impossible to hold that Palestine itself was the homeland of the *Didascalia*. However, this is not the only possible hypothesis regarding its origin. Other pieces of evidence would place the document farther east, in Arabia, or perhaps even farther north in Coele-Syria, in Edessa, in Mesopotamia.[37] Personally, I would favor one of these more eastern locations.

[30] J. G. Davies, ibid.

[31] F. Nau, op. cit., pp. xix–xx. In chapter 12 of the *Didascalia*, the description of the liturgy seems to imply that there are only two deacons.

[32] R. H. Connolly, op. cit., p. xl.

[33] Ibid., pp. lxxviii, lxxxviii. The deaconess is considered by him to be the "type" of the Spirit, because, as we have already explained above, in Syriac the word "spirit" is feminine.

[34] F. Nau, op. cit., pp. xx–xxii, xxviii–xxix; R. H. Connolly, op. cit., pp. lvii–lix, lxxxviii.

[35] F. Nau, op. cit., p. xxv; R. H. Connolly, op. cit., pp. lxxv–lxxvii.

[36] J. Daniélou, *Théologie du judéo-christianisme* (Tournai: Desclée, 1957), pp. 31–33.

[37] F. Nau, op. cit., p. xxi: "The *Didascalia* is thus a Mesopotamian work of the third century. Nevertheless it is possible that a number of modifications were made in the document before the beginning of the fourth century." Baumstark, *Geschichte der syrischen Literatur*, p. 263: "[a translation] of a production of the third century originating in Palestine, in the neighboring province of Arabia or Coele-Syria". R. H. Connolly, op. cit., p. lxxxix: ". . . I agree in the main with Achelis' conclusion and would locate the *Didascalia*, roughly speaking, between Antioch and Edessa, yet without excluding the possibility of lower Syria or even Palestine." J. Quasten, *Patrologia*, ed. española, vol. 1 BAC 206 (Madrid, 1961), p. 438: "The *Didascalia* was . . . composed . . . by a community of Christians converted from paganism in northern Syria. . . ." A. Vööbus, *Découverte de nouvelles sources de la Didascalia syriaque*, RechSR 64 (1976): 459: "This combination of sources indicates that, objectively, we must consider that the document originated either in Palestine or in northern Syria."

The fact is that it was the churches on the confines of the Empire—Mesopotamia and beyond—that most consistently preserved the characteristics of the Jewish-Christians—particularly in the liturgy. For example, the "Acts of Judas Thomas", which were probably composed in Edessa and were also probably closely contemporaneous with the *Didascalia*, describe a ritual for the baptism of women that is quite similar to the one described in the *Didascalia*.[38] It was in these same eastern regions that the *Didascalia* had its greatest influence—in fact, its influence spread rapidly and endured. Certain sects long invoked its authority.[39] The Persian sage Aphraate seems to have been acquainted with and made use of it; this means that the date of its composition must have been quite early. At the very least, we must note the similarity between it and the works of this particular Persian sage.[40] Furthermore, its original form includes archaic terms and ideas found in the most ancient sources traceable to Syria and Mesopotamia.[41] Finally, it is in the ancient baptismal rituals of the Nestorians that we will find the role of deaconesses persisting as first described in the *Didascalia*. On the other hand, as we shall see, it seems that their functions and role were certainly not included in the ancient rites of Jerusalem.[42]

[38] R. A. Lipsius and M. Bonnet, *Acta Apostolorum apocrypha*, vol. 2:2 (Leipzig, 1903), pp. 266–67 (Greek text); W. Wright, *Apocryphal Acts of the Apostles*, vol. 2 (London, 1871), p. 289 (Syriac text): "At the time of the baptism of Vizan and his sisters, the apostle first invoked the name of the Lord over the oil; Mygdonia undressed the women and anointed them after the apostle had first anointed the head of each one with oil and had also anointed Vizan himself. Then all three of the candidates for baptism descended at his request into the water in the name of the Father, Son and Holy Spirit. However, when the author earlier described some baptisms of women, notably that of Mygdonia herself, there was no mention of any woman present to perform the anointments; Mygdonia received an anointing on her head from the apostle before she was undressed; then she was undressed [and was anointed over her whole body?] by her nurse, who covered her loins with a cloth": Greek text, op. cit., pp. 230–31, Syriac text, op. cit., p. 258. The Syriac text is the original here; it dates from the first half of the third century: J. Quasten, op. cit., p. 139. R. H. Connolly, "The Liturgical Homilies of Narsai", TS 8:1 (1909), from p. xlii.

[39] F. X. Funk, *Didascalia et Constitutiones Apostolorum*, 2: 3–8; F. Nau, op. cit., pp. xx–xxi; R. H. Connolly, *Didascalia Apostolorum*, p. lxxxvii.

[40] R. H. Connolly, op. cit., pp. xvii–xviii, xlviii, lxxiv–lxxv, lxxxvii, 265–67; A. Vööbus, CSCO 402, p. 28; Vööbus does not reject the comparisons with the Persian sage Aphraate.

[41] A. Vööbus, op. cit., pp. 46–48.

[42] I do not think it is worthwhile to consider the Pseudo-Clementine *Homilies* and *Recognitiones*, although they were composed in the same region as the *Didascalia* and in roughly the same era. The texts of the *Homilies* (*Homélie* 11, 36:2, ed. B. Rehm, GCS 42, p. 172) and of the *Recognitiones* (6:15, ed. B. Rehm, GCS 51, p. 197) deal with widows, of the "order of widows" (χηρικόν) in a sense that had already become traditional. Kalsbach, in *Altkirchliche Einrichtung*, p. 21, proposes a reconciliation that is entirely gratuitous; the same

2. "THE TESTAMENT OF OUR LORD JESUS CHRIST"
(TESTAMENTUM DOMINI)

Chronological order, as well as concern for logic, might have suggested that we should go on immediately to deal with the *Apostolic Constitutions* after the *Didascalia of the Apostles*. The first six books of the *Apostolic Constitutions* reproduce, develop and sometimes modify the text of the *Didascalia*. However, as we shall see, the *Apostolic Constitutions* cannot be localized in an eastern region in the same way as could the *Didascalia*. The *Apostolic Constitutions* can thus have had only an indirect influence on the liturgy and discipline of the churches of the East under consideration here—through the *Octateuch of Clement*, for example. There is, on the other hand, another document that attempted to harmonize the *Didascalia* with the *Apostolic Tradition* of St. Hippolytus of Rome, while including many other things as well. This document is an ecclesiastical ordinance entitled the "*Testament of Our Lord Jesus Christ*" (*Testamentum Domini*). It is possible to come upon entire chapters of this *Testamentum* in later Syriac editions of the *Didascalia*.[43] The *Testamentum* is a work invoked as an authority by Jacobite collections of canons in particular.

Now that we have reached the point of dealing with documents such as the *Apostolic Constitutions* and the *Testament of Our Lord Jesus Christ*, we should first remind ourselves what sort of documents they are. Dom Bernard Botte described with appropriate caution the approach and method to employ in dealing with these ancient collections of canons:

> Except for the *Didascalia* and the *Apostolic Tradition* of St. Hippolytus, all these collections are apocryphal works that represent the ideals of their compiler more than they do any authentic living reality in the church in which they originated. No doubt they contain some elements that reflect the usages of their particular church. But it is really only when they stray somewhat from the written sources they are using that they become real and authentic witnesses of their own particular milieu. To take the *Testamentum Domini* or the *Apostolic Constitutions* as faithfully reflecting Syrian liturgy of their time and place would be an error. They are really a melange of apostolic fictions; they represent their authors' ideal reforms. Hence they can only be employed as sources if a watchful, critical spirit is also present.[44]

Practically speaking, the *Testament* has only been preserved for us within another collection of eight volumes called the *Octateuch of Clement*. Several

---

thing is true of the widow referred to in *Epist. II de Virginitate* 4 (F. Diekamp, *Patres Apostolici*, vol. 2 [Tübingen: Laup, 1913], p. 35); the widow in question exercises a service of both hospitality and charity (Kalsbach, *Altkirchliche Einrichtung*, p. 20).

[43] A. Vööbus, *Didascalia*, CSCO 402, pp. 39–41, 27–43, etc.

[44] B. Botte, *Les plus anciennes collections canoniques*, OS 5 (1960): 346.

versions of this work exist: a Syriac version, a double Arabic version and an Ethiopic version. However, as in the case of the *Didascalia*, there is general agreement that the text was originally written in Greek. The *Testament* was known to the patriarch Severus of Antioch (d. 538 A.D.), and, according to the colophon on one of the manuscripts, the Syriac version was the work of James of Edessa, completed in 687 A.D.[45] A great variety of dates have been proposed for this work, but there seems to be an almost unanimous opinion that the *Testamentum* was written in the fifth century and, indeed, in the second half of the fifth century,[46] somewhere in the eastern part of Syria.[47]

When the author of the *Testament* wanted to describe the rite of baptism, he generally tried to follow the *Apostolic Tradition* of St. Hippolytus of Rome. However, he was even more preoccupied than the author of the *Didascalia* with the problems of decency and modesty that arose in connection with the baptism of women. He was troubled by the rite as it was described by Hippolytus and, somewhat clumsily, inserted a rubric concerning the baptism of women after the first postbaptismal anointing rite, which had appeared in the *Apostolic Tradition*. There is reason to believe that this rubric is not a purely bookish addition: it may in this case reflect a real practice, since in it are registered two differences from the discipline as described in the *Didascalia*:

> The women must be anointed by the widows who have precedence while the
> priest recites the prayers over them. Similarly, the widows will cover them

[45] On the subject of the various extant manuscripts and on the problems of a possible critical edition, see A. Vööbus, *Nouvelles sources de l'Octateuque Clémentin syriaque*, in *Le Muséon* 86 (1973): 105–9; R. G. Coquin, *Le Testamentum Domini, problèmes de tradition textuelle*, in *Paroles de l'Orient* 5 (1974): pp. 165–88.

[46] The first editor of the *Testament*, Patriarch Ignatius Rahmani, believed that he "*posse demonstrari nostrum librum iam ante medium tertium saeculum exstitisse*" and he even went on to provide "*haud exigua neque levia momenta ad probandum* Testamentum *ad saeculum Ecclesiae secundum merito referendum esse*", *Testamentum* (Moguntiae, F. Kirchheim, 1899; reprinted, G. Olms, 1968), pp. xliii, xlviii. F. Nau, *La version syriaque de l'Octateuque de Clément*, in *Le canoniste contemporain* 30 (1907): 467, gives the views of the various patrologists: Baumstark, *Geschichte der syrischen Literatur*, p. 252: "Fifth century"; J. Quasten, op. cit., p. 475: "The work dates, according to the views of many, from the fifth century, and appears to have been composed in Syria"; A. Vööbus, CSCO 402, p. 39: "The document originated in the second part of the fifth century in Syria." Cf. M. Arranz, *Les rôles dans l'assemblée chrétienne d'après le "Testamentum Domini"*, in *L'assemblée liturgique et les différents rôles dans l'assemblée*, Conferences Saint Serge, XXIII *Semaine d'études liturgiques*, Bibliotheca EL, Subsidia (Rome, Edizioni liturgiche, 1977), pp. 43–77, especially pp. 43–46.

[47] See in the preceding note, the opinions of Quasten and Vööbus. However, the fact that by means of the *Octateuch* the *Testament* was diffused also in Egypt caused Hanssens to hesitate on this point: J. M. Hanssens, *La liturgie d'Hippolyte*, vol. 1, OCA 155 (Rome, 1959), p. 60; and, following him, also P. Ciprotti, *La version syriaque de l'Octateuque de Clément* (Paris: Lethielleux, 1967), p. 1.

with a veil while the bishop reads out what they must confess and what they
must deny.[48]

The precautions required here are much more strict than those in the
Didascalia, since the participation of a feminine minister is here considered
obligatory; in addition, a veil must hide the nudity of the baptismal
candidates from the eyes of the bishop while he is carrying out the
baptismal interrogations. On the other hand, the female ministry is
confided here not to deaconesses but to "the widows who have precedence".

The *Testament* prescribes another feminine ministry in line with the
Didascalia of carrying out visits to women who are ill. Again, it is a widow
who carries out this task: "Each Sunday, she will go out with a deacon or
two, and she will assist them."[49] Actually her task of pastoral solicitude
for other women is conceived quite broadly and is in no way limited to the
neophytes:

> May she strive for perfection in the Lord, as if visited by the Holy Spirit. May
> she carry out with piety and with zeal the things she is commanded to do.
> May she exhort the women who are disobedient; may she instruct those who
> are ignorant; may she convert sinners and teach them how to be modest. . . .[50]
> She will teach those entering [into the church] how they are to behave,
> and she will instruct those going out. She will patiently impart to the
> [female] catechumens what is appropriate and necessary; after three re-
> primands she will no longer deal with those who are disobedient. She will
> love and cherish those who aspire to live a life of purity or virginity; she will
> reprimand with modesty and reserve those who are hostile and rebellious; she
> will maintain a peaceful disposition with all; she will reprove in particular
> those who are prolific with vain words, and if they will not listen to her, she
> will return to them with an older person or else report the whole incident to
> the bishop. . . .[51]

---

[48] *Testament*, bk. II, 8:12, translated into French by F. Nau, in *Le canoniste contemporain* 32,
1909, p. 533, or in P. Ciprotti, op. cit., p. 63. The Latin translation by I. Rahmani, op. cit.,
pp. 129–31, reads: "*Mulieres a viduis habentibus praecedentiam sessionis ungantur, cum presbyter
recitat super illas (formulam). Item in collatione baptismi eaedem viduae intra velum teneant mulieres
obducto velo, cum episcopus profert formulas professionis itemque dum profert formulas abrenuntiationis.*"

[49] Bk. I, 40:2, translated into French by F. Nau, in *Le canoniste contemporain* 31 (1908): 589,
in P. Ciprotti, op. cit., p. 53. I. Rahmani, op. cit., p. 97: "*Visitet aegrotas, omni die dominico
secum adducens diaconum unum aut duos, easdemque adiuvet.*"

[50] I leave aside here for treatment later on the clause that F. Nau has translated "may she
follow in the footsteps of the deaconesses" and that I. Rahmani has more accurately rendered
as "*diaconissasque perquirat*".

[51] Bk. I, 40:2, translated into French by F. Nau, in *Le canoniste contemporain* 31, 1908, p.
589, in P. Ciprotti, op. cit., pp. 52–53. Cf. the Latin translation by I. Rahmani, op. cit., pp.
95–97.

This particular text is a part of four long chapters where the author of the *Testament* obviously bases his treatment very heavily on both the *Apostolic Tradition* of St. Hippolytus[52] and the *Didascalia*.[53] But he also modifies quite significantly the classic image of the widow and the place she occupies in the Church. In both of the earlier sources, widows had no ministerial functions; instead, they were to lead a life of silence and spiritual perfection in which their principal activity was prayer. The *Testament* maintains a concern for these spiritual activities; indeed, it elaborates upon them by describing the forms and rhythms of the prayers to be carried out by widows.[54] But it adds pastoral responsibilities and also a liturgical role that the *Didascalia* assigned to deaconesses instead of widows. Could we therefore conclude from all this that what the document describes as "the widows who have precedence" were in reality deaconesses under another name? The answer to this question is no, for a number of reasons.

First, we must note that the author expressly distinguishes widows from deaconesses. In one place he even says that "the widow must supervise the deaconesses".[55] Deaconesses are mentioned frequently in the text of the *Testament*: in the liturgical assembly, for example, they were "to be stationed near the principal door of the church".[56] At the oblation they were to be behind the screen with the clergy, but "after the subdeacons".[57] In the diaconal litany included in the universal prayer they are named after both subdeacons and lectors.[58] As was the case for all the faithful, deacons were "to call out the names of the sister or deaconess arriving late and therefore obliged to remain outside, so that the people might pray for them."[59] It is clear that deaconesses occupied a very humble place in this scheme of things: at Communion they presented

---

[52] Hippolytus of Rome, *Tradition apostolique*, no. 10, éd. B. Botte, LQF 39, pp. 30–31.

[53] *Didascalie*, cc. 14–15.

[54] Bk. I, 42–43, translated into French by F. Nau, in *Le canoniste contemporain* 31 (1908): 590–92, in P. Ciprotti, op. cit., pp. 54–55; Syriac text and Latin translation by I. Rahmani, op. cit., pp. 100–105.

[55] This is the clause that we left aside earlier, cf. n. 50 to this chapter. I have checked the meaning of the Syriac verb *'aqqeb*; it corresponds to the definition provided by Gryson, *Ministère des femmes*, p. 118, n. 8: "The Syriac verb that is employed here literally means to follow the tracks of someone but figuratively it also means 'to examine or look carefully into something, to superintend or supervise'." It is thus correctly that I. Rahmani translates this as "*diaconissasque perquirat*" in op. cit., p. 97.

[56] Bk. I, 19:7, trans. F. Nau, in P. Ciprotti, op. cit., p. 33: "*Maneant apud portam domus dominicae*", I. Rahmani, op. cit., p. 27. Cf. *Constitutions apostoliques*, II, 57:10, Chapter 3, n. 19, below.

[57] Bk. I, 23:1, I. Rahmani, op. cit., pp. 36–37; P. Ciprotti, op. cit., p. 36.

[58] Bk. I, 35:5, I. Rahmani, op. cit., pp. 86–87; P. Ciprotti, op. cit., p. 50.

[59] Bk. I, 36:4, I. Rahmani, op. cit., pp. 90–91; P. Ciprotti, op. cit., p. 51.

themselves, not with the lower clergy, but with the men of the congregation, the first of the women so to be served.[60] Nothing at all is said about their designation or about the activities normally associated with them, with one exception: if a pregnant woman was unable to attend the Easter Mass, the deaconess was to "bring Communion to her".[61] The hesitation exhibited by the author in mentioning deaconesses in his descriptions of the liturgy indicates that he derived his material from other source documents.

In contrast, widows appear to have played a much more important role than deaconesses. It is true that, in his treatment of widows, the author of the *Testament* also makes ample use of his two sources, the *Apostolic Tradition* and the *Didascalia*. For example, it is possible to deduce an order of precedence from the fact that St. Hippolytus lists widows before lectors, virgins and subdeacons; this order of precedence is explicitly brought out in the way that the author of the *Testament* presents widows as precisely "the widows who have precedence".[62] This is confirmed by the προκαθήμεναι of the eleventh canon of Laodicea[63] and also by the place that widows occupy in the assembly.[64]

Following the First Epistle to Timothy, St. Hippolytus assumed a specific hierarchical action to "institute" or install (καθιστάναι) widows in their function, and he made it clear that this institution took place by pronouncing certain words. Thus all that was required was the text of a prayer for this ritual. It was introduced by a rubric similar to the one used to introduce the rite of ordination of priests and deacons: "The ordination

---

[60] Bk. I, 23:14, I. Rahmani, op. cit., pp. 46–47; P. Ciprotti, op. cit., p. 39. Cf. *Constitutions apostoliques*, VIII, 13:14, Chapter 3, n. 40.

[61] Bk. II, 20:7, I. Rahmani, op. cit., pp. 142–43; P. Ciprotti, op. cit., p. 66.

[62] Bk. I, 19:7; 34:4; 41:1; 43:2; bk. II, 4:4; 8:12. It is no doubt widows that the diaconal litany mentions under the name that corresponds to Greek πρεσβύτιδες, bk. I, 35:5, I. Rahmani, op. cit., pp. 86–87; P. Ciprotti, op. cit., p. 50.

[63] H. T. Bruns, *Canones Apostolorum et conciliorum*, vol. 1 (Berlin: Reimer, 1839), p. 74; Joannou, vol. 1:2, p. 135.

[64] "The place of the bishop will be near to the place called 'in front'; so will that of the widows who are said to be 'seated in front' ": bk. I, 19:7, trans. F. Nau, who understands προσκήνιον [= our "proscenium"—Trans.] as "in front"; in P. Ciprotti, op. cit., p. 32; I. Rahmani, op. cit., pp. 26–27. During the eucharistic offering, they too were to be behind the screen "after the priests, on the left side", that is symmetrically with the deacons, who were on the right side: bk. I, 23:1, I. Rahmani, op. cit., pp. 36–37; P. Ciprotti, op. cit., p. 36. They took Communion after the deacons and before the subdeacons and the lectors: bk. I, 23:14, I. Rahmani, op. cit., pp. 46–47; P. Ciprotti, op. cit., p. 39. There is the same order of enumeration in the diaconal litany—we should take due note that this is the order of St. Hippolytus of Rome—if, at any rate, widows are the ones being designated under the term "old women" (French: "anciennes" [Tr.]): bk. I, 35:5, I. Rahmani, op. cit., pp. 86–87; P. Ciprotti, op. cit., p. 50.

(*mettasr'honûto*) of widows is carried out in the following manner. . . ." It would be incorrect, however, to conclude anything special from the use of this introductory word,[65] for the rite or ritual itself does not allow us to confuse it with the rite of ordination of the bishop, priest or deacon. Even if we did not recall the express interdiction of St. Hippolytus, which he repeated, of not employing laying on of hands in the case of widows, we cannot fail to note that the author of the *Testament* expressly provides for this in the case of the three sacerdotal orders but not in the case of widows.[66] In the latter case, instead of including the prayer of the laying on of hands, he presents a euchological text under the title "Prayer for the Institution of Widows".[67] This, of course, represents the strictest fidelity to the principles of St. Hippolytus. It is thus an error to speak of the ordination of widows. As for the euchological text itself, the prayer makes no mention of the pastoral role that, a few paragraphs earlier, the author of the *Testament* assigned to widows; the prayer itself seems to assume that they will be confined to convents and hence provides a rule of life and an outline of an ideal of contemplative solitude for them:

High and holy God, who contemplates humble things, who chooses the weak as well as the powerful, Venerable, who created vile things as well as noble: give, Lord, to your servant the spirit of power and fortify her in your truth, in order to enable her to carry out your precepts and work in your holy house. May she be a vessel of honor for you and may you glorify her on the day you glorify your poor and humble, O Lord. Give her the strength cheerfully to fulfill the rules you have given her, your servant, to live her life. Give her, Lord, the spirit of humility, strength, patience and sweetness to enable her to endure with inexpressible joy the fatigue of bearing your yoke.

Yes, Lord God, you who know our weakness, sanctify your servant for the glory of your house and for edification also and good example. Fortify her, sanctify her, teach her, O God, for your Kingdom is blessed and

---

[65] It is not legitimate simply to underline the use of this introductory word as if it signified something extremely important, as does M. Arranz (art. cit., n. 46 to this chapter, p. 64); besides the word is quite neutral, and means "designation" or "election" as well as "ordination". Similarly, Gryson (*Ministère des femmes*, pp. 114–15) confuses the reader by asserting without explanation that "a widow could only be ordained after having been *chosen*" and by underlining the mention of this "choice" in chap. 40 as a "parallelism with the case of the bishop, the priest and the deacon". In this case, *'armalṭō dein tettasrah* corresponds to I Tim 5:9: χήρα καταλεγέσθω, and even more closely to προχειρίζω, according to the Hexapla Bible. See n. 7 to this chapter.

[66] For the bishop: *s'yōm* (I, 21) and *kirûtûniya* (χειροτονία) (I, 22). For the priest: *soyem efisqofō* (ἐπίσκοπος) *'ideh 'al rîseh* (I, 30:1) and, again, *kirûtûniya* (I, 30:2). For the deacon: *efisqofō balhûdo n'sîm 'law(y) 'ido* and, again, always *kirûtûniya* (I, 38).

[67] *S'lûto da-mqîmōnûto d-'arm'lōtō* (I, 41:2). *Mqîmōnûtō* means "institution." I owe the philosophical information to the competence of my colleague, Fr. Simon Légasse, professor in the faculty of theology of Toulouse, to whom I am happy to express my gratitude here.

glorious, God the Father, and to you is due all glory as it is also to your
Son. . . .[68]

Our final important point in this section is that, even if the author of the
Testament placed widows symmetrically with deacons at the eucharistic
celebration, he at no time equated widows to deacons. He did not even
borrow from the *Didascalia* that which concerned the baptismal functions
ascribed to them in that document or mention their ministry to women
who were ill. In this respect, he was more faithful to Hippolytus. It would
be a mistake, however, to attribute to him any intention of reacting
against the institution of deaconesses,[69] nor can we speak of "widow-
deaconesses" in connection with this "*Testament of Our Lord Jesus Christ*".[70]

3. THE PRACTICE OF THE CHURCHES OF CHALDEA AND PERSIA

The communities of Chaldea and Persia were located outside the Roman
Empire. They were nevertheless evangelized very early out of Edessa.
These were, of course, regions where Greek was not spoken. Gradually,
as a result of political events and the Church's christological disputes,
most of these churches came to constitute separate bodies that came under
the authority of the Catholics of Seleucia-Ctesiphon in Mesopotamia; a
small number of them coming from within the Roman Empire were
represented within the Syrian Jacobite church.

---

[68] Bk. I, 41:2–3. I. Rahmani, op. cit., pp. 98–99; P. Ciprotti, op. cit., pp. 53–54.

[69] Cf., the remarks of J. G. Davies, art. cit., p. 6.

[70] Kalsbach speaks of "widow-deaconesses" in *Altkirchliche Einrichtung*, pp. 43, 45.
Regarding this *Testamentum Domini*, our analysis is thus in many respects closer to that of
Gryson, *Ministère des femmes*, pp. 110–19. Let us note also that the so-called *Didascalia of
Haddai*, or *Canons of the Apostles Compiled by Haddai*, another work that no doubt was
originally written in Greek, but that has come down to us in a number of other versions as
enumerated below, makes no mention in its eleventh canon of any order except bishops,
priests, deacons and subdeacons. This particular work has come to us in a Syriac version
from the Nestorians (A. Mai, *Scriptorum veterum nova collectio*, vol. 10, first part [Rome:
Typis Collegii Urbani, 1838], pp. 3–7, 169–73); in a Syriac version from the Jacobites
(P. de Lagarde, *Reliquiae iuris ecclesiastici antiquissimi syriacae* [Leipzig: Teubner, 1856], pp.
32–44; W. Cureton, *Ancient Syriac Documents* [London, 1864], pp. 24–35); a Coptic-
Arabic version (cf. W. Riedel, *Die Kirchenrechtsquellen des Patriarchats Alexandrien* [Leipzig:
Deichert, 1900], pp. 159–64); an Arabic-Melkite version (cf. J. B. Darblade, *La collection
canonique arabe des Melkites*, CCOF, ser. 2, fasc. 13, pp. 51–53); and an Armenian version (ed.
H. Ghedighian, CCOF, ser. 2, fasc. 21, pp. 1–41). This collection probably dates from
before the separation of the eastern churches, but its liturgy cannot be dated earlier than the
middle of the fourth century; cf. Baumstark, *Geschichte der syrischen Literatur*, pp. 82–83;
translation of these canons by F. Nau, *Didascalie*, pp. 223–37.

A. "The Ordo [τάξις] and the Canons concerning Ordination [χειροτονίαι] in the Holy Church"

This document has been transmitted to us by means of the Jacobite tradition. It was copied from a Syriac manuscript of the eighth or ninth century, but it is generally recognized that it is much more ancient than that; it probably dates from some time before the end of the fifth century. It was quite evidently aimed at a non-Greek-speaking community; for this reason, it was necessary to explain the meaning of Christian terms in Greek. The mention of a "catholicos" points in the direction of Persia, perhaps to one of the churches united to the Metropolitan of Tagrit on the Tigris; these churches were Jacobite and had their own special rite.[71]

The "Ordo" lays out, in its first part, the duties of bishops, priests, deacons, subdeacons, lectors and exorcists (canons 5–11; Rahmani 1–7). It then presents the ordination rites of these same ministers (canons 12–17; Rahmani 8–13). Then it adds (canon 18; Rahmani 14) the following prescriptions concerning deaconesses:

Canon 18. The deaconess is brought into the diaconicon, or place set apart for deaconesses, and the bishop prays over her; when he has placed her before the altar and she has bowed her head, the bishop then lays his hand upon her head and prays using a prayer that is known and that in no way resembles the prayer used in the ordination of a deacon. The deaconess should not approach the altar; her task lies principally in assisting with the anointing at baptisms. When women are called to receive by baptism the seal of life, this should not give rise to any impurity which might soil or blemish the Church of God; on the contrary, everything should be carried out with good order, preserving purity and chastity. It is not fitting for deacons to anoint women and thus see their nudity, and it was for this reason that the blessed apostles transmitted to us the discipline that men coming to receive the seal of the new life should be brought forward by deacons and be anointed by them with the oil of sanctity. They should not be approached by anyone else, not subdeacon, lector or exorcist. Lay people, men or women, must not so much as cast their glance on anyone being anointed by the deacons for fear that our holy mysteries might thereby be exposed to ridicule and contempt. It was for this same reason that the blessed apostles transmitted these mysteries to us not in writing but by a purely oral tradition; it was appropriate that these mysteries be known only by deacons and priests, not by just anybody. Deaconesses, for their part, were instituted [ett^e sîm(y)] in order to anoint the women coming to receive the seal of baptism. Since it is not fitting that a priest who is

---

[71] A. Baumstark, *Geschichte der syrischen Literatur*, p. 55; I. Ortiz De Urbina, *Patrologia syriaca* (Rome: Pontificium Institutum Orientalium Studiorum, 1958), p. 51; A. Vööbus, *Syrische Kanonessammlungen, ein Beitrag zur Quellenkunde*, I, *Westsyrische Originalurkunden*, 1. A. CSCO 307 (1970), pp. 146–56.

baptizing women should view their nudity, he should extend his hand
toward them from behind a veil serving as a screen. The deaconess brings
forward a woman who is to be baptized to the hand of the priest, and he lays
his hand on her head without directly seeing her; he then pronounces the
threefold baptismal invocation in the name of the Father and of the Son and of
the Holy Spirit. This action is carried out in exactly the same fashion as when
the deacons bring forward male candidates to the priest to be baptized.
Laying his hand upon their heads, he does thus baptize them.

In addition, at the moment of the service of the offering, the deaconesses
station themselves at the church door leading into the part of the church
occupied by the women; this is to prevent men from coming to mingle there
with the women, which would allow impurity right there in the Church of
God. The deaconesses also separate out those women who have not yet
received the seal of baptism which allows them to view with their own eyes
the holy mysteries being carried out or to hear the sacred words with their
own ears. Finally, it is the responsibility of the deaconesses to exhort the
daughters of the covenant as well as lay women in general to behave
themselves properly.[72]

This rather lengthy text is of very great interest. The mention of a laying
on of hands for the ordination of a deaconess is all the more remarkable in
that it was expressly forbidden in earlier canons, in both that of St.
Hippolytus of Rome and the "*Testament of Our Lord Jesus Christ*". It is true
that the case of deaconesses was hardly envisaged in either of these two
documents: the "*Testament*", of course, included a ritual for blessing
widows but with no mention of laying on of hands. We can perhaps see in
this document a kind of intermediate stage between the ordinations of
Hippolytus and the "*Testament*" on the one hand and the rite of the
Apostolic Constitutions on the other. Yet it in no way appears that this
"*Ordo*" derives from the *Apostolic Constitutions*, although the latter document
dates from at least a century earlier.

The role assigned to deaconesses in the "*Ordo*" was threefold. First,
they assisted in the baptism of women, as was the case in the prescriptions
of the *Didascalia*; the detail of the veil used to hide the women's nudity,
however, was found in the ritual described in the "*Testament*". Second,
they watched the church doors—a particularity also of the "*Testament*".
Third, they had a teaching, or educative, function, since they were
required to exhort other women to chastity; this function was also one
that had appeared in the *Didascalia*. In the "*Ordo*", however, a new
dimension was added to the educative task of the deaconesses; perhaps it
was even a primary task: teaching "the daughters of the covenant", the

[72] Both the Syriac text and a Latin translation are to be found in I. Rahmani, *Studia syriaca*,
fasc. 3, *Vetusta documenta liturgica*, Scharfé (1908), pp. 29–31, 60–62.

benat-qeyâmâ. This was the first recorded mention of a mission that was to become progressively more exclusive to deaconesses: the direction of women religious. In this regard, it does not seem that the *"Ordo"* was inspired by the *Apostolic Constitutions*.[73]

B. Questions on the Sacraments of Catholicos Ishô'yahb I

The British Museum Royal Library manuscript Addendum 7181 includes, after the final prayers of the *Ordo Baptismi* of Ishô'yahb III, a text that the copyist says he took from a document entitled "Questions Resolved by the Catholicos Ishô'yahb I". Ishô'yahb I, a former student of the school of Nisib in (modern Nusaybin), was the Bishop of Arzon, and then, from 580 to 596 A.D., Catholicos of Seleucia-Ctesiphon.[74] Of his "XXII Questions on the Sacraments", only a few extracts remain. If the attribution of this document is correct, the description that it provides of the baptism of adult women shows how far beyond even the *Didascalia* the Nestorian tradition went in trying to ensure that modesty would be maintained:

> But if it happens to be women who are to be baptized, it is necessary that special precautions be observed in order that no immodesty be introduced into the Church of God. For this purpose, there should be set apart to assist a chaste deaconess of at least sixty years of age, as Paul prescribed in the case of widows. There should even be a separate place for women candidates for baptism, hidden from view: this place should be a special room adjoining the baptistery. There should be an elongated basin along one side, crossing the double baptistery in such a way that one part of the baptistery can be used for men and another for women. The eyes of the priests should not behold the scene at the moment of the nudity of the women being baptized. To avoid this, there should be a window in the wall above the basin; at the moment when (the woman) is ready to be anointed, the priest should dip three fingers into the oil and then extend his hand through the window. The deaconess

[73] Some scholars find a relationship between this *"Ordo"* and the collection called the "Arabic Canons of Nicaea", and the fact is that both documents exhibit a common concern to explain Greek terms to non-Greek readers. A compiler of the Eastern *Synodicon* even thought these canons should be added to the authentic canons of the Council of Nicaea, influenced by the origin attributed to them by their name; they were supposed to have been transmitted by Marutha de Maiperqat, but there are too many anachronisms in the account attesting to this for it to be considered in any way plausible. They were not utilized by the Chaldeans prior to the Synod of 554, and, today, there is general agreement that they originated in Antioch or, at any rate, were originally set down in Greek. See on this subject: J. Dauvillier, *Chaldéen* (law), in *Dictionnaire de droit canonique*, vol. 3 (Paris: Letouzey, 1938), col. 302; Baumstark, *Geschichte der syrischen Literatur*, pp. 53–54; J. B. Darblade, *La collection canonique arabe des Melkites* (XIII–XVII centuries), introduction, CCOF, ser. 2, fasc. 13, (1946), 81–89.

[74] On Ishô'yahb I and his responses to Jacques de Darai, cf. Baumstark, *Geschichte der syrischen Literatur*, p. 126; J. Dauvillier, op. cit., col. 324–25.

who has been selected for this service should then guide the hand of the priest to the forehead of the woman. She should be anointed on the forehead and not on the chest. The priest should anoint her in the manner that has been described above, with the sign of the cross. The deaconess is on the head [*sic*; no doubt: "puts her hand on the head"] of the woman to be baptized and plunges her three times into the water. The priest, meanwhile, invokes over her the three adorable names. The deaconess then brings her back up out of the water and clothes her in her baptismal robes—all except the crown, for it is for the priest to crown her.

If there is no deaconess available, the bishop should ordain one, and she should perform this service fittingly. If there is no bishop available to ordain a deaconess, then the service should be performed by one of the daughters of the covenant bearing witness to chastity, virginity, modesty and being of a suitable age.[75]

Farther on in the text, speaking of the baptism of the sick, the author specifies that it can be performed by a deacon, but there is no longer any question of a deaconess, no doubt because there is no immersion in the case of the sick. In any case, the deaconess would not be able to invoke the "three adorable names".

As was the case in the *Didascalia*, a substitute could perform the ministry of the deaconess. In this case, however, her place is not to be taken by just any matron. Rather one of "the daughters of the covenant" is to be chosen; this institution was by this time well established. Moreover, deaconesses were required by this particular discipline to fulfill the Pauline role of being more than sixty years of age. It must be added that the science of archeology has not yet actually discovered any Nestorian baptisteries constructed as this ritual required,[76] except possibly in the church of Tâhra at Mosul.[77] It is true, of course, that many of these edifices, in their present condition, probably were built after the disappearance of the practice of baptizing adults.

[75] Syriac text and German translation in G. Dietrich, *Die nestorianische Taufliturgie ins Deutsche, übersetzt und unter Verwertung der neuesten handschriftlichen Funde historisch-kritisch erforscht* (Giessen: Töpelman, 1903), pp. 94–96 (Syriac), 96–99 (German).

[76] There are several descriptions of baptisteries in J. M. Fiey, *Mossoul chrétienne. Recherches publiées sous la direction de l'Institut des lettres orientales de Beyrouth*, 12 (Beirut: Imprimerie catholique, 1959); cf. J. Dauvillier, *L'archéologie des anciennes églises de rite chaldéen*, in *Parole de l'Orient*, 6–7 (1975–76): 357–86. There are few examples of Nestorian church buildings in the church plans collected by A. Khatchatrian, *Les baptistères paléochrétiens, Ecole pratique des Hautes Etudes . . . , Collection chrétienne et byzantine* (Paris: Klincksieck, 1962). In any case the identification of the baptistery space is often very problematical.

[77] J. M. Fiey, op. cit., p. 73.

C. "The Nicene-Arabic Canons"

There is yet another enigmatic collection of canons. It has been preserved in Syriac, Arabic and Ethiopic. This is the collection known as "the Nicene-Arabic Canons". The Syriac edition includes seventy-three canons; it has been wrongly attributed to Marutha de Maiperqat, a prelate who supposedly presented these canons to the Synod of Seleucia-Ctesiphon in 410 A.D. as canons of the Council of Nicaea. It is now generally agreed that Marutha did in fact present the authentic canons of the Council of Nicaea to the Mesopotamian council. However, this collection of seventy-three canons was not among them; it was composed in both Syriac and Greek toward the end of the fifth century. The fact is, though, that it never had any influence in the Greek world. Rather, it became a part of the Nestorian collection of canons and, later, in its Arabic translation, of the Melkite collection of canons.[78] Canon 41 of "the Nicene-Arabic Canons" presents a discipline on the subject of deaconesses that is very close to the discipline that, as we shall see, was to be mandated by the Synod of 676 A.D.:

> 41. *On the Subject of the Daughters of the Covenant and of Deaconesses.* It is the will of this general synod that the churches of the cities should not be without the class of sisters [among whom there must be widows].[79] They must have a zealous director and receive instruction in the Scriptures and, especially, in psalmody. From among this class of sisters, let there be chosen some who have been without reproach from their youth, and who have attained the age of sixty, as the blessed Paul specified in instructing his disciple; let these women be made deaconesses, for the sole purpose of carrying out the service of baptism. Synod decision without anathema.[80]

D. The Synod of Mar George I in 676 A.D.

The fact that deaconesses belonged to the class of "daughters of the covenant" was officially confirmed by canon 9 of the Synod of Mar George I in 676 A.D. The heading of canon 9 reads: "Of the daughters of

[78] On the subject of these collections of canons, see O. Braun, *De sancta Nicaena Synodo* . . . , *Kirchengeschichtliche Studien*, vol. 4, bk. 3 (Münster: Schöningh, 1898); J. B. Chabot, *Synodicon orientale, Notices et extraits des manuscrits de la Bibliothèque Nationale* . . . , vol. 37 (Paris: Imprimerie Nationale, 1902), pp. 4–5, 259–60; Baumstark, *Geschichte des syrischen Literatur*, pp. 53–54; J. B. Darblade, op. cit., pp. 81–89.

[79] This insertion is found in the collection of Macarius, Vatican Arabic ms. 149, and also in the editions of Turrianus and Echellensis; it is lacking, however, in Vatic. Arabic Borgian, 82.

[80] Syriac text and English translation in A. Vööbus, *Syriac and Arabic Documents regarding Legislation Relative to Syriac Asceticism* . . . , *Papers of the Estonian Theological Society in Exile*, 11 (Stockholm, 1960), pp. 125–26. German translation in O. Braun, op. cit., p. 87, following the Vatican Arabic mss. 149, 153, especially Vatic. Arabic Borgian, 82 (K VI 4).

the covenant, also called virgins: What is their ministry [literally, 'their carrying out'] in the Church?" The canon reads as follows:

> Women who have vowed themselves to virginity and to the chaste life of religion must be distinguished by their form of dress as well as by the cut of their hair. Above all, they must know how to recite the psalms, to observe carefully the divine office of the Church and to sing hymns at the proper time. They should chant hymns for the dead on the day of burial as well as on days designated to commemorate the dead. They should also chant the hymns on vigil days. However, they are not permitted to go into the cemetery to chant the hymns. The vigilance employed in watching over the weak should be employed in their regard. They should be assembled in one or two places in the city, in their convents; direction over all of them should be confided to one of the older sisters who can bear witness to a chaste life. They must not do anything [literally: "they must neither go out nor come in"] without her permission. She must see that the rules are applied and that the sisters will not engage in idle conversation. She must preserve them from murmuring and slander, whether originating inside or outside the convent.
>
> The most virtuous of these sisters should be set apart [tèt^{h}paraš] to carry out the ecclesiastical ministry. She should be instituted [or "ordained", tètt^{e}sîm] as a deaconess. Her task is to anoint with the holy oil adult women being baptized; she must always carry out this task, the ceremony of baptism, in the way that modesty requires.[81]

In fact, however, baptism of adults had probably become quite rare by this time, especially when we consider that the ritual reforms of Ishô'yahb III, the predecessor of George I, had consisted principally of eliminating a number of the ceremonies concerned with adults. The description of the baptism of adults provided by Emmanuel bar Shahhare in his *Memra* on baptism (tenth century) shows, by the anachronisms that it contains, that this rite had by then fallen into disuse.[82]

---

[81] Professor J. Dauvillier helped me to correct and make more precise the translation of J. B. Chabot, op. cit., p. 486.

[82] He does not indicate who carried out the anointing over the whole body. See W. de Vries, *Zur Liturgie der Erwachsenentaufe bei der Nestorianern*, OCP 9 (1943): 460–73.

CHAPTER THREE

The *Apostolic Constitutions*:
Meeting Place of Diverse Traditions

Among all the ancient collections of canons, the most voluminous is no doubt the one entitled Διαταγαὶ τῶν ἁγίων ἀποστόλων διὰ Κλήμεντος.[1] This collection includes—with a number of important additions and modifications—another work already examined herein: the *Didascalia*. The *Didascalia* comprises the first six books of this collection. The collection also includes the *Didache*, which along with a number of extracts from various rituals makes up the seventh book of the collection as a whole. It includes also the *Apostolic Tradition* of St. Hippolytus of Rome. Finally, its eighth book includes several series of canons, of which the collection of eighty-five so-called apostolic canons was destined to enjoy a later independent existence and life of its own.[2]

In the form in which the Greek text of this work has come down to us, this compilation has generally been attributed to an Arian or Arianizer, who could also have been the author of an edition of the Epistles of St. Ignatius of Antioch containing many additions and interpolations. The date of the work is believed to be around 380 A.D., and the place of its composition could have been Antioch itself or even Constantinople.[3] It

[1] The mention of Clement here is not part of the original but seems to have been traditionally applied to this collection following the Trullan Synod (see n. 6 to this chapter); and also the canon 85 of bk. VIII of the *Apostolic Constitutions*, ed. F. X. Funk, p. 592. [The Trullan Synod of 692–693 A.D. was a continuation by the Orthodox church of the Third General Council of Constantinople of 680 A.D. (Tr.).]

[2] According to the study of C. H. Turner, *Notes on the Apostolic Constitutions II, The Apostolic Canons*, JTS 16 (1915): 523–38, the original compilation of these 85 canons was the work of the same person who compiled the *Apostolic Constitutions* as a whole, and who also produced an interpolated edition of the Epistles of St. Ignatius of Antioch.

[3] This dating is suggested both by the liturgical calendar that is described in it and by its utilization of the canons and councils and synods up to that of Laodicea. On the subject of both the dating and the author, see F. X. Funk, *Didascalia et Constitutiones apostolorum*, vol. 1 (Paderborn: Schöningh, 1905), pp. xv–xx; J. M. Hanssens, *La liturgie d'Hippolyte* I, OCA 155 (Rome, 1959), p. 52; J. Quasten, *Patrologia*, ed. española prep. por I. Oñatiba, vol. 1, BAC 206 (Madrid, 1961), pp. 473–74; B. Altaner, *Précis de patrologie*, adapté par H. Chirat, Mulhouse Salvator (1961), pp. 99–102; G. Wagner, *Zur Herkunft der Apostolischen Konstitutionem*, in *Mélanges liturgiques offerts au R. P. Dom Bernard Botte* . . . (Louvain: Mont César, 1972), pp. 525–37.

does not seem to have circulated widely in the eastern regions.[4] However, by contrast, its euchology exerted an enormous influence on Egyptian liturgy.[5] In spite of the condemnation issued by the Trullan Synod of 691–692 A.D., which judged the document "falsified by heretics",[6] its prestige continued, at least to some extent, owing especially to the eighty-five "apostolic canons" with which it concluded.

The historian encounters some difficulty locating and identifying the reflection of a real, living Church in this document. We must remind ourselves of the caution voiced by Dom Bernard Botte on the use of these collections of canons as sources generally. Furthermore, the fact that this collection consists of eight volumes does not mean that all of the documents thus brought together have been properly harmonized; the very vocabulary encountered in the work betrays the diversity of the sources from which it has been compiled. In this case, instead of seeking to arrive at a synthesis of the whole, we should aim rather at analyzing separately any collection of documents as diverse as this. This approach impels us, however, to adopt a method different from that employed by Roger Gryson.[7] Also, we should be aware that increasing doubts have been expressed about the classic text of the document, the edition prepared by F. X. Funk published in 1905. There are numerous indications that an earlier edition of the document, or at least an earlier text of book VIII, must have existed. Between the *Apostolic Tradition* of St. Hippolytus of Rome and book VIII of the *Apostolic Constitutions* as found in Funk's edition, this text seems to have existed in two intermediate states. One of these states is represented by the *Epitome*, as it is called: Ἐπιτομὴ τοῦ βιβλίου ἢ τῶν διαταγῶν τῶν ἀποστόλων, of which a parallel edition was also prepared by Funk.[8] The other state is represented by all the variants that exist in the various manuscripts and versions of the document.[9]

---

[4] At least not in the churches of Mesopotamia and Persia. See J. Dauvillier, *Chaldéen* (law), in *Dictionnaire de droit canonique*, vol. 3 (Paris, Letouzey [fasc. 13–14], 1938), col. 297. Among the western Syrians, however, its bk. VIII, with numerous abridgements, was included in the *Octateuch of Clement*.

[5] E. Lanne, *Les ordinations dans le rite copte, leurs relations avec les Constitutions apostoliques et la Tradition d'Hippolyte*, OS 5 (1960): 81–106.

[6] Can. 2, Joannou, vol. I, I, p. 121: "Since in these [85] canons we are asked to receive constitutions from the holy apostles set down by Clement that formerly were modified by heretics, to the detriment of the Church, with false teachings alien to the true faith . . . , we have decided to reject these constitutions . . . , disapproving absolutely of the composition of heretical untruths. . . ."

[7] Op. cit., pp. 95–109. The same defective method is found in P. Rentinck, *La cura pastorale in Antiochia nel IV secolo*, Analecta Gregoriana 178 (Rome, 1970), pp. 230–34.

[8] Op. cit., vol. II, pp. 72–96. On the subject of the earlier editions of the *Epitome*, ibid., p. xii.

[9] See especially J. M. Hanssens, op. cit., pp. 48–52, 202–16; E. Lanne, art. cit. and in sec. 3 of this chapter. The article of A. Baumstark, *Die nichtgriechischen Paralleltexte zum Buch VIII der apostolischen Konstitutionen*, OC I (1901): 98–137, has aged considerably, but it still

I. THE FIRST SIX BOOKS OF THE
"APOSTOLIC CONSTITUTIONS" AND THE "DIDASCALIA"

The compiler of the *Apostolic Constitutions* found two texts concerning deaconesses in the *Didascalia*. When including them in his compilation, he made a certain number of changes, which we must now examine.

We will recall that chapter 9 of the *Didascalia* laid out a typology of the various groups and functions within the Church that deserved the respect of the faithful. According to this typology, those who under the old Jewish law were called Levites were under the new dispensation called variously deacons, priests, widows and orphans.[10] The author of the *Apostolic Constitutions* completed this list: bishops, priests, "deacons, lectors, cantors, doorkeepers, your deaconesses [αἱ διακονοι ὑμῶν], widows, virgins and your orphans".[11] Developing the themes of the *Didascalia*, the author went on: the bishop must be honored as God is honored, the deacon must be at the bishop's side in the same way that Christ is at the side of the Father, the deaconess (ἡ διάκονος) must be honored as the Holy Spirit is honored. Here the author/compiler seizes the occasion to comment that "the deaconess says nothing and does nothing apart from the deacon, just as the Paraclete says nothing and does nothing on his own, but rather glorifying Christ, he is even attentive to Christ's will; and just as it is not possible to believe in Christ apart from the teaching of the Spirit, so it is that, apart from the deaconess, no woman should approach the deacon or the bishop."[12] This phraseology suggests, on the one hand, that the author is making the deaconess subject to the deacon, and, on the other, that he is echoing some of the precautions adopted in a number of churches around the end of the fourth century in order to safeguard the reputation of the priests.[13]

Especially on the subject of the diaconal ministry, is it necessary to compare closely what the *Didascalia* says in its sixteenth chapter with what the compiler of the *Apostolic Constitutions* has set down in his book III. At first the parallelism between deacon and deaconess will seem less rigorous:

Didascalia	*Apostolic Constitutions*
This is why, O bishop, you must take to yourself workers for justice, helpers	This is why, O bishop, you must choose [προχειρίζου] your collabora-

---

retains a certain interest.

[10] See Chapter 2, n. 1.

[11] *Const. apost.*, II, 26:3, Funk, pp. 103, 105.

[12] *Const. apost.*, II, 26:6, Funk, p. 105.

[13] St. Jerome, *Lettre 52 à Népotien* (in 394), ed. L. Bayard (*Belles Lettres*), 2:179: "*Solus cum sola secreto et absque arbitro non sedeas*". Cf. Gryson, *Ministère des femmes*, p. 105.

who will cooperate with you in guiding others toward life. Those among the people who must please you in this respect should be chosen and instituted as deacons: on the one hand, a man for the administration of the many necessary tasks; on the other hand, a woman for ministry among the women.[14]

tors, workers for life and justice, deacons agreeable to God, those from the ranks of the people whom you believe to be most worthy and zealous in fulfilling the needs of their service [τῆς διακονίας]. Choose [προχείρισαι] also a deaconess who is faithful and holy for the service [ὑπηρεσίας] of the women.

We should not overestimate the significance of the differences between these two texts. Immediately following this passage, the author of the *Apostolic Constitutions* returned to the very text of the *Didascalia* itself: "For there are houses where you may not send male deacons [ἄνδρα διάκονον] on account of the pagans, but to which you may send deaconesses [γυναῖκα διάκονον], on account of the evil-minded, and also because the service of a deaconess is required in many other domains."

The description of the rite of baptism that follows evidences a distinct liturgical and disciplinary development. The liturgical development involves a postbaptismal anointing with *myron*, or chrism, while the prebaptismal anointing seems to have become more complicated: to the action of the bishop, who in laying on his hands (ἐν τῇ χειροθεσίᾳ) anoints the head, and to the action of the deaconess in continuing the anointing over the rest of the body, as in the *Didascalia*, the compiler rather clumsily then added that "the deacon anoints the forehead only".[15] The disciplinary development here is that the function of the deaconess is without doubt now so firmly established that it is no longer necessary either to justify her presence or to provide for an appropriate substitute for her in case of her absence; it was considered sufficient to recall that "it is not good for women to be viewed by men". On the other hand, no other mission was any longer being confided to the deaconess comparable to the task of catechizing women after their baptism, which the *Didascalia* had confided to her. Here it is merely stated that after emerging from the baptismal waters "the man will be received by the deacon, the woman by the deaconess [ἡ διάκονος], so that the unbreakable seal will be affixed with gravity and dignity." Similarly, the compiler omitted any mention of a ministry to the sick carried out by deaconesses—a ministry to the sick described in such detail in the *Didascalia*. Perhaps the reason for this was that by this time there was no real difference between the deacon and the deaconess with regard to many of the kinds of service the bishop might require of them:

---

[14] See Chapter 2, above.

[15] Cf. also *Ex Constitutionibus Capitula*, 19, Funk, 2:140: ὁ δὲ διάκονος τὸ στόμα καὶ τὸ στῆθος.

Deacons ought to be without reproach in all things, like bishops; having more activities, they ought to exist in numbers proportioned to the total number of members in the church. This is so that they might serve the invalids of the congregation in a way that is totally free of fault. And the women [ἡ μὲν γυνή] will similarly be concerned with the care of the women. Both [ἀμφότεροι δέ] will carry out tasks related to messages, journeys and other services in accordance with what the prophet Isaiah foretold about our Lord.[16]

Nevertheless the *Apostolic Constitutions* do repeat the prohibitions of the *Didascalia* with regard to women. Women were not to be permitted to teach nor, with stronger reason, to baptize. The practice of the Lord Jesus was taken as normative in this regard.[17] But there is one slight difference between the two documents. We read in the *Didascalia*: "We do not permit women to teach in the assembly [ἐν ἐκκλησίᾳ]," thus referring back to 1 Corinthians 14:34. But we should not place too much emphasis on this variant.[18] It is not the only variant of this type in that part of the *Didascalia* of which we possess only the Syriac text. The most original thing about the compiler of the *Apostolic Constitutions* in supplementing his source is the way in which he extended the argument drawn from the example of the Lord Jesus to include the more general considerations contained in the statement that "the head of a woman is her husband" (1 Cor 11:3); it was not right that the head should be commanded by the rest of the body. This was the reason why women could not be permitted to teach; it would have been considered even more strongly against nature (παρὰ φύσιν) to have permitted them to baptize: "It was impiety and culpable ignorance on the part of the Greeks to ordain priestesses for female divinities." Christ would never have permitted any such thing. He who was the author of nature would never have permitted the violation of the order of nature that he had created.

The compiler of the *Apostolic Constitutions* did not limit himself merely to reproducing the *Didascalia*—and even then, as we have seen, he was quite liberal in the way that he allowed himself to use this source. In a number of places he made mention of deaconesses where no such mention was made in the original *Didascalia*; his purpose was to locate them properly within all the categories of membership and functions within the Church. Thus, in repeating the basic description of the assembly contained in the *Didascalia*, the compiler inserted further information about the place and role of the lector and also about the homily of the

---

[16] *Const. apost.*, III, 16 and 19, Funk 1:209, 211, 213, 215.

[17] *Const. apost.*, III, 6, Funk, p. 191, reproducing *Didascalia* 15, trans. Connolly, p. 133, trans. Vööbus, CSCO 408, p. 145. *Const. apost.*, III, 9–11, ed. Funk, pp. 199, 201, reproducing *Didasc.* 15, trans. Connolly, p. 142, trans. Vööbus, p. 151.

[18] Gryson, *Ministère des femmes*, p. 97.

priest and the bishop. He then went on to add: "Let the doorkeepers remain at the entrances for men in order to guard them, and let the deaconesses [αἱ δὲ διάκονοι] remain at the entrances for women like those who round up sailors for a voyage [δίκην ναυστολόγων], for in the Tent of the Testimony the same usage was followed."[19] We should take note of the fact that this kind of biblical typology will recur in the course of this collection. In the Pseudo-Ignatius of Antioch, we read: "I greet the women guardians of the holy doors, saintly deaconesses in Christ" (τὰς ἐν Χριστῷ διακόνους).[20] The ministry of deaconesses continued inside the assembly, where they occupied themselves with placing the women, whether rich or poor; this function, however, was considered parallel not to that of the doorkeepers but rather to that of the deacons.[21] The shift here indicates the artificiality of this particular addition. Where the author of the *Didascalia* merely required widows to be submissive to the bishops and to the deacons, the author of the *Apostolic Constitutions* added: "and, to be sure, submissive to the deaconesses as well" (ἔτι μὴν καὶ ταῖς διακόνοις).[22]

Up to this point we have seen the compiler of the *Apostolic Constitutions* employing the term ἡ διάκονος as his normal word for "deaconesses". This was certainly the word that he found in his source, the *Didascalia*. However, he employed this term only one more time—that is, if, like Funk, we ignore the variant in the Vatican Greek manuscript 838 (which is a very important one, by the way).[23] Henceforth the compiler adopted the term διακόνισσα, a neologism to which the Council of Nicaea itself had already accustomed Greek ears. It is true, of course, that henceforth the compiler was dealing with source documents that had nothing to do with the *Didascalia*. Two of these variant usages were nevertheless inserted by him into parts of the text still based upon the *Didascalia*. This occurs in book III, in the middle of the chapter on widows. Here the insistence the author placed upon the prohibition of baptism by women motivated him to go on to develop an entire list of sacred actions that could not be carried

---

[19] *Const. apost.*, II, 57:10, Funk, p. 163; cf. *Testament*, I, 19:7, Chapter 2, n. 56, above. In *Didasc.* 12, trans. Connolly, pp. 119–20, trans. Vööbus, CSCO 408, pp. 130–31, it was one of the two deacons who was responsible for watching those who came into the church. Comparing the functions of deaconesses with the guarding of the Tent of Meeting [Cf. Ex 27:21 (Tr.).] is an idea that will recur in bk. VIII. See sec. 3 of this chapter, below.

[20] *Ad Antiochenses* 12:2, ed. F. Diekamp, *Patres apostolici*, vol. 2 (Tübingen: Laup, 1913), p. 222.

[21] *Const. apost.* II, 58:6, Funk, p. 171, addition with respect to *Didasc.* 12, trans. Connolly, pp. 122–25, trans. Vööbus, CSCO 408, p. 134.

[22] *Const. apost.* III, 8:1, Funk, p. 197, addition with respect to *Didasc.* 15, trans. Connolly, pp. 139 (Latin text), 138 (trans. from Syriac), trans. Vööbus, CSCO 408, p. 149.

[23] *Const. apost.*, VIII, 13:14, Funk, p. 516.

out either by lay people or by those in the minor clerical orders. Only the bishops and priests, for example, could baptize, with the help of the deacons. The author continued: "We do not permit priests to ordain [χειροτονεῖν] either deacons, deaconesses [διακονίσσας], lectors, sub-deacons, cantors or doorkeepers; only the bishop can carry out ordinations; such is required for ecclesiastical order and harmony."[24] In book VI and elsewhere, the author / compiler followed the order of the final chapters of the *Didascalia* less faithfully; he also inserted a number of warnings about heresy, apocryphal books and disciplinary errors and added prescriptions concerning the monogamy of bishops, priests and deacons as well as a prohibition of marriage after ordination. The lower orders of the clergy were not subject to this last prohibition, but they too had to be mono-gamous; neither the higher nor lower clergy could marry either a widow or a prostitute, in accordance with Leviticus 21:4. As for the deaconess, she had to be "a chaste virgin, or the widow of a single marriage, faithful and deserving of honor".[25]

2. THE BAPTISMAL RITUALS OF BOOK VII

We have already seen how, in dealing with the ministry of deaconesses in book III, the author of the *Apostolic Constitutions* described the ritual of Christian initiation. In book VII the author went on to describe two other rituals. The first of these, very brief, came on the occasion of the author's inclusion of what the *Didache* had said about baptism; the first thirty-two chapters of that document were adopted *in toto*, and, on baptism, the author of the *Apostolic Constitutions* then wrote: "You will first anoint with the holy oil, then you will baptize with water, and you will complete the process with the seal of chrism. . . ."[26] The author's second description of baptism is a complete ritual (chapters 34–35) inserted among the other diverse documents that have been brought together here; there is no order in these documents, as was the case with the author / compiler's treatment of the *Didache* earlier. The baptismal ritual comes after a long prayer proclaiming the Providence of God. This prayer seems to have been inspired by a Jewish euchology; at any rate, its resemblance to Jewish models is striking.[27] In any case, it is not easy to conjecture about the true

[24] *Const. apost.*, III, 11:3, Funk, p. 201.

[25] *Const. apost.*, VI, 17:4, Funk, p. 341.

[26] *Const. apost.*, VII, 22:2, Funk, p. 406; cf. *Didache* 7.

[27] L. Bouyer, *Eucharistie* (Tournai: Desclée, 1966), pp. 33, 122–36, and also the references indicated there, to which should be added E. Peterson, *Henoch im jüdischen Gebet und in jüdischer Kunst*, in *Miscellanea liturgica in honorem L. Cuniberti Mohlberg*, vol. I, *Bibliotheca EL*, 22 (Rome, 1948), pp. 413–17.

source of this ritual. The formula for the baptismal creed resembles the one promulgated by the Synod of Antioch in 341 A.D.[28] The text of the renunciations is similar to the one contained in the Jerusalem and Antioch catechisms. While awaiting the results of possible future research on this subject, we can venture with some assurance to say that the compiler of the *Apostolic Constitutions* was inspired by the usage of Antioch but that he added a few personal touches of his own.[29] There is a difference between this baptismal ritual and the ones for ordination and the Eucharist that we will find in book VIII; in this ritual, the prayers are not given in set formulas immediately usable by the celebrant. Instead, there is a simple outline indicating the themes the celebrant must develop in blessing the oil and the water. Only the formula that accompanies the postbaptismal anointing with chrism is given in a specific form.[30] If we compare this ritual of initiation with the two earlier descriptions given in the *Apostolic Constitutions*, we will recognize that the structure is identical; it includes prebaptismal anointing with oil, immersion in water and postbaptismal anointing with chrism. The ritual contains a mention of the laying on of hands, although this is almost incidental.[31] It does not indicate how the prebaptismal anointing is to be carried out; it does not allude in any way to the nudity of the baptismal candidates; nor does it provide the slightest indication that deaconesses might any longer be present at baptisms or what their role might be if they were—it does not mention deacons in any such connection either, for that matter.

---

[28] F. X. Funk, op. cit., n. on pp. 445–49.

[29] L. Mitchell, *Baptismal Anointing*, *Alcuin Club Collections* 48 (London, 1966), p. 46, reporting the opinion of E. C. Ratcliff. But which "usage of Antioch" is meant here? In the second half of the fourth century, the church of Antioch underwent all the turmoil of dissidence caused by the three different schisms that occurred then: L. Ligier, *La confirmation, sens et conjoncture oecuménique hier et aujourd'hui*, *Théologie historique* 23 (Paris: Beauchesne, 1973), p. 176.

[30] *Const. apost.*, VII, 42 (blessing of the oil), 43 (blessing of the water), 44 (anointing with chrism), Funk, pp. 448, 450. The author added to the prayer with chrism: ταῦτα καὶ τὰ τούτοις ἀκόλουθα λεγέτω.

[31] *Const. apost.*, VII, 44:3, Funk, p. 450. Cf. D. Van Den Eynde, *Baptême et confirmation d'après les Constitutions apostoliques*, RechSR 27 (1937): 196–212; L. Mitchell, op. cit., pp. 45–48; L. Ligier, op. cit., pp. 177–79.

3. BOOK VIII OF THE "APOSTOLIC CONSTITUTIONS"
AND THE "APOSTOLIC TRADITION" OF HIPPOLYTUS OF ROME

After an introduction in which the compiler of the *Apostolic Traditions* indicated that he would like to fill the gap by the Περὶ χαρισμάτων of St. Hippolytus of Rome,[32] a work that he did not have (and that in fact has probably been irretrievably lost to posterity), he went on at great length to treat and develop the prayers and prescriptions of the *Apostolic Tradition* of St. Hippolytus of Rome. No doubt he was not the first to do this—or else the text that we possess is not the original one. Let us recall that we also possess the *Epitome of Book VIII*, which is quite often much closer to the text of St. Hippolytus, including the very title with which it describes that text: Διατάξεις τῶν ἁγίων ἀποστόλων περὶ χειροτονιῶν διὰ 'Ιππολύτου.[33]

Like Hippolytus himself, the author / compiler began by describing first the election of a bishop and then his ordination. The *Epitome* preserves the exact text of this, without the addition of the "Prayer of Hippolytus"; the *Apostolic Constitutions*, however, contain a broad development of the whole idea, beginning with a "theology" that seems to have been borrowed from a Syrian euchology.[34] As is the case in the text of Hippolytus, the ceremonial of the Mass follows the ritual for the ordination of a bishop; the ceremonial has assumed such vast proportions, however, that it is difficult to imagine how it might ever have been carried out exactly as it has been set down.[35]

In this Mass ceremonial, the listing of the various categories of membership in the assembly is repeated frequently. The deacon's litany in the universal prayer invites the faithful to pray ὑπὲρ πάσης τῆς ἐν Χριστῷ διακονίας καὶ ὑπηρεσίας.[36] Are we to understand that, in employing this unusual turn of phrase, the author intended to include deaconesses? This question arises all the more insistently in that the preceding prayer is not for the *presbyterion* but rather ὑπὲρ τῶν πρεσβυτέρων, and in the following prayer it is proclaimed that ὑπὲρ ἀναγνωστῶν, ψαλτῶν, παρθένων, χηρῶν τε καὶ ὀρφανῶν δεηθῶμεν. Thus, if the author did intend to include

---

[32] *Const. apost.*, VIII, 1–2, Funk, pp. 460–70.

[33] In Funk, 2:77. The Syriac version, which constitutes bks. IV–VII of the *Octateuch of Clement*, seems, on the contrary, to be later than bk. VIII of the *Apostolic Constitutions*; cf. J. M. Hanssens, *La liturgie d'Hippolyte* (I), OCA 155 (Rome, 1959), pp. 75–87, 207–8.

[34] E. Lanne, art. cit. (see n. 5 to this chapter), pp. 94–95.

[35] Ibid., pp. 87–88, concludes, however, following the evidence in what remains of the Great Euchology of the White Monastery, that this Mass ceremonial was actually in use; this view is contrary to the received opinion.

[36] *Const. apost.*, VIII, 10:9, Funk 1:490.

deaconesses, he was very discreet about it. In the prayer of intercession, in the course of the anaphora, the bishop-celebrant prays for himself, for the presbyterate, for the deacons (ὑπὲρ τῶν διακόνων) and for all the clergy.[37] Then he invokes the saints: patriarchs, prophets, just ones, apostles, martyrs, confessors, bishops, priests, deacons, subdeacons, lectors, cantors, virgins, widows, lay people. . . .[38] There is no express mention of deaconesses as such. Only at the moment of Communion are we truly able to discern their presence. For at that point it is stated "that the bishop should first take Communion himself; then come the priests, deacons, subdeacons, lectors, cantors, ascetics and, among the women, the deaconesses [αἱ διάκονοι],[39] virgins and widows; then come the children and, after that, all the people with due order, reverence and decorum and without undue noise".[40] This is the same order of precedence indicated by the *Testament of Our Lord Jesus Christ*.[41] Whether the *Testament* was inspired by the *Apostolic Constitutions* on this point, or whether—and this seems to me more likely—both documents utilized the same source, the point itself seems clear: deaconesses were not members of the clergy, even the lower clergy; they were merely the first in order of precedence among the women.

The ritual for the ordination of priests and deacons follows the model, if not the actual text, of the *Apostolic Tradition*. Shortly thereafter, however, the author of the *Apostolic Constitutions* departed completely from the model of St. Hippolytus as well as from the doctrine justifying it. With regard to the model, St. Hippolytus had presented in succession[42] confessors, widows, lectors, virgins, subdeacons and those possessing the gift of healing. In the *Apostolic Constitutions*, however, as in the *Epitome*, we find deaconesses (διακόνισσα) placed directly after the ordination of deacons; then come subdeacons, lectors and after them confessors, virgins, widows and exorcists.[43] Exorcists have thus taken the place of those possessing gifts of healing in the *Apostolic Tradition*, and confessors have lost their ancient precedence.[44] Deaconesses, who were not even listed in the

---

[37] *Const. apost.*, VIII, 12:41, Funk, p. 510.

[38] *Const. apost.*, VIII, 12:43, Funk, p. 512.

[39] It is true that the word διάκοναι appears in Funk's edition, p. 516, but as we indicated above (see n. 23), the best manuscript reads διακόνισσαι.

[40] *Const. apost.*, VIII, 13:14, Funk, p. 516.

[41] Cf. *Testament*, Chapter 2, n. 60, above.

[42] At least this was the order followed by St. Hippolytus if we accept the Arabic and Ethiopic versions, and, except for the subdeacon, also in the *Testamentum*, B. Botte, does, op. cit., p. xxxi.

[43] *Const. apost.*, VIII, 19–20 (deaconess), 21 (subdeacons), 22 (lectors), 23 (confessors), 24 (virgins), 25 (widows), 26 (exorcists), Funk, pp. 524–28.

[44] Confessors disappear entirely from the list contained in the *Testamentum*.

Apostolic Tradition, have taken the place occupied by widows in that document and in the *Testament of Our Lord Jesus Christ*. The ordination of deaconesses has assumed a place between the ordination of deacons and that of subdeacons, and widows have been relegated to a position following virgins.

More than merely this order of precedence, it is the very doctrine that St. Hippolytus employed to justify his way of proceeding that is eliminated in the *Apostolic Constitutions*. St. Hippolytus was very clear about his theology of inferior orders. He distinguished very clearly between the ordinations of bishops, priests and deacons, effected by the laying on of hands and the recitation of an epiclesis, and the "institution", or installation, of widows, lectors and subdeacons, to whom he expressly denied any laying on of hands. Now, however, both the laying on of hands and the invoking of the coming of the Holy Spirit are prescribed for the deaconess, subdeacon and lector. These two actions are excluded only in the case of confessors, virgins, widows and exorcists. Perhaps this ritual assimilation took place progressively rather than abruptly and suddenly; one indication that this might be so is that the *Epitome* preserved intact the ritual of Hippolytus for the institution or installation of a lector, without any change whatsoever.[45] The compiler of the *Apostolic Constitutions*, however, linked the bishop with the entire series of ministers all the way through that of lector, including, of course, the deaconess. In considering this, however, we must never lose sight of the fact that whatever conclusions the theologian may draw from the phenomenon of the deaconess receiving a laying on of hands along with an invocation to the Holy Spirit to descend upon her, he must necessarily draw in the case of the subdeacon and the lector as well.

We can nevertheless imagine that there were differences in the respective rituals as they were actually carried out, differences suggesting a greater or lesser degree of solemnity. The laying on of hands received by the priest was effected by the bishop himself, surrounded by his priests and deacons. The laying on of hands received by the deaconess also assumed that the bishop was surrounded by his priests, deacons and the other deaconesses (τῶν διακονισσῶν). No such assumption arises, however, in the case of the subdeacon or lector.

The *Apostolic Constitutions* include the texts of the epiclesis intended to accompany the laying on of hands in the course of the ordination of the

---

[45] *Epitome* 13, Funk, 2:82. It is to be noted that, following F. Nau, in P. Ciprotti, *La version syriaque de l'Octateuque de Clément* (Paris: Lethielleux, 1967), p. 82, the Syriac version does not apply the Greek term χειροτονία to deaconesses but reserves it for bishops, priests and deacons; on the other hand, it also omits any specific mention of a laying on of hands—did the latter omission result from the inadvertence of a scribe or was it a voluntary omission?

deaconess, the subdeacon and the lector; comparable texts are totally absent from St. Hippolytus. We shall limit ourselves to citing the prayer recited over the deaconess:

> Eternal God, Father of Our Lord Jesus Christ, Creator of both man and woman, you who filled Miriam, Deborah, Anna and Huldah with the Spirit, you who did not judge it unworthy for your only Son to be born of a woman, you who in the Tent of the Testimony and in the Temple designated [προχειρισάμενος] women to guard your holy doors; let your gaze now fall upon your [female] servant here present, who has been designated [τὴν προχειριζομένην] for the diaconate [εἰς διακονίαν],[46] and give her a holy spirit, cleanse her "from every defilement of body and spirit" [2 Cor 7:1], that she may carry out in a worthy fashion the task confided to her, for your glory and for the praise of your Christ, with whom. . . ."[47]

It is very difficult to decide whether this prayer is the work of the compiler himself, or whether—and we shall have to return to this point—he has here reproduced a formula found elsewhere. Let us look for a moment at the mention of women designated "to guard your holy doors". We have already encountered a reference to this particular task in the Pseudo-Ignatius of Antioch.[48] As in book II, the model proposed is that of the Old Testament Tent of the Testimony ("Tent of Meeting"). In Exodus 38:8, we read that Moses "made the laver of bronze . . . from the mirrors of the ministering women who ministered at the door of the Tent of Meeting".[49] This reference, of course, is very vague and enigmatic. The compiler also made reference to the Temple in this prayer. Nowhere in the Bible, however, is it indicated that women ever functioned as guardians of the doors of the Temple.[50] Miriam, the sister of Aaron; Deborah the prophet-

---

[46] Gryson, *Ministère des femmes*, p. 108. The word translated "diaconate" here gives a meaning that is perhaps too technical; this is the case here, as it is in the prayer for the ordination of a deacon. Funk, 1:524, translates it *"ministerium"*. On the other hand, this technical meaning seems to be justified when the compiler of the *Apostolic Constitutions* united it to ὑπηρεσία, "diaconate and subdiaconate".

[47] *Const. apost.* VIII, 20, Funk, p. 524. There is an almost identical text in *Epitome*, 10, Funk, 2:81 (ὁ πληρώσας πνεύματος, add: ἁγίου). There is an identical text in the *Octateuque syriaque*, V, 12, trans. Nau, in P. Ciprotti, op. cit., p. 82.

[48] See n. 19 to this chapter.

[49] In the Septuagint, 38:26: ἐκ τῶν κατόπτρων τῶν νηστευσασῶν, αἱ ἐνήστευσαν παρὰ τὰς θύρας τῆς σκηνῆς τοῦ μαρτυρίου. In the Hebrew text of 1 Sam 2:22, apropos of the sons of Eli, a gloss recalls those "women who kept watch at the entrance of the Tent of Meeting", but this is missing in nearly all the Greek manuscripts. Origen, however, in the Hexapla, cites three, PG 15, col. 1277–78: τῶν γυναικῶν τῶν παρεστηκυιῶν, or τὰς γυναῖκας παρεστῶσας παρὰ τὴν θύραν τῆς σκηνῆς τοῦ μαρτυρίου.

[50] Perhaps this is really a reference to the gloss cited in the previous note, since this gloss was inserted into a context where the ancient Tent of Meeting had already been replaced by a Temple constructed with doors.

ess; Anna, the daughter of Phanuel (or Hannah, mother of Samuel) and Huldah the prophetess were all selected as representing women to whom special charisms were given.[51] We should take note of the fact that the author of the prayer provided no examples from the apostolic period and made no reference to a baptismal ministry. Rather, he sought to outline the plan of God in general: God created woman as well as man and had certainly not considered it unworthy for his Son to have been born of a woman. Was this approach dictated by a need to reply to objections or dissipate prejudices—the very prejudices, indeed, for which the compiler himself had taken responsibility in book III, thus burdening the argumentation of the *Didascalia*? It is evident from this kind of discrepancy that the *Apostolic Constitutions* are indeed a patchwork of different documents of diverse origins, which the author/compiler scarcely even attempted to bring into any kind of consistency or coherence. In the explanation of the preparations for baptism that the *Apostolic Constitutions* provide at the end of the part based on the *Apostolic Tradition*, deacons are alluded to only in passing, while deaconesses are not mentioned at all.[52] And since the compiler had already included treatments of the baptismal ceremonies three different times, he simply excised the detailed baptismal ritual in St. Hippolytus of Rome, no doubt because the ritual described there was too different from the one he was accustomed to seeing performed.

4. THE CANONS INSERTED INTO BOOK VIII[53]

After having set forth and explained ordinations, the compiler inserted an initial series of canons into the text before going on to describe, following Hippolytus, how new adherents to the Faith were to be received. Already in book III he had introduced a summary of these canons concerning the

[51] Origen, in his Commentary on St. Paul's First Epistle to the Corinthians (see below, Chapter 4, n. 18), had already considered together the prophetic charisms of Deborah (Jg 4–5); of Miriam, sister of Aaron (Ex 15:20–21); of Huldah (2 Kings 22:14–20) and of Anna, daughter of Phanuel (Lk 2:36). Was the author of this prayer inspired by Origen? This is quite possible. The works of Origen were widely diffused and universally utilized. In spite of the authority of this source, however, I believe that the "Anna" mentioned here was actually "Hannah", mother of Samuel (1 Sam 2), for the author appears to have been following a chronological order here. In bk. VIII of Funk's edition, p. 470, there is a more extended list of prophetesses: Miriam; Deborah; Huldah; Judith; Mary, the mother of Christ; Elizabeth; Anna, daughter of Phanuel and the daughters of Philip (Acts 21:9).

[52] *Const. apost.*, VIII, 32:2, Funk, 1:534.

[53] On the subject of these canons: A. Baumstark, *Die nichtgriechischen Paralleltexte zum achten Buch der Apostolischen Konstitutionem*, OC 1 (1901): 127–37; J. M. Hanssens, op. cit., pp. 82–85.

requirement for collegial action in the ordination of a bishop;[54] also contained is an explanation of the powers, and their limits, of the various members of the clergy. After explaining the powers of the bishop, priest and deacon, the compiler added:

> No other category of clergy is allowed to carry out the functions of the deacon. The deaconess [διακόνισσα] does not give blessings; in fact, she does nothing that the priests and deacons do. All that she does is watch the doors and carry out her ministry [ἐξυπηρετεῖσθαι], assisting the priests in the baptism [ἐν τῷ βαπτίζεσθαι] of women for the sake of decency and decorum [διὰ τὸ εὐπρεπές]. The deacon has the power to excommunicate the subdeacon, the lector, the psalmist and the deaconess if this is required and the priest is absent. But neither the subdeacon, the lector, the psalmist nor the deaconess is allowed to excommunicate anyone, whether clerical or lay, for those in these categories are the servants [ὑπηρέται] of the deacons.[55]

Immediately following these canons, the author of the *Apostolic Constitutions* inserted a series of new additions, among which we must notice in particular a prescription regarding a surplus in the offerings [περὶ περισσευμάτων]. This prescription had already appeared in the *Didascalia* and in book II of the *Apostolic Constitutions* themselves; here it is found in a more elaborate form and contains a specific mention of deaconesses:

> Deacons should distribute to the clergy in accordance with the directives of the bishop or the priests any surplus in the offerings made at the time of the Eucharist: four parts to the bishop, three parts to the priest, two parts to the deacon and one part to each of the others: subdeacons, lectors, psalmists and deaconesses [διακονίσσαις]. It is good and agreeable to God to honor each in accordance with his dignity [κατὰ τὴν αὐτοῦ ἀξίαν] for the church is not a school of disorder but rather one of a good order.[56]

Other canons in this series of additional canons, however, simply pass over deaconesses in silence in their enumeration of the ministries of the Church.[57] This fact is particularly remarkable in chapter 46, which serves as a kind of preamble to the eighty-five "apostolic canons" and prescribes that each holder of office in the Church must remain in his proper place and not go beyond the limits of that place: "You know well that the

---

[54] *Const. apost.*, VIII, 27, ed. Funk, p. 530; cf. III, 20:1, ibid., p. 217; *Epitome* 18, Funk, 2:83; *Octateuque syriaque* VI, 1, in P. Ciprotti, op. cit., p. 84.

[55] *Const. apost.*, VIII, 28:5, Funk, 1:530. The same text in the *Epitome* 19, Funk, 2:83–84, and in the *Octateuque syriaque*, VI, 1, P. Ciprotti, op. cit., pp. 84–85.

[56] *Const. apost.*, VIII, 31, Funk, 1:532–34. Cf. *Didasc.* 9, ed. Connolly, pp. 90–91 (trans. Nau; p. 83; trans. Vööbus, CSCO 402, p. 101) and *Const. apost.*, II, 28, ed. Funk, p. 109; *Epitome* 21, ed. Funk, 2:84; *Octateuque syriaque*, VI, 2:2, in P. Ciprotti, p. 85.

[57] None of the ministries below that of deacon is mentioned in VIII, 30: τῶν λοιπῶν κληρικῶν, Funk, 1:532; cf. *Epitome* 20, ed. Funk, 2:84; VIII, 44, τῶν ἐν κλήρῳ, Funk, 1:554; *Octateuque syriaque*, VI, 2:1, VI, 7:1, in P. Ciprotti, pp. 85, 87.

bishops, priests and deacons named by us became such by means of prayer and of the laying on of hands [χειρῶν ἐπιθέσει]."[58] Thus we encounter here the same vision of a sacred order that we found earlier in St. Hippolytus of Rome, one presented in the perspective of that same "good order" that St. Clement admired so much in the hierarchy of the Old Testament (as he also did in that of the New Testament).[59] In this particular vision, there is no place in the Church for others besides the three orders of bishops, priests and deacons to receive the laying on of hands. Having described the functions and limits of those three sacred orders recognized by him here, the author of this text went on to say: "We have established in common priests, deacons, subdeacons and lectors."[60] The author added nothing about how this choice was effected, but the fact remains that the ministries he listed are precisely those found in St. Hippolytus of Rome. Moreover, having merely listed the other ministries, he immediately reverted to describing the institution of bishops, priests and deacons.

As for the eighty-five "apostolic canons" themselves, nearly every one of them legislates for this inevitable trilogy of bishops, priests and deacons; other ministries such as subdeacons, lectors, psalmists or cantors are scarcely ever even mentioned.[61] Never at any place in all of these canons is there ever a question of deaconesses or of any of the other ecclesiastical offices.

5. DOCUMENTARY VALUE OF THE "APOSTOLIC CONSTITUTIONS"

From the analysis that we have conducted, we can easily see that two major traditions are juxtaposed in the *Apostolic Constitutions*, both of them, however, somewhat at the mercy of all the documents that happen to be thrown together to make up the whole collection. Moreover, as we

---

[58] *Const. apost.*, VIII, 46:9, Funk, 1:560; *Epitome*, 28:9, ed. Funk, 2:94; *Octateuque syriaque* VI, 9:4, in P. Ciprotti, op. cit., p. 89.

[59] St. Clement of Rome, *Lettre aux Corinthiens* 40, ed. A. Jaubert, SC 167, pp. 166–67.

[60] *Const. apost.*, VIII, 46:13, Funk, 1:560; *Epitome*, 28:13, Funk, 2:95; *Octateuque syriaque* VI, 9:5, in P. Ciprotti, op. cit., p. 89.

[61] Canon 26: lectors and psalmists; canons 43 and 69: subdeacon, lector, psalmist; often there is mention of clerical orders in general. Also found is the expression ἐκ τοῦ καταλόγου τοῦ ἱερατικοῦ, for example, in canons 8, 17, 18, 63, etc. With regard to the 85 "apostolic canons" generally, see: Joannou, vol. I, 2, pp. 1–7. Joannou does not give an opinion on the origin of these canons: "Is the author of these canons also the compiler of the *Apostolic Constitutions*, or did the letter, as is more probable, pass through several revisions?" The first of these hypotheses is the opinion of C. H. Turner, *Notes on the Apostolic Constitutions, II, The Apostolic Canons*, JTS 16 (1915): 523–38; the second is the opinion of W. M. Plöchl, *Geschichte des Kirchenrechts*, I, 2nd ed. (Vienna, 1959), p. 110.

have seen, the author / compiler of the collection never, apparently, made the slightest effort to achieve a coherent synthesis of the materials that he had at hand.

When he reproduced the *Didascalia*, for example, he followed that document in pairing the deaconess with the deacon and in attributing to the deaconess a ministry of visits to homes and of lending assistance with baptisms analogous to services normally carried out by deacons, though on a more limited scale—indeed, the author / compiler limited the ministry attributed to deaconesses more severely than had been the case in the *Didascalia* itself.[62] At the same time, he added absolutely nothing that might be considered a personal testimonial to the existence of a usage or practice.

The other principal tradition represented in the *Apostolic Constitutions* was surely the tradition that we also find in the *Testament of Our Lord Jesus Christ*, although, as we saw, we are unable to affirm that the *Testament* derived this tradition from the *Apostolic Constitutions* themselves. This tradition included pointedly locating deaconesses at the end of the list of ministries and assigning to them the task of watching the church doors.[63] In other words, this tradition assigned to deaconesses a task already assigned to another office present in the early Church, that of porters; where the office of porters did not exist, the task was usually confided to one of the deacons.[64]

Side by side with these two principal traditions, however, the author / compiler included a new element: a ritual of institution that represented a kind of compromise between the two traditions. In effect, the prayer of institution in this case seems to have been inspired by the second of the two traditions, since it gives as a model for the deaconesses the supposed female guardians of the Old Testament Tent of the Testimony and of the doors of the Temple. Under the influence of the other of the two traditions, however, the ordination of the deaconess was placed between that of the deacon and the subdeacon, replacing the mention of widows made by St. Hippolytus and, more than that, replacing the prayer of institution contained in the *Testament*.

Probably this ritual of institution in the *Apostolic Constitutions* would not have attracted the attention of historians that it has if it did not uniquely include the two particularities we have observed: the extension to deaconesses, subdeacons and lectors of the laying on of hands, which St. Hippolytus of Rome had expressly denied to them; and the obligatory

[62] This is a fact emphasized by Kalsbach, *Altkirchliche Einrichtung*, p. 31.

[63] The *Testament*, I, 19:7, merely says that deaconesses "should remain near the principal door of the edifice" (trans. F. Nau) or "*apud portam domus dominicae*" (trans. Rahmani).

[64] *Didascalie*, 12, ed. Connolly, p. 120; trans. Nau, p. 113; trans. Vööbus, CSCO 408, p. 131.

presence of priests, deacons and deaconesses at the ordination of a deaconess, while no such requirement was mentioned for the subdeacon or the lector. The fact of the laying on of hands for these three minor ministries is far from universally accepted. This is perhaps understandable, considering that the practice is plainly contradicted by some of the other documents included in the same book VIII of the *Apostolic Constitutions*; these other documents, of course, conform in this respect to the tradition of St. Hippolytus' *Apostolic Tradition*. As for the extra solemnity that would have been lent to the ritual by the presence of the entire clergy, this is a subject about which we are unable to arrive at any firm conclusions— unless we elect to explain and justify this dimension of the ritual by making reference, anachronistically, to the example of the Byzantine rite and its medieval commentators, as Fr. Cipriano Vagaggini has attempted to do in a most seductive presentation of the case.[65] However, the Byzantine rite postdated the ritual under consideration here by several centuries. Nevertheless, it was perhaps under the influence of the *Apostolic Constitutions* that the Byzantine rite maintained the practice of laying on of hands for all of the various ministries and even added features linking the ordination of deaconesses more closely with that of deacons, distinguishing both more sharply from the ordinations employed for the lower ministries.

On the other hand, the text of this unusual prayer of institution does not appear to have been actually used anywhere. Was it the artificial creation of our author / compiler? Or was it actually used in a local church somewhere? It is very difficult to say. Because of the very fact that its actual use did not spread anywhere, I would be inclined to attribute it to the author / compiler. The case for this conclusion is all the stronger if it is true that we must identify the author / compiler of the *Apostolic Constitutions* as the same person who falsified the Epistles of St. Ignatius of Antioch.[66]

---

[65] C. Vagaggini, *L'ordinazione delle diaconesse nella tradizione greca e bizantina*, OCP 40 (1974): 163–73.

[66] I have already noted above the divergence in method which separates me from R. Gryson; this divergence becomes all the more marked when we consider the "Note" that he included in his *L'Ordination des diaconesses d'après les Constitutions apostoliques*, in *Mélanges de science religieuse* 31 (1974): 41–45. According to him, the *Apostolic Constitutions* are in no way the work of a "forger" but rather a compilation like the *Testament of Our Lord Jesus Christ* and so many of the other collections of canons that we will be considering in the course of this study. However, the remark of B. Botte (Chapter 2, n. 44), seems to me more and more to be right on the mark when we examine these collections in detail. With regard to the question of whether or not the ordination of deaconesses had any sacramental value, it is evident that no decisive theological conclusion can be reached on the evidence of the *Apostolic Constitutions* without falling into a serious anachronism. For my part, I prefer to defer this theological question until we have completed our historical survey. See Conclusion below.

CHAPTER FOUR

There Were No Deaconesses in Egypt or Ethiopia

This is a fact of considerable significance that we must put on record at the outset: we have never discovered any trace of the institution of deaconesses in any of the documents or inscriptions of the Church in Egypt. Nor can any of the deaconesses whose memory has been preserved in hagiography or in various inscriptions be identified as belonging to this particular region.[1] Nevertheless, we must study the whole situation in considerable detail because some historians have claimed that the testimony of Clement of Alexandria and of Origen alone firmly establishes the existence, if not of deaconesses, at least of widows exercising a similar ministry—indeed, this ministry was supposedly carried out from the third century on.[2] Furthermore, some of the canonical treatises originally composed in the East mentioning deaconesses came to be included also in some of the Alexandrian collections.

1. THE EXEGESIS OF CLEMENT OF ALEXANDRIA AND OF ORIGEN

The testimony of these two Alexandrian theologians of the third century deserves to be examined, especially when we consider that their works represent the earliest attempt to provide a suitable exegesis of the New Testament texts that we have considered at the beginning of this book.

---

[1] G. Lefebvre, in *Recueil des inscriptions grecques chrétiennes d'Egypte* (Cairo: Institut français, 1907), p. 22, mentions under no. 98 an inscription preserved by the Cairo Museum (no. 8696): μαριαμ διακονια. It has not been decided where this inscription actually came from, and its meaning was considered doubtful by W. E. Crum, *Catalogue général des antiquités égyptiennes du Caire, Coptic Monuments* (Cairo: Institut français, 1902); in the index to this work the word *"diakonia"* is followed with a question mark. Gryson, in *Ministère des femmes*, p. 148, following Du Cange and Kalsbach, recalls that in the *Life of St. Eupraxia* (or *Euphrasia*), nos. 7, 10, AASS *Martii*, 2:729, Theodula, the religious superior of the Thebaid convent, to which the saint repaired, is called a "deaconess" (ἡ διάκονος). However, this *Life* is a work of Byzantine origin; it cannot be cited as evidence for the existence of Egyptian ecclesiastical institutions in the Thebaid, not even for the later period when the *Life* itself was composed; cf. G. Lucchesi, in *Bibliotheca Sanctorum*, vol. 5 (1964), col. 233–35.

[2] Kalsbach, *Altkirchliche Einrichtung*, pp. 32–36.

These two Alexandrians show how the Greek-speaking Christians of the third century understood these New Testament passages.

A. Clement of Alexandria

Clement of Alexandria was a contemporary of St. Hippolytus of Rome. Let us glance first at a phrase of his found in his work entitled *The Tutor*:

> Prescriptions concerning those specific persons [πρόσωπα ἐκλεκτά] singled out for mention in the holy books are innumerable: there are those pertaining to bishops and deacons, and those pertaining to widows.[3]

There is no reason to be surprised at a mention of widows here alongside that of bishops and deacons, for that is exactly what is found in 1 Timothy[4]—as it is also found in the *Apostolic Tradition* of St. Hippolytus. But Πρόσωπα ἐκλεκτά really says no more than did χήρα καταλεγέσθω.[5]

However, there is a passage in Clement's *Miscellanies* that interests us rather directly. In this passage, Clement was attempting to clear up any difficulties that might have arisen on the subject of the sanctity of marriage from misunderstanding the observation of St. Paul in 1 Corinthians 9:5: "Do we not have the right to be accompanied by a wife, as the other apostles and the brothers of the Lord and Cephas?"[6] Clement proceeded to explain this passage as follows:

> Those who dedicated themselves entirely to the preaching of the gospel, as was required by this ministry [τῇ διακονίᾳ], took their women along with them, not as spouses, but rather as sisters, so that they might serve as their collaborators in their ministry [συνδιακόνους], serving women who were confined to their homes. Through them, the Lord's teaching was also able to enter the restricted women's houses [εἰς τὴν γυναικωνῖτιν], without causing ill will. We are also aware of all the things that the noble Paul prescribed on the subject of female deacons [περὶ διακόνων γυναικῶν] in one of the two Epistles to Timothy.[7]

Clement was affirming three points here. First, the apostles made their wives collaborators in their ministry. In this regard, the word συνδιακόνους

---

[3] *Pédagogue*, 3, 12, 97:2, trans. C. Mondésert and C. Matray, SC 158 (1970), p. 183; text, ibid., p. 182 (= ed. Staehlin, 3rd ed., GCS 12 [1972]: 289).

[4] In his footnote at the bottom of p. 183 of SC 158, H. I. Marrou underlines this fact.

[5] Kalsbach, in *Altkirchliche Einrichtung*, p. 36, greatly exaggerates the importance of this.

[6] Modern exegesis understands "women" in 1 Cor 9:5 as "believing women" [the Greek contains two words, *adelphēn*, a sister, and *gunaika*, a wife (Tr.)] and does not see it as referring in any way to marriage or to the natural use of marriage. In fact, doubts have often been expressed about whether the word (ἀδελφήν) was actually included in the original text of the Epistle: Gryson, *Ministère des femmes*, p. 59.

[7] *Stromate*, 3, 6, 53:3–4, ed. O. Staehlin, GCS 52 (15), 3rd ed. (1960), p. 220. We have reproduced the translation given by Gryson in *Ministère des femmes*, p. 58.

provided an intentional response to τῇ διακονίᾳ. Second, Clement was trying to explain and justify the female collaboration with the apostles that was required in order to reach women who were confined to restricted residences and did not appear in public. Any attempt by the apostles themselves to reach these women would have generated enormous ill will; only other women could succeed in introducing the Lord's teaching into such houses or in having any contact with the women who lived in them. Up to this point, the term Clement used to describe the activities carried out by women in collaboration with the apostles was the term used in general for "ministry" or "service"; St. Paul similarly employed διάκονος in this very general sense.[8] Suddenly, however, we find Clement resorting to the use not only of διακονία but even of συνδιακόνους, and then going on to use διακόνων γυναικῶν, which was, precisely, the technical term "women deacons" or "female deacons". Clement also made direct reference to 1 Timothy in explanation of all this.

To which passage of this Epistle was he referring? This is a question that has inspired a considerable amount of scholarly discussion. According to Kalsbach (following Clement's editor Staehlin), the passage in question could only be 1 Timothy 5:9, the text referring to widows of not less than sixty who had been the wives of only one husband. He believes this is the only possible passage because it lays down an age requirement as well as specifying a relationship to the institution of marriage. Thus 1 Timothy 3:11, which enumerates the requisite qualities of "the women", cannot be the passage referred to since these two features cannot be predicated of it; the thesis that the latter passage could be the passage referred to is thus "considered to be without any foundation", according to Kalsbach.[9] Also, according to this line of reasoning, Clement's reference to "women deacons" really can only refer to the "widows" of 1 Timothy 5:9. Roger Gryson, however, has critically examined this historical prejudice of Kalsbach's and has shown the weakness of the reasoning that supports it.[10] Gryson pointed out that the wives of the apostles were not, in fact, widows, nor were the widows of 1 Timothy 5:9 charged with the task of evangelization, and where 1 Timothy 3:11 simply speaks of "the women", using the Greek word γυναῖκας, Clement understands instead "women deacons", διακόνους γυναῖκας, from the general context of the passage. Many exegetes have interpreted the passage in exactly this same way.

It is also to be noted that Clement justified this female ministry by the insurmountable obstacles that would have prevented the apostles from entering restricted houses where women were, in effect, confined. This,

---

[8] See Chapter 1, above.
[9] Kalsbach, *Altkirchliche Einrichtung*, pp. 32–33.
[10] Gryson, *Ministère des femmes*, pp. 59, 61.

of course, was one of the very tasks that the author of the *Didascalia* assigned to deaconesses, as we have seen; and the author of the *Didascalia* was a near contemporary of Clement of Alexandria. Was there a possible influence of one upon the other? Certainly there are clearly manifested differences in the perspectives of the two: the *Didascalia* was attempting to deal with an actual concrete pastoral situation, and thus it proposed that the bishop institute deaconesses to deal with that situation. Clement, however, was merely an exegete seeking to provide the proper meaning of a scriptural text; he was not attempting to describe the situation that obtained in the Egypt of his day but rather the one that supposedly obtained in the apostolic era, according to the passage in front of him. He did not look to any contemporary institutions to explain or justify his choice, and he simply referred to "one of the two Epistles to Timothy" (ἐν τῇ ἑτέρᾳ πρὸς Τιμόθεον ἐπιστολῇ).

B. Origen

It has been pointed out how Origen, too, emphasized the dignity of the position occupied by widows in the Church. Like Clement of Alexandria, he mentioned them more than once, usually along with the three orders of the hierarchy:

> There is a debt proper to the widow assisted by the Church, just as there is a debt proper to the deacon, and one proper to the priest and one proper to the bishop—a very considerable debt, in fact, which is claimed by the Savior from the whole Church, and the Savior will demand an accounting if that debt is not discharged.[11]
>
> Not only fornication, but even second marriages prevent us from enjoying any ecclesiastical dignity. For the fact is that neither a bishop, nor a priest, nor a deacon nor a widow can be married more than one time. . . .[12]

The assistance provided by the Church referred to here is certainly in conformity with 1 Timothy 5 and indeed in conformity with the entire biblical tradition; thus there is nothing new to be concluded from this passage from Origen. Nor is the precept of monogamy laid down here anything new; we have already encountered it in Tertullian. It is true that in his *Commentary on Saint John*, in connection with the washing of the disciples' feet, Origen referred to one of the conditions specified by St. Paul for the selection of a widow: "one who has . . . washed the feet of the

---

[11] *De Oratione*, 28:4, ed. P. Koetschau, GCS 3 (1899), p. 377; I have again used the translation of Gryson, p. 52.

[12] *Homélies sur Luc* 17:10 (we have only the Latin translation of this work), ed. M. Rauer, GCS 49 (35), 2nd ed. (1959), p. 110; trans. H. Crouzel, F. Fournier, P. Perichon, SC 87 (1962), p. 263.

saints".[13] Declining to take this text literally, Origen observed that it would be absurd, in the absence of this single condition, to deny a holy widow "admission to this ecclesiastical dignity" (μὴ κατατετάχθαι εἰς ἐκκλησιαστικὴν τιμήν).[14] It would be a serious anachronism to attribute to this expression the meaning associated with it in our modern thought categories.[15] However, in his *Commentary on St. Matthew*,[16] after having cited the Pauline prescriptions concerning the monogamy of bishops, deacons and widows—that is, of those who were accorded "a certain preeminence [ὑπεροχήν τινα] by the Church", Origen did break new ground. As Roger Gryson has aptly remarked,[17] Origen went on "from the consideration of mere literary texts to a consideration of the life of the Church. Suddenly he was no longer concerned with anything except the bishops, presbyters and deacons; the actual hierarchical order of the living Church that he knew superseded in his mind his usual biblical texts—and we hear nothing more about widows." Unlike Tertullian, Origen did not have before his eyes any image based on his actual experience of widows sitting in the special part of the church reserved for them.

He certainly never saw them exercising any such ministry as Clement had attributed to the wives of the apostles. Of course, there was no doubt in his mind that women could receive the grace of prophecy: that they could was evident from the cases of Deborah, Aaron's sister Miriam and the prophetess Huldah in the history of the Old Testament,[18] and also from those of Anna, the daughter of Phanuel, and of the four daughters of Philip in the history of the New Testament.[19] The last example mentioned here was the one that interested Origen the most; this was true because the Montanists cited it in support of their position. The Alexandrian theologian was thus obliged to protest vigorously: none of the women mentioned in the Holy Books ever taught in public, and could thus not be

[13] 1 Tim 5:10.

[14] *In Ioannem comment*. 32:12 (7), ed. E. Preuschen, GCS 10 (1903), p. 444.

[15] This is a defect from which, in my opinion, Kalsbach, in his *Altkirchliche Einrichtung*, does not entirely escape. See p. 36 of his work. The same thing applies to his work in general, especially with respect to the nuances with which he qualifies his opinion; see H. J. Vogt, *Das Kirchenverständnis des Origenes, Bonner Beiträge zur Kirchengeschichte*, vol. 4 (Cologne: Böhlau, 1974), pp. 55–56.

[16] *In Matthaeum comment*. 14:22, ed. E. Klostermann, GCS 40 (1937): 336–38; trans. Gryson, *Ministère des femmes*, pp. 53, 63.

[17] Op. cit., p. 62.

[18] "Fragment 74 on the First Epistle to the Corinthians", text in C. Jenkins, JTS 10 (1908–9): 41–42; Fr. trans. in Gryson, op. cit., pp. 56–57; cf. Chapter 3, n. 51, above, on the possible utilization of this text by the *Apostolic Constitutions*; cf. also *In Iudic. homilia* 5:2, ed. W. A. Baehrens, GCS 30 (1921): 492.

[19] Acts 21:9. This text and the following one are commented on in "Fragment 74", described in the previous note.

cited as instances where the Pauline prohibition did not apply. That
prohibition was clear: "The women should keep silence in the churches."[20]
A church in which a woman could be found preaching was not authentic.[21]
No more could women teach or direct men.[22] Nor did Origen even any
longer confide to them the task of evangelizing those women who did not
appear in public. Basing himself exclusively on the charge given to "the
older women" (πρεσβύτιδες) in the Epistle to Titus, he limited their
function to what was specified in this Epistle: "to teach what is good"
(καλοδιδασκάλους εἶναι).[23] They were to teach the good

> in the sense that they have the responsibility to teach chastity not to young
> men but to young women. It is not fitting that a woman should be the one to
> teach a man, but women should inculcate in young women both chastity and
> the love of their husbands and of their children.[24]

This is "to teach what is good" in the same fashion that widows were
supposed to wash "the feet of the saints", that is, by means of a mere
mechanical type of conformity to a Pauline formula that should have been
understood more in a spiritual sense than in a material one.[25]

Origen, like Clement, also encountered a feminine ministry in the
course of his commentary on the New Testament. Unlike Clement,
however, it was not in either of the Epistles to Timothy; rather it was the
case of Phoebe, which he dealt with in his *Commentary on the Epistle to the
Romans*. Unhappily, we possess only the Latin version of this work:

> Et hic locus apostolica auctoritate docet etiam feminas in ministerio Ecclesiae
> constitui. In quo officio positam Phoeben apud ecclesiam quae est in Cenchris,
> Paulus cum laude magna et commendatione prosequitur, enumerans etiam
> gesta ipsius praeclara, et dicens: Quia in tantum omnibus astitit, hoc est, in
> necessitatibus praesto fuit, ut etiam mihi ipsi in necessitatibus meis aposto-
> licisque laboribus tota devotione mentis astiterit. Simile autem opus eius
> dixerim hospitalitati Lot, qui dum semper hospites suscepit, meruit aliquando
> et angelos hospitio suscipere. Similiter et Abraham, dum semper occurrit
> hospitibus, meruit ut et Dominus cum angelis diverteret ad tabernaculum
> eius. Ita et haec religiosa Phoebe, dum astat omnibus et omnibus obsequitur,
> assistere et obsequi etiam Apostolo meruit. Et ideo locus hic duo pariter
> docet, et haberi, ut diximus, feminas ministras in Ecclesia, et tales debere

---

[20] I Cor 14:34.

[21] Cf. H. J. Vogt, op. cit., p. 57.

[22] Cf. I Tim 2:12.

[23] Titus 2:3.

[24] *In Isaiam homilia* 6:3, ed. W. A. Baehrens, GCS 33 (1925), p. 273; trans. in Gryson,
Ministère des femmes, pp. 54–55.

[25] *In Isaiam homilia* 6, ibid.: *In Ioannem comment.*, 32:12 (7), ed. E. Preuschen, GCS 10
(1903): 444; cf. Gryson, op. cit., pp. 53–58; H. J. Vogt, op. cit., p. 56.

assumi in ministerium, quae adstiterint multis, et per bona officia usque ad
apostolicam laudem meruerint pervenire. Hortatur etiam illud, ut qui bonis
operibus in Ecclesiis dant operam, vicem recipiant a fratribus et honorem,
ut in quibuscumque necessarium fuerit sive carnalibus officiis, honorifice
habeantur.[26]

As Roger Gryson has emphasized, it is easy to translate back into Greek
the expression *feminas in ministerio Ecclesiae constitui*. This is because Phoebe
is described in the exergue of Origen's commentary in a way that conforms
to the usual Latin translation of the New Testament, that is, as one *"quae
est in ministerio Ecclesiae quae est [in] Cenchris"*. This had to be "γυναῖκας
διακόνους τῆς ἐκκλησίας καθίστασθαι".[27] And the affirmation *"haberi . . .
feminas ministras in Ecclesia"* must be translated as "εἶναι γυναῖκας διακόνους
ἐν τῇ Ἐκκλησίᾳ". Finally, *"Assumi in ministerium"* corresponds more or
less to "προσκαλεῖσθαι εἰς τὴν διακονίαν".[28]

The case of Phoebe thus proved two things, as far as Origen was
concerned. First, women were called to serve in the Church just as Phoebe
had been called to serve—that is, in a ministry for which they could be
designated by a positive act of the authorities of the Church. What was
that ministry? Nothing more and nothing less than the ministry carried
out by Phoebe, because the second thing that this Pauline example
proved, as far as Origen was concerned, was that service to the community
was an honor that offered, as recompense for the performance of numerous
acts of charity and dedication, the opening up of the possibility of an even
more noble dedication along the very same lines. Abraham and Lot were
recompensed for having so often practiced hospitality by being granted
the honor of offering hospitality to the Lord himself and his angels.
Phoebe, having rendered service and assistance to all (*dum astat omnibus et
omnibus obsequitur*)—that is, having helped them in their needs (*hoc est in
necessitatibus praesto fuit*)—merited being given the further charge of aiding
and assisting the apostle Paul with all her dedication in his apostolic needs
and labors (*ut etiam mihi ipsi in necessitatibus meis apostolicisque laboribus tota
devotione mentis astiterit; assistere et obsequi etiam Apostolo meruit*). Although
St. Paul gave Phoebe public praise and asked that she too be given
appropriate assistance, it was nevertheless necessary that "those who do
good works in the churches should receive the same honor [*honorem*]
from their brethren in all things whatever that may be necessary; and that
even in the matter of their material needs, they should be treated with

---

[26] *In Epistolam ad Romanos comment.*, 10:17, PG 14, 1278; Fr. trans. in Gryson, op. cit., p. 60.

[27] Gryson, op. cit., ibid., n. 2. Yet I hesitate regarding καθίστασθαι: this term, familiar to
us from Hippolytus, cannot be referred back to the New Testament except to Titus 1:5: ἵνα
. . . καταστήσῃς . . . πρεσβυτέρους.

[28] Cf. Acts 13:3: εἰς τὸ ἔργον ὃ προσκέκλημαι αὐτούς.

honor [*honorifice habeantur*]." It appears that the "ministry" or "*diakonia*" that we are dealing with here is thus the consecration by the Church of charitable activities performed for the sake of one's Christian brethren.

Did Origen believe that these γυναῖκες διάκονοι were "women deacons"— women who carried out the same ordained ministry as their male deacon counterparts? This very real question falls outside the perspective that Origen had on these questions, since his purpose was limited to providing an appropriate exegesis of the text of the Epistle to the Romans. He did not even make any attempt to clarify the issue by reference to 1 Timothy; as it happens, he left us no commentary on that Epistle at all. Thus when he declared, "there are women deacons in the Church", it is inadmissable to infer from this statement that he was talking about an institution that existed in the church in Alexandria of his day or, indeed, in any other particular church of that time. This point has been strongly emphasized by R. Gryson,[29] following a number of other scholars;[30] it has been confirmed by H. J. Vogt.[31] Origen was not confused about the relationship of exegesis to ecclesiology—we saw that in the case of his treatment of widows. He could move easily from one subject to another, as he demonstrated in his "Homily XXII on the Book of Numbers".[32] In this homily, he covered the laying on of hands by Moses upon Joshua; to him, the incident suggested episcopal ordination. It is true that this kind of analogy is more understandable in a homily destined for the people than in a scholarly exegetical commentary. Nowhere, however, did he provide the slightest hint or allusion that there were any hierarchical orders in the Church other than those of bishops, priests and deacons. And all of these were bound by the scriptural rule that required each one of them to be "the husband of one wife" (1 Tim 3:2).[33] Neither widows nor deaconesses were in his mind included in the sacred hierarchy.

---

[29] Gryson, *Ministère des femmes*, pp. 60–64.

[30] Notably by an unsigned article that appeared under the title "On the Early History and Modern Revival of Deaconesses", in *Church Quarterly Review* 47 (1898–99): 302–41 (308–9); L. Zscharnack, *Der Dienst der Frau in den ersten Jahrhunderten der christlichen Kirche* (Göttingen, 1902), pp. 108–9.

[31] H. J. Vogt, op. cit., p. 55.

[32] *Homélies sur les Nombres*, 22:4, Lat. trans. Rufinus, ed. W. A. Baehrens, GCS 30 (1921), p. 209; Fr. trans., A. Méhat, SC 29 (1951), p. 432.

[33] See n. 20 to this chapter. The Bohairic apocryphal manuscript "The Falling Asleep of Mary", ed. F. Robinson, *Coptic Apocryphal Gospels*, TS 4:2 (Cambridge University Press, 1896), p. 52, pictures an apparition of Christ ordaining Peter an archbishop and the disciples, priests, and then goes on to deacons, lectors, psalmists and porters; deaconesses are not mentioned.

2. THE ANCIENT COLLECTIONS OF CANONS

The church in Alexandria showed itself quite willing to accept canonical ordinances originating in other regions. These included such documents from the East as the *Apostolic Tradition* of St. Hippolytus of Rome; the *Didascalia*, the *Testament of Our Lord Jesus Christ*, the "Apostolic Rules", or book VIII of the *Apostolic Constitutions*, with its "Apostolic Canons". Alexandria accepted a number of the existing collections and also re-grouped them in a number of different ways. A special tripartite collection was put together in Alexandria, in fact, and remained particular to the Alexandrian church: the *Synodos*. Our task here must be to examine all the various documents as they relate to the Alexandrian church to determine if any special legislation concerning deaconesses really existed. Our task is also to determine how existing treatment of deaconesses in Church documents taken over from other areas may have been confirmed, modified or eliminated in Alexandria.

A. *The Ecclesiastical Canons of the Holy Apostles*

The *Ecclesiastical Canons of the Holy Apostles* is a collection known under a number of different names. The title of the principal Greek manuscript is κανόνες ἐκκλησιαστικοὶ τῶν ἁγίων ἀποστόλων.[34] Scholars who have studied this particular collection have named it variously *Apostolische Kirchenord-nung*,[35] "Apostolic Church: Order or Ordinance",[36] *Canons Apostoliques*,[37] *Canones Ecclesiastici*[38] and *Ordonnance Apostolique*.[39] The Greek text of the collection has been preserved. As we shall see, the collection is the first of the documents making up the Alexandrian *Synodos*; it is also one of the eight books of the Arabic and Syriac *Octateuch of Clement*.[40] Finally, it was translated into Latin along with the *Didascalia* and the *Apostolic Tradition* in the collection whose valuable fragments are contained in the Verona manuscript (*Bibl. Capitolare* LV).[41]

---

[34] Vienna, Nationalbibliothek, *Hist. graec.* 7 (anciennt. 45).

[35] According to its first editor, J. W. Bickell, *Geschichte des Kirchenrechts*, vol. I (Giessen, 1843), pp. 107–32.

[36] J. P. Arendzen, in JTS 3 (1901–2): 59ff.; E. Peterson, in *The Catholic Encyclopedia*, 2nd ed., I (1936): 683.

[37] B. Botte, *Les plus anciennes collections canoniques*, OS 5 (1960): 332, 334ff.

[38] E. Tidner, *Didascalia apostolorum canonum ecclesiasticorum, Traditionis apostolicae versiones latinae*, TU 75 (Berlin: Akademie Verlag, 1963), p. 105.

[39] J. M. Hanssens, *La liturgie d'Hippolyte* (I), OCA 115 (Rome, 1959), pp. 62–65.

[40] See the table presented by P. Ciprotti, *La version syriaque de l'Octateuque de Clément* (Paris: Lethielleux, 1967), p. 5.

[41] The most recent edition of the Greek text is that of T. Schermann, *Die allgemeine*

Concerning the origin and date of this collection of canons, there has been considerable debate about whether it originated in Syria or in Egypt and whether it dates from the third or the fourth century. Today the preponderance of opinion is inclined to favor an Egyptian origin and to date the collection at the beginning of the fourth century.[42]

The apostles are represented in this document as having come together in a council in order to make decisions in accordance with an order that the Savior supposedly delivered to them in these terms: "Divide up the provinces by lot, regulate their boundaries and the dignities of the bishops [ἐπισκόπων ἀξίας], the seats of the priests [πρεσβυτέρων ἕδρας], the auxiliary functions of the deacons [διακόνων παρεδρείας], the wisdom of the lectors [ἀναγνωστῶν νουνεχίας], the irreproachable qualities of the widows [χηρῶν ἀνεγκλησίας] and everything else that is necessary for the foundation of the Church."[43] From this listing, it becomes clear that the priests and deacons were classified in accordance with the place they occupied in the liturgical assembly. There were no subdeacons. Neither were there any deaconesses or virgins. Following the first two canons presented in the name of all the apostles,[44] canons III–XXX are attributed to one or another of the apostles individually.[45] Canons IV–XIV

Kirchenordnung, frühchristliche Liturgien und kirchliche Überlieferung, vol. 1, *Die allgemeine Kirchenordnung des zweiten Jahrhunderts, Studien zur Geschichte und Kultur des Altertums*, 3. suppl. vol. (Paderborn: Schöningh, 1914); E. Tidner, op. cit., pp. 107–13, covers what remains of the Latin text. Regarding the Sahidic, Bohairic, Arabic and Ethiopic versions in the *Synodos*, see n. 62 to this chapter below. The Syriac version in the *Octateuch* was edited by J. P. Arendzen, "An Entire Syriac Text of the Apostolic Church Order", JTS 3 (1901–2): 59–80.

[42] Harnack proposed already in the last century a date around the beginning of the fourth century; he believed that canons 16–21 utilized a third-century source and that canons 22–28 or 29 utilized a source from the second century: A. Harnack, *Die Quellen der sogenannten Apostolischen Kirchenordnung*, TU 2, 5 (Leipzig, 1886), p. 55; F. X. Funk, in *Doctrina duodecim Apostolorum* (Tübingen: Laup, 1887), pp. lv–lvi, thought that the work could not have been composed after the first half of the third century and added: "*Cum autem libellus in ecclesia Aegyptiaca auctoritatem adeptus sit, eum in Aegypto compositum esse concludere licet*"; E. Peterson, op. cit., said: "The work was compiled in Egypt or possibly in Syria in the third or, at the latest, in the early part of the fourth century"; J. M. Hanssens, op. cit., p. 46, wrote: "The *Ordonnance apostolique* is . . . very probably Egyptian"; B. Botte, art. cit., p. 350, merely noted: "Third or fourth century, uncertain origin"; J. Quasten, *Patrología*, vol. I, trans. I. Oñatibia, BAC 206 (Madrid, 1961), p. 413: "Probably dates from the beginning of the fourth century . . . appears to have been composed in Egypt, although some believe it to have come from Syria"; Gryson, *Ministère des femmes*, p. 80: "There is general agreement on recognizing that *The Ecclesiastical Canons of the Holy Apostles* first saw the light of day in Egypt around the beginning of the fourth century."

[43] *Canons ecclésiastiques des saints Apôtres I*, ed. Schermann, op. cit., p. 13.

[44] The list of the apostles contains a number of curious anomalies, which have been the subject of the research of J. M. Hanssens, op. cit., pp. 63–65.

[45] According to the numbering of the Greek and Sahidic versions. It is canons 2–20

seem to recapitulate a part of the *Didascalia* and to propose "a way of life". From canon XV to canon XXI the subject is the rules for the institution of the bishop, the priests, the lectors, the deacons and the widows; in each case the author utilized the verb καθιστάναι. The local church that emerges from this description was evidently one without a large number of members, resembling in this respect the local church on which the *Didascalia* was also evidently based. The number of priests required was three; the number of deacons required was the same; perhaps there was only one lector. Cephas is reported to have said, apropos of the widows:

> Three widows are to be instituted [καθιστανέσθωσαν]; two of them will persevere in prayer for all those who are being put to the test and for all that is necessary in the light of revelation [πρὸς τὰς ἀποκαλύψεις περὶ οὗ ἂν δέῃ]. The other one will aid those women who are suffering illness. She must be fit for good service [εὐδιάκονος], sober; she must inform the priests of what is needed; she must shun dishonest profit; she must be moderate in her intake of wine so that she can be watchful during night services and carry out the other good works that might be asked of her, for the initial treasures of the Lord are very good.[46]

The number of widows envisaged corresponds to the number of priests and deacons. Also, the alert reader will have noticed that several of the qualities required of the widow were the same as those required of the deacon by 1 Timothy 3:8: "Not addicted to much wine, not greedy for gain" (μὴ οἴνῳ πολλῷ προσέχοντας). Because of these similarities, F. X. Funk concluded that the author of this canon was really thinking about deaconesses and not about widows.[47] J. W. Bickell went considerably farther: he thought he could find in the use of the word ἀποκαλύψεις ("revelation", "disclosure") an allusion to baptismal nudity![48] This shows a bit too much imagination, I think. The widows who devoted them- selves to prayer were doing exactly what they should have been doing according to 1 Timothy. The widow who devoted herself instead to helping women who were ill was performing a service. It is true that in the *Didascalia* this kind of service was attributed to deaconesses. But it would

according to the Arabic version and the Syriac version in the *Octateuch*; 2–21 according to the Ethiopic version; for a table showing the correspondences, see P. Ciprotti, op. cit., p. 16.

[46] Canon 21, ed. Schermann, pp. 29–30; J. M. Hanssens, in *La liturgie d'Hippolyte* (II) (Rome: Univ. Gregoriana, 1970), pp. 58–61, placed in parallel tables (no. 17) a Latin translation of the various witnesses. On the interpretation of the last two lines of this quotation, see J. P. Arendzen, op. cit., p. 71, or Gryson, *Ministère des femmes*, pp. 82–83. But the Vienna ms. says ταῦτα πρῶτα, as E. Tidner has reinterpreted it, op. cit., p. 108, following F. X. Funk, op. cit., p. 68.

[47] F. X. Funk, *Doctrina duodecim Apostolorum*, p. 68.

[48] J. W. Bickell, *Geschichte des Kirchenrechts*, vol. I (Giessen: Heyer, 1843), p. 127; on the place of "revelations" in the *Octateuch*, see Gryson, *Ministère des femmes*, p. 116.

be a serious error to assume that two documents of such differing origins would be based upon exactly the same assumptions.

This collection of canons does go on to speak of another female ministry—but only in order to exclude it. It is possible, of course, that canons XXII–XXVIII come from a different source, as Harnack originally suggested. However that may be, after having again mentioned deacons in order to underline the responsibility they have for doing good works and organizing the material assistance provided by the Church (canon XXIII), the author of these canons imagines a conversation among the disciples (canons XXIV–XXVIII):

Andrew: It would be useful, brothers, to institute [καταστῆσαι], a ministry for women.

Peter: We decided earlier about this. In what concerns the offering of the Body and the Blood, we must give very precise indications.

John: You must have forgotten, brothers, that when the Master asked for the bread and the cup, and when he blessed them and said, "This is my Body and Blood", he did not allow women to assist us [συστῆναι ἡμῖν].

Martha: Mary was the cause of it. He saw her smiling.

Mary: It was not because I laughed. He foretold, when he was teaching, that the weak would be saved by the strong.

Cephas: You should all remember some of the things he said: that women should not pray standing but rather seated on the ground.

James: How can we establish a ministry [διακονίαν] where women are concerned, unless it is a ministry of comfort to those who are in need?[49]

What is the meaning that we must assign to διακονία in this text? The presence of the verb καταστῆσαι here suggests that some kind of liturgical ministry must be envisaged. The train of thought that is pursued in the dialogue tends to confirm this: the apostles immediately raise the subject of the Eucharist only to exclude just as immediately any ministry of women connected with it. Precisely what ministry is it that is being excluded here? According to Roger Gryson, συστῆναι ἡμῖν here means "stand at the side of the apostles", hence, exercise the role of celebrant.[50] Cephas, in order to support the exclusion, recalls a curious precept obliging women to pray seated rather than standing.

I have some difficulty agreeing that this interpretation is entirely well founded, however. It was the deacon, especially, who stood during the celebration—even while the other celebrants were seated. In fact, no seat

---

[49] E. Tidner, op. cit., pp. 110, 112, rather than Schermann, pp. 31–33. Cf. the Tables of J. M. Hanssens, op. cit., 2:62–65.

[50] Gryson, *Ministère des femmes*, pp. 84–85.

was provided for the deacon. In the verb συνίστημι, it is the prefix that normally has the greatest importance, hence the meaning "to assist".[51] The author of the canon certainly could have wished to condemn those sects which allowed women to be priestesses. However, it seems much more plausible and natural that the author was aiming at the institution of deaconesses, as Robinson long ago concluded.[52] As we have seen, the institution of deaconesses existed by this time in some of the churches of the East. However that may be, the passage was understood to have been aimed at deaconesses by the Latin and Coptic translators, if only because of a copyist's variant in the Greek text.[53] The end result was that the only ministry[54] allowed to women was a ministry of charity or assistance to those in need—the ministry assigned by Cephas in our earlier quotation from this collection of canons to one of the three widows who were to be instituted.

B. *The Canons of Hippolytus*

The document known as the "Canons of the Church Written by Hippolytus, Archbishop of Rome" were surrounded by a number of uncertainties for more than a century.[55] Some of them were cleared up, however, by the critical edition accompanied by an important study published by R. G. Coquin in 1956. One of the problems was always that we possessed only an Arabic version of the document transmitted along with Egyptian collections of canons from the Middle Ages, but it has now been established

---

[51] Thus has it been translated: Latin version: *"nobiscum adstarent"*, Tidner, p. 111; Sahidic version: "To assist with them", G. Horner, *The Statutes of the Apostles, or Canones Ecclesiastici* (London: Williams and Norgate, 1904), p. 305; the Arabic version: "He did not direct women to give their assistance", J. and A. Périer, *Les 127 Canons des Apôtres*, PO 8:4 (Paris: Firmin-Didot, 1912), p. 588; the Syriac version: "To remain with us", J. P. Arendzen, op. cit., JTS 3 (1901–2): 73 (F. Nau, in P. Ciprotti, op. cit., p. 74: "To join themselves to us").

[52] C. Robinson, *The Ministry of Deaconesses* (London: Methuen, 1898), pp. 192–93. I was unable to consult the second edition, published in 1914.

[53] Latin version: *"Diaconissam ordinare"*, Tidner, op. cit., p. 111; Coptic version: "Women to be made deacons", G. Horner, op. cit., p. 305. The Syriac version, however, corresponds to the Greek: "If we established ministries for the women", J. P. Arendzen, op. cit., p. 73. The *lamma* is lacking in both the Arabic and Ethiopic. We should add that Arendzen, op. cit., pp. 79–80, thought that the lesson to be derived from the Sahidic, Bohairic and Syriac versions was that the remark of Cephas had a primitive meaning, namely: "It does not beseem women that they should approach the sacrifice with heads uncovered but rather with heads covered."

[54] This time all the versions agreed on *diakonia*.

[55] R. G. Coquin, *Les Canons d'Hippolyte, édition critique de la version arabe, introduction et traduction française*, PO 31:2 (Paris: Firmin-Didot, 1966). Cf. also, since 1956, the lucid position adopted by B. Botte, *L'origine des Canons d'Hippolyte*, in *Mélanges en l'honneur de Mgr. Michel Andrieu* (Strasbourg: Université, 1956), pp. 53–63.

that this Arabic version was based on a Sahidic one that, in turn, was based on an earlier Greek text. Moreover, the title is not really a falsification, since the document is indeed a rather free adaptation of the *Apostolic Tradition* of St. Hippolytus of Rome, with a number of different additions from other sources, notably the *Didascalia* and perhaps even the *Ecclesiastical Canons of the Holy Apostles* just examined. From his examination of the text, Coquin concluded that it was drafted in the patriarchate of Alexandria some time between 336–340 A.D.[56]

These *Canons* are entirely devoid of any mention of deaconesses; they adhere faithfully to the hierarchical degrees recognized by Hippolytus. However, the canon concerned with widows does not precede those concerned with lectors and subdeacons; it follows them, as is, in fact, the case in the Sahidic version of the *Apostolic Tradition*:

> Those who are established as widows should not be ordained. Already in effect for them are the precepts of the apostle. They should not be ordained. Prayers should be said over them, but ordination is for men. The function of widows is important because of the responsibilities laid upon them: frequent prayer, services rendered to those who are ill and frequent fasting.[57]

While St. Hippolytus himself envisaged an entirely contemplative life for widows, the *Canons* assign them a double mission: both prayer and service to the sick, this second task having no doubt been inspired by *The Ecclesiastical Canons of the Holy Apostles*; but the two functions are here united in one vocation.

It is also necessary to note that, in describing the rites of baptism, the author of the *Canons* insisted even more pointedly than did Hippolytus on the fact of baptismal nudity and on the way in which modesty and decency had to be safeguarded. However, he made no allusion whatsoever to any possible assistance rendered by a woman to the bishop, the priests and the deacons in this regard:

> Those who are making the responses for little children should undress them first; then those who will be making the responses for themselves should undress. Finally, the women should be the last to disrobe: they should remove their jewelry, whether of gold or other material; they should also untie the hair lest anything partaking of an alien spirit should descend with them into the water of the second birth. . . . The priest will anoint [the baptismal candidates] with the oil of exorcism. . . . The candidate will be brought by a deacon to the priest, who will be situated next to the water.[58]

[56] R. G. Coquin, op. cit., pp. 318–31.
[57] Canon 9, op. cit., p. 363.
[58] Canon 19, op. cit., p. 379.

It is not specified whether the prebaptismal anointing had to be done over the whole body: it was an unction with the oil of the Eucharist, which was spread over the whole body when the neophyte came up out of the water. The neophyte "then wiped himself with a cloth, which he kept for himself" (although this translation is not certain).[59]

The *Canons of Hippolytus* continued to be included in the medieval canonical collections of the Coptic church in both Egypt and Ethiopia.[60]

C. The Synodos *of the Church in Alexandria*

There is a compilation of canons preserved in Sahidic Coptic, Bohairic Coptic, Arabic and Ethiopic which has, in its Ethiopic edition, the title: *Synodos of Our Fathers the Apostles, Who Established the Direction of the Church*. The numbering of the canons in this compilation differs according to the edition, but their content is the same. Although the various translations do not make this clear, the *Synodos* is really a compilation of the *Ecclesiastical Canons of the Holy Apostles*, the *Apostolic Tradition* of St. Hippolytus of Rome and the equivalent of book VIII of the *Apostolic Constitutions*. All of these collections are presented one after the other without any attempt to establish continuity, and they are then followed by all or part of the eighty-five Greek *Canons*. This entire compilation was also included in the great medieval Egyptian canonical collections.[61] The manuscripts we have of the Bohairic version were copied around the beginning of the nineteenth century. The oldest manuscript of the Sahidic version dates from the year 1006 A.D., but the translation from the original Greek in this manuscript can itself hardly be dated later than the seventh century. The Arabic version was made from the Coptic version, and the Ethiopic version was based on the Arabic version. However, a complete outline of the relationships of dependency between the various versions cannot be made on the basis of the manuscripts that have been preserved.[62]

---

[59] Op. cit., p. 383, n. 19.

[60] Op. cit., pp. 277–307.

[61] Notably: the *Nomocanon* of Michael of Damietta; the *Lamp in the Shadows* of Abu il-Barakat; the collection of canons of Macarius; the *Nomocanon* of Ibn al-'Assal, W. Riedel, *Die Kirchenrechtsquellen des Patriarchats Alexandrien* (Leipzig: Deichert, 1900; reprint. Aalen, Scientia Verlag, 1968), pp. 20–28, 92, 115–19, 124.

[62] A complete modern study of the *Synodos* as a whole remains to be done. The work by W. Riedel cited in the previous note is essential, of course, but it is difficult to use since it lacks tables and identifies manuscripts by their ancient classifications. This work must be supplemented by reference to J. M. Hanssens, *La liturgie d'Hippolyte* (I), OCA 155 (Rome, 1959), pp. 31–47, and, especially for the Coptic manuscripts, to W. Till and J. Leipoldt, *Der koptische Text der Kirchenordnung Hippolyts*, TU 58 (Berlin: Akademie Verlag, 1954), pp. VII–XX; for the Arabic manuscripts, to J. and A. Périer, *Les 127 Canons des Apôtres*, PO 8:4 (Paris: Firmin-Didot, 1912), pp. 554–71; and for the Ethiopic manuscripts to H. Duensing,

Nevertheless it is of the greatest interest to try to determine how the church of Alexandria, and the church of Ethiopia that was so closely dependent upon it, either transmitted or modified those texts concerning the ministry of widows or deaconesses.

There is a single variant in the transmission of the *Ecclesiastical Canons of the Holy Apostles*; it concerns the ministry of widows. According to the Ethiopic version, the nocturnal service of the widows did not consist of their care and comforting of the sick but rather of a mission of prayer.[63]

We must take notice of another anomaly in the Sahidic version. The translator of the imagined dialogue of the apostles had Andrew saying not, as we saw earlier, "it would be useful . . . to institute a ministry [διακονίαν] for women", but instead, "it would be good to decide to make women deacons [διάκονος]."[64] The Bohairic version preserves the same reading.[65] This misreading, we know, recurs in the Latin version. It certainly becomes corrected by the context, of course, by the remark made by James, but in the Arabic and Ethiopic versions it was seen as a problem to the point where the phrase was simply omitted, making the reference to the Eucharist and the remarks of Mary and Martha unintelligible. In the Ethiopic version, the reference to the Eucharist was also modified, turning it into a recommendation for greater reverence thereto. But all the versions are in agreement in limiting the ministry of women to the assistance provided by them to the sick and the indigent.[66]

Where the *Synodos* reproduces the chapter of the *Apostolic Tradition* on widows, it reproduces it integrally: the text has not been modified in any way and there is no variant worthy of mention.[67] We have already noted that in the Sahidic version widows were presented after lectors and subdeacons, while in the others they came before these ministries; the latter order no doubt conformed to the original order of Hippolytus.[68] As for baptism, it is only through the Alexandrian *Synodos* that we

---

Der aethiopische Text der Kirchenordnung des Hippolyts, (Abhandlungen der Akademie der Wissenschaften in Göttingen, Philol.-hist. Klasse, 3, Folge, Nr. 32) (Göttingen: Vandenhoeck and Ruprecht, 1946), pp. 5–13. The publications of Till-Leipoldt and Duensing are limited to the part of the *Synodos* based upon the *Apostolic Tradition*, and hence for the other parts of the Ethiopic version of the *Synodos*, it is necessary to turn to G. Horner, op. cit., and for those of the Sahidic version to P. de Lagarde, *Aegyptiaca* (Göttingen: Dieterich, 1883).

[63] G. Horner, op. cit., p. 136; cf. J. M. Hanssens, *La liturgie d'Hippolyte* (II) (Rome: Univ. Gregoriana, 1970), no. 17, pp. 58–61.

[64] G. Horner, op. cit., p. 305; J. M. Hanssens, op. cit., no. 20, pp. 62–65.

[65] G. Horner, op. cit., p. 447.

[66] Ibid., pp. 137, 305; J. and A. Périer, op. cit., pp. 588–89.

[67] B. Botte, *La tradition apostolique de saint Hippolyte*, LQF 39 (Munster W., 1963), pp. 30–31.

[68] Op. cit., pp. xxx–xxxi.

are acquainted with the rituals that preceded the ritual of immersion according to Hippolytus. The total nudity prescribed was only qualified with a single requirement, namely, that infants and children be baptized first, then men and finally women; no feminine ministry assisting the deacons in the baptism of women was mentioned, nor was any exact description given of how the anointing with oil was carried out.[69] However, in the Ethiopic version there has been introduced, rather clumsily, right in the middle of Hippolytus' chapter treating of offerings, another baptismal ritual, and a very well developed one at that. We will examine it later.

The canons treating of deaconesses corresponding to book VIII of the *Apostolic Constitutions* have undergone modifications and corrections in some of the versions of the *Synodos*, though not in all.[70] Thus, Sahidic canon 64 (Arabic 52, Ethiopic 53) has the charge of watching over the women's part of the church being carried out by subdeacons rather than by deaconesses.[71] Sahidic canon 65 (Arabic 52, Ethiopic 53) omits any mention of deaconesses in order for the distribution of Communion.[72] Sahidic canon 66 lays the groundwork for a significant reworking, which was to undergo some curious vicissitudes both in the Arabic version (canon 53) and the Ethiopic version (canon 54):

> On the subject of the ordination [χειροτονία], of priests and deacons: You, O bishop, when you ordain a priest, place your hand upon his head, surrounded by all your priests at your sides and all your deacons as well. Pray over him and ordain [χειροτονεῖν] him. You must also ordain [χειροτονεῖν] the deacon in accordance with the same ritual. But as regards subdeacons [ὑποδιάκονος], lectors [ἀναγνώστης] and women deacons [διάκονος], we have already said that they are not to be ordained [again, χειροτονεῖν].[73]

It is well known that, in reproducing the *Apostolic Constitutions*, the *Synodos* omits all the ordination prayers. The reason for this, no doubt, was that there was already an Egyptian pontifical containing all of them.[74] Nevertheless, the Sahidic edition that we have, in order to be faithful to Hippolytus, clearly rejects the laying on of hands in the case of the lower

---

[69] B. Botte, op. cit., pp. 44–53; G. Horner, op. cit., pp. 152–55, 316–19; J. and A. Périer, op. cit., pp. 602–5; J. M. Hanssens, op. cit., pp. 110–15, no. 39.

[70] Although his article has aged considerably, it is still worth consulting: F. X. Funk, *Das achte Buch der Apostolischen Konstitutionen in der koptischen Überlieferung*, in *Theologische Quartalschrift* 86 (1904): 429–42.

[71] G. Horner, op. cit., pp. 199, 342; J. and A. Périer, op. cit., p. 635: two Arabic manuscripts have "subdeaconesses", "*al-abodiakonat*"; one has "subdeacon", "*al-abodiakon*"; another "subdeacons", "*al-abodiakonion*".

[72] G. Horner, op. cit., pp. 200, 344; J. and A. Périer, op. cit., pp. 636–37.

[73] P. de Lagarde, *Aegyptiaca*, p. 277; Eng. trans. G. Horner, op. cit., p. 345; M. Lafontaine, professor at the University of Louvain, has checked my French translation.

[74] E. Lanne, *Les ordinations dans le rite copte*, OS 5 (1960): 86–87.

ministries, and it is only in connection with these lower ministries that
deaconesses are even mentioned (in the Arabic and Ethiopic versions):

> On the subject of the ordination of priests and of deacons. On the subject of
> subdeacons [this second sentence omitted in the Arabic version]. On the
> subject of deaconesses, subdeaconesses and female lectors: You, O bishop. . . .
> As for deaconesses, subdeaconesses and female lectors, we have already
> expressed ourselves on this subject.[75]

Apparent hesitations on the part of various copyists show how surprised
they must have been to encounter such an unusual listing of ecclesiastical
orders.[76] However, J. M. Hanssens has provided a satisfactory explanation
of what must have occurred to get the readings we find in the Arabic and
Ethiopic versions. The Arabic translator must have had before his eyes a
Coptic text where he read, literally, "as regards subdeacons, lectors and
women deacons. . . ." Hanssens explained thus: "Instead of associating
the word 'women' with the third order only, that of deacons, he associated
it with the first two orders as well; and, after having mistakenly feminized
the orders of subdeacons and lectors, he then quite logically placed them
after the 'deaconesses'."[77]

We need to say a word on the subject of the last clause of this quotation:
"We have already expressed ourselves on this subject." The texts of
Hippolytus on the two offices of subdeacons and lectors appeared earlier
in the document, of course. But deaconesses? There is no earlier mention
of them in the *Synodos* except in the part that reproduces the *Ecclesiastical
Canons of the Holy Apostles*.

With respect to widows, the three versions—Sahidic, Arabic and
Ethiopic—reproduce the text of book VIII of the *Apostolic Constitutions*,
which, in any case, is very close to the reading of Hippolytus.[78]

The canons of the *Synodos* similarly transcribe without any change the
text of book VIII, 28:6, of the *Apostolic Constitutions*:

> The deaconess does not bless, nor does she carry out any of the functions of
> the priests and deacons; she merely watches the doors. She must also serve
> [ὑπηρετεῖ] the priests when women are being baptized, for that is what is
> most fitting [πρέπει].[79]

[75] J. and A. Périer, op. cit., pp. 638–39; G. Horner, op. cit., p. 201.

[76] See the variants identified by G. Horner, op. cit., p. 406.

[77] J. M. Hanssens, *La liturgie d'Hippolyte* (I), OCA 155 (Rome, 1959), p. 113.

[78] Sahidic canon 69, Arabic 55, Ethiopic 56, G. Horner, op. cit., pp. 202, 346; J. and A.
Périer, op. cit., p. 640. Cf. *Const. apost.* VIII, 25, Funk, p. 528.

[79] Sahidic canon 71, Arabic 58, Ethiopic 59, G. Horner, op. cit., pp. 204, 348; J. and A.
Périer, op. cit., pp. 642–43; cf. *Const. apost.*, VIII, 28:6, Funk, p. 530.

On the other hand, the texts that follow immediately in the *Apostolic Constitutions* (book VIII, 28:7–8), concerning the power of the deacon over the lower ministries and the denial of this same power to the subdeacon, were reproduced exactly in the Sahidic version but made the Ethiopic scribes hesitate and were omitted entirely in the Arabic version.[80] In the canons, however, there is again reproduced without change the prescription in book VIII (31:2) of the *Apostolic Constitutions*, giving the lower ministries, including that of deaconesses, a share in any surplus from eulogies.[81]

It thus plainly appears that when the translators of the various versions of the *Synodos* included mentions of deaconesses that they found before them in book VIII of the *Apostolic Constitutions*, they did so simply as copyists and compilers.[82] Often enough, though, aware that these mentions of deaconesses had no application to the actual discipline of their own churches, they attempted to introduce changes, usually quite ineptly.

D. *The Arabic and Ethiopic* Didascalia

A document that the Arabic and Ethiopic manuscripts and their editors referred to as the *Didascalia* is extant in two different versions.[83] One of them is found in the Borgian Arabic manuscript 22 of the Vatican Library, and the other is found in five Ethiopic manuscripts of the Royal Library of the British Museum.[84] This document is an adaptation of the first seven

---

[80] G. Horner, op. cit., p. 348 (Sahidic), pp. 204–5 (Ethiopian), p. 407 (variant). Cf. *Const. apost.* VIII, 28:7–8, Funk, p. 530.

[81] Sahidic canon 73, Arabic 60, Ethiopic 61, G. Horner, op. cit., pp. 205, 349; J. and A. Périer, op. cit., p. 644. Cf. *Const. apost.* VIII, 31:2, Funk, p. 532. It should be mentioned that there is no reference to deaconesses in the documents corresponding to bk. VIII (46) of the *Apostolic Constitutions* reproduced by the Sahidic (78), the Arabic (71) and the Ethiopic (72) versions.

[82] Thus vainly does G. Giamberardini claim that "the canons of the apostles in the Coptic version include deaconesses within their scope". This statement occurs in a joint work edited by G. Concetti, *Il prete per gli uomini d'oggi* (Rome: A.V.E., 1975), p. 129. We shall return later to consideration of this particular error. See n. 111 to this chapter.

[83] On the subject of the Arabic and Ethiopic manuscripts of the *Didascalia*, see: F. X. Funk, *Die apostolischen Konstitutionen* (Rottenburg: W. Bader, 1891), pp. 207–42; A. Baumstark, *Die Urgestalt der arabischen Didascalia der Apostel*, OC 3 (1903): 201–11; F. X. Funk, *Didascalia et Constitutiones Apostolorum* (Paderborn: Schöningh, 1905), vol. 2, pp. xxviii–xxxii; F. Nau, *La Didascalie des douze Apôtres*, 2nd ed., *Ancienne littérature canonique syriaque*, I (Paris: Lethielleux, 1912), pp. ix–x, xxii–xxiii; J. M. Harden, *The Ethiopic Didascalia, Translations of Christian Literature*, ser. 4, *Oriental Texts* (London: Macmillan, 1920), pp. xi–xx; especially J. M. Hanssens, *La liturgie d'Hippolyte* (I), OCA 155 (Rome, 1959), pp. 35–36. The Ethiopic version enjoys an integral English translation by J. M. Harden, op. cit.; only a part of this text was published by T. Pell Platt, *The Ethiopic Didascalia* (London, 1834); as for the Arabic version, there are accessible only the fragments translated into Latin by F. X. Funk, op. cit., 2:120–36.

[84] Nos. 752, 793, 797, 798, 799, and also the incomplete manuscript belonging to an

books of the *Apostolic Constitutions* with a certain number of lacunae in it.[85] All the passages mentioning deaconesses have been reproduced without significant change, although the text as a whole has generally been abridged by comparison with the Greek version.[86] The rendering of the prescription requiring the presence of deaconesses during the baptism of women deserves to be reproduced here:

> This is why, O bishop, you must test the deacons who are to assist you. Help them perform their good works. They must be prompt in exercising their ministry to the whole people. A deaconess should be designated to exercise the ministry to women. The woman chosen should be pure, irreproachable. The deacon should not exercise the ministry to women for fear that he might provoke calumny from unbelievers. This is why there needs to be a deaconess for ministering to women: she should anoint them and dress them again following baptism. You, bishop, anoint the foreheads of those being baptized, men and women; anoint them with oil in accordance with the ritual of holy baptism. Following that, O bishop and priests, pray over those who are before [beneath] you, and baptize them in the name of the Father and of the Son and of the Holy Spirit. Then the deacon should take the men, and the deaconess the women, for the seal that they have received, and which none dare break, must remain pure and holy. After they have been baptized, the bishop should anoint them with the oil of balsam, for they have been baptized into the death of Christ.[87]

As can easily be seen, this is an abridgement of the text from the *Apostolic Constitutions* and not a direct adaptation from the *Didascalia*.

As for the other version, it does not include book VII of the *Apostolic Constitutions* but adds to the content of the first six books some chapters derived from the *Testament of Our Lord Jesus Christ*. It is for this reason that it contains other mentions of deaconesses.[88]

This Arabic and Ethiopic *Didascalia* figures, in whole or in part, in several of the collections compiled in the Middle Ages by the Egyptian canonists Taj al Riyasa, Ibn al-'Assal and Macarius and also in the *Fatha*

English Bible society, which T. Pell Platt made known.

[85] See the table of J. M. Harden, op. cit., pp. XVIII–XIX.

[86] Chap. 8, Eng. trans., in Harden, p. 48 = *Const. apost.* II, 26:3 (Funk, 1:103); same chapter, Harden, p. 49 = *Const. apost.* II, 26:6 (Funk, p. 105); chap. 12, Harden, p. 75 = *Const. apost.* II, 57:10 (Funk, p. 163); same chapter, Harden, p. 78 = *Const. apost.* II, 58:6 (Funk, p. 171); chap. 14, Harden, p. 90 = *Const. apost.* III, 8:1 (Funk, p. 197); chap. 16, Harden, p. 92 (missing in the manuscript utilized by Pell Platt) = *Const. apost.* III, 11:3 (Funk, p. 201); chap. 23, Harden, p. 154 = *Const. apost.* VI, 17:4 (Funk, p. 341).

[87] Chapter 17, Harden, pp. 95–96. Compare with the *Didascalia* 16, Chapter 2 above, and with *Const. apost.* III, 16:1, 4 (Funk, pp. 209, 211).

[88] Chap. 35:17, Latin trans., in F. X. Funk, *Didascalia et Constitutiones Apostolorum*, 2:125 = *Testamentum Domini* 1:19 (I. Rahmani, op. cit., p. 27); Chapter 38:21, Funk, p. 132 = *Testamentum Domini* 1:23 (I. Rahmani, op. cit., pp. 35–37).

Nagast of the Ethiopians.[89] It was the inclusion of this kind of text that has led some historians to believe that the institution of deaconesses did, after all, exist in Egypt. However, this kind of text was an importation from the East and, in fact, had no practical influence on the local institutions, either in Egypt or in Ethiopia, and has left no trace of such influence.

E. *The* Octateuch of Clement

This document, the *Octateuch of Clement*, represents yet another collection of canons imported from Syria and simply translated in Egypt. There exists an Arabic version, still unpublished, as well as a Bohairic version, published with an English translation prepared in the middle of the last century; this second version must have been made from an older Sahidic version. There must also have been an Ethiopic version, although no manuscript of it has ever been found.[90] Here, again, all these translations served no other purpose except to respond to the concern of canonists for proper documentation; they had no practical effect on the institutions of Egypt and Ethiopia.

3. EUCHOLOGIES AND RITUALS

No Egyptian euchologies (books of prayers) and pontificals (books of rituals) ever provided for the ordination or institution of deaconesses. This fact can hardly be considered in any way surprising in the so-named Euchology of Serapion,[91] for this work was certainly influenced heavily by the *Apostolic Tradition*; traces of the latter can be found in this euchology's prayers of ordination for the deacon, the priest and the bishop. It is not that the lower orders or ministries were unknown to the author of this work; the universal prayer preceding the Eucharist mentions—after the deacons—subdeacons, lectors and translators (ἑρμηνέων). It goes on to enumerate states of life: *monazontes* and virgins (τῶν παρθενευουσῶν).[92] This order reflects a Palestinian community such as described by Egeria in the *Journal* of her travels. However we look at it, this particular euchology is rather difficult to fit into the Alexandrian tradition.

[89] J. M. Hanssens, op. cit., pp. 35–37; W. Riedel, op. cit., pp. 115–19, 124 (no. 14); and F. Nau, loc. cit., n. 83 of this chapter.

[90] On the subject of the Arabic and Bohairic *Octateuch*: J. M. Hanssens, op. cit., pp. 55–58; P. Ciprotti, *La version syriaque de l'Octateuque de Clément* (Paris: Lethielleux, 1967), pp. 1–5; W. Riedel, op. cit., pp. 155–57.

[91] Ed. in F. X. Funk, *Didascalia et Constitutiones Apostolorum*, vol. 2, pp. 158–95.

[92] Chapter 11:4–5, ibid., pp. 168–70.

The absence of deaconesses from the Egyptian euchologies, which so closely reflected the authentic practices in the churches of Egypt, is a remarkable fact. Many of these euchologies had taken the prayers they contained from a version of book VIII of the *Apostolic Constitutions* that was anterior to the Greek text of the work that we know.[93] The great Euchology of the White Monastery, from the tenth century,[94] has come down to us in too fragmentary and scattered a state; we do not possess the part that contained the prayers for ordinations. In the prayer of intercession of the anaphora, however, we nevertheless find the classic mention of the bishops, priests, deacons, subdeacons, lectors, psalmists, monks, virgins, celibates, widows, orphans and lay people. . . .[95] Porters and exorcists were eventually added to this list.[96] But there were no deaconesses. No more can mention of any ceremony concerning deaconesses be found in the *Rituale*, which the Jesuit Athanasius Kircher translated into Latin in 1647.[97] The same thing is true of the pontifical published by Tuki in 1761, which E. Lanne meticulously compared with the manuscripts of the Vatican, one of which dated from the first decades of the fourteenth century.[98]

Nor is there any question of deaconesses in the treatises of the medieval canonists and liturgists *The Order of the Priesthood* of the first half of the thirteenth century[99] and *The Pearl of Great Price of Ecclesiastical Science*, a work of Johanna ibn abi Zakaria ibn Sibah, who lived at the beginning of the fourteenth century.[100] There is the same silence in the liturgical ordinances of the patriarch Gabriel V (1409–27 A.D.).[101]

---

[93] E. Lanne, *Les ordinations dans le rite copte*, OS 5 (1960): 81–106.

[94] Edited by E. Lanne, PO 28:2 (Paris: Firmin-Didot, 1958).

[95] Ibid., pp. 298–99; cf. 322–23.

[96] Ibid., pp. 300–301.

[97] *Rituale ecclesiae Aegyptiacae sive Cophtitarum quod . . . ex lingua Copta et Arabica in Latinam transtulit Athanasius Kircherius . . . anno 1647*, published in *Leonis Allatii Σύμμικτα, sive Opusculorum Graecorum et Latinorum, libri duo, Coloniae Agrippinae* (J. Kalchovium, 1653), pp. 236–67.

[98] E. Lanne, *Les ordinations dans le rite copte*, OS 5:91. The Coptic texts are accessible in the translations of Kircher, op. cit.; of J. S. Assemani (A. Mai, *Scriptorum veterum nova Collectio*, vol. 5, pt. 2, pp. 209–19); and of Denzinger, 2:1–64. Cf. description of the euchologies of the Vatican Library in A. Mai, op. cit., pp. 143–49.

[99] J. Assfalg, *Die Ordnung des Priestertums, ein altes liturgisches Handbuch der koptischen kirche, Publications du Centre d'études orientales de la Custodie franciscaine de Terre-Sainte, Coptica*, 1 (Cairo, 1955).

[100] Ed. with Latin trans. by V. Mistrih, *Studia orientalia christiana, Aegyptiaca* (Cairo: *Centrum franciscanum studiorum orientalium christianorum*, 1966). See in particular c. 29 (the "orders" of Christ), 44–52 (explanation of various ecclesiastical orders), 74–83 (ordinations).

[101] A. Abdallah, *L'ordinamento liturgico di Gabriele V, Studia orientalia christiana, Aegyptiaca* (Cairo: Edizioni del Centro francescano di studi orientali cristiani, 1962).

Almost all of the Coptic and Ethiopic baptismal rituals published by various scholars[102] are of relatively late date and are, in practice, at least, devoid of any provision for an adult catechumenate. They do not contain particular rubrics intended to preserve feminine modesty even when they mention the tradition of baptismal nudity in formulas recalling the *Apostolic Tradition* or prescribe an anointing over the whole body.

We must, however, mention at least two rituals that continued to assume that catechumens could be adults. The first of these rituals was an interpolation in the Alexandrian *Synodos*; it made its appearance right in the middle of the text of the *Apostolic Tradition*. This ritual prescribes the following with regard to prebaptismal anointing: "If it is a man, he should be anointed by a deacon or priest; if a woman, she should be anointed by one of the female faithful who has preserved her virginity."[103] The function of ensuring modesty and decency was thus, in this case, assigned neither to a deaconess nor to a widow.

The second of these rituals raises a much more formidable problem. It is found in the Arabic canonical collection compiled to Taj al Riyasa abu Isaac ibn Fadl Allah toward the end of the thirteenth century.[104] Its contents are as follows: a prayer for episcopal ordination, a mystagogy, an *Ordo* of the Mass, prayers for the ordination of priests, deacons and widows and, finally, a rite of Christian initiation. All of these materials were inserted between the *Testamentum Domini* and the Arabic *Didascalia*; these two documents had been translated from a Coptic (Bohairic) manuscript dated to 926 A.D. This particular ritual is manifestly and quite narrowly dependent on the *Testamentum Domini* for its mystagogy and for

[102] Denzinger, 1:192–214 (according to Assemani), 214–21 (according to the papers of Renaudot), 222–33 (according to the *Bibliotheca maxima Patrum*, Martène and PL 138, col. 911ff.), 233–35 (according to Assemani); V. Ermoni, *Rituel copte du baptême et du mariage* in *Revue de l'Orient chrétien* 5 (1900 to 9, 1904) according to Bibl. Nat., ms. copte 72); M. Chaine, *Le rituel éthiopien, Rituel du baptême*, in *Bessarione* 29 (1913): 38–71; S. Grébaut, *Ordre du baptême et de la confirmation dans l'Eglise éthiopienne*, in *Revue de l'Orient chrétien* 26 (1927–28): 105–89; O. H. E. Khs Burmester, *The Baptismal Rite of the Coptic Church, a Critical Study*, in *Bulletin de la Société d'archeologie copte* 11 (1945): 27–86; G. Kretschmar, *Beiträge zur Geschichte der Liturgie, insbesondere der Taufliturgie in Aegypten*, in *Jahrbuch für Liturgik und Hymnologie* 8 (1963): 1–54.

[103] C. 39, ed. H. Duensing, *Der aethiopische Text der Kirchenordnung des Hippolyts* (Göttingen: Vandehoeck and Ruprecht, 1946), p. 102 (*texte éthiop.*), p. 105 (Ger. trans.). In the *Bulletin de littérature ecclésiastique* 60 (1959): 57–62, I gave the reasons why it was impossible to accept the dating and the reconstitution of this ritual by A. Salles, in *Trois antiques rituals du baptême*, SC 59 (Paris: Ed. du Cerf, 1958); on this ritual see also J. M. Hanssens, *La liturgie d'Hippolyte* (I), pp. 43–44.

[104] Bibl. Vatic., Ms. *Borgian. arab.* 22 (K IV 24). On the subject of this ms., J. M. Hanssens, op. cit., pp. 71–73.

the prayers of ordination. The *Ordo* of the Mass, however, and also the ritual of baptism, published and commented upon by Anton Baumstark,[105] present the true characteristics of the Egyptian liturgy as it was actually celebrated.[106] Baumstark thought that the *Ordo* dated from the sixth century; however, the arguments he used to reach this conclusion are scarcely decisive. He assimilated the *Ordo* to canon 105 of the Arabic version of the *Canons of Basil*.[107] Yet, although canon 105 of Basil did not in any way mention baptismal nudity,[108] we find the contrary in the canon Baumstark has presented:

> Following this, they are disrobed and they turn toward the East when receiving baptism—or at least the men do. As for the women, the deaconesses [*al-sammasah*] disrobe them behind a cover and cover them with a cloth.[109]

This strongly resembles the rubric found in the *Testamentum Domini*, except that "deaconesses" have taken the place of the former "widows who have precedence"—that is, if the translation is correct (from Syriac into Coptic and then into Arabic).[110] No doubt this correspondence has come about under the influence of the Arabic *Didascalia*, which was included in the same collection. However, we have no evidence about whether this rubric was ever actually applied.

At the end of the twelfth century—an entire century before the compilation of Taj al Riyasa—the patriarch of Alexandria Mark III (1164–89 A.D.) was taken completely by surprise when he came upon a mention of deaconesses in the ancient Church canons. He had never heard of this feminine

---

[105] A. Baumstark, *Eine aegyptische Mess- und Taufliturgie vermutlich des 6. Jahrhunderts*, OC 1 (1901): 1–45.

[106] Ibid., pp. 5–6; I particularly thank Dom Emmanuel Lanne, a specialist in Coptic liturgy, who, in a letter dated July 16, 1980, kindly pointed out to me two characteristic particularities: the formula of adherence after renunciation and the baptismal formula itself.

[107] The Arabic version of the *Canons of Basil* includes 95 Greek canons, of which at least canons 1–92 are authentic extracts from St. Basil (Joannou, 2:85–199); but this collection shows modifications in 11 canons that describe the liturgy; it is a Coptic liturgy; Abû'l-Barakât, however, indicated that it differed from the liturgy of his day: W. Riedel, *Die Kirchenrechtsquellen des Patriarchats Alexandrien* (Leipzig, 1900), pp. 232–83; cf. I. Rahmani, *I fasti della Chiesa patriarcale Antiochena* (Rome: Accademia dei Lincei, 1920), pp. xiv–xvii; G. Graf, *Geschichte der Christlichen-Arabischen Literatur*, vol. 1, ST 118 (Vatican City, 1944), pp. 606–8.

[108] W. Riedel, op. cit., p. 281.

[109] A. Baumstark, op. cit., p. 41. Msgr. J. M. Sauget of the Vatican Library kindly confirmed for me the exactness of this translation; he also verified that in the ms. Vatic. *Borgian. arab.* 22, ff. 40v–41r the "Prayer over the Widow" is in fact the prayer of the *Testamentum Domini*.

[110] Cf. Chapter 2, above.

institution and was obliged to seek information about it from the Byzantine canonist Theodore Balsamon.[111]

[111] T. Balsamon, *Responsa ad interrogationes Marci*, 35, PG 138, col. 988, also cited Chapter 8, n. 38, below. I do not see how C. de Clercq, in *L'ordre, le mariage, l'extrême-onction, Bibliothèque catholique des sciences religieuses* (Paris: Bloud and Gay, 1939), p. 47, could ever claim that, among the Ethiopians, "there were deaconesses". Father Alphonse Raes, prefect emeritus of the Vatican Library, whom I consulted on this subject, wrote to me as follows in a letter dated April 5, 1973: "All my research efforts to find evidence for the existence of deaconesses among the Ethiopians have proved to be fruitless." To complete the picture, I should cite the information that the review *Proche Orient Chrétien* published in its "*Chronique d'Egypte*" 22 (1972): 90: "A novelty in the Coptic Church: the creation of deaconesses. Henceforth women are to be admitted as cantors in the churches but without partaking in any way of the sacrament of holy orders. A villa at Menchia-el-Bakry, in Cairo, has been made available to the Patriarchate to serve as a training institute for candidates." This information was disseminated by G. Giamberardini, art. cit., above, n. 82 to this chapter, and by G. Viaud, *La liturgie des coptes d'Egypte* (Paris: Maisonneuve, 1978), p. 85. I wrote to Cairo inquiring about this and received a reply dated February 22, 1980, to the effect that "the term employed to designate those women who are dedicating themselves in a greater degree to the service of the Church, of the parishes and in carrying out various good works is a feminine noun derived from *chammas*, the word for those who serve at the altar and carry out other forms of service to the Church and do good works; they are not deacons nor even cantors; they are the helpers of the lower ranks of the clergy. The feminine noun that was translated as 'deaconesses' has no canonical value, since the Coptic church has never had any deaconesses." Patriarch Shenouda III, speaking in London on January 28, 1979, replied to a question about deaconesses by saying that a decision "could only be made by the Church after a serious, in-depth study of the matter". Reported in *Le monde copte*, 4th quarter (1979), p. 8.

CHAPTER FIVE

Deaconesses in the Other Churches of the Greek-Speaking and Eastern Regions Of the Roman Empire
(End of Fourth to Sixth Centuries)

I. IN CHURCH TEACHING AND LEGISLATION

From the last quarter of the fourth century on, the presence of deaconesses in the Greek-speaking and eastern regions of the Roman Empire became a notable public fact, well known and attested to by Church councils, laws enacted by Christian emperors and the works of Christian authors.

1. DEACONESSES IN OFFICIAL CHURCH LEGISLATION

A. The First General Council of Nicaea (325 A.D.)

Is it even necessary to mention a date as late as the last quarter of the fourth century? The First General Council of the Church, held in the East at Nicaea in 325, was already employing the neologism διακόνισσα, and in this way bore public witness to the existence of deaconesses. However, as we shall see, the use of this term did not come in connection with a decision affecting the universal Church, or even a specific local church; its use arose in connection with a dissident sect, the Paulianists, a sect that grew up following the deposing of Paul of Samosata from the See of Antioch in 272.

This, then is what the Fathers of Nicaea decided in their canon 19:

> With regard to the Paulianists returning to the Catholic Church, it has been decided that they absolutely must be rebaptized. If some of them were formerly members of [their] clergy [ἐν τῷ κλήρῳ ἐξητάσθησαν], they must be rebaptized and then ordained by the bishop of the Catholic Church, provided, however, that their lives are spotless and irreproachable. If inquiry

reveals that they are unworthy, though, then they must be excluded from the clergy [καθαιρεῖοθαι]. The same thing must be done with respect to deaconesses [περὶ τῶν διακονισσῶν] and, in general, the same rule must be observed in the case of all those fulfilling an official role [τῶν ἐν τῷ κανόνι ἐξεταζομένων]. We spoke about deaconesses enrolled in these ranks [ἐν τῷ σχήματι ἐξεταοθεισῶν], since they have received no laying on of hands [χειροθεσίαν τινά] and are thus therefore to be counted among the laity.[1]

It is well known that Paul of Samosata was only able to become and maintain himself as bishop of Antioch through the protection afforded to him by the queen of Palmyra while she exercised authority over the city of Antioch. When Emperor Aurelian reconquered the city (271–272 A.D.) and expelled the deposed bishop Paul therefrom,[2] the schismatic community of his followers undoubtedly also fled toward the East, to Samosata itself or to Palmyra, near the Euphrates; that is to say, into the very regions where the ecclesiastical institutions corresponded to what the *Didascalia* has already described for us and where deaconesses actually existed and functioned.

Paul of Samosata, who was originally from the same area, had perhaps already introduced them into Antioch when he became bishop there in 260 A.D. Who and what were these deaconesses? What was the import of the decision of the Council of Nicaea concerning them? The variants and marginal corrections to be found in the Greek manuscripts in which this canon has been handed down to us from antiquity indicate that, from the very beginning, manifold difficulties have been perceived therein. In the same way, many modern readers have read the passage with a desire to find in it a justification for their own favorable opinions concerning deaconesses.[3]

However, if we look at this canon without preconceptions and without trying to project upon it our knowledge of later practices, we must note that the Paulianists employed no laying on of hands in the case of

---

[1] Greek text in H. T. Bruns, *Canones apostolorum et conciliorum veterum selecti* (Berolini, typis G. Reimeri, 1839), 1:19, rather than in Joannou, vol. I, pt. 1, pp. 40–41. I have corrected the translation of Joannou, bearing in mind, in particular, certain remarks of Gryson, *Ministère des femmes*, p. 86. However, I do not think it is necessary (or well founded) to give ἐπεί a concessive meaning.

[2] Eusebius, *Ecclesiastical History* VII:30:19—from Fr. ed., G. Bardy, *Eusèbe Hist. eccles.*, SC 41 (1955), p. 219. On this whole subject, see G. Bardy, *Paul de Samosate*, DTC 12 (1932), col. 46–51. I note that Bardy translates the relevant portion of the canon of Nicaea as follows: "The same thing must be done with respect to deaconesses . . . who have not received any laying on of hands, and thus they are counted among the laity . . . they should be rebaptized and they should retain their functions."

[3] This point of view is thoroughly set forth in Kalsbach, *Altkirchliche Einrichtung*, pp. 46–49, and an adequate summary can be found in Gryson, op. cit., p. 87, and, more recently, in C. Vagaggini, *L'ordinazione delle diaconesse nella tradizione greca e bizantina*, OCP 40 (1974): 155–60.

deaconesses. Were deaconesses then counted among the laity in their own community, or was it the Great Church that denied to them any share in the clerical state that they perhaps did share among the Paulianists? The latter interpretation would only be possible if we considered the three different formulas employed by the Council of Nicaea to be completely synonymous with one another:

$$ἐν τῷ κλήρῳ ἐξετάζεσθαι$$
$$ἐν τῷ κανόνι ἐξετάζεσθαι$$
$$ἐν τῷ σχήματι ἐξετάζεσθαι$$

This is exactly what Fr. Cipriano Vagaggini claims is the case. Unfortunately, this is impossible. The two Greek terms κλῆρος and κανών are distinguished from each other in Nicene canons 16 and 17, where κανών is accorded a broader meaning than κλῆρος. Canon 16, after listing priests and deacons, adds ἢ ὅλως ἐν τῷ κανόνι ἐξεταζόμενοι. Similarly, in canon 19, deaconesses and all those enrolled in an official role (ἐν τῷ κανόνι) are added to the κλῆρος and to the ranks of those who have received the χειροτονία. Roger Gryson, it seems to me, provides the best definition of "canon" that I have seen: "The list of all those carrying out one of the functions recognized in the ecclesiastical legislation, thereby receiving in some measure a subsidy from the Church".[4] As for σχῆμα, this is a word with a very imprecise meaning. Following Gryson, I have translated it as "rank" or "degree". Dionysius Exiguus understood it as "*in eodem habitu*", while Syriac documents understood it to be "state" or "condition".[5]

The upshot of all this was that the deaconesses of the Paulianists, once they had returned to the Great Church and had been rebaptized, were able, if they possessed the requisite characteristics, to continue to carry out the same functions that they had carried out before. No more than before, however, did they receive any laying on of hands or become a part of the κλῆρος. Thus, at the time of the Council of Nicaea, the same practices were observed with regard to all the Church ministries below the diaconate (the members of which were still an integral part of the "*kanon*"), as had been laid out a century before in the *Apostolic Tradition* of St. Hippolytus of Rome; these minor ministries were not conferred by the laying on of hands. The precision employed in the language of the Council of Nicaea on this subject did not have as its aim to oppose the usage of the Paulianists to that of the Great Church, but rather merely to make clear exactly what

---

[4] Gryson, *Ministère des femmes*, p. 86. The Syriac version renders the term κανών by *qeyama* which A. Vööbus translated as "a covenant, the minor orders" in *The Synodicon in the West Syrian Tradition*, CSCO, 368, p. 101.

[5] In the *Novellae* of Justinian (3:1; 123:10), σχῆμα denotes one's rank among the various ministries of the Church (cleric, deaconess, porter, etc.), but the very same word was also constantly used to designate the distinctive vestment used by celebrants or monks.

deaconesses were, since they were really little known and hardly existed
outside the eastern regions.

B. The Canons of Laodicea

It has been held—without justification—that one of the canons of Laodicea
contains a decision concerning deaconesses. Thus, canon 11 is worded as
follows: Περὶ τοῦ μὴ δεῖν τὰς λεγομένας πρεσβύτιδας ἤτοι προκαθημένας ἐν
ἐκκλησίᾳ καθίστασθαι.[6] The compilers of the Greek collections interpreted
this as Περὶ τοῦ ἐν ἐκκλησίᾳ πρεσβυτέραν ἐν γυναιξὶ μὴ καθίστασθαι.[7] The
Latin commentators exhibited the same kind of embarrassment in trans-
lating this text.[8] Modern scholars have added yet another difficulty by
questioning both the date of the Council of Laodicea and the certain
identification of this particular council as the authentic source of these
canons.[9]

The fact is, however, that all the terms encountered here can be
explained by means of texts that we have already examined in the course
of this work. Πρεσβυτίδες is to be found in Titus 2:3–5, and in a context
where it can only refer to older women—to the virtues that they must
possess, to the role that they must play with respect to the younger
women—προκαθημέναι, of course, refers to "the widows who have
precedence" in the Testamentum Domini.[10] And this canon expressly
forbids "instituting" them (καθιστάναι), going contrary to both the Testamentum Domini and the Apostolic Tradition of St. Hippolytus of Rome in
this respect, both of which envisaged, precisely, such an "instituting" of
them. For in both of these two documents, καθιστάναι was used, in

---

[6] H. T. Bruns, op. cit., 1:74.

[7] Joannou, vol. I, pt. 2, p. 135. Cf. the Syriac version, A. Vööbus, op. cit., p. 120.

[8] Dionysius Exiguus: "Quod non oporteat eas quae dicuntur presbyterae vel presidentes in
ecclesia constitui"; the Collection Hispana: "Mulieres, quae apud Graecos presbyterae appellantur,
apud nos autem viduae seniores, univirae et matriculariae nominantur, in ecclesia tamquam ordinatas
constitui non debere." H. T. Bruns, op. cit., p. 74, n. 10.

[9] The authenticity of these canons is maintained by Joannou, vol. I, pt. 2, pp. 127–28, and
by B. Botte, in Miscellanea liturgica in onore di S.E. il Cardinale Giacomo Lercaro, vol. 2 (Rome:
Desclée, 1967), pp. 799–800; if these authorities are correct, the date of the council would be
between 380–450 A.D.; but there are serious reasons for doubting this, following this
A. Boudinhon, Note sur le Concile de Laodicée, in Comptes rendus du Congrès scientifique
international des catholiques, vol. 2 (1888): 420–27; and E. Amann, Laodicée (Concile de), DTC 8
(1925), col. 2611–14. Gryson, in Ministère des femmes, p. 92, sums up the state of the question
aptly: "It is generally agreed, after all, that the canons of Laodicea constitute a kind of
summary of the canonical rules that applied in Phrygia; it is a summary that was perhaps
approved by one or two successive synods held in that province. The discipline reflected in
these canons, however, persuades us to situate them generally towards the end of the fourth
century."

[10] See Chapter 2, n. 62 above.

contrast to χειροτονία, the term strictly reserved to describe the ordination of bishops, priests and deacons by a laying on of hands.[11]

Thus, the correct translation of this canon is: "Those called 'older women' or 'widows who have precedence' should not be 'instituted' in the Church."[12]

What is clear is that it is not the deaconesses who are being referred to here; in fact, the phenomenon of deaconesses fell outside the normal range of the consciousness of the bishops who drafted the canon.[13] It is even possible to conclude from the canon that deaconesses did not exist in Phrygia at the time of the Council of Laodicea [380 A.D.?]; and that, a fortiori, they would not have been accepted if they had been suggested.

C. The Canons of St. Basil

These canons existed from at least the second half of the fourth century (375 A.D.), in both Cappadocia and Lycaonia; they reflected the authentic thinking of St. Basil of Caesarea. In one of his replies to the bishop of Iconium, Amphilocus, St. Basil resolved a disciplinary case concerning deaconesses; his solution assumed the existence of deaconesses as an ecclesiastical institution that was established so solidly as to be henceforth beyond discussion; and the "canon" in which St. Basil spoke of them became a fixture in the various canonical collections, being placed on the same level as some conciliar canons:[14]

> Canon 44. The deaconess [ἡ διάκονος] who has committed fornication with a pagan [τῷ Ἕλληνι] will be admitted to penance [εἰς μετάνοιαν], but she will not be admitted back to the offering again except after the passage of seven years, and only provided that she has continued to live a chaste life during that time. As for the pagan [ἕλλην] who reverts back to impiety after having professed the Christian Faith, he should be considered as having returned to his own vomit. For our part, we cannot tolerate the prospect that the bodies of the deaconesses, which have been consecrated to the Lord, should serve as the means to carnal pleasures.[15]

[11] See Chapter 1, n. 57 above. Joannou, in his work, has wrongly translated the following, on page 135: "There should be no *ordination* in the Church of those called *presbytides* or *presidents*" [the latter in the feminine gender in French (Tr.)].

[12] Gryson, in *Ministère des femmes*, p. 94, prudently wonders if canon 45 in the same collection of the canons of Laodicea that prohibits women from entering the sanctuary was perhaps framed in order to eliminate the usage described in the *Testamentum Domini*, which placed the "widows who have precedence" behind the sanctuary curtain during the Eucharist.

[13] Gryson, op. cit., pp. 92–95; Kalsbach, *Altkirchliche Einrichtung*, p. 53.

[14] Joannou, vol. II, pp. 85–199.

[15] Trans. Joannou, p. 136; for an identical translation as far as meaning is concerned, see Gryson, op. cit., pp. 90–92. On one point, as we shall see, we must reject the translation of Y. Courtonne in St. Basil's *Lettres*, collection Budé, vol. 2 (Paris: Belles Lettres, 1961), p. 162.

The mention of "Hellene", or "Greek", has been translated here as "pagan", in accordance with the common usage of the Septuagint and the New Testament, both of which used this word to designate both "pagans" and "gentiles".[16] The reading εἰς μετάνοιαν, which was adopted by both Joannou and Gryson, was actually an insertion in three of the manuscripts made by some subsequent party to replace κοινωνίαν, which is to be found in most of the source documents. However, it is a reading that seems to be imperative, unless we are prepared to leave standing a gross contradiction in the thought of St. Basil: the deaconess could not at one and the same time be received back into Communion and yet be denied access to the offering (προσφορά); she had to do seven years of penance. As Roger Gryson has pointed out, this fact alone proves that deaconesses were not a part of the clergy, because members of the clergy guilty of the same sin of unchastity were definitively reduced to the lay state; they were not, however, denied Communion since, according to the law, "He will not take vengeance twice on his foes" (Nahum 1:9). Also, the punishment of the clergy being reduced to the lay state was perpetual, whereas the penances assigned to the laity were not perpetual.[17] St. Basil did not give any indication in this reference of his to deaconesses about what the functions and activities of deaconesses were or what their place in the community was. Only one conclusion can therefore be drawn from this mention of deaconesses, and that is that they belonged to a group vowed to continence; their bodies are described as "consecrated" (ὡς καθιερωμένον) and hence could not serve for any carnal purpose. Any deaconesses who nevertheless did fall into the sin of fornication could only be reconciled to the Church after a penance of seven years, and then only "provided that she . . . continued to live a chaste life during that time". The state of life depicted here was not, however, a life of virginity, about which St. Basil wrote in the same letter, although it did involve a "consecration" similar to the consecration undergone by those vowing themselves to a life of perpetual virginity.[18] But this "consecration" was in no way an "ordination".[19] Certainly no such conclusion can be derived from this text.

[16] A. Bailly, *Dictionnaire grec-français*, 11 ed. (Paris: Hachette, 1935), p. 648. Y. Courtonne did not understand the basic meaning of the word without which the canon cannot be correctly interpreted.

[17] *Canons de Basile*, 3, 32, 51, Joannou, pp. 100, 131, 142 (= *Lettres* 188, 199, 217, ed. Y. Courtonne, op. cit., pp. 124–25, 161, 209–10).

[18] Canon 18: νύμφη ἐστὶ τοῦ Χριστοῦ καὶ σκεῦος ἱερὸν ἀνατεθὲν τῷ Δεσπότῃ, Joannou, p. 119; Y. Courtonne, op. cit., p. 156.

[19] There is a pertinent critique made by Gryson, op. cit., p. 91, against Kalsbach, *Altkirchliche Einrichtung*, p. 109, who saw in this canon of St. Basil and in the letter of St. Epiphanius that we will encounter farther on (Chapter 5) the beginnings of a rite of institution and ordination of deaconesses.

D. *Imperial Legislation: The Theodosian Code*

Fifteen years after the letter of St. Basil on which the canon we have just examined was based, the institution of deaconesses became a subject of imperial concern. It appears that some abuses had become manifest; it is possible that widows possessing inheritances became subjected to pressure from members of the clergy aiming to gain control of these inheritances; it could also have been that the admission of women who were too young to be deaconesses had introduced a greater risk of the relaxation of moral standards.[20] It was for this reason that a law of Theodosius I, Valentinian II and Arcadius was issued on June 21, 390 A.D.:

> Nulla nisi emensis sexaginta annis, cui votiva domi proles sit, secundum praeceptum apostoli ad diaconissarum consortium transferatur.[21]

This law makes explicit reference to the precept of 1 Timothy 5:9 that widows should only be enrolled if they are not less than sixty years of age—and deaconesses are, of course, assimilated to widows in this case.

With regard to the possessions of the deaconesses who were enrolled, this law stipulates a disposition of this property similar to the stipulations of an earlier law of July 30, 370,[22] concerning the disposition of the property of widows. On August 23, 390, two months after the issuance of the 390 law quoted above, another law was published easing up on the first law's provisions.[23] Moreover, whenever the emperors henceforth had occasion to deal with the question of the Church's worldly goods, they included the category of deaconesses in their stipulations. This does not mean that they considered deaconesses to be members of the clergy; it merely means that the property of deaconesses raised the same civil and juridical questions as were raised by the disposition of the property of all the other categories of those who dedicated their lives to Christ and to the Church:

> Legem quae de diaconissis vel viduis nuper est promulgata. . . .[24] Ut sive vidua, sive diaconissa, sive virgo Deo dictata, vel sanctimonialis mulier, sive quocumque alio nomine religiosi honoris vel dignitatis femina nuncupatur, testamento vel codicillo suo. . . .[25]

---

[20] This is what the historian Sozomen gives us to understand: see *Histoire ecclésiastique* 7, 16, 11, GCS 50, p. 324.

[21] *Codex Theodos.*, Lib. 16, tit. 2, no. 27, ed. T. Mommsen and P. Meyer, *Theodosiani libri XVI* (Berolini, Weidmann, 1905), vol. I, pt. 2, pp. 843–44. Cf. Gryson, op. cit., pp. 120–21.

[22] *Codex Theodos.*, Lib. 16, tit. 2, no. 20, ed. Mommsen-Meyer, 1–2, p. 841.

[23] *Codex Theodos.*, Lib. 16, tit. 2, no. 28, ed. Mommsen-Meyer, 1–2, p. 844.

[24] Ibid.

[25] *Novelle de Marcien*, tit. 5, ed. Mommsen-Meyer, vol. 2, p. 195.

However, let us take note of the place that deaconesses occupied according to a law of Theodosius II and Valentinian III that was issued on December 15, 434:

> Si quis episcopus aut presbyter aut diaconus aut diaconissa aut subdiaconus vel cuiuslibet alterius loci clericus aut monachus aut mulier quae solitariae vitae dedita est, nullo condito testamento discesserit. . . .[26]

The deaconess is here named after the deacon but before the subdeacon. This could be the beginning of a development that, as we shall see, achieved its end in the legislation of Justinian.[27]

E. The Council of Chalcedon (451 A.D.)

A short time later, in 451 A.D., the General Council of Chalcedon, legislating about ecclesiastical discipline generally, also dedicated a canon to deaconesses. This canon came after the Council had first fixed the rules for bishops, monks and clerics, the marriage of lectors and psalmists and immediately before the council turned its attention to virgins:

> Canon 15. Deaconesses are not to be ordained [διάκονον μὴ χειροτονεῖσθαι γυναῖκα] before the age of forty, and then only after a rigorous probation period. After receiving ordination [τὴν χειροθεσίαν] and carrying out her ministry [τῇ λειτουργίᾳ] for any period of time, if she then marries, thus spurning the grace of God, she must be anathematized along with the one she marries.[28]

The manuscript tradition here reveals a hesitation between διάκονον and διακόνισσαν and between χειροτονίαν and χειροθεσίαν. However, for the period in question, these variations are without any special significance.[29] It is indeed a question of laying on of hands that we encounter here. The Council of Chalcedon seems to have tacitly permitted a ritual similar to that of the *Apostolic Constitutions*. The verb χειροτονεῖσθαι is applied to canon 6 not only to the priest and the deacon but to clerical orders in general: μήτε ὅλως τινὰ τῶν ἐν τῷ ἐκκλησιαστικῷ τάγματι. Dionysius Exiguus similarly translated the canon 15 quoted above with "*suscipiens manus impositionem*".

---

[26] *Codex Theodos.*, Lib. 5, tit. 3, no. 1, ed. Mommsen-Meyer, 1–2, p. 220. Cf. Gryson, op. cit., pp. 121–22.

[27] See pt. F of this chapter below.

[28] E. Schwartz, *Acta Conciliorum oecumenicorum*, vol. 2, *Concilium universale Chalcedonense*, vol. I, pt. 2 (Berlin: W. de Gruyter, 1939), p. 161 (357); H. T. Bruns, op. cit., vol. I, p. 29; Joannou, vol. I, pt. 1, pp. 81–82. The translation follows Joannou, ibid.

[29] C. Vogel, *L'imposition des mains dans les rites d'ordination en Orient et en Occident*, in *La Maison-Dieu* 102 (1970): 60–65 (= *Ordinations inconsistantes et caractère inamissible* (Turin: Bottega d'Erasmo, 1978), pp. 120–25).

The Council of Chalcedon did not specify what the *leitourgia*, or ministry, of deaconesses was. However, a number of the things that are involved, such as the location of the canon following those on lectors and psalmists and immediately before the one on virgins, as well as the rigor of the life of chastity prescribed, suggests that we are dealing with a state of life similar to the one prescribed for widows among the Paulianists. Nevertheless, the requirement that deaconesses be not less than sixty years of age, earlier maintained in imperial legislation, was lowered to forty years of age. It is no doubt true that, in practice, very little attention was paid to these limitations.[30]

F. The Novellae *of Justinian*

Like his predecessors, Emperor Justinian often got involved in questions of ecclesiastical organization and in the affairs of the clergy from both the legal and the financial standpoints. It was in exactly this fashion that he came to make mention of deaconesses and to give us some indication both of what their canonical situation was in the second half of the sixth century and of what their status was from the point of view of the civil law.

Number 3 of Justinian's *Novellae*, dated March 16, 535, and addressed to Epiphanius, Archbishop of Constantinople, aimed to put an end to the number of clerics drawing salaries from the churches; this number could exceed by quite a bit the resources available to these churches. Henceforth, in the Great Church of the imperial capital, there were to be no more than sixty priests, one hundred male deacons (διακόνους δὲ ἄρρενας), forty female deacons (θηλείας), ninety subdeacons, one hundred and ten lectors and twenty-five cantors—which amounted to four hundred and twenty-five clerics (κληρικῶν)—plus one hundred porters. In the other churches, it was specified that no new ordinations could be made until the number of priests, of deacons, both male and female (διακόνων ἀρρένων τε καὶ

---

[30] In 691 A.D., the Trullan Synod could only repeat the prescriptions of the Council of Chalcedon on the subject of deaconesses: in its canon 14, after having specified that a priest could not be ordained before the age of thirty, and a deacon before the age of twenty-five, the Council declared that a deaconess (διακόνισσα) cannot be ordained (χειροτονείσθω) before the age of forty. Canon 15 fixed twenty as the age for the subdeacon to enter upon his ministry. It is worth noting several interesting features of this particular legislation: the Council rejected the Latin tradition that limited the number of deacons to seven. In its canon 40, it seems to have accurately identified and distinguished widows and deaconesses respectively. Finally, it is worth quoting canon 48: "The wife of the one who has been promoted to the episcopacy, having separated from her husband by mutual agreement, will enter after his ordination into a convent located at some distance from his episcopal residence where, however, she will continue to enjoy material support from the bishop; if she is worthy, she herself may be promoted to the dignity of becoming a deaconess [πρὸς τὸ τῆς διακονίας ἀναβιβαζέσθω ἀξίωμα]", Joannou, vol. I, pt. 1, p. 186; cf. pp. 143–48, 175–76.

θηλείων), of subdeacons, of lectors, of cantors and of porters was reduced to the number existing when these churches were founded.[31]

Number 6 of Justinian's *Novellae* of the same date sets forth the rules that must govern the creation of bishops, priests and deacons, both male and female (διακόνους ἄρρενας καὶ θηλείας). What the sovereign emperor said on the subject of clerics—that is, bishops, priests, male deacons, subdeacons and lectors—he specified also (chapter 6) "should be observed equally as far as deaconesses (διακόνισσαι), beloved of God, are concerned". They were not to be recruited too young because of the greater risk of a fall, but rather they were to be enrolled "in conformity with the divine rule at the age of around fifty", and in such wise that they have merited sacred ordination (τῆς ἱερᾶς χειροτονίας), being either virgins or wives of one husband.[32]

Number 123 of Justinian's *Novellae*, dated May 1, 546, contains a disciplinary code for clerics, monks and virgins. Here the age required for becoming a deacon has been lowered to forty (chapter 13). Those who fail to live right will be removed from performing any service within the Church (τῆς ἐκκλησιαστικῆς ὑπηρεσίας); their goods will be forfeit; and they will be enclosed within a convent (chapter 30).[33]

In the same number 123 of the *Novellae* (chapter 21), the privilege of internal forum, or conscience, is preserved in the case of any actions "against a cleric, a monk, a deaconess, a nun or an ascetic".[34]

All of these texts have quite naturally been the subject of many commentaries, by both ancient authors and modern.[35] Taken all together, they certainly afford us a glimpse into certain aspects of the institution of deaconesses, but they also leave us in a state of uncertainty on numerous points. According to the *Novellae*, the state of life of deaconesses was more demanding than that of clerics. They had to be either virgins or widows, and widows of only one husband at that. Their state of life, once entered upon, was irrevocable; this fact was solemnly communicated to them

---

[31] R. Schoell and G. Kroll, *Novellae*, 5th ed., *Corpus iuris civilis*, 3 (Berlin: Weidmann, 1928), pp. 18–22. Cf. a decision of the same type but with different figures (fifty deacons, forty deaconesses) was made by Emperor Heraclius (610–14); Photius, *syntagma canonum*, cap. 30, PG 104, col. 555–56.

[32] Schoell-Kroll, op. cit., pp. 35, 43–45.

[33] Ibid., pp. 604, 616.

[34] Ibid., p. 609. St. Gregory the Great, in *Regestum* 13:50, ed. Ewald-Hartmann MGH, *Epistolarum* 2:414, cites no. 123 of the *Novellae*, to which he makes reference in a case concerning a priest. This reference constitutes the only citation of the word *diakonissa* in the entire edition of L. Hartmann.

[35] On the ancient commentaries, see Chapter 8 below; on the modern commentaries, see Kalsbach, *Altkirchliche Einrichtung*, pp. 65–69; Gryson, *Ministère des femmes*, pp. 122–26; C. Vagaggini, art. cit., n. 3 to this chapter, above, pp. 174–77.

before all the other deaconesses. It was for this reason that they were not to be enrolled except at a mature age—about which age, however, the emperor seems to have remained curiously undecided. In requiring them to be "around fifty years of age", he seems to have been ignorant of the fact that, eighty years earlier, the Council of Chalcedon had allowed them to become deaconesses at forty—an age to which the emperor himself eventually reverted.

Some of these deaconesses no doubt possessed personal fortunes. This can be seen from the fact that Justinian, like Theodosius before him, made provisions for dealing with these fortunes. Most deaconesses, however, drew a salary from the budget of the churches. Were they thereby considered by the emperor to be members of the clergy? This question has often been asked, but it is an equivocal one. It is equivocal because the privileges of the churches extended also, for example, to monks and to other pious and charitable organizations. It is to be noted that these texts frequently distinguish deaconesses from members of the clergy.[36] Moreover, the place of deaconesses in the listings of Church roles varies considerably from document to document and sometimes even within the same document; sometimes deaconesses are named just after the clergy, sometimes they are named among "states of life", and sometimes, it is true, they are indeed named among the clergy.

The most surprising of all the formulas is the one that occurs three times in number 3 of the *Novellae*: "male and female deacons". This formula inevitably reminds us of chapter 16 of the *Didascalia of the Apostles*; but the formula otherwise appears only in number 6 of the *Novellae* and not at all in any of the subsequent numbers. Nevertheless, the ritual by which deaconesses were instituted was considered by the *Novellae* to be a "sacred ordination", ἱερὰ χειροτονία; it was this consideration that, as St. Basil had already taught, entailed the obligation of strict continence; it also justified the heavy penalties meted out both to the deaconesses who failed in this requirement and to their partners in unchastity.

According to the *Novellae* of Justinian, there were deaconesses who lived in convents, but not all of them did so; some lived alone or with their own families, as long as conditions were such that no suspicion could arise as to any compromise of their virtue. But exactly what ministry did they

---

[36] For example, no. 3 of the *Novellae*: εὐλαβεστάτων κληρικῶν καὶ γυναικῶν γε μὴν διακόνων. This is a formula that comes down to a question of the declension of cases. There is especially to be noted, however, in no. 123 of the *Novellae*, cap. 19: τοὺς δὲ πρεσβυτέρους καὶ διακόνους καὶ ὑποδιακόνους καὶ ἀναγνώστας καὶ ψάλτας, οὓς πάντας κληρικοὺς καλοῦμεν. See Schoell-Kroll, op. cit., p. 608. It is simply not possible to subscribe to the formula of Gryson, op. cit., p. 122, where he declares: "It emerges clearly from the legislation of Justinian that deaconesses were counted among the clergy."

carry out? In what activities did they engage? This was in no way a matter
for a Roman emperor to decide, and, on that subject, it is merely stated in
the *Novellae* that they should "exercise the sacred ministry, assist at the
revered rites of baptism and participate in the other hidden tasks that they
normally carry out in connection with the most venerable mysteries": ἐπὶ
τὴν ἱερὰν παριέναι διακονίαν καὶ τοῖς τε προσκυνητοῖς ὑπηρετεῖσθαι βαπτίσμασι,
τοῖς τε ἄλλοις παριέναι τοῖς ἀπορρήτοις ἅπερ ἐν τοῖς σεβασμιωτάτοις μυστηρίοις
δι' αὐτῶν εἴωθε πράττεσθαι.[37]

2. DEACONESSES IN THEOLOGICAL TREATISES
AND EXEGETICAL COMMENTARIES

A. St. Epiphanius

St. Epiphanius was a native of Judaea, but for around thirty years he
directed a monastery at Eleutheropolis. In 367 A.D. he became bishop of
Salamis on the island of Cyprus. He was a fervent defender of orthodoxy
who, in his zeal, may have even gone a bit too far. Between 374 and 377
A.D. he composed a monumental work "against eighty heresies" entitled
Panarion (or *Kibotios*)—a "box" or "chest" of remedies, a medicine chest.
For the authors of antiquity, this work was a gold mine of information
about the sects and heresies of the early centuries of Christianity. St.
Epiphanius dealt with the subject of deaconesses in two different places.

First of all, he dealt with the subject in treating of the seventy-ninth
heresy, that of the Collyridians, who, it seems, offered sacrifices to the
Virgin Mary; this heresy was found in Arabia, Thrace and upper Scythia.
St. Epiphanius declared emphatically that the priesthood was not conferred
upon women in either the Old or the New Testaments. According to
him, women functioned only as prophetesses. He went on as follows:

> There is in the Church, however, the order of deaconesses [διακονισσῶν
> τάγμα], but it does not exist for the purpose of exercising priestly functions
> [οὐχὶ εἰς τὸ ἱερατεύειν] or for the purpose of confiding certain tasks to
> women. It exists for the purpose of preserving decency for the female sex,
> whether in connection with baptism [λουτροῦ] or in connection with the
> examination of [women undergoing] sufferings or pain, or whenever the
> bodies of women are required to be uncovered, so that they need not be
> exposed to the gaze of the men officiating [ἱερουργούντων], but instead be
> viewed only by the deaconess [διακονούσης], who receives from the priest
> the order to take care of the woman at the time of her nudity. Thus it is that
> the ecclesiastical rule and discipline is wisely and solidly assured by this
> particular canon. It is for this reason too that the Divine Word neither permits

---

[37] No. 6 of the *Novellae*, cap. 6, Schoell-Kroll, op. cit., pp. 43–44.

a woman to speak in the assembly nor allows her to exercise authority over a man. There is a great deal to be said on this subject.

Furthermore, it is necessary to verify with some care that the ecclesiastical organization [τάγμα] actually needed only deaconesses [διακονισσῶν]; the Church also has widows among whom the older ones are called πρεσβύτιδας, but the Church has never admitted priestesses [πρεσβυτερίδας ἢ ἱερίσσας]. Deacons [διάκονοι] themselves in the ecclesiastical order [τάξει] have not been given the charge of administering any sacrament, but only the charge of assisting those who do administer the sacraments [διακονεῖν τὰ ἐπιτελού-μενα].[38]

The second text relating to deaconesses to be found in St. Epiphanius appears in his *Exposition of the Catholic Faith*, which followed the *Panarion*. After having described the different states of the Christian life—virginity, life of solitude, continence, marriage and widowhood—he pointed out the necessity for continence even in marriage and for the exclusion of any second marriage for the members of the ἱεροσύνη, namely bishops, priests, deacons and subdeacons. The same requirement was not imposed upon the order of lectors (ἀναγνωστῶν τάγμα), because the lector was not a priest (ἱερεύς). St. Epiphanius then went on to add:

Deaconesses [διακόνισσαι] are instituted [καθίσταται] solely for service [ὑπηρεσίαν] to women, to preserve decency as required, whether in connection with their baptism [λουτροῦ] or in connection with any other examination of their bodies. Deaconesses can only have been married once, and they must lead continent lives or else be the widows of a single marriage or else have remained perpetual virgins.

In addition to the ministries already enumerated, St. Epiphanius went on to mention exorcists, translators (ἑρμηνευταί) of readings and homilies from one language to another, gravediggers and porters—all the various orders.[39] There can be no doubt that, in the mind of St. Epiphanius, deaconesses constituted a distinct group. They were listed after deacons, subdeacons and lectors but ahead of such shifting and unstable categories as exorcists, translators, gravediggers and porters. Can we say that deaconesses, as described in St. Epiphanius, were part of the clergy?[40] The question is pointless: to answer it, it would first be necessary to specify what we mean by the word "clergy". It is extremely difficult in any case to determine the precise meaning of ἐκκλησιαστικὸν τάγμα each time that we encounter it.[41] In the text of the *Panarion* that we have just been considering, it appears to refer to the entire organization of the Church.

[38] Ed. K. Holl, GCS 37 (1933): 478; PG 42, col. 744–45.

[39] Ed. K. Holl, GCS 37, p. 522; PG 42, cols. 824–25.

[40] Gryson, op. cit., p. 134.

[41] Cf. G. W. H. Lampe, *A Patristic Greek Lexicon* (Oxford: Clarendon, 1961), pp. 1370–71; C. Vagaggini, op. cit., p. 162.

Also, it will have been quite evident to the reader that St. Epiphanius strictly limited the functions of deaconesses to working with other women, performing those services, either liturgical or charitable, that modesty and decency forbade to men. Moreover, their activities were limited to what a priest directed them to carry out, assisting at the baptisms of women where nudity was required, for example; it was not considered proper for women's bodies to be exposed to the authorized administrator of the sacrament. St. Epiphanius also envisaged cases where women's bodies had to be "examined"; this would have been the case not only in connection with preparation for baptism and anointing but also in some cases of illness.

The account that St. Epiphanius provided about deaconesses thus resembled that of the *Didascalia*, although St. Epiphanius was even more limited in his conception of the role, since he said nothing at all about any catechetical role. But the very description that he provided poses a problem for us, as we shall see in the next chapter. The question is: Is his description of deaconesses purely literary, bookish? Or does it correspond to the actual practice of the churches with which he was acquainted in Judaea or on Cyprus?

We should add that the question has been raised about whether the account of St. Epiphanius provides any new information on the ritual of investiture of deaconesses.[42] In his *Exposition of the Catholic Faith*, as we have seen, he employed only the word καθίστανται; in the context in which it appears, however, it cannot be considered as opposed to χειροτονεῖν.

A letter of St. Epiphanius from the year 393 A.D., preserved for us in a Latin version found among the correspondence of St. Jerome, speaks of a dispute that St. Epiphanius had with John, bishop of Jerusalem, the successor of St. Cyril of Jerusalem. St. Epiphanius had ordained a monk—perhaps from the monastery that he directed before becoming a bishop. He had ordained this particular monk first as a deacon, then as a priest, thereby encroaching upon the jurisdiction of Bishop John. He justified his proceeding by declaring that he had done no more than many other bishops were wont to do. Then he went on to say: "*Numquam autem ego ordinavi diaconissas et ad alienas misi provincias, neque feci quidquam ut ecclesiam scinderem.*"[43]

No firm conclusions can be drawn from the fact that the same verb *ordinare* was employed in describing the ordination of priests and deacons and that of deaconesses; but when St. Epiphanius admits, as he does in the passage just quoted, that if he had done for deaconesses what he did for a

---

[42] Kalsbach, op. cit., pp. 50–51; Gryson, op. cit., p. 134; C. Vagaggini, op. cit., p. 161.

[43] Saint Jerome, *Lettres*, Text edited and translated by J. Labourt, vol. 2, *Collection des Universités de France*, Guillaume Budé (Paris: Belles Lettres, 1951), p. 159, cf. pp. 203–4.

monk, he would have thereby divided the Church, we may imagine that not all the "provinces" of the Church recognized the institution of deaconesses. Alternatively, we may conjecture that we are already dealing with the deaconess-nuns that we will in fact encounter later on.

B. Pseudo-Dionysius

It is only for the sake of reminding ourselves of his work that we include Dionysius the Areopagite, or Pseudo-Dionysius, here. It is generally agreed that his writings date from somewhere near the end of the fifth to the beginning of the sixth centuries.[44] But Pseudo-Dionysius made not the slightest allusion to deaconesses in his entire *Ecclesiastical Hierarchy*. In point of fact, the systematic presentation he makes for the necessity of a threefold sacerdotal order (τῶν ἱερουργῶν) does not allow for any other degrees (τάξις), except for (1) those who purify, that is, ministers (λειτουργῶν); (2) those who illuminate, that is, priests (ἱερέων); and (3) those who perfect, that is, bishops or high priests (ἱεραρχῶν).[45]

> The order of ministers [ἡ δὲ τῶν λειτουργῶν τάξις] is charged with purifying and sifting out those who do not possess the divine resemblance before they approach the holy sacerdotal liturgies [τὰς τῶν ἱερέων ἱερουργίας]. He purifies those who present themselves to him. In sanctifying them, he removes from them any trace of participation in evil. He prepares them for the rite of initiation [ἐποψίαν] as well as for sacred Communion. It is for this reason that in the course of the ceremony through which the Divine Rebirth [θεογενεσίας] is effected, it is the ministers [οἱ λειτουργοί] who remove [ἀπογυμνοῦσιν] from the candidate his old clothing, and who undo his belt and make him face west for renunciation [ἀποταγήν] and then make him face east.[46]

In the description of this baptismal liturgy, no allusion whatsoever is made to the problem of nudity of women candidates, nor is mention made of any feminine ministry aiming to preserve modesty and decency. Of course, the total silence on these subjects could always be explained and justified by the fact that Pseudo-Dionysius characteristically left aside the details of rituals that did not contribute to illustrating his scheme. But another function was also envisaged for "the order of ministers" by his particular scheme:

[44] R. Bornert, *Les commentaires byzantins de la divine liturgie du VIIᵉ au XVᵉ siècle*, *Archives de l'Orient chrétien*, 9 (Paris: Institut français d'études byzantines, 1966), p. 66; see the summary exposition of the various opinions on the date and origin of the *Ecclesiastical Hierarchy* in B. Altaner, *Précis de patrologie* (Mulhouse, Salvator, 1961), p. 697.

[45] *Hiérarchie ecclésiastique* 5, 1, 3, PG 3, col. 504C; cf. trans. by M. de Gandillac, *Oeuvres complètes du pseudo-Denys l'Aréopagite*, *Bibliothèque philosophique* (Paris: Aubier, 1943), p. 296.

[46] *Hiérarchie ecclésiastique* 5, 1, 6, PG 3, col. 508. I correct the translation of Gandillac, op. cit., p. 298. Cf. also the baptismal ritual in *Hiérarchie ecclésiastique* 2, 2, 6–7.

He separates the profane from the priests [or from the holy things?]. This is why the prescriptions of the bishop [ἡ ἱεραρχικὴ θεσμοθεσία] puts this order in charge of the sacred doors [ταῖς ἱεραῖς αὐτὴν ἐφίστησι πύλαις].[47]

What, then, was this "order of ministers"? If we examine his description of ordination into this particular "order of ministers", and interpret it in the light of known liturgical tradition, we will be persuaded that ordination into the diaconate alone is what we are dealing with here. Pseudo-Dionysius was faithful to the principles of St. Hippolytus of Rome as regards the laying on of hands. He is even more strict than Hippolytus, in that he made no mention at all of any lower ministries. Nevertheless, his description of the liturgy in general gives us to understand that, under the generic name of "ministers", he included lectors and possibly even psalmists and porters. According to him, after the catechumens were sent out,

> from among the ministers [τῶν λειτουργῶν], certain ones station themselves at the doors of the sanctuary and insure that they are closed. The other ministers carry out those functions that correspond to their order; those who possess the highest dignity among the ministers [οἱ δὲ τῆς λειτουργικῆς διακοσμήσεως ἔκκριτοι] help the priests [σὺν τοῖς ἱερεῦσιν] spread out on the altar the sacred bread and the chalice of benediction of the divine sacrifices.[48]

Then there is this excerpt from the liturgy of the word assigned for the rite of burial of the deceased:

> The ministers [οἱ λειτουργοί] read the text of the true promises contained in the divine Scriptures on the subject of our sacred resurrection; they also sing the psalms bearing on the same theme. The first among the ministers [τῶν λειτουργῶν ὁ πρῶτος] sends the catechumens out; then he proclaims the names . . . then he exhorts all the assistants to pray.[49]

There is nothing here to suggest that deaconesses could not have been included, like lectors, among these "ministers", thus finding their place within the rigid structure of the scheme of Pseudo-Dionysius. But there is also nothing to suggest that they were present.

C. Antiochian Exegetical Commentaries

Three of the exegetes of the Antiochian school wrote commentaries on the Epistles of St. Paul. They include Theodore of Mopsuestia, ordained a priest in 383 A.D., who in 393 became bishop of Mopsuestia in Cilicia, the

---

[47] Ibid.; cf. Gandillac, op. cit., p. 299 (I have also corrected this translation).
[48] Hiérarchie ecclésiastique 3, 2, PG 3, col. 425; cf. Gandillac, op. cit., p. 264.
[49] Hiérarchie ecclésiastique 7, 2, PG 3, col. 556; cf. Gandillac, op. cit., pp. 315–16.

province that bordered Upper Syria; Theodore's contemporary, John—
called Chrysostomos, "golden-mouthed", after his death—ordained a
deacon in 381 and a priest in 386, who in 397 became archbishop of
Constantinople; and, finally, Theodoret, who was the junior of the two
previous Antiochian exegetes by some forty years, and who in 423
became the bishop of Cyrrhus, a small town to the east of Antioch.

Apropos of Phoebe, St. Chrysostom wrote only this: "See how Paul
honors her, for he mentions her ahead of everybody else, and he calls her
his sister: it is no small thing to be called the sister of Paul." He added a
mention of her dignity: διάκονον.[50] St. John Chrysostom did not go any
deeper into the matter than that: he enumerated none of the activities by
which Phoebe merited the praise of Paul, and he certainly made no
connection between the title of διάκονος given to her by Paul and any
ecclesiastical institution of the church of Antioch.

Theodoret, however, was much more specific:

> Cenchreae is a great agglomeration adjoining Corinth. The effectiveness of
> the preaching is to be admired: in a very short period of time, not only were
> the cities filled with piety but the countryside around them as well. The
> Church assembly at Cenchreae was already so considerable as to have a
> woman deacon [γυναῖκα διάκονον], prominent and noble. She was so rich
> in good works performed as to have merited the praise of Paul.[51]

Theodoret went on to comment on the hospitality she must have extended
to St. Paul. According to Theodoret, only large communities (τοσοῦτον
. . . σύστημα) had deaconesses. Was he trying to suggest that the dignity
accorded to her—to use the phraseology of St. John Chrysostom—was
only conferred upon noble people, and that being "rich in good works"
(πλοῦτον κατορθωμάτων) presupposed being just rich, plain and simple?

We only have some fragments of Theodore of Mopsuestia's commentary
on the Epistle to the Romans, and these fragments do not include his
treatment of the sixteenth chapter.[52]

As for 1 Timothy 3, the mention of "the women" there seemed
perfectly straightforward to all three of the Antiochian exegetes; there was
apparently no doubt in their minds that "the women" about whom the
apostle spoke were indeed women deacons. Theodore of Mopsuestia
expressed himself on this subject as follows:

> Since Paul was speaking immediately before about deacons, and since this
> name applies also to women given to similar tasks, he quite logically added

[50] St. John Chrysostom, *Comment. in Epist. ad Rom.*, 30:2, PG 60, col. 665.

[51] Theodoret, *Interp. Epist. ad Rom.* 16:1, PG 82, cols. 217D, 220A.

[52] PG 66, cols. 787–876; K. Staab, *Pauluskommentare aus der griechischen Kirche aus
Katenenhandschriften* (Münster: Aschendorff, 1933), pp. 113–72.

that the women also should be chaste. This does not mean that the wives of deacons were established in this service, but that any women who were established in it to exercise the same office as the deacons had to be as distinguished in their zeal for virtue as those same deacons. . . . After having mentioned cases of women given the responsibility of the diaconate, a mention which is explicable because of the similarity of the names, [Paul] went on to pick up the thread again of what he had been saying about deacons. And he added: "Let deacons be the husband of one wife."[53]

St. John Chrysostom was briefer in his comment but no less clear:

"The women likewise". He meant the [women] deacons. There are those who say he was talking about women in general. No, that is not the case. It would have made no sense to have inserted here something about women in general in this particular place. He was referring to those having the dignity of deaconesses [ἀλλὰ περὶ τῶν τὸ ἀξίωμα τῆς διακονίας ἐχουσῶν λέγει]. "Let deacons be the husband of one wife." This too is appropriately said also of woman deacons [περὶ γυναικῶν διακόνων], for this is necessary, useful and proper in the highest degree in the Church.[54]

Theodoret wrote:

"The women likewise", that is to say, the [woman] deacons (diakonous), "must be serious, no slanderers, but temperate, faithful in all things." What he prescribed for men, [he prescribed] in similar [παραπλησίως] terms equally for women. For just as he required deacons to be "serious", so he required women to be serious. Just as he required deacons not to be "double tongued", so he required the women to be "no slanderers". Just as he required deacons not to be "addicted to much wine", so he required the women to be temperate.[55]

Theodore of Mopsuestia, however, certainly went counter to the prevailing confusion between deaconesses and widows. In commenting on 1 Timothy 5:9, "Let a widow be enrolled if she is not less than sixty years of age, having been the wife of one husband", he explained as follows:

[53] Theodore of Mopsuestia, In Epistolas b. Pauli Commentarii, ed. H. B. Swete, vol. 2 (Cambridge University Press, 1882), pp. 128–29. We do not have the Greek text of this commentary, only the Latin text. Theodore goes on to say that we shouldn't be surprised that Paul mentioned neither subdeacons nor lectors since these degrees must have been created later in response to the needs of the ministry, but they were not degrees that were conferred before the altar because their conferral involved no service before the altar (ibid., pp. 132–34).

[54] St. John Chrysostom, In Epist. 1 ad Timoth. 3, Homil. 11:1, PG 62, col. 553. Cf. J. Lécuyer, Saint Jean Chrysostome et l'ordre du diaconat, in Mélanges liturgiques offerts au R. P. Dom Bernard Botte (Louvain: Mont César, 1972), p. 309.

[55] Theodoret, Interp. Epist. I ad Tim. 3:11, PG 82, col. 809.

The apostle believed himself above all to have indicated the age that must be attained by those to be received into the order of widows. Certain people, however, paying little attention to his motive in providing this indication, have wondered if it was possible to ordain deaconesses at a younger age, imagining that deaconesses somehow necessarily had to be received into the higher order of widows. These people have not understood that if [the apostle] had wished to prescribe such an age rule for ordination, he would certainly have prescribed it first of all for priests and bishops. But this is manifestly not the case. Paul never believed that function should be determined in accordance with age. Timothy, after all, was very young.

The point here is that widows performed no functions, but they did receive a subsidy from the Church that was supposed to enable them to live a contemplative life.[56] St. John Chrysostom went even farther on this particular point: "Just as today there are what are called 'choirs of virgins' [παρθένων χοροί], so formerly [τὸ παλαιόν] there were 'choirs of widows' [χηρῶν χοροί]."[57] It is, therefore, a no longer existing institution. By his time this "order" consisted merely of the needy being helped by the Church.[58]

All in all, if we possessed no other documentation on the subject of deaconesses than what we have just reviewed, we would be very little informed about them. It is not enough merely to take note of their existence. Considering the very great differences in discipline that existed from one local church to another, we must carefully examine the situation on a case-by-case basis: What were these deaconesses? What was their mission, and what were the activities in which they engaged? What was their position in the community? Did they carry out the same function as the deaconesses we have already encountered functioning on the eastern frontiers of the Roman Empire and within the Persian Sassanid Empire? In order to respond to such questions as these, it is fortunate that we possess other sources of information.

---

[56] Theodore of Mopsuestia, op. cit., pp. 158–60.

[57] St. John Chrysostom, *In illud "Vidua eligatur non minus sexaginta annis"*, PG 51, col. 323. Cf. Gryson, op. cit., pp. 141–42.

[58] Gryson, op. cit., p. 142.

CHAPTER SIX

Deaconesses in the Other Churches of the Greek-Speaking and Eastern Regions of the Roman Empire
(End of Fourth to Sixth Centuries)

II. IN THE LIFE AND PRACTICE OF THE CHURCH

In order to locate deaconesses properly within the life and practice of the churches of these regions of the Roman Empire, two types of documents are especially valuable for us. First of all, there is the correspondence of the great bishops such as St. Basil, St. John Chrysostom, Theodoret and Severus of Antioch. There are also biographies and edifying narratives composed along the same lines. These biographies and narratives, however, unless they were the work of contemporaries, were often in great part purely legendary; nevertheless, even then, they serve to represent some of the institutions that existed as well as the mentality of the time and place of the author. With regard to this kind of literature, we can scarcely improve upon the inventories compiled by Charles Du Fresne Du Cange[1] in the seventeenth century and by Jean Gaspard Schweitzer[2] in the eighteenth century; we need merely add new documents discovered since then and make reference to more modern editions.

But all of this literature constitutes only one of the types of documents valuable for us in our survey. The other type consists of the abundant epigraphic evidence now accessible in the great collections of inscriptions available in libraries. Although these collections have already been

---

[1] Ioannis Cinnami, *Historiarum libri sex* . . . , Accedunt Caroli du Fresne du Cange, *in Nicephori Bryennii Caesaris Annae Comnenae Caesarissae et eiusdem Ioannis Cinnami historiam Comnenicam Notae historicae et philologicae* (Parisiis, ex typ. Regia, 1670), pp. 416–21, sub v. Διακονισσῶν; C. du Fresne du Cange, *Glossarium ad scriptores mediae et infimae Graecitatis* (Lugduni, Anisson etc., 1688), v. Διακόνισσα.

[2] J. C. Suiceri, *Thesaurus ecclesiasticus e Patribus Graecis*, 3rd ed., vol. 1 (Trajecti, 1746), col. 864–69.

thoroughly mined by A. Kalsbach, E. D. Theodorou[3] and R. Gryson,[4] I believe they constitute a source well worth revisiting.[5]

1. GEOGRAPHICAL EXTENSION OF THE INSTITUTION OF DEACONESSES

We will recall that number 3 of Justinian's *Novellae* attempted to limit the number of deaconesses in the Great Church of Constantinople to forty.[6] The existence of this piece of legislation surely indicates that there were more than forty deaconesses there at the time. These excessive numbers evidently characterized all the Church ministries at that time in Constantinople, since the emperor's legislation also envisaged holding the number of deacons to sixty. The normal number of deacons, at least in the churches of the West, was only seven, in keeping with the tradition of the Acts of the Apostles.

We are not in a position to establish the numbers of deaconesses or occupants of other ministries in the other great churches of that time. In Antioch, for example, the very existence of deaconesses is known to us merely from literary documents that yield up only a few names, not any numbers: Sabiniana, the aunt of St. John Chrysostom,[7] who lived toward the end of the fourth century; and Anastasia, Jannia, Eugenia and Valeriana, who corresponded with the patriarch Severus of Antioch toward the beginning of the sixth century.[8] When Severus went into exile, foreseeing

[3] Notes by A. Kalsbach published by O. Casel in *Jahrbuch für Liturgiewissenschaft* 11 (1931): 277–78: E. Δ. Θεοδώρου, Ἡ χειροτονία ἢ χειροθεσία τῶν διακονισσῶν, in Θεολογία 25 (1954): 600–601.

[4] Gryson, *Ministère des femmes*, pp. 149–50.

[5] I have principally made use of the eight volumes of *Indices* in MAMA; and those in *Inscriptions grecques et latines de la Syrie*, a publication begun by Louis Jalabert and René Mouterde, and continued by the Institut Fernand Courby (Paris: Geuthner, 1929–70), 7 pts. in 8 vols. (Institut français d'archéologie de Beyrouth, *Bibliothèque archéologique et historique* 12, 32, 46, 51, 61, 66, 78, 89) and the *Table*, which appeared in 1970, of vols. 11–20 (1950–64) of *Supplementum epigraphicum Graecum*, which has been published in Leyden since 1923. Other collections utilized will be indicated in the course of the present chapter.

[6] See Chapter 5, 1F, the *Novellae* of Justinian.

[7] St. John Chrysostom, *Lettres à Olympias*, 6 (13), 1, SC 13b, p. 130: ἡ κυρία μου Σαβινιανὴ ἡ διάκονος, compared with Palladius, *Histoire Lausiaque* 41, ed. C. Butler, TS 4:2 (1904): 129, trans. A. Lucot, *Textes et documents* 15 (Paris: Picard, 1912), pp. 292–93: "At Antioch I met a most venerable woman, on intimate terms with God; she was the deaconess Sabiniana, the aunt of the bishop, John."

[8] Severus of Antioch, *A Collection of Letters*, ed. E. W. Brooks, PO 14, fasc. 1 (Paris: Firmin-Didot, 1920), pp. 245–88 (= 75–117), letters 69–72 (Anastasia) and pp. 443–44

the difficulties that would be brought about by the absence of bishops, he attempted to reinforce the established rules governing ordinations. Concerning deaconesses, he happened to add a sentence to the effect that "the practice of devout women . . . being ordained deaconesses is very usual and is diffused, if I may say so, over the whole world."[9]

In Jerusalem, the only trace of the existence of deaconesses we have ever found consists of two funerary inscriptions.[10] No trace of them can be discerned in the descriptions of the Jerusalem liturgies provided to us by Egeria. It is the tenth or eleventh century before they began to be mentioned in the Greek liturgy of St. James.[11]

Outside of these great archepiscopal sees, perhaps even more understandably, we encounter only individual cases of deaconesses, most of which come to our attention through inscriptions. It is interesting to try to chart the spread of deaconesses throughout the Roman Empire by means of these inscriptions. However, we should remember that the existence of a greater or lesser number of these inscriptions is a result of both the hazards of any archeological investigation and the nature of the excavations that actually were carried out. The reality, once lived, of the institution of deaconesses is not necessarily accurately reflected in the partial and uneven evidence testifying to it that is available to us.

For example, Palestine, Upper Syria, Lower Syria and the Euphrates

---

(= 273–74), letter 110 (Eugenia); E. Brooks, *The Sixth Book of the Selected Letters of Severus, Patriarch of Antioch*, vol. 2 (London: Williams and Norgate, 1904, The Text and Translation Society), pt. 1, pp. 411–14 and pt. 2, pp. 364–68 (Letter to Valeriana); pt. 1, pp. 415–18 and pt. 2, pp. 368–71 (letter to Jannia). Theodoret, in *Hist. eccl.* 3:14, GCS 44, pp. 190–92, speaks of a pious woman from what appears to have been Antioch "who had merited the grace of the diaconate" (τοῦ τῆς διακονίας ἠξιωμένη χαρίσματος). There is also a legendary story in the *Vita Cypriani* about a deaconess Justa who became Justine; it already existed around the end of the fourth century. See n. 93 to this chapter below. Also legendary is the story of the deaconess Roma: see A. Kalsbach, *Altkirchliche Einrichtung*, p. 54.

[9] E. W. Brooks, op. cit., vol. 2, pt. 1, letter 49, p. 139: ". . . the practice of devout women living in their houses, being ordained deaconesses, is very usual and is diffused, if I may say so, over the whole world."

[10] The first of these inscriptions is that of Sophia (doubtless sixth century): see P. Thomsen, *Die lateinischen und griechischen Inschriften der Stadt Jerusalem und ihrer nächsten Umgebung* (Leipzig: Hinrich, 1922), no. 130; the second is that of Eneon (tomb in the vicinity of Jerusalem): see J. Germer-Durand, *Epigraphie chrétienne de Jérusalem*, in *Revue biblique* 1 (1892): 560–88, no. 10. But also see the final inscription in the list of inscriptions included in the Supplementary Note at the end of this chapter, below.

[11] "Remember, Lord, the priests, deacons, deaconesses (*diakonissōn*), subdeacons, lectors, exorcists, interpreters, cantors, monks, virgins, orphans, celibates . . . , ed. B. C. Mercier, PO 26:2 (1946), pp. 218–19; the Vatic. Greek ms. 2282, from the ninth century, and two mss. from the twelfth reproducing the same text, do not include the mention of deaconesses (H, A, E); nor is it to be found in the Syriac Anaphora (tenth century), ed. O. Heiming, *Anaphorae Syriacae*, vol. 2, fasc. 2 (Rome, P. Istituto Orientale, 1953), pp. 166–67.

Valley have yielded almost no inscriptions at all on this subject.[12] The correspondence of St. Basil is the source of our knowledge of the daughters of Terentios, who were deaconesses at Samosata.[13] The correspondence of Theodoret provides the names of two deaconesses in Cyrrhus, Axia and Casiana, whom he consoled because each of them had lost a child, and also the name of a third deaconess, Celerina.[14] Palladius, in his *Historia Lausica*, mentioned a deaconess in Caesarea in Palestine.[15] Mark the Deacon, in his *Life of Porphyry, the Bishop of Gaza*, spoke of a deaconess named Manaris.[16] In Isauria in Cilicia, Egeria visited one named Marthana.[17] If we add to all these names the inscriptions discovered at Korykos in Upper Cilicia,[18] we then have the complete list for the Roman Diocese of the East as far as the present state of our knowledge is concerned. Later on, we may be able to find an explanation for the rarity of occurrence of these names of deaconesses.

The Roman diocese of Pontus similarly has not yielded a very rich harvest of inscriptions that mention deaconesses.[19] A single inscription found at Aksaray in Cappadocia eulogizes a deaconess named Mary in terms that will merit a closer look.[20] Yet we know from the letter of St. Basil to Amphilocus of Iconium that the institution of deaconesses was rather common in Cappadocia.[21] St. Gregory of Nyssa, in his *Life of St. Macrina*, speaks of a certain Lampadion ἐν τῷ διακονίας βαθμῷ at Annisa.[22] In Greater Armenia, Bishop Elpidius of Satala was deposed by

[12] In the eight vols. of *Inscriptions grecques et latines de la Syrie* (see n. 5 to this chapter), I found only inscriptions referring to male deacons: Εὐσεβίς, *Eusebis* (n. 458, 555A, 559) was an architect: εὐσεβής.

[13] St. Basil, Letter 105 (from the year 372 A.D.), ed. Y. Courtonne, *Coll. Budé* (Paris: Belles Lettres, 1961), 2:6–7.

[14] Theodoret, *Correspondance*, ed. Y. Azema, vol. I, SC 40, p. 118, cf. 44; vol. 2, SC 98, pp. 62–64; vol. 3, SC 111, pp. 18–20.

[15] Palladius, *Histoire Lausiaque*, ed. C. Butler, TS 4:2 (1904): 166; ed. A. Lucot, *Textes et documents* 15 (Paris: Picard, 1911), pp. 394–95.

[16] Mark the Deacon, *Vie de Porphyre*, c. 12, nos. 100–102, ed. H. Grégoire and M. A. Kugener, *Coll. byzantine . . . Budé* (Paris: Belles Lettres, 1930), pp. 77–78.

[17] Egeria, *Journal de voyage* 23, ed. H. Pétré, SC 21, p. 184; CCL 175 (1965): 66.

[18] MAMA, 3:133 (no. 212: Athanasia), 158 (no. 395: Theodora), 161 (no. 418: Theophila), 208 (no. 744: Timothea), 209 (no. 759: Charitina).

[19] G. Jacopi, *Missione archeologica italiana in Anatolia. Relazione sulla prima campagna esplorativa*, in *Bollettino del Reale Istituto di archeologia e storia dell'arte* 7 (1937): 3–26; *Esplorazioni e studi in Paflagonia e Cappadocia*, ibid., 8 (1938): 3–43.

[20] Ibid. 8 (1938): 34–36 and figs. 135–36; cf. A. Merlin, *Année épigraphique* (1941): 351–52, n. 164.

[21] See Chapter 5, 1C, above.

[22] St. Gregory of Nyssa, *Vie de sainte Macrine*, ed. P. Maraval, SC 178 (1971), pp. 236–37. Installation in the female diaconate has been wrongly predicated of St. Macrina herself: see P. Maraval, op. cit., pp. 55–56.

the Synod of Constantinople of 360 A.D. for having admitted into the female diaconate a certain Nectaria, who had been excommunicated and hence necessarily should have been excluded from that dignity in accordance with ecclesiastical law.[23] In Lesser Armenia, according to Cyril of Scythopolis, the widow Dionysia, mother of St. Euthymius, was, in 378, ordained a deaconess of the holy Church by Otreios, the bishop of Melitene.[24]

It was the Roman diocese of Asia that has proved to be the richest in inscriptions mentioning deaconesses. There are at least ten of them from Phrygia and Galatia.[25] In Pisidia, the city of Laodicea Combusta alone furnished four.[26] The center of the Encratite heretics, Nevinna, provided another one, signed by one Elaphia, who was a deaconess of the Encratite sect.[27] In Lycaonia, two inscriptions originated in Lystra[28] and two in Iconium, one of the latter mentioning the deaconess Basilissa.[29] As far as Iconium itself is concerned, we have St. Basil's letter to Amiphilocus. We should also mention the inscription of Agalliasis on the isle of Melos, one of the Cyclades Islands;[30] and another one from Arete; and a third from Aphrodisias in Caria.[31] A legendary life of St. Xenia, written by a native of Caria, depicts the Apostle Paul coming to Milasa in Caria to ordain St. Xenia a deaconess.[32] A later life of the bishop of Lampsacus on the Hellespont, St. Parthenios (tenth century?) speaks of a visit paid to this saint by the deaconess Theophila of Chersonesus,[33] but Chersonesus (modern Crimea) was outside the boundaries of the Roman Empire.

Finally, we possess only two inscriptions that indicate that there were deaconesses in Achaia: one concerning a certain Athanasia from Delphi[34] and another concerning Nicagora from Mount Hymettus.[35]

---

[23] Sozomen, *Hist. eccl.* 4, 24, 16, ed. Bidez-Hansen, GCS 50, p. 181.

[24] Cyril of Scythopolis, *Vie de sainte Euthyme* 3, ed. E. Schwartz, TU 49:2 (1939), pp. 10–11; cf. A. J. Festugière, *Les moines d'Orient*, III, 1 (Paris, Ed. du Cerf, 1962), pp. 60–61.

[25] MAMA, vol. 1, nos. 323 (Nunes), 324 (Strategis), 326 (Pribis, rather than Leontiana), 383 (Matronia); vol. 7, nos. 120 (Celsa), 186 (Severa), 471 (Domma), 539 (Nonna), 585 (Messalina). The meaning of *diakonō* in inscription no. 556 of vol. 7 appears doubtful to me.

[26] MAMA, vol. 1, nos. 178 (Masa), 194 (Aurelia Faustina), 226 (Paula); vol. 7, no. 75 (Magna).

[27] MAMA, vol. 7, no. 69; cf. vol. 1, p. xxv.

[28] MAMA, vol. 8, nos. 64, 91.

[29] MAMA, vol. 8, nos. 318 (Basilissa), 321.

[30] H. Grégoire, *Recueil des inscriptions grecques chrétiennes d'Asie Mineure*, fasc. 1 (Paris: Leroux, 1922), no. 209 (first half of the fourth century, in a catacomb).

[31] Ibid., no. 258.

[32] *Vita s. Eusebiae seu Xenae*, ed. T. Nissen, in *Analecta Bollandiana* 56 (1938): 11.

[33] Crispinus, *Vita s. Parthenii*, c. 2, no. 8, PG 114, col. 1357.

[34] J. Laurent, *Delphes chrétien*, in *Bulletin de correspondance hellénique* 23 (1899): 273–78; DACL 4, cols. 570–71.

[35] At the Monastery of Kareas: C. Bayet, *De titulis Atticae christianis antiquissimis commen-*

As for the Diocese of Thrace, except for the city of Constantinople itself, there are no inscriptions to be considered.

2. WHO WERE THE DEACONESSES?

The idea of the institution of deaconesses that emerges from a study of all these texts is fairly uniform. The methods of recruitment also seem to have been similar. All this was true in spite of local differences.

First of all, we are obliged to notice the dignity (διηκονίης τιμήν)[36] that attached to being a deaconess: deaconesses were respected. It was an honor (ἀξίωμα διακόνου) that Nicarete of Bithynia, in her humility, did not seek to gain for herself.[37] It was a grace, merited by a pious woman (τοῦ τῆς διακονίας ἠξιωμένη χαρίσματος).[38] We cannot take too literally the praise and encomiums that were typically included in these inscriptions on tombs or steles,[39] but a constant theme of the ancient historians and hagiographers was that the diaconate typically crowned a life of piety, prayer and contemplation. We find such inscriptions or references as "Athanasia most pious, who led an irreproachable life";[40] Dionysia, "ardently attached to God and to divine things";[41] Sabiniana, "a most venerable woman, on intimate terms with God".[42] We also find such titles as "deaconesses of the Great Church",[43] or διάκονος πανμάκαρος Χριστοῦ.[44]

At least twice we find Pauline reminiscences invoked in connection with deaconesses. Sophia, whose funerary inscription was found on the Mount of Olives, was "the second Phoebe".[45] Mary, whose richly decorated tombstone was found at Aksaray in Cappadocia, "according to the text of the apostle, raised children, practiced hospitality, washed the

tatio historica et epigraphica (Paris: Thorin, 1878), p. 113, no. 105; Corpus inscriptionum Graecarum, no. 9318. C. Spicq, in Saint Paul, les Epîtres pastorales, 4th ed., vol. 1, Etudes bibliques (Paris: Gabalda, 1964), p. 460, mistakenly believed that he had identified a deaconess under the name of Euthychiane in a Corinthian inscription: from Supplementum epigraphicum Graecum 11 (1950), p. 23, no. 172.

[36] MAMA, vol. 8, no. 321.

[37] Sozomen, Hist. eccl. 8, 23, 7, GCS 50, p. 381.

[38] Theodoret, Hist. eccl., 3, 14, GCS 44, pp. 190–92.

[39] See especially the one published in MAMA, vol. 8, no. 321.

[40] See the inscription referred to in n. 34 to this chapter, above.

[41] See n. 24 to this chapter, above.

[42] Σεμνοτάτη γυναικὶ καὶ τῷ Θεῷ προσομιλούσῃ, Palladius, Histoire Lausiaque 41, ed. C. Butler, TS 6:2 (1904); ed. A. Lucot (Textes et documents 15), pp. 292–93.

[43] Basilina: Cyril of Scythopolis, Vita s. Ioannis solitarii, ed. E. Schartz, TU 49:2 (Leipzig, 1939), p. 218; Dionysia, see n. 24 to this chapter, above.

[44] MAMA, vol. 1, no. 226.

[45] Ἐνθάδε κεῖται ἡ δούλη καὶ νύμφη τοῦ Χριστοῦ Σοφιά ἡ διάκονος, ἡ δευτέρα Φοίβη, P. Thomsen, loc. cit., n. 10 to this chapter, above.

feet of the saints and distributed her bread to those in need".[46] Doing good works seems to have been the dominant trait of this Mary,[47] as it doubtless was also of Sophia. The same thing must have been true of Pentadia, a correspondent of St. John Chrysostom; she too is supposed to have done an enormous amount of good work around her,[48] and this was also true of Eneon, "deaconess of this hospital".[49] All of this supposes that these women had some wealth. The ideal of the widow has here become the ideal of the deaconess as well.

In fact, in the case of a good number of these deaconesses, it is made clear that they were also widows. Those inscriptions gathered in the small towns and villages of Asia and Pontus suggest that deaconesses lived at home with their families. Some were members of what we may be so bold as to call "clerical families". Domna was the daughter of the priest Theophilus.[50] Aurelia Faustina was the mother of a lector.[51] Nonna was the mother of the priest Alexander.[52] Sabiniana was the aunt of St. John Chrysostom.[53] Masa was perhaps both daughter and wife of priests.[54] Messalina was the sister of a priest.[55]

It must have sometimes happened that a deaconess was instituted at the same time that a ministry was conferred upon her son. This was at any rate the case for Dionysia, the widow of St. Euthymius, if we are to believe the account of Cyril of Scythopolis: Bishop Otreios baptized her son, gave him the tonsure and made (ἐποίησεν) him a lector of his church; at the same time he ordained (ἐχειροτόνησεν) the mother a deaconess.[56] Then there are some apocryphal acts, supposedly at the second generation (fourth/fifth century), called *The Martyrdom of Matthew*, in which a conversation is reported with a persecuting king that supposedly took place after the death of the apostle; the latter was then reported to have appeared and to have ordained (κατέστησεν) the king a priest, his son a deacon and his wife and daughter-in-law deaconesses.[57] It is, of course, always possible that

---

[46] Cf. 1 Tim 5:10.

[47] Jacopi, *Esplorazione e studi*, art. cit., p. 34, n. 19 to this chapter, above.

[48] St. John Chrysostom, Letter 104, PG 52, cols. 663–64.

[49] J. Germer-Durand, art. cit., n. 10 to this chapter, above. But see the final item in the Supplementary Note to this chapter, below.

[50] MAMA, vol. 7, no. 471.

[51] MAMA, vol. 1, no. 194.

[52] MAMA, vol. 7, no. 539.

[53] See n. 7 to this chapter, above.

[54] MAMA, vol. 1, no. 178.

[55] MAMA, vol. 7, no. 586.

[56] Cyril of Scythopolis, cited in n. 24 to this chapter, above.

[57] R. A. Lipsius and M. Bonnet, *Acta Apostolorum Apocrypha*, vol. 1, pt. 2 (Lipsiae: H. Mendelsohn, 1898), pp. 258–59. It is to be noted that the Bibl. Nat. Greek ms. 880 (10th

the author of a legend such as this was inspired by a real usage in the church with which he was familiar.

In 691, the Trullan Synod provided that "the wife of the one who has been promoted to the episcopacy, having separated from her husband by mutual agreement, will enter after his ordination into a convent . . . if she is worthy, she herself may be promoted to the dignity of becoming a deaconess [καὶ πρὸς τῆς διακονίας ἀναβιβαζέσθω ἀξίωμα]".[58] But this route for arriving at the dignity of becoming a deaconess logically flowed from a very different discipline than the one we have been observing being practiced in the East.

3. FUNCTIONS OF DEACONESSES

From the evidence that we have already examined, it emerges that the deaconesses who lived and functioned within the confines of the Roman Empire did not bear a very close resemblance to the deaconesses described in the *Didascalia* or in the documents emanating from Chaldea or Persia. This is a question that we must examine more closely—first of all, by trying to ascertain whether the deaconesses within the Roman Empire played any pastoral or liturgical role in connection with the baptism of women.

A. Did the Deaconesses of the Greek-Speaking and Eastern Regions of the Empire Exercise Any Function in Connection with the Baptism of Women?

We should remind ourselves of the affirmation made by St. Epiphanius around the year 375 A.D.: "Deaconesses are instituted *solely* for service to women, to preserve decency as required, whether in connection with their baptism or in connection with any other examination of their bodies."[59] As we know, nearly two centuries later, one of the *Novellae* of Justinian echoed this affirmation of St. Epiphanius and stated that deaconesses should "exercise the sacred ministry, assist at the revered rites of baptism and participate in the other hidden tasks that they normally carry out in connection with the most venerable mysteries".[60]

---

century) gives the queen the title *presbutida* instead of *diakonissan*, but the reading *diakonissan* is attested to by the Latin version (mss. of the 8th and 9th centuries) and by a second family of Greek mss. (10th–11th centuries).

[58] Joannou, vol. I, pt. 1, p. 186; see n. 30, Chapter 5, above.

[59] See Chapter 5, 2A.

[60] See Chapter 5, 1D.

However, Justinian also legislated on the subject of deaconesses who lived in monasteries. A letter from Severus, the patriarch of Antioch, written some time between 519 and 538 A.D., provides a very different viewpoint from that of St. Epiphanius. Those with whom Severus was in correspondence were in anguish concerning "the times of confusion and of persecution" in which they were living. Severus himself was in exile. His correspondents feared that they might have to face the problem, in the place where they lived, of having no bishop who could perform ordinations. Severus was asked to distinguish between the ordination of male priests and deacons, who were necessary for the holy Sacrifice, and the ordination of deaconesses. Severus replied:

> In the case of deaconesses, especially in convents, ordination is performed less with regard to the needs of the mysteries than exclusively with regard to doing honor.

He added:

> In the cities, deaconesses habitually exercise a ministry relating to the divine bath of regeneration in the case of women who are being baptized.[61]

Could it be that Severus was writing to correspondents living in the East, where deaconesses were in fact actively involved in baptisms of women? Could it be that St. Epiphanius or Emperor Justinian were aiming to provide general principles, keeping in mind the diversities within the Church? Most modern historians of the liturgy have not asked themselves these questions. They have often assumed that the evidence of the *Didascalia* and the *Apostolic Constitutions* was in itself enough to establish that a practice was universal within the Church. However, the fact is that this assumption is vulnerable to a considerable number of objections.

The first of these objections is the silence on the subject of the baptismal catechisms, which have been preserved for us from both Antioch and Jerusalem and which date from the end of the fourth century. These baptismal catechisms are contemporaneous with the *Panarion* of St. Epiphanius. Neither St. John Chrysostom, nor Theodore of Mopsuestia nor the bishop of Jerusalem—whether St. Cyril of Jerusalem or his successor—made mention of any assistance rendered by deaconesses at baptism, even though adult catechumens were almost certainly still in the majority in their day. All three of these prelates, however, did specify that

[61] E. W. Brooks, *The Sixth Book of the Selected Letters of Severus*, vol. 2, pt. 1 (London: Williams and Norgate, 1903), pp. 193–94, letter 62. This letter does not have a specific addressee; however, the Syriac version employs the feminine pronoun with reference to these addresses, P. Hindo, *Disciplina antiochena antica*, Siri, vol. 2, CCOF, ser. 2, fasc. 26 (Tipog. Vaticana, 1951), p. 333, is in error when he attributes this letter to the same addressees as the previous letters in the series.

candidates for baptism were obliged to disrobe completely[62]—according to St. John Chrysostom, it was the priest who disrobed them.[63] They also specified that the prebaptismal anointing was done over the whole body,[64] "from the hair on their heads down to their toes", according to the bishop of Jerusalem.[65] It appears that the bishop himself did not carry out the anointing, according to St. John: "ἅπαν τὸ σῶμα ἀλείφεσθαι παρασκευάζει".[66] Theodore of Mopsuestia was more explicit:

> You receive the sacred anointing, while the one on whom the pontifical dignity has fallen says: "Be anointed, [name], in the name of the Father and of the Son and of the Holy Spirit." Those who are designated for this service must anoint the entire body.[67]

However, Theodore provided no hint of who was "designated for this service". As for the bishop of Jerusalem, he did not specify who performed the anointing. Some commentators have been quite surprised at this silence on the subject of deaconesses; some have even considered themselves authorized to fill in the gap caused by the lack of any mention of deaconesses. Wenger, for example, confidently wrote: "The deacons and the lower clergy anointed the men; the anointing of the women was carried out by deaconesses."[68] Mitchell was less positive; he wrote: "Perhaps those who were 'designated for this service' were the deacons

---

[62] Theodore of Mopsuestia, *Homélies catéchétiques*, 14, 1 and 8, trans. R. Tonneau-R. Devreesse, ST 145, Bibl. Apost. Vaticana, pp. 401, 417; Cyril (or John) of Jerusalem, *Catéchèse mystagogique* 2, 2, ed. A. Piédagnel, SC 126 (Paris: Le Cerf, 1966), p. 104. Total nudity was only required for the prebaptismal anointing that preceded the immersion; for the exorcisms, the catechumens removed only their outer garment and stood barefooted upon a hair cloth.

[63] St. John Chrysostom, *Catéchèse III*, in A. Papadopoulos-Kerameus, *Varia Graeca sacra* (Saint Petersburg, 1909), p. 173: τότε ἀποδύσας σε τὸ ἱμάτιον ὁ ἱερεύς. Cf. *Catéchèse Stravonikita II*, 24, in A. Wenger, *Jean Chrysostome, huit catéchèses baptismales inédites*, SC 50 (Paris: Le Cerf, 1957), p. 147: ὁλόκληρον ἀποδύσας τὸ ἱμάτιον.

[64] St. John Chrysostom, *Catéchèse Stravonikita II*, 24, Wenger, p. 147: ἅπαν τὸ σῶμα; Theodore of Mopsuestia, *Homélie* 14, nn. 1, 8, ed. Tonneau-Devreesse, pp. 401, 419: "anointed all over".

[65] St. Cyril of Jerusalem, *Catéchèse mystagogique* 2, 2, p. 106: ἀπ' ἄκρων κορυφῆς τριχῶν ἕως τῶν κατωτάτων.

[66] St. John Chrysostom, *Catéchèse Stravonikita II*, Wenger, p. 146. In "Catechism III" in the edition of Papadopoulos-Kerameus (p. 173) it is Christ himself who σφραγίζεσθαι κελεύει.

[67] Theodore of Mopsuestia, *Homélie catéchétique* 14, 8, Tonneau-Devreesse, p. 419.

[68] A. Wenger, op. cit., n. 62, p. 93. In a note referenced to C. Baur, *Johannes Chrysostomus und seine Zeit*, vol. I, *Antiochien* (München: Max Hueber, 1929), p. 65; but Wenger admitted at the same time that "Baur indicated the fact [of deaconesses] and made reference to 'Homily VI on Colossians', PG 62, 342, where a description of baptism is in fact to be found, but without any mention of deaconesses." If Wenger continued to maintain his position in spite of this admission, it was because "deaconesses in the time of Chrysostom constituted an order of women consecrated to the service of the Church (see 'Homily XI on 1 Timothy', PG 62, col. 553D)".

and deaconesses mentioned in the *Didascalia* and the *Apostolic Constitutions*."[69] Piédagnal, for his part, concluded with a little more rigor: "The silence on the subject in the majority of catechisms can be explained in two ways: either their participation was taken for granted to such a point that it didn't occur to anyone to mention it, or their participation was not in fact established in every area."[70]

We should add that, a century later, Pseudo-Dionysius, who was normally very precise in his description of rituals, attributed expressly to priests the responsibility for carrying out the prebaptismal anointing of the catechumen over his or her whole body, while he assigned the responsibility for disrobing candidates to deacons:

> The ministers [τῶν λειτουργῶν] then disrobe him entirely [τελείως ἀπαμφιεσάντων], and the priests [οἱ ἱερεῖς] bring the holy oil required for anointing. The bishop [ἀρχιερεύς] begins the anointing with three sacred signs, and then leaves it to the priest to anoint the entire body of the man [ἱερεῦσι τὸν ἄνδρα χρῖσαι πανσώμως παραδούς].[71]

There was the same silence on the subject of deaconesses in the baptismal rituals coming from the Antioch region. Some of these rituals, among them the older ones at that, did, however, specify that the prebaptismal anointing had to be carried out over the entire body and that it was carried out or continued by deacons.[72]

It is important to note that in neither these catechisms nor these rituals is there ever any particular concern indicated about any precautions needing

---

[69] L. Mitchell, *Baptismal Anointing*, Alcuin Club Collections 48 (London, S.P.C.K., 1966), p. 40.

[70] A. Piédagnel, op. cit., n. 62, above, pp. 108–9.

[71] Pseudo-Dionysius, *Hiérarchie ecclésiastique* 2, 2, 7, PG 3, col. 396BC. There is also the text of 5, 1, 6 already cited, Chapter 5, n. 46, above.

[72] *Ordo* attributed to Timothy of Alexandria (6th century), S. Brock, "A New Syriac Baptismal *Ordo* Attributed to Timothy of Alexandria", in *Le Muséon*, 1970, p. 388, n. 40; *Ordo* called Basil's *Ordo*, Denzinger, 1:325; ms. Royal Library, British Museum Add. 14493 (10th century), S. Brock, "Studies in the Early History of the Syrian Orthodox Baptismal Liturgy", JTS 23 (1972): 30. C. du Fresne du Cange, in *Ioannis Cinnami . . . historiarum libri sex* (Parisiis: typ. Regia, 1670), p. 417, reported the complaints that arose at the Council of Constantinople in 536 A.D. against, among others, the bishop of Apamea in Syria, Peter, who was supposed to have entered the baptistery with a certain Mary and to have remained alone with her there while she was stark naked awaiting baptism. This accusation is found in the Latin acts of the council published by S. Binius, *Conciliorum*, vol. 2, pt. 1 (Coloniae Agrippinae, 1618), p. 751. In reality, at the council, Peter of Antioch was reproached for having ejected from the baptistery both the priests and the catechumens who were in the process of being exorcised, that is, in the process of undergoing the final steps prior to baptism; these catechumens were not entirely stripped as for baptism, although they were barefooted and minus their outer garments, as was normal. Peter is supposed to have spent several hours in the baptistery with the κανονικαί, virgins and widows living in the world. See E. Schwartz, *Acta Consiliorum oecumenicorum*, vol. 3, *Collectio Sabaitica* (Berlin: W. de Gruyter, 1940), p. 99.

to be taken in case of the baptisms of women. On the contrary, the custom of baptismal nudity was precisely intended to be a sign of a return to the state of innocence that obtained in paradise before the Fall of Man. The Antioch catechisms expressed the idea in this fashion:

> Adam and Eve were naked and they did not know shame before they were cloaked in the garment of sin—the garment of abundant shame. Consequently, there is no reason for shame here either. For the baptismal pool is preferable to paradise itself. Here there is no serpent present, but Christ, who here exercises his office of mystagogue with regard to the rebirth to be brought about by water and the Holy Spirit. Here there are no beautiful trees, agreeable to the sight. Here there is no tree of knowledge of good and evil. Here there is neither law nor commandments, but rather grace and the gifts. [73]

> Since Adam was naked at first and did not blush for shame for himself, but required a garment separate from himself only after having sinned against the commandment of God and become mortal thereby, you, who are presenting yourself for the gift of holy baptism, so that you may henceforth be born of this baptism and become immortal in a prefigured way, must remove the garment separate from yourself—this garment that is the index of your mortality, the convincing proof of the judgment that sentenced [man] to have to wear a garment. [74]

We encounter the same language in the Jerusalem Catechism:

> As soon as you entered, then, you divested yourself of your garment; this gesture symbolized the divesting yourself of the old man in you with all his practices. Disrobed, you were naked, symbolizing in this Christ who was nailed naked to the Cross, and by his very nudity defeated the principalities and powers, dragging them into his triumphal cortege. . . . O marvelous thing, you were naked before everyone and yet you did not blush for shame. Truly you represented in this the image of the first man, Adam, who in paradise was naked but was not ashamed. [75]

Thus, if neither St. John Chrysostom, nor Theodore of Mopsuestia, nor

[73] St. John Chrysostom, *Catéchèse III*, no. 8, ed. Papadopoulos-Kerameus, pp. 173–74, trans. in A. Wenger, *Huit catéchèses*, p. 93. Cf. n. 85 to this chapter below.

[74] Theodore of Mopsuestia, *Homélie catéchétique* 14:8, ed. trans. Tonneau-Devreesse, pp. 417–19.

[75] St. Cyril of Jerusalem, *Catéchèse mystagogique* 2:2, ed. A. Piédagnel, pp. 104–7. In a note on p. 105 of this referenced work, Piédagnel expressed the typical modern opinion: "It is probable", he declared, "that precautions were taken to preserve modesty." He pointed out that, during the exorcisms, men and women were separated, but, of course, they were not naked during the exorcisms but only without their outer garments. Pseudo-Dionysius ascribed to nudity an exclusively moral symbolism, but he did so in connection with the ritual of renunciation, which took place according to a distinct sequence, prior to both that of the prebaptismal anointing and that of immersion and which did not require total nudity (see n. 62 to this chapter): "In removing so to speak the neophyte from the sin of his earlier life, in rooting out of him all desires and attachments to this world and in placing him facing east, body and feet uncovered, in order that he might thereby renounce", PG 3, 401A, trans.

the Antiochan rituals nor the Jerusalem Catechism made any mention of deaconesses in the celebration of baptisms, this silence seems to indicate that, in the particular churches represented by these writers, there was no perceived need to confer any such ministry upon deaconesses. Only on this hypothesis is it comprehensible that we would encounter no mention at all of their supposed role in these churches.

These considerations must lead us to the conclusion that the apparently strange incident recounted in John Moschus' *Spiritual Meadow* was not in fact so exceptional.[76] The incident took place in the Palestinian monastery of Penthoucla, situated to the west of the Jordan River,[77] during the time of the archbishop Peter (524–548 A.D.). The priest Conon, a native of Cilicia and a monk of great merit, who was doubtless the same monk who later became hegumen of this very same monastery,[78] was responsible for performing baptisms; and he was so embarrassed by having to anoint the bodies of women that he actually wanted to leave the monastery because of it:

> One day a girl from Persia came to be baptized. She was so beautiful and so youthful and blooming that the priest could not summon up the courage to anoint her with the holy oil. Since she remained there for two days, the archbishop Peter learned about it, and he was so struck by it that he wanted to designate a deaconess [ἠθέλησεν ἀφορίσαι διάκονον γυναῖκα ἐπὶ τὸ αὐτό].

This was an obvious solution, which could well have been suggested by the baptismal candidate herself since it was, after all, the custom that prevailed in the Christian communities of her own country. But—continues the narrative of John Moschus—"[the archbishop] did not do this because it was not permitted in that place" (ἀλλὰ τοῦτο οὐκ ἐποίησεν, διὰ τὸ μὴ ἐπιδέχεσθαι τὸν τόπον). Or: "the place did not permit this." *Ton topon* is indeed the reading of the manuscripts and not the mistaken emendation of the editors: τρόπον. The term *Topos*, "place", can refer either to the region or to the monastery of Penthoucla.[79] After an

---

M. de Gandillac, p. 259.

[76] John Moschus, *Le Pré spirituel*, c. 3. The text is to be found in Migne, PG 87, col. 2853, and is very defective. I owe thanks to Professor Philip Pattenden for communicating to me the results of his work of John Moschus that he is preparing. I have corrected in the sense indicated by him the translation of M. J. Roüet de Journel in SC 12 (1946): 48–50. I have also benefitted greatly from the judicious remarks of Charles Astruc, curator at the Bibliothèque Nationale.

[77] S. Vailhé, *Répertoire alphabétique des monastères de Palestine*, in *Revue de l'Orient chrétien* 5 (1900): 41–42.

[78] John Moschus, *Pré spirituel*, chap. 15.

[79] The two meanings appear to be equally possible, as Messrs. Pattenden and Astruc have helped me to understand.

initial flight, the priest, who had meanwhile been comforted by a vision of St. John the Baptist, returned

> to the monastery, where he anointed and baptized the young Persian woman the next day without even perceiving that she was a woman. He carried on in the same way for a dozen years, anointing and baptizing, without experiencing any movement of the flesh and without paying particular attention to any woman.

There is no reason to doubt the authenticity of this anecdote; all the best manuscript traditions are in agreement with placing it here in our narrative. Even if we limit the geographical extent of the *topos* involved, and even if we agree that the archbishop Peter did not designate a deaconess because he did not believe that this would be appropriate in a monastery, it is nevertheless the case that this anecdote fits perfectly into the baptismal rituals of Jerusalem and of Antioch as we know them.

There is another anecdote that, though coming from a different angle, points to the same conclusion. This anecdote is recounted in the *Life of Porphyry*, who was the bishop of Gaza in Palestine at the beginning of the fifth century; this *Life* was not, in fact, written by the bishop's deacon, Mark, but is "a reworking doubtless done in the sixth century".[80] Porphyry sent a priest, Timothy, to a house where a paralyzed woman resided in order to sign her with the sign of the cross and to prepare her for baptism; after having been briefly catechized, she received baptism, along with her little daughter, Salaphta. Porphyry also conferred upon the latter the canonical habit (τὸ κανονικὸν σχῆμα) and recommended her (παρέθετο) to the pious Manaris, a deaconess (τὴν διάκονον).[81] Thus it was not because of any shortage of deaconesses that Bishop Porphyry sent a priest to care for a sick woman. The fact is that the deaconess in question fulfilled another and different function.[82] This should be immediately apparent from this narrative. As for Constantinople, where we know that deaconesses were quite numerous in the middle of the sixth century, there is not the slightest bit of evidence concerning any possible role that they

[80] B. Altaner, *Précis de patrologie* (Mulhouse: Salvator, 1961), p. 330; Cf. *Clavis Patrum Graecorum*, vol. 3, n. 6722.

[81] Mark the Deacon, *Vie de Porphyre, évêque de Gaza*, c. 12, nos. 100–102, ed. H. Grégoire and M. A. Kugener, Coll. byzantine, Budé (Paris: Belles Lettres, 1930), pp. 77–78.

[82] It was at Antioch that the incident occurred that is cited by Theodoret in *Hist. eccl.* 3:14, GCS 44, pp. 190–92, and repeated by du Cange, Kalsbach and Gryson: a deaconess was responsible for converting to Christianity the son of a pagan priest. But this was not because the deaconess had any official role as a catechist. Rather, she was the friend of his mother, and she influenced the boy on the occasion of social visits to his mother. After the death of his mother, the boy continued to come to the house of the deaconess in order to receive instruction in the Faith.

might have played in connection with baptism. We do not possess any complete baptismal ritual earlier than the one in the Barberini euchology (eighth century), and that is not a ritual of Constantinople but rather one from southern Italy.[83] The *Mystagogical Catechism for Baptism* of the patriarch Proclus describes only the renunciation ceremony.[84] Nevertheless, it appears that the baptismal liturgy of Constantinople in the fifth century was no different from that of Antioch,[85] and there are only two indications in the literature suggesting that deaconesses in Constantinople ever had anything to do with baptism.

According to Palladius, the deaconess Olympias, among other highly meritorious actions, "catechized many women".[86] Again according to Palladius, when St. John Chrysostom was obliged to leave Constantinople to go into exile, he first left his episcopal palace and went into the church, where he said farewell to the other bishops gathered in the sacristy; from there he proceeded into the baptistery, where he had Olympias, Pentadia and Procla summoned so that he could say good-bye to them.[87] Why into the baptistery? Was it because they normally carried out some of their activities there? More plausibly, it was simply because of the soldiers who were waiting for John in order to take him off into exile. These two unique indications of a possible link between deaconesses and baptism are truly too tenuous to allow us to base any conclusions on them. As we shall see, there is abundant evidence from Constantinople and elsewhere pointing to another, entirely different role for deaconesses.

B. Deaconesses in Charge of Convents of Women

We should remind ourselves here of the remark of Severus of Antioch on the subject of deaconesses. Severus wrote: "Especially in convents,

[83] The Barberini Euchology mentions only the activity of the deacon: καὶ τότε ὑπὸ τοῦ διακόνου χρίται ὅλον τὸ σῶμα, J. Goar, *Euchologion sive Rituale Graecorum*, 2nd ed. (Venice: Javarina, 1730), p. 294. Cf. A. Strittmater, "*The Barberinum sancti Marci of Jacques Goar*", EL 47 (1933), p. 349, no. 130 (210).

[84] F. J. Leroy, *L'homilétique de Proclus de Constantinople*, ST 247 (Vatican City, 1967), pp. 184–94.

[85] St. John Chrysostom, in *Homélie VI sur Colossiens*, PG 62, col. 342, gives some indications on the baptismal ritual; he indicates that nudity was the practice, and this was specifically contrasted to the nudity of Adam, of which the latter was "ashamed". Anointing was contrasted with the application of oil on the body of an athlete before his entrance into the stadium. This particular homily supplying these indications about the baptismal ritual was preached in Constantinople, no doubt in 399 A.D.: J. Quasten, *Patrologia*, vol. 2, BAC 217, p. 469.

[86] Palladius, *Histoire Lausiaque* 56, ed. C. Butler, TS 6:2 (1904), p. 150; ed. A. Lucot, *Textes et documents* 15 (Paris: Picard, 1912), pp. 350–51.

[87] Palladius, *Dialogus de vita s. Ioannis Chrysostomi*, ed. P. R. Coleman-Norton (Cambridge University Press, 1928), p. 61: εἰσελθὼν δὲ ἐν τῷ βαπτιστηρίῳ καλεῖ τὴν Ὀλυμπιάδα, ἀναπάλλακτον οὖσαν τῆς ἐκκλησίας σὺν Πενταδίᾳ καὶ Πρόκλῃ ταῖς διακόνοις.

ordination is performed less with regard to the needs of the mysteries than exclusively with regard to doing honor."[88] There is an inscription from Korykos in Upper Cilicia that reads simply, "Timothea, deaconess of the convent".[89] The literary documents are even more explicit in what they tell us; from the end of the fourth century, there was a hegumenē (ἡγουμένη), or mother superior, in charge of a convent, and she was a deaconess.

Thus, that Marthana, the "holy deaconess", whom Egeria visited in Isauria in Cilicia, "directed convents of apotactites or virgins" near the sanctuary of St. Thecla. We should take due note of the plural here: convents (*monasteria*); for, surrounding the church, there were "a number of monasteries for both men and women".[90] At Caesarea in Palestine, according to Palladius, a lector placed his pregnant wife in a convent and asked the deaconess of that female community (τὴν αὐτόθι διάκονον τῆς ἀδελφότητος) to take care of her until it was time for her to give birth.[91] At Annisa, according to St. Gregory of Nyssa, there was "one of those who directed the choir of virgins, a deaconess by the name of Lampadion".[92] From Severus of Antioch, we have a letter "to Jannia, deaconess and hegumenē" and another one "to Valeriana, deaconess and hegumenē"; he rejoiced that Valeriana "was placed at the head of these holy virgins"; and to both of them he gave counsel with regard to the carrying out of their responsibilities.[93] It is also to Antioch that the legendary story of St. Justine has become attached, but this legend already existed at the end of the fourth century. According to the story, the bishop Cyprian, "after

[88] See 3A and n. 61 of this chapter, above.

[89] MAMA, vol. 3, no. 744: Σωματοθήκη τιμοθέας διακ μονῆς.

[90] *Itinerarium Egeriae*, 23:3: "Ibi autem ad sanctam ecclesiam nichil aliud est nisi monasteria sine numero virorum ac mulierum. Nam inveni ibi aliquam amicissimam michi et cui omnes in Oriente testimonium ferebant vitae ipsius, sancta diaconissa nomine Marthana, quam ego apud Ierusolimam noveram, ubi illa gratia orationis ascenderat: haec autem monasteria aputactitum seu virginum regebat," CCL 175, p. 66; SC 21, pp. 182–84.

[91] Palladius, *Histoire Lausiaque*, ed. C. Butler, TS 6:2 (1904), p. 166; ed. A. Lucot, *Textes et documents* 15 (Paris: Picard, 1912), pp. 394–95.

[92] St. Gregory of Nyssa, *Vie de sainte Macrine* 29, ed. P. Maraval, SC 178 (Paris: Le Cerf, 1971), pp. 236–37 (PG 46, col. 988D): καὶ ἦν τις προτεταγμένη τοῦ χοροῦ τῆς παρθενίας ἐν τῷ τῆς διακονίας βαθμῷ, Λαμπάδιον ὄνομα αὐτῇ.

[93] E. W. Brooks, *The Sixth Book of the Selected Letters of Severus, Patriarch of Antioch*, The Text and Translation Society (London: William and Norgate, 1904), vol. 1, pt. 2, pp. 411–18 (Syriac text), vol. 2, pt. 2, pp. 364–71 (English trans.). In the letter no. 69, addressed to Anastasia, ed. E. W. Brooks, *A Collection of Letters of Severus of Antioch*, PO 14, fasc. 1 (Paris: Firmin-Didot, 1920), p. 75 (245), Severus rendered homage to Anastasia for "walking in the way of justice, I mean the way of asceticism and of the monastic life", but he made no allusion to her functioning in the role of a superior. In the Coptic version of this same letter, Anastasia is called "the venerable virgin (*parthenos*), Anastasia, the deaconess (*diakon*)", see M. Chaine, *Une lettre de Sévère d'Antioche à la diaconesse Anastasie*, OC, new series, vol. 3 (1913): 36.

having added Justine to the community of deaconesses, gave her the
headship of those who were in the convent and put her in charge of the
others as a mother".[94] This same theme recurs in a number of similar
legends, most of which, though, are of rather late vintage. One of them is
that St. Susanna, whom the bishop sent to Eleutheropolis in Palestine,
placing her at the head of a convent of virgins after having made her "a
deaconess of this holy Church".[95] Another legend was that of St. Xenia,
whom St. Paul, visiting the convent of Milasa in Caria, supposedly
ordained a deaconess.[96]

It was in Constantinople itself that the link between being a deaconess
and being in charge of a convent became manifest; this resulted from the
celebrity gained by Olympias because of the prestige of her relationship
with St. John Chrysostom and the correspondence she exchanged with
him while he was in exile. She was born around 368 A.D. into a family that
belonged to the high society of Constantinople and was married toward
the end of 384 A.D. to Nebridius, who became the prefect of the city two
years later and then died suddenly shortly thereafter. Olympias thus
found herself already a widow at the age of twenty, although up to then
she had been "fortunate in her birth, her wealth and her education,
endowed by nature with the happiest of dispositions, being still in the
flower of her age".[97] Emperor Theodosius wanted to see her married to
someone else, but she determinedly refused this prospect and, over the
course of some four years, suffered the loss of all her worldly goods by
seizure as a consequence.

When she finally recovered the use of her wealth, she used it to found a
hostel for priests as well as a number of hospitals; in carrying out these
enterprises, she surrounded herself with considerable reserves of female
dedication and zeal. It was then that, in spite of her youthfulness—καίπερ
νέαν χήραν γενομένην, a widow of less than thirty—the archbishop Nectarius
ordained her a deaconess (διάκονον ἐχειροτόνησε).[98] Was it before or after
becoming a deaconess that she founded her convent? Whichever it may
have been, vocations proved to be abundant; very soon there were 250

---

[94] *Vita et Martyrium sanctorum Cypriani et Justinae*, ed. E. Blampignon (= PG 115, col.
868): καὶ ταῖς διακόνοις ἐγκαταλέξας, τὴν προστασίαν αὐτῇ τῶν κατὰ τὸ ἀσκητήριον ἐγχειρίζει καὶ
ὡς μητέρα ταύταις ἐφίστησι. On the subject of this *Vita*, see A. Amore, in the *Bibliotheca
Sanctorum*, vol. 3 (1963), col. 1284.

[95] AASS, Septembris, 6:157. Cf. J. M. Sauget, in *Bibliotheca Sanctorum*, vol. 12 (1969),
col. 77.

[96] Text in *Analecta Bollandiana* 56 (1938): 111. Cf. C. de Clerq, in Bibliotheca Sanctorum,
5 (1964), col. 245.

[97] Palladius, *Dialogus de vita Ioannis Chrysostomi* 17, ed. P. R. Coleman-Norton (Cambridge
University Press, 1928), p. 108; PG 47, col. 60. Cf. A. M. Malingrey, *Introduction à Jean
Chrysostome, Lettres à Olympias*, 2nd ed., SC 13 bis (Paris: Le Cerf, 1968), p. 18.

[98] Sozomen, *Hist. ecclés.* 8, 9, GCS 50, p. 361.

nuns. After St. John Chrysostom succeeded Nectarius as archbishop in 397, he ordained as "deaconesses of the holy Church" the sisters of Olympias, Martyria and Palladia as well as Elisanthia, another of Olympias' relatives (συγγενὶς αὐτῆς). Three of these women were members of the convent community, and the presence of the four of them made it possible for their four services [of praise] to ensure uninterrupted worship at the holy convent of Olympias.[99]

Along with all the others who remained loyal to St. John Chrysostom, Olympias was a victim of the same persecution that was incited against him, and she too was exiled. She went into exile "after having committed her flock into the hands of Marina".[100] However, the author of the *Life of Olympias* did not expressly say that Marina was also ordained a deaconess. Then, "after the death of Marina, it was Elisanthia, beloved of God, who had already been named deaconess [ἡ διάκονος] who was then chosen hegumenē of this holy flock of Christ".[101] It was apropos of this election (προχειρίζεται) that Mademoiselle Malingrey thought she could discern "a rapid institutional development: instead of deaconesses ordained by the bishop for the service of his Church, we find an autonomous convent headed by an abbess."[102] In reality, if there was indeed such a development, it involved merely the fact that the hegumenē was no longer imposed by the bishop but was elected from among the three already ordained deaconesses who, after the death of Marina, were charged with responsibilities over the other nuns.

While St. John Chrysostom was making his farewells to his spiritual daughters, two other deaconesses were also present: Pentadia and Procla. We know very little about Pentadia, even though she was the addressee of three of the letters of the saintly archbishop.[103] Two of his other letters were addressed "to the deaconess Amprocla and those who are with her" (Ἀμπρούκλῃ διακόνῳ καὶ ταῖς σὺν αὐτῇ).[104] This salutation would lead us to believe that she too was the head of a community.

[99] *Vie d'Olympias* 7: χειροτονεῖ διακόνους τῆς ἁγίας Ἐκκλησίας καὶ τὰς τρεῖς αὐτῆς συγγενίδας Ἐλισανθίαν, Μαρτυρίαν, καὶ Παλλαδίαν ἐπὶ τὸ τὰς τέσσαρας διακονίας εἰς τὸ διηνεκὲς ἔχιν τὸ συστὰν ὑπ' αὐτῆς εὐαγὲς μοναστήριον, in A. M. Malingrey, op. cit., p. 420, who translated, p. 421: "So that the four services of praise might unfold without interruption in the holy convent established by her". Malingrey explained, ibid., n. 5, why she interpreted *diakonia* here as a "*laus perennis*". I don't dare acquiesce in this explanation.

[100] *Vie d'Olympias* 10, ed. A. M. Malingrey, in op. cit., pp. 426–27; cf. 12, pp. 432–33.

[101] *Vie d'Olympias* 12, op. cit., pp. 432–33.

[102] Op. cit., p. 433, n. 4.

[103] *Lettres* 94, 104, 185; letter 104 gives us to understand that Pentadia did much good around her. She was mentioned incidentally in "Letter 9 to Olympias", ed. A. M. Malingrey, SC 13 bis, p. 234.

[104] *Lettres* 96 and 103. Letter 191 has as its title only Ἀμπρούκλῃ διακόνῳ. On the subject of all these correspondents of St. John Chrysostom, see C. Baur, *Joannes Chrysostomus und seine Zeit* (München: Max Hueber, 1930), 2:89–90.

More and more, we are brought up against the link between the dignity of the female diaconate and the charge of being the hegumenē over a convent of religious women. This was the situation that came about in those great capitals of the Eastern Church that were Antioch and Constantinople, and it obtained elsewhere as well, from about the end of the fourth century on—in other words, in roughly the same era when the compiler of the *Apostolic Constitutions* seemed to know nothing of this discipline—the function of deaconess being related to the authority exercised within the religious life. How did this particular discipline come about? What was its origin? Doubtless the fact that the prescriptions in the Epistles of St. Paul concerning religious widows had so often been confused with and applied to the ministry of deaconesses made easier the eventual combining of these two states of life, and the helping ministry that the female diaconate had originally been became transformed into a religiously consecrated state of life, as we have already seen expressed in the "Canons of St. Basil".

At first there was probably no special ritual for the blessing of the hegumenēs of religious communities, such as might have been used for Olympias.[105] Even if she had not already been the head of her community, her institution as a deaconess would still have been the only available way to recognize officially the consecration of her life and her special religious merit. There is yet one other consideration that might possibly have played a role, and that is that we have found traces of abbots in both East and West who were also deacons.[106] This was no doubt a sporadic occurrence; it may also have been a relatively late one. But it is possible that the ritual of ordination of the deaconess was seen as the equivalent of the ritual of blessing of an abbess. This is merely a hypothesis.

4. THE CASE OF DEACONESSES
IN THE MONASTERIES OF THE REGION OF EDESSA

It seems useful to treat separately the case of the deaconesses of the region of Edessa (modern Urfa). This region was included at various times in different administrative divisions of the Empire. Eventually it lost nearly

---

[105] The East did not adopt the Roman usage of consecration by the bishop, which was a veritable matrimonial rite for a consecrated virgin living in the world.

[106] There is an inscription concerning a deacon archimandrite in Syria: see L. Jalabert, R. Mouterde, C. Mondésert, *Inscriptions grecques et latines de Syrie*, vol. 4 (Paris: Geuthner, 1955), n. 1632; in Italy at the end of the sixth century there are mentions made of deacon-abbots in St. Gregory the Great, *Registrum* 7:18 and *Dialogi*, 2:35:1.

all the features of the liturgy that were proper to it.[107] Earlier in this work, we advanced the hypothesis that it was in this region that the *Didascalia of the Apostles* was composed. Yet from about the fifth century on, we no longer find any evidence that deaconesses or widows played any role in connection with baptism.[108] It is true that James of Edessa does mention this function in his *Canonical Resolutions* at the end of the seventh century: "[the deaconess] anoints adult women being baptized; she visits sick women and takes care of them". We must come back to these *Canonical Resolutions*, but, at the moment, we have to ask ourselves whether this author is referring to a real discipline familiar to him, or whether he is merely repeating information gathered from a careful reading of the *Didascalia* or the *Testamentum Domini*, or both. What is beyond doubt is that, from the fifth century on, the churches of this region had a different conception of what a deaconess was; as in Antioch and Constantinople, she was a woman religious exercising a function of authority in a religious community.

This is what Rabbula, the bishop of Edessa between 412–435 A.D., prescribed in his "Ordinances and Notifications Relative to Priests and *Benai Qeyāmā* ('Sons of the Covenant')":

> Canon 37 (Nau 62). Religious men (*benai qeyāmā*) may not attend meetings or go elsewhere without being accompanied by priests, nor may religious women (*benat qeyāmā*) without being accompanied by a deaconess.[109]

Between 532 and 534 A.D., some "holy fathers"—Jacobite bishops in exile in Antioch and under Severus of Antioch—answered a number of questions posed to them "from the East",[110] no doubt from Jacobite communities

---

[107] There is an excellent discussion of the problem of the liturgy of Edessa in W. F. Macomber, "A Theory of the Origins of the Syrian, Maronite and Chaldean Rites", OCP 39 (1973): 235–42.

[108] It is true that, to my knowledge, we possess no baptismal ritual coming from this region; all of those published come from Antioch: S. Brock, "Studies in the Early History of the Syrian Orthodox Baptismal Liturgy", JTS 23 (1972): 16–64; J. M. Sauget, Le "Codex liturgicus" of J. L. Assemani et ses sources manuscrites pour les 'Ordines' de l'initiation chrétienne selon la tradition syro-occidentale, in Gregorianum 54 (1973): 339–52.

[109] French trans. F. Nau, Les canons et les résolutions canoniques, Ancienne littérature canonique syriaque 2 (Paris: Lethielleux, 1906), p. 89; ed. and English trans., in A. Vööbus, "Syriac and Arabic Documents regarding Legislation relative to Syriac Asceticism", Papers of the Estonian Theological Society in Exile 11 (Stockholm, 1960), p. 45. On the subject of ordinances, cf. A. Vööbus, Syrische Kanonessammlungen, CSCO 307, pp. 128–38; cf. another series, 317, pp. 307–15. This text is often cited incorrectly following J. Pien (Pinius), Tractatus praeliminaris de Ecclesiae diaconissis, AASS, Septembris vol. 1 (Antuerpiae 1746), pp. v–vi.

[110] Chapitres qui furent écrits de l'Orient, leurs questions furent présentées aux saints Pères et elles reçurent les réponses suivantes, in I. Rahmani, Studia syriaca 3 (Sharfé, 1908), pp. 5–23 (ed. Syr. following the Paris Syriac ms. 62) and pp. 24–33 (Latin trans.); French trans., in F. Nau,

in contact with the churches of Persia. They answered as follows, on the subject of deaconesses:

> Canon 9. The custom of the East, namely, that the superiors of female monasteries should be deaconesses and should share the mysteries with those who are under their power, should be preserved everywhere there is a deaconess, if there is no priest or deacon in the place where the mysteries are shared; but if there is in the vicinity a pure priest or a deacon, then the superiors should not give out [Communion].
>
> Canon 11. The ordination (χειροτονία) of the deaconess will take place according to the custom of the country. We have also learned that the bishop casts an *orarion* on the shoulder of the candidate, as is the case for the deacon.[111]

We are here dealing with convents situated far from the large urban agglomerations—communities without a regularly assigned priest or deacon to give out Communion to the members of the community. By ordaining a superior of the community as a deaconess, the Church was permitting her to fulfill the same ministry in her religious community that the *Testamentum Domini* allowed to the deaconesses who took Communion to the sick.[112] As for the ordination of the deaconess, not the slightest detail has come down to us; and as for the *orarion*, insofar as the available documents allow us to fix its usage, it is not correct that it was employed as in "the case of the deacon".[113]

Only a few years later, in 538 A.D., John bar Qursos, bishop of Tella Mauzelat, replied to some "Questions Asked by the Priest Sargis".[114] Tella was in Osrhoene, halfway between Edessa and Mardin.[115] In this case, it was certainly an authentic local discipline that the bishop was describing to his correspondent; moreover, some of his replies show that, beyond the faculties that the "Holy Fathers" granted to the deaconess-religious superior, numerous casuistical problems were raised by the existence of convents of women religious:

Ancienne littérature syriaque 3 (1909): 39ff. On these manuscripts—and on the origin and dating of these *Chapitres*, see also A. Vööbus, *Syrische Kanonessammlungen*, CSCO 307, pp. 167–75. These *Chapitres* were included in the Syriac *Synodicon* of the year 1204 A.D., ed. A. Vööbus, CSCO 367, and English trans. CSCO 368, pp. 157–68.

[111] I. Rahmani, op. cit., p. 33; F. Nau, op. cit., p. 40.

[112] See Chapter 3, 2, above, especially n. 61.

[113] See Chapter 7, 1, C, below, especially n. 37.

[114] On the subject of this document, see A. Vööbus, *Syrische Kanonessammlungen*, CSCO 317, pp. 263–69.

[115] Tella was called at different times Constantina and Antoniopolis. Today the town is called Wiranschehir and is in Turkish territory. Professor Jean Dauvillier kindly supplied me with this geographical information.

33. *Question*. Is it permitted to the deaconess to give out Communion to the sick, three years and older?

Answer. It is not permitted to the deaconess to give Communion to children five years old and more.

34. *Q*. Can she assume any of the functions pertaining to the service of the altar for others besides herself and for the other sisters who reside with her in the community?

A. The law does not permit her to enter into the sanctuary if there is a priest or deacon, but does permit it where there is no deacon to assist the priest in their convent.

35. *Q*. Is she permitted to cense with the thurible and raise her voice aloud and to impart the prayer of incense over and above the prayer of the penitent soul, which is an avowal of conscience?

A. It is not permitted to her to raise her voice aloud when she censes with the thurible; it is forbidden to her to say the prayer over the thurible; she may, however, offer to God in silence and with contrite heart the prayer of the penitent soul.[116]

36. *Q*. Is it permitted to her to wash the sacred vessels?

A. It is permitted to her to wash the sacred vessels.

37. *Q*. Is it permitted to her during the time of her menses to give out Communion or offer the chalice, if necessary?

A. It is not permitted to her during the time of her menses to enter [into the sanctuary] or to touch the holy Eucharist.

38. *Q*. Is it permitted to her to pour the wine and water into the chalice?

A. With the permission of the bishop, she may pour the wine and water into the chalice.[117]

39. *Q*. In case of illness, is it permitted to her to charge another sister to handle the sacred vessels?

A. It is not permitted to her to allow another sister to touch the sacred vessels except in the case of a serious illness and an urgent necessity.

40. *Q*. Is it permitted to her to charge another sister with the responsibility

---

[116] Both F. Nau, op. cit., p. 16, n. 5, and A. Vööbus, CSCO 368, p. 203, n. 11, see in this description the penitential rite of the beginning of the Syrian Mass. This is impossible, for this is not an ancient ritual. Rather, we are dealing here with the incense prayers for the evening and morning prayers of the liturgy of the hours; the antiquity of these are well attested: see J. Mateos, *"Sedre" et prières connexes dans quelques anciennes collections*, OCP 28 (1962): 239–87; cf. the canons attributed by Bar Hebraeus to James of Edessa, cited under nos. 107, 110, 111 by F. Nau, op. cit., pp. 73–74.

[117] This part of the ritual was carried out by the deacon: *Canons sur le diacre* of John bar Qursos, in I. Rahmani, *Liturgies orientales et occidentales*. Beirut: Imprimerie, patriarcale syrienne (1929), pp. 149–50; J. M. Hanssens, *Institutiones liturgicae de ritibus orientalibus*, vol. 3, pt. 2, p. 30. However, this part of the ritual was carried out at the *diaconicon*, not at the altar.

of disposing of the candles and hence entering into the sanctuary to appropriate them? If the deaconess cannot give this permission, is it permitted to the priest to give such permissions without recourse to the bishop?

A. If she is ill and cannot get up, then it is permitted to do what is necessary in the way of entering into the sanctuary and disposing of the candles. Urgent necessity allows these things to be done without specific ecclesiastical permission.

41. Q. Is it permitted to the deaconess to enter without permission into the sanctuary when she comes into a μαρτύριον[118] outside her own convent, in a monastery of either men or women?

A. It is not permitted to the deaconess to enter without permission into the sanctuary of the μαρτύρια of men, or even into those of women, outside of her own convent, except in cases of urgent necessity.

42. Q. Is it permitted to her habitually to read the Gospels and the holy books in an assembly of women meeting in common?

A. This is permitted to her.[119]

It should be clear from these responses that the deaconesses served, at one and the same time, as a kind of sacristan as well as an auxiliary to the deacon in celebrations of the liturgy of the hours when celebrated without a priest in sacred orders present. This certainly emerges from a reading of the answer to question 42; I think the same thing is also true of the answer to question 35.

Finally, James of Edessa dealt with the subject of deaconesses around a century and a half later, some time between 683 and 708 A.D., in his *Canonical Resolutions*.[120] We have mentioned this work before; here is the complete text dealing with the subject of deaconesses:[121]

---

[118] *Marturia* were chapels consecrated to martyrs, whose relics they enclosed, situated to the left of the altar in Jacobite churches: see J. M. Fiey, *Mossoul chrétienne* (Beirut, 1959), *Recherches publiées sous la direction de l'Institut de lettres orientales de Beyrouth* 12, p. 100.

[119] French trans. by F. Nau, *Ancienne littérature canonique syriaque* 2 (Paris: Lethielleux, 1906), pp. 16–18. The Syriac text, with a Latin translation, is to be found in T. J. Lamy, *Dissertatio de Syrorum fide et disciplina in re eucharistica* (Lovanii: Valinthout, 1859), pp. 62–97. The *Questions diverses* have been reproduced with their variants in the Syrian *Synodicon*, ed. A. Vööbus, CSCO 367, and English trans. CSCO 368, pp. 197–205.

[120] *Questions que le prêtre Addai a posées à Jacques, évêque d'Urhāi et ses réponses*, ed. P. de Lagarde, *Reliquiae iuris ecclesiastici antiquissimi syriace* (Lipsiae, 1856), pp. 117–34; T. J. Lamy, op. cit., pp. 98–170 (with Latin trans.); French trans., F. Nau, *Les canons et les résolutions canoniques*, *Ancienne littérature canonique syriaque* 2 (Paris: Lethielleux, 1908), pp. 38–66. On the subject of this work, see Baumstark, p. 249; A. Vööbus, *Syrische Kanonessammlungen*, CSCO 317, pp. 273–84. It has been reproduced in the Syrian *Synodicon*, ed. A. Vööbus, CSCO 367, and English trans. CSCO 368, pp. 235–44.

[121] Although, on the whole, I follow the translation of F. Nau, op. cit., pp. 48–49, I have nevertheless had to make a number of corrections on the advice of my colleague, Fr. Simon Légasse; these corrections are corroborated by the English translation of A. Vööbus, CSCO

23. *Addai*: Does the deaconess, like the deacon, have the power to put a portion of the sacred Host into the consecrated chalice?

James: In no way can she do this. The deaconess did not become a deaconess in order to serve at the altar but rather for the sake of women who are ill.

24. *Addai*: I would like to learn in a few words what the powers of a deaconess in the Church are.

James: She has no power over the altar, because when she was instituted (*mettasr^eho*: "ordained" or "instituted"), it was not in the name of the altar, but only to fulfill certain functions in the Church.[122] These are her sole powers: to sweep the sanctuary and to light the lamps, and she is only permitted to perform these two functions if no priest or deacon is available. If she is in a convent of women, she can remove the sacred Hosts from the tabernacle [= cabinet], only because there is no priest or deacon present, and give them out to the other sisters only or to the small children who may also be present. But it is not permitted to her to take the Hosts up off the altar, nor carry them to the altar nor indeed in any way to touch the table of life [the altar]. She anoints adult women when they are baptized; she visits women who are ill and cares for them. These are the only powers possessed by deaconesses with regard to the work of priests.

This description by James of Edessa was reproduced in the Syrian *Synodicon*, and, much less accurately, in the *Nomocanon* and the *Book of Rays* of Bar Hebraeus as well as in the pontifical of Michael the Great.[123]

SUPPLEMENTARY NOTE

While the present work was in press, Monsieur Michel Chalon, of Paul Valéry University in Monpelier, kindly sent to me the texts of a number of additional Greek inscriptions with mention of deaconesses, thus very generously putting at my disposal the results of some of the research that he carried out especially for me. In particular, he furnished the important list of inscriptions contained in the work of A. Christophilopoulos, Θέματα βυζαντίνου ἐκκλησιαστικοῦ δικαίου ἐνδιαφέροντα τὴν σύγχρονον πρακτικήν (Athens: Tzaka-Delagrammatica, 1957, pp. 20–21). In addition to the inscriptions covered above, therefore, we must add the following inscriptions on the subject of deaconesses:

368, p. 242. The term *mettasr^eho* can be translated by "established" or "instituted" as accurately as by "ordained". Vööbus, in fact, preferred "appointed".

[122] T. J. Lamy, op. cit., p. 126, gave this reading in Latin for this passage: "Diaconissae in ecclesia et non in sanctuario ordinari, quia intra cancellos altaris non admittebantur. Olim tamen ordinabatur diaconissa in gradibus altaris constituta, ut statuitur in canonibus apostolorum."

[123] See Chapter 7, 2, below.

From Arabia, the epitaph to Mahaiy from a deaconess named Maria (seventh century): R. Canova, *Iscrizioni e monumenti protocristiani del paese di Moab*, (Roma: P. Istituto di Archeologia Cristiana, 1954, no. 391).

From Pontus, two inscriptions, one from Amisos, dated 562 A.D., concerning one Aeria, "who lived her life as a deaconess of the saints": H. Grégoire, *Recueil des inscriptions grecques et latines du Pont et de l'Arménie*, Studia Pontica 3 (Bruxelles: Lamertin, 1910), p. 22, no. 12; the other one, in the neighborhood of Andrapa, concerning one Basilike: F. Cumont, ibid., p. 57, no. 44.

From Galatia, near Ankara, an inscription mentioning one Philogones, deaconess, a daughter and sister of priests: G. De Jerphanion, *Inscriptions grecques de la région d'Alishar*, in *Mélanges de l'Université Saint-Joseph* 19 (1935), pp. 94–95, no. 25.

From Pisidia, near modern Armutlu, an inscription concerning one Kyrie, deaconess, wife of the priest Conon: J. R. Sitlington Sterret, "The Wolfe Expedition to Asia Minor", in *Papers of the American School of Classical Studies at Athens* 3 (1884–85), p. 198, no. 326.

From Lycaonia, near modern Bademli, an epitaph of a deaconess whose name has disappeared along with that of her husband: H. Swoboda, J. Keil and F. Knoll, *Denkmäler aus Lykaonien, Pamphylien und Isaurien* (Brunn, Rohrer, 1935), p. 42, no. 96.

From Lydia, near Daldis, an inscription concerning Epiphaneia: H. Grégoire, *Recueil des inscriptions grecques chrétiennes d'Asie Mineure*, fasc. 1 (Paris: Leroux, 1922), no. 341.

From the province of Rhodope (diocese of Thrace), at Nicopolis, an epitaph of 538 A.D. concerning the deaconess Eugenia, "who erected a place of worship dedicated to St. Andrew": V. Beševliev, *Spätgriechische und spätlateinische Inschriften aus Bulgarien* (Berlin, 1964), pp. 164–66, no. 231.

From Thrace, an epitaph of the deaconess Posidonia at Philippi: P. Lemerle, *Philippes et la Macédoine orientale à l'époque paléochrétienne et byzantine* (Paris, 1945), p. 92.

From Macedonia, in the cathedral at Stobi, an inscription dating from before the beginning of the fifth century: "Fulfilling her vow, it was Matrona, the most pious deaconess, who had the mosaic of the exedra built": J. and L. Robert, *Bulletin épigraphique*, in *Revue des études grecques* 86 (1974), no. 336.

From Macedonia, an epitaph of one Agathocleia, "virgin and deaconess", from Edessa: J. H. Mordtmann, in *Mitteilungen des deutschen archäologischen Instituts, Athenische Abteilung* 18 (1893), pp. 416–17, no. 3.

From the island of Thasos, an inscription from which the name of the deaconess has been almost completely effaced: C. Delvoye, *Chronique des fouilles*, in *Bulletin de correspondance hellénique* 75 (1951), p. 160.

From ancient Epirus, at Drymos, an epitaph concerning "the servant of the Lord Theoprepia, virgin and deaconess of Christ": J. and L. Robert, *Bulletin épigraphique*, in *Revue des études grecques* 85 (1972), pp. 412–13, no. 240.

From Thessaly, at Thebes, an epitaph of Irene, a deaconess: N. Giannopoulous, in *Byzantinische Zeitschrift* 21 (1912), p. 152; and at Volo, Tetradia, a deaconess: N. Giannopoulos: Παλαιοχριστιανικὴ ἐπιγραφή in Ἐπετηρὶς Ἑταιρείας βυζαντινῶν σπουδῶν, 12 (1936), p. 401.

From Achaia, at Klauseios, in the Basilica of St. Leonidas, a votive inscription concerning "Polygeros, the most pious lector, and Andromache, the beloved deaconess of God": J. and L. Robert, *Bulletin épigraphique*, in *Revue des études grecques* 79 (1966), p. 386, no. 229; and at Elis, an epitaph of the daughter of the deaconess Alexandra, ibid., p. 381, no. 213.

On the other hand, we are obliged to eliminate from consideration the inscription concerning "Eneon, deaconess of this hospital", which was discussed above; this reading was a mistaken interpretation made by J. Germer-Durand of an inscription from the neighborhood of Jerusalem: J. T. Milik, *La topographie de Jérusalem vers la fin de l'époque byzantine*, in *Mélanges de l'Université Saint-Joseph* 37 (1961), p. 149; cf. already F. M. Abel, "Jerusalem", in DACL 7 (1927), col. 2362.

CHAPTER SEVEN

The Liturgy for the Ordination of Deaconesses

The first liturgical ritual or rite created to consecrate women into a special religious state of life could well have been "the blessing of a widow". We saw earlier how St. Hippolytus of Rome did not believe that any special hierarchical action was required in the case of consecrated virgins, but he did prescribe that widows should be the object of a special "institution" (καθίστασθαι). This "institution" was certainly different from "ordination" (χειροτονία), which was conferred only upon the bishop, the priest and the deacon, but at the same time it was something more than a simple administrative act, since Hippolytus explained that "the widow should be instituted by means of the word only, and then she should join herself to the others." This language suggests that a liturgical ceremony was involved.[1] At any rate, the text of such a ceremony was included in the document called the *Testament of Our Lord Jesus Christ*, or *Testamentum Domini*,[2] from which it became widely disseminated through various collections of canons.[3] Of course, the mere fact that it appeared in such collections of canons is never in itself proof that a ritual widely used. The fact is that this ritual for the institution of widows was never, to my knowledge, included in the Greek, Syrian or Chaldean euchologies; in any case, it was quickly superseded by a ritual for the ordination of a deaconess.[4]

The two terms generally employed for "institution", καθιστάναι and κατάστασις, used only for widows by Hippolytus, the *Didascalia*, canon 11 of Laodicea and the *Testamentum Domini* were occasionally used elsewhere

---

[1] St. Hippolytus of Rome, *Apostolic Tradition*, ed. B. Botte, LQF 39 (1963), pp. 30–31. I don't think it is possible to agree with Botte that the "institution" of deaconesses was "a simple naming of someone, not an ordination". The problem is not at all one of a ritual versus a nonritual in this context, but rather whether or not a laying on of hands was employed.

[2] See Chapter 2, 2, above, especially n. 68.

[3] There is a prayer for the ordination of a widow in the canonical collection of Taj al Riyasa (13th century). It is in Vatic. Borgian Arabic ms. 22; no doubt it is that of the *Testamentum Domini*, but it remains unpublished. Cf. Chapter 4, 3, above, especially n. 109.

[4] P. Hindo, *Disciplina Antiochena antica, Siri, II, Les Personnes*, CCOF II, 26 (1951), p. 557 of the Index, which refers the reader from *Viduitas* to *Diaconissa*.

to designate also the ritual for the ordination of a deaconess.[5] On the whole, however, it appears that the distinction between "institution" and "ordination" prevailed. Nevertheless from the beginning of the fifth century on, χειροτονεῖν and χειροτονία were used with respect to the ordination of deaconesses. Thus, the *Apostolic Constitutions*, where this usage also occurred, were consistent with the usage of Antioch and Constantinople in this respect.[6] The Council of Chalcedon, in its canon 15, made this usage official, although in the manuscripts there is some hesitation between χειροτονία and χειροθεσία.[7]

It is important to remark that the rules laid down by Hippolytus were not necessarily observed in and throughout the regions of Antioch and Constantinople. This may have been because these rules were not even known in those regions. In any case, χειροτονεῖν and χειροτονία were frequently employed in these regions also in the ritual formulas concerned with the lesser ministries.[8]

According to the *Novellae* of Justinian, the obligation of chastity incumbent upon the deaconess was solemnly conveyed to her in the presence of the other deaconesses.[9] A public ceremony was thus certainly required. This ceremony was described for us in summary fashion, as it existed in the sixth century in the metropolitan See of Tagrit (Tikrit), by the *Ordo and the Canons for Ordinations in the Holy Church* that were cited

---

[5] For example, in St. Epiphanius (Chapter 5, 2A, above), in *le Martyre de Matthieu* (Chapter 6, 2, above), and also in the inscription from Delphi (Chapter 6, 1, above): Ἡ εὐλαβεστάτη διακόνισσα Ἀθανασία ἄμεμπτον βίον ζήσασα κοσμίως, κατασταθῖσα δὲ διακόνισσα παρὰ τοῦ ἁγιωτάτου ἐπισκόπου Πανταμιανοῦ.

[6] Palladius, Sozomen and the *Life of Olympias*, apropos of the deaconess of Constantinople (Chapter 6, 3B, above, especially n. 97), and also doubtlessly in those texts of which we possess only single versions: St. Epiphanius (Chapter 5, 2B, above) and Theodore of Mopsuestia (Chapter 5, 2C, above).

[7] See Chapter 5, 1E, above. Cf. Canons 6 and 14 of the Trullan Synod of 691 A.D., Joannou, vol. I, pt. 1, pp. 132, 143–44.

[8] Without mentioning the *Apostolic Constitutions*, the *Epitome* and the "Canons of the Twelve Apostles" (Chapter 3, 2–3, above), we should mention canons 2 and 6 of the Council of Chalcedon, Joannou, vol. I, pt. 1, pp. 70, 74: χειροτονήσοι ἐπὶ χρήμασιν . . . ἢ ἕτερόν τινα τῶν ἐν τῷ κλήρῳ καταριθμουμένων; χειροτονεῖσθαι . . . μήτε ὅλως τινὰ τῶν ἐν τῷ ἐκκλησιαστικῷ τάγματι. But the Council employed προβάλλειν and προβολή (canon 2) for housekeepers and other functionaries. Theodore of Mopsuestia certainly employs χειροτονία for subdeacons and lectors: *In Epist. ad. 1 Tim.* 3:14–15, Swete, 2:132: ὅθεν οὐδὲ νενόμισται αὐτοὺς πρὸ τοῦ θυσιαστηρίου τὴν χειροτονίαν δέχεσθαι. However, the Council of Antioch of 341 A.D., distinguished in its canon 10: καθιστᾶν ἀναγνώστας καὶ ὑποδιακόνους καὶ ἐξορκιστὰς . . . μήτε δὲ πρεσβύτερον μήτε διάκονον χειροτονεῖν τολμᾶν, Joannou, vol. I, pt. 2, p. 112. At the Trullan synod of 691 A.D., canon 6, χειροτονία was applied indiscriminately to the subdeacon, deacon and priest, the subdeacon being subject to the same law with respect to marriage; Joannou, op. cit., p. 132.

[9] Justinian, no. 6 of the *Novellae*, chap. 6, ed. R. Schoell and G. Kroll, *Novellae*, 5th ed.

earlier.[10] An allusion to this ceremony is also found in the "Replies of the
Holy Fathers", from which we quoted in the last chapter, dealing with
usages in the same general region.[11] Since, as was decided earlier, we
cannot depend upon the *Apostolic Constitutions* as a firm foundation for the
existence of a particular usage or practice, we must go all the way to the
eighth century before we can find a complete and authentic ritual for the
ordination of deaconesses. The ritual in question is the one to be found in
the euchology reproduced in Barberini Greek manuscript 336 in the
Vatican Library.

1. THE BYZANTINE RITUAL
FOR THE ORDINATION OF DEACONESSES

The Barberini Greek euchology contained in the Vatican Library manuscript
336 (formerly, III, 55) was originally part of the library of St. Mark's
Convent in Florence. That is why Jacques Goar named it the *Codex Sancti
Marci Florentini*, or *Barberinum Sancti Marci*. André Jacob, who prepared
the integral edition of this work, believed that "it could have been copied
in southern Italy, perhaps in Calabria or Sicily. The document must be
dated to the eighth century, according to Pitra and Wilmart."[12] After the
prayers for the liturgy of St. Basil, the liturgy of St. John Chrysostom, the
prayers of the liturgy of the hours and the rituals for Christian initiation
and the consecration of the church and the altar, this euchology includes
successively the rituals for the ordination (χειροτονία) of bishops, priests,
deacons, deaconesses and subdeacons. This is followed by the designation
(ἐπὶ προχειρίσεως) of lectors, psalmists and hegumens.[13]

We should take note of the distinction made in the titles of these
different ceremonies. The term χειροτονία was used for "ordination"
down through the rank of subdeacon but was not used for that of lector,
just as was the case in the *Epitome*.[14] For the lector, as for the psalmist and
the hegumen, the word used was προχείρισις.[15]

---

[10] Chapter 2, 3A, above.

[11] Chapter 4, 4, above.

[12] A. Jacob, *Les euchologes du fonds Barberini grec de la Bibliothèque Vaticane*, in *Didaskalia* 4
(1974), pp. 154–57.

[13] For a rather complete description of the contents of this Euchology, see: A. Strittmatter,
"The '*Barberinum S. Marci*' of Jacques Goar", EL 47 (1933): 329–67.

[14] Chapter 3, 3, above.

[15] We have already noted the usage of *procheirizein* for the election of Elisanthia, the
second hegumenē of the convent of Olympias, Chapter 6, 3B, above.

A. Text of the Barberini Greek Euchology 336[16]

For the ordination of a deaconess:

After the holy anaphora has been completed, and the doors have been opened, and before the deacon says, "Πάντων τῶν ἁγίων", the deaconess who is to be ordained is presented [169v] *to the bishop. The bishop recites aloud the formula:* "'Η θεία χάρις", *while the candidate herself bows her head* [ἐπιτίθησιν τὴν χεῖρα αὐτοῦ ἐπὶ τὴν κεφαλὴν αὐτῆς], *and, making three signs of the Cross, he prays, as follows:*

Holy and all-powerful God, you who sanctified the female sex [τὸ θῆλυ] by the birth according to the flesh of your only Son and our God from a virgin, and who granted the gift of your grace and the coming of the Holy Spirit not only to men but also to women [γυναιξί], you, Lord, look kindly on this maidservant now before you [170r], call her to the work of the diaconate [εἰς τὸ ἔργον τῆς διακονίας σου], and cause to descend upon her the precious gift of the Holy Spirit; preserve her in the orthodox Faith and in conduct that is irreproachable according to what is pleasing to you, while in all things she continually fulfills her ministry [τὴν ἑαυτῆς λειτουργίαν διὰ παντὸς ἐκπληροῦσαν]. For to you is due all glory and honor.

After the "Amen", one of the deacons prays:

In peace, let us pray to the Lord.

For the peace that comes from above. . . .

For the peace of the whole world. . . .

For our bishop, his priesthood, his responsibility, his long life [170v], his health and also for the work of his hands. . . .

For this deaconess who is now being set apart [τῆς νῦν προχειριζομένης] and for her salvation. May the God who loves mankind give her the grace to fulfill her diaconate [τὴν διακονίαν] without either spot or stain—for all these things, let us pray to the Lord.

And for our most pious king, beloved of God. . . .

While this prayer is said by the deacon, the bishop, once again with his hand on the head of the deaconess who is being ordained [χειροτονουμένης] *prays as follows:*

You, Lord, our Master, you who do not reject women who are consecrated to you [ἀναθεμένας] in order to serve [λειτουργεῖν] in your holy places with a fitting holy desire [171r], but who accept them into the ranks of your ministers [ἐν τάξει λειτουργῶν], grant also to your servant here present—who has wished to consecrate herself to you [ἀναθεῖναί σοι ἑαυτήν] perfectly to fulfill the gift of the diaconate [τὴν τῆς διακονίας . . . χάριν]—[grant] the grace of your Holy Spirit, just

---

[16] Bibl. Vatic. ms. Barberini grec 336, ff. 169r–171v. Dr. Vittorio Peri, scriptor at the Vatican Library, has kindly looked over and made comparisons for me on this text. Except for a few minor variants, it corresponds to the one edited by J. Goar, *Euchologion sive Rituale Graecorum*, 1st ed. (Lutetiae Parisiorum, S. Piget, 1647), pp. 262–63; 2nd ed. (Venetiis, B. Javarina, 1730; reprint. Graz, 1960), pp. 218–19; J. Morin, *Commentarius de sacris Ecclesiae ordinationibus* (Paris: G. Maturas, 1655), pp. 69–70; also several other editions, among them the Amsterdam edition, marked Antuerpiae, H. Desbordes (1695), pp. 56–57.

as you gave the gift of your diaconate [τὴν χάριν τῆς διακονίας σου] to Phoebe, whom you called to the work of ministry [λειτουργίας]. Grant her the grace to persevere without reproach in your holy temples, O God. May she apply herself to household government [τῆς οἰκείας πολιτείας]. May she, especially, be temperate in all things. May she be your perfect [171v] servant [δούλην σου] in order that, presenting herself before the judgment seat of your Christ, she may receive the worthy reward of her just stewardship. Through the mercy and love of mankind of your only Son, with whom. . . .

After the "Amen", he places around her neck the diaconal orarion *(below the* maforion*), bringing its two ends out in front.*

Then the deacon, standing at the ambo, *says: "*Πάντων τῶν ἁγίων μνημονεύσαντες*", and the rest.*

After having received the sacred Body and the precious Blood, the bishop gives her the holy chalice; she takes it and puts it down on the sacred table.

B. *Other Greek Euchologies*

The ritual described in this text of the Barberini Greek euchology maintained itself for a long time in the euchologies that followed it; at least that appears to be the case to the extent that we can verify it today in the following:[17] the Sinai Greek manuscript 956, of the tenth century;[18] the euchology of the Great Church of Constantinople, Bibliothèque Nationale, Paris, ms. Coislin 213, dated 1027;[19] the euchology of Bessarion, Grottaferrata Γ.β.I., which originated in Constantinople and dates back to the eleventh or twelfth century;[20] the Vatican Greek euchology 1872 from southern Italy, dating from the twelfth century;[21] the Vatican Greek euchology 1970, from the same region and the same era (from Santa Maria del Patire, to be precise);[22] the euchology of Our Holy Savior of Messina, dating from around 1130 and preserved in the Bodleian Library at Oxford, Auct. E 5.13;[23] and, finally, two euchologies from the fourteenth century:

[17] I particularly thank André Jacob for the references that he supplied to me and also for the details he has provided on the euchologies published by J. Morin, op. cit., and by A. Dmitrievskij, *Opisanie liturgitseskich rukopisej*, vol. 2, Εὐχολόγια (Kiev: Typ. University, 1901; repr. Hildesheim, G. Olms, 1965).

[18] A. Dmitrievskij, op. cit., p. 16.

[19] F. 32; A. Dmitrievskij, op. cit., p. 996; cf. R. Devreesse, *Le fonds Coislin, Catalogue des manuscrits grecs*, 2 (Paris: Imprimerie Nationale, 1945), pp. 194–95.

[20] J. Morin, op. cit., 1655 edition, pp. 80–81; 1695 edition, p. 65.

[21] Ff. 47v–49v; J. Morin, op. cit., 1655 edition, pp. 99–100; 1695 edition, pp. 80–81; cf. P. Canart, *Codices Vaticani graeci, Codices 1745–1962*, vol. 1 (1970), p. 423.

[22] Ff. 193r–195r; cf. G. Mercati, *L'Eucologio di S. Maria del Patire*, RevBen 46 (1934): 233–34 (= G. Mercati, *Opere minori*, vol. 4, ST 79 [1937], pp. 479–80).

[23] Ff. 147v–149r; A. Jacob, *Un euchologe du Saint-Sauveur "in lingua Phari" de Messine, le Bodleianus auct. E. 5.13*, in *Bulletin de l'Institut historique belge* (1980), pp. 283–364. The rubrics

Cairo, Bibliothèque Patriarcale 104[24] and Mount Athos, Xenophonti 163.[25]

In these books the ritual for the ordination of deaconesses is found right after the ritual for deacons, whether the various minstries are listed in ascending order (from subdeacon up to priest and bishop) or in descending order (from bishop down to subdeacon). There is only one exception, and that is in the Sinai Greek manuscript 956. In this document, the *Ordo* for the deaconess is placed after the ceremony for the evening prayer of Pentecost and not among the rituals for ordinations. The text of the prayers does not undergo any change; however, the rubrics become gradually more precise.

Thus, apropos of the tradition of taking the chalice after Communion: "She does not give Communion to anyone [οὐδενὶ μεταδίδωσι]."[26] In the manuscripts from southern Italy and Mount Athos, the ritual for the ordination of deacons envisages a case where the ordination might take place in the course of a liturgy of the catechumens; the rubric adds: "The same ritual will be observed for the ordination of a deaconess, except that she does not make the genuflection [ἄνευ τὸ γονυκλῖναι] but merely inclines her head; after Communion, having received the holy chalice, she does not give Communion to anybody but sets it down immediately on the sacred table."[27]

Finally, in the euchologies of Bessarion and Cairo, there is this entire *Ordo* of rubrics preceding the ritual:

> *The order that is employed for the ordination of a deaconess.* She must be at least forty years of age, a chaste virgin, and, according to the custom that prevails today, she must be a nun in habit, tonsured, having attained to such a high degree by the virtues that have flowered in her—namely, that she is a worthy rival to virtuous men and thus has proved herself worthy of this great dignity. All the rites must then be carried out in the case of a deacon being ordained, with the exception of a few points that have to be modified. For example, she should be conducted to the sacred table with her head veiled

---

are identical to those of the Barberini Greek Euchology 336. Cf. H. D. Coxe, *Bodleian Library Quarto Catalogues*, I, *Greek Manuscripts* (Oxford: Bodleian Library, 1969; reprint of the ed. of 1853 with corrections), col. 661–62, no. 78.

[24] F. 6, A. Dmitrievskij, op. cit., pp. 346–47.

[25] A. Dmitrievskij, op. cit., p. 361. I have no information on the Euchology Athens Ethnike Bibliotheke 662 from the twelfth century: see I. Sakkelion and A. Sakkelion, *Katalogos tōn cheirographōn tēs ethnikēs bibliothekēs* (Athens, 1892), p. 123; cf. E. D. Theodorou, art. cit., chap. 6, n. 3, p. 580.

[26] *Euchology of Bessarion*: οὐ μεταδίδωσι; Vatic. Greek 1872 and Cairo 104: οὐδενὶ μεταδίδωσι.

[27] *Euchologe de S. Maria del Patire*, f. 193r, G. Mercati, op. cit., pp. 233–34 (= 480); Vatic. Greek 1872, f. 47v, J. Morin, op. cit., ed. 1695, p. 80; *Zenophonti 163*, cit. by E. D. Theodorou, op. cit., p. 581.

with the *maforion*, with the two ends kept apart in front. After the "Ἡ θεία χάρις" has been pronounced, she does not bend the knee, as the deacon does, but rather inclines her head. The bishop signs her three times and, with his hand on her head, prays thus. . . .[28]

C. The Meaning of These Rituals

The authors of the Byzantine *Ordo* for the ordination of deaconesses plainly wanted it to be as symmetrical as possible with the one for the ordination of deacons.[29] This can be seen both from the way it is placed in the majority of euchologies and from the structure that it has been given.

The *Ordo*, for both deaconesses and deacons, was placed at the same point in the eucharistic celebration, namely, after the doxology terminating the anaphora and ahead of the diaconal litany preceding the recitation of the Our Father.[30] Those euchologies that provide for the ordination of deacons in the course of the liturgy of the catechumens mention the ordination of deaconesses in parallel fashion.[31] Even if the place of ordination was not always specified, as it usually was for deacons, that place was evidently the sanctuary, because the doors remained open and the candidate had to advance toward the bishop; nowhere is it specified that the bishop had to leave the altar. By contrast, the ordination of subdeacons took place neither at the altar nor during the eucharistic celebration.[32]

[28] A. Dmitreivskij, op. cit., pp. 346, 996.

[29] This is the aspect of the matter that is underlined by C. Vagaggini, op. cit., pp. 177–85, who, however, passes over in silence the differences that exist.

[30] Cf. J. Goar, op. cit., ed. 1647, pp. 79 (liturgy of St. John Chrysostom), 173 (liturgy of St. Basil); ed. 1730, pp. 64, 147.

[31] See the example in pt. B of this chapter, where the Barberini Greek Euchology 336 makes reference to the Liturgy of the Catechumens: J. Goar, op. cit., ed. 1647, p. 254; ed. 1730, p. 211. (It is erroneously that C. Vagaggini, op. cit., refers to J. Morin, op. cit., p. 80.)

[32] C. Vagaggini, op. cit., pp. 181–84. However, Vagaggini exaggerated the significance of the fact that the deaconess was ordained within the sanctuary, while subdeacons and lectors had to remain outside, either in the nave or in the *diaconicon*. Certainly the distinction between ordinations carried out inside the sanctuary and those carried out outside is a classic distinction. Simeon of Thessalonica several times insisted on this distinction in his *De sacra liturgia*, cap. 99, PG 155, col. 301A; in *De sacris ordinibus*, cap. 156, 169, ibid., col. 361D–363A, 372D. This distinction is even an ancient tradition attested to by Theodore of Mopsuestia, who noted in his commentary on 1 Tim 3:14–15: "We need not be surprised if the apostle seems not to have mentioned either subdeacons or lectors. The fact is that these functions were added later to the ministries necessary for the good functioning of the Church; this was because the multitude of believers demanded that these ministries be performed by others. For this reason subdeacons and lectors do not receive ordination before the altar [πρὸ τοῦ θυσιαστηρίου τὴν χειροτονίαν δέχεσθαι] because they are not ministers of the mysteries, properly speaking. Lectors do the readings; subdeacons prepare in the

The ceremony began, as in the ordination of bishops, priests and deacons, with a proclamation recited by the bishop: "'Η θεία χάρις." Dom Bernard Botte saw in this formula the essence of the ordination prayer; however, his opinion in this matter has not been adopted by most liturgists.[33] Even though the Byzantine rite did not employ this formula for the subdeacon or lector, other traditions did accept it.[34] More than that, the Barberini euchology 390 ("*Codex Allatianus*"), although it is a late document—sixteenth century—showed rituals for the προχείρισις of a hegumen and a steward that also began with an 'Η θεία χάρις.[35] However, it was followed by a special text, which proves that such an *incipit* does not prejudice the authenticity of the use of this formula. Not a single existing manuscript contains the complete text of the 'Η θεία χάρις for the ordination of deaconesses. Surely this text could not have been the same one as was used at other ordinations,[36] where the supposition always existed that the candidate already possessed the preceding degree of ministry.

Two rites, coming at the end, seemed to have contributed to assimilating the ritual for the ordination of the deaconess to that for the ordination of the deacon: they were the conferring of the *orarion*, or deacon's stole, and the presentation of the chalice. However, these two rites indicate differences

---

diaconicon that which is necessary for the deacons' work and watch over the lighting for the church. Only priests and deacons carry out the ministry of the mysteries as such: the priests accomplish this through the exercise of their sacerdotal ministry, and the deacons by providing service for the accomplishment of these holy things. We take note of all these things so that nobody will believe that Paul was forgetful": Greek text in the series of Coislin 204 (Cramer VII, 30) and ancient Latin translation (VI, s.) in H. B. Swete, *Theodori episcopi Mopsuestensis in Epistolas beati Pauli Commentarii* (Cambridge University Press, 1882), 2:132–34. The same motif appears in Simeon of Thessalonica: ordination at the altar was conferred only upon those destined to serve at the altar. And the deaconess had no role at the altar, as all the ancient and medieval authors attested. It is true that Theodore spoke of deaconesses in connection with the Pauline texts; Simeon, as we shall see, did not mention them at all. Thus it is not possible to find a theological reason for conducting the ordination of deaconesses in the Byzantine rite within the sanctuary. Cf. J. Tchekan, *Eléments d'introduction à l'étude de la liturgie byzantine des ordinations*, in *Bulletin du Comité des études* (de la Compagnie de Saint-Sulpice) 10 (1968): 196. Moreover, as we have already seen, the deaconess was forbidden to touch the altar during her ordination.

[33] B. Botte, *La formule d'ordination "La grâce divine" dans les rites orientaux*, OS 2 (1957): 288–96; E. Lanne, *Les ordinations dans le rite copte*, OS 5 (1960): 81–106; P. M. Gy, *Les anciennes prières d'ordination*, in *La Maison-Dieu* 138 (1979): 93–122.

[34] For example, the Palestinian euchology published by M. Black, *Rituale Melchitarum*, Bonner orientalische Studien 22 (Stuttgart: Kohlhammer, 1938), pp. 91, 94.

[35] J. Morin, op. cit., ed. 1655, pp. 114, 118; ed. 1690, pp. 93, 96.

[36] J. Goar, op. cit., ed. 1647, pp. 265–66; ed. 1730, pp. 220–21, *nota* 3, reports on this subject the unhelpful diatribes of P. Arcudius, *Libri VII de Concordia ecclesiae occidentalis et orientalis in septem sacramentorum administratione* (Lutetiae Parisiorum: Cramoisy, 1626), lib. 6, cap. 10.

as much as similarities between the two ordination rituals. The conferring of the *orarion*, we will recall from the Jacobite "Replies of the Holy Fathers", was a rite practiced "in the East" (and thus not at Antioch). Moreover, the wearing of the *orarion* quite rapidly extended to subdeacons[37] in spite of the prohibition of the Canons of Laodicea.[38] The description of the entire rubric already included in Barberini Greek euchology 336 demonstrates that the deaconess did not wear the *orarion* in the same way as did the deacon; it was not wrapped all the way around her neck, and the two ends were brought out in front. As for the chalice, it was made absolutely clear that as soon as it was presented to the deaconess, she was to place it back upon the altar without giving Communion to anyone. This was precisely different from the practice at the ordination of the deacon. When the chalice was given to the deacon, he immediately went down to distribute Communion to the faithful.

There is no point in exaggerating the significance of the triple signing and laying on of hands. These actions are common to all ordinations in the Byzantine rite, including those of subdeacons and lectors.[39] As far as the laying on of hands is concerned, it must have been established practice by about the beginning of the fifth century, at least in Constantinople, and doubtless elsewhere also, as both the vocabulary[40] and the ritual of the *Apostolic Constitutions* attest.

However, we should take due note of one of the other differences between the ordination of deaconesses and that of deacons. These are points that could appear to be simple minutiae; in the symbolic system of Pseudo-Dionysius, however, they are charged with meaning. The candidate for ordination as a deacon genuflected or knelt on one knee; while the candidate for ordination to the priesthood knelt on both knees[41] —but both of them rested their heads against the altar. The candidate for ordination as a deaconess, however, remained standing; she did not bend her knee at all but simply bowed her head.

For the ordination of a subdeacon, the bishop pronounced one single prayer. For the ordination of a deaconess, as for the ordination of a deacon, a priest or a bishop, the officiating bishop pronounced two prayers, separated by a diaconal litany, and during each one he kept his

---

[37] A. Vööbus, *Syrische Kanonessammlungen*, CSCO 307, p. 154; A. Raes, *Introductio in liturgiam orientalem* (Rome: P. Institutum studiorum orientalium, 1947), pp. 236–38.

[38] Canon 22 (subdeacons) and 23 (lectors and psalmists), Joannou, vol. I, pt. 2, pp. 139–40.

[39] At least if lectors were the ones being referred to in the Barberini Greek Euchology 336, J. Goar, op. cit., ed. 1647, p. 235; ed. 1730, p. 195. C. Vagaggini, op. cit., p. 180, fully recognized this.

[40] See the introductory portion to this chapter.

[41] Pseudo-Dionysius, *Hiérarchie ecclésiastique*, c. 5, II, III, 2, 7, 8, PG 3, cols. 509, 516. Cf. Simeon of Thessalonica, *De sacris ordinationibus*, cc. 169, 179, PG 155, cols. 376, 388.

hand on the head of the ordained.[42] Is it necessary to point out, however, that the prayers pronounced in the case of the deaconess did not represent a simple transposition of those pronounced for the ordination of a deacon?

In the first place, the role of women in the economy of salvation was affirmed once and for all by the Virgin Birth, according to the flesh, of the Son of God, and by the gift of prophecy more than once accorded to women by God. This constitutes a point of contact between the Byzantine formulary and that of the *Apostolic Constitutions*, but it is really the only point of contact. In response to the need for a biblical paradigm for the deaconess, the euchology did not limit itself, as did the *Apostolic Constitutions*, to the model of women as "guardians of the holy doors" (which also shows that the euchology assigned no such role to deaconesses). Rather, the euchology used the example of Phoebe, just as St. Stephen was used as the example for the deacon. Phoebe, of course, was "called to the work of ministry" and received "the gift of the diaconate" of God. The ordination assumed an initiative on the part of the candidate. Women who were accepted by God "into the ranks of [his] ministers" consecrated themselves to *him* to serve in *his* "holy places with a fitting holy desire". They "wished to consecrate" themselves to the Lord. All this is completely consistent with the teaching of St. Basil[43] on the subject and also with the attestation of Justinian[44] that deaconesses were entering upon a state of life aimed at perfection.

It was for this reason that the deaconess' head had to be covered with the *maforion*. The grace of the Holy Spirit was invoked upon her for the same reason. This epiclesis again shows how similar in some respects were the rituals for the ordination of deacons, priests and bishops to that of deaconesses. But we must nevertheless recall that the *Apostolic Constitutions* called down the Holy Spirit upon subdeacons and lectors as well. In the judgment of Fr. Cipriano Vagaggini,[45] this fact relativizes whatever theological judgment one might attempt to draw from this invocation of the Holy Spirit upon deaconesses. However, it is clear that, in the Byzantine rite, the Holy Spirit is invoked upon neither lectors nor subdeacons.

According to the prayers employed in each of the rituals, the function of the deaconess was very different from that of the deacon. Deacons were to be "servants of Christ and stewards of the mysteries of God"

---

[42] On the usage in the ordinations of the grouping of the two prayers: see J. M. Hanssens, *Les oraisons sacramentelles des ordinations orientales*, in his book *La liturgie d'Hippolyte* (II), *Documents et études* (Rome: Univ. Gregoriana, 1970), pp. 263–85.

[43] Chapter 5, 1C, above.

[44] Chapter 5, 1F, above.

[45] C. Vagaggini, op. cit., p. 180.

(1 Cor 4:1). They were to "hold the mystery of faith with a clear conscience" (1 Tim 3:9). In this the commentators have always discerned a clear reference to the ministry of distributing Communion from the chalice. Moreover, immediately after his ordination, the deacon proceeded immediately to carry out this and other tasks proper to his ministry: he shook the *rhipidion*, or fan intended to keep flies away, which was given to him by the bishop; he gave out the Precious Blood to the faithful in Communion; and he also chanted the final litany.

The deaconess, however, was to "persevere without reproach in [God's] holy temples"; she was to "apply herself to household government", which was the proper work, precisely, of the hegumenē of a convent of contemplative nuns but implied no other outside work or service; certainly it implied no liturgical role. Even the vocabulary in the two rituals, for the ordination of the deacon and the deaconess, respectively, were not the same. For the deacon, the language employed made reference to "τὴν τοῦ διακόνου λειτουργίαν" and "τὸ τοῦ διακόνου ἔργον". For the deaconess, however, reference was made only to διακονία, which was a very general and very imprecise term, translated as readily by "service" as by "diaconate". Of course, the deaconess was accepted "into the ranks of God's ministers" (ἐν τάξει λειτουργῶν), but we must remember that the term λειτουργός was used in Pseudo-Dionysius for the diaconate as well as for the lower ministries.[46]

However solemn may have been the ritual by which she was initiated into her ministry, however much it may have resembled the ritual for the ordination of a deacon, the conclusion nevertheless must be that a deaconess in the Byzantine rite was in no wise a female deacon. She exercised a totally different ministry from that of the deacons.

2. THE CHALDEAN RITUAL FOR THE
ORDINATION OF DEACONESSES

The oldest Chaldean pontifical that we possess is Berlin Syriac manuscript 38, which dates from 1496. However, in its current state, it contains ordinations only for a lector, subdeacon, deacon and priest and the prayer for the consecration of an altar.[47] The pontifical contained in Vatican Syriac manuscript 66, from 1529, and copied from a manuscript of 1276, similarly makes no provision for the ordination of a deaconess.[48] The

---

[46] Chapter 5, 2B, above.

[47] I. M. Vosté, *Pontificale iuxta ritum Ecclesiae Syrorum orientalium, id est, Chaldaeorum, Versio latina* (Typis polyglottis Vaticanis, 1937–38), pp. 82–83.

[48] Ibid., pp. 189–90.

oldest *Ordo* that we possess making such a provision, in the present state of our knowledge, is the pontifical contained in Vatican Syriac manuscripts 45–46 (*olim* 18–19).[49]

This ritual has only been described for us very recently, and its history and antecedents are impossible to reconstruct. We may recall that in the various Chaldean rite documents that dealt with the institution of deaconesses—the "Questions on the Sacraments of Catholicos Ishô'yahb I", the "Nicene-Arabic Canons", canon 9 of the 676 Synod of Mar George I[50]—not one provided an actual ritual by which this institution might be carried out.

The anonymous work entitled *Exposition of the Offices of the Church*, erroneously attributed to George of Arbela but which evidently dates from only the eleventh century, mentions deaconesses in passing, but in a way that does not even correspond to the authentic Nestorian tradition. According to this work, subdeacons supposedly exercised the role of the angels in the parable, separating the wheat from the tares; then, the work went on, "among women an order of deaconesses has also been chosen and, from among them, those who close the doors; for the lineage of Adam is one and the same always, although there is a diversity of fecundity and natural faculties".[51] The logic of this train of thought gives deaconesses the task of being guardians of the doors, and it would thus certainly take us back to the *Apostolic Constitutions* and the *Testamentum Domini*.[52] However, this can only be a purely literary reference because, a few pages further on, the author has not deaconesses but rather the daughters of the covenant, the *benâth qeyâmā*, functioning as guardians of the women's doors for the purpose of excluding from the mysteries those who have not yet been initiated into the ranks of the faithful.[53] With respect to baptism, this anonymous work mentioned the anointing of catechumens over their entire bodies and indicated that it was not the priest who carried out this anointing.[54] But the description is too brief and

---

[49] Ibid., p. 83. Detailed description in S. E. and J. S. Assemani, *Bibliothecae apost. Vaticanae codicum manuscriptorum Catalogus, II, Codices Chaldaici sive Syriaci* (Rome: Barbielli, 1758), pp. 302–7.

[50] Chapter 2, 3B, 3C, 3D, above.

[51] *Expositio officiorum Ecclesiae* 4:13, Latin trans. by R. H. Connolly, CSCO 76 (1915; reprint. 1953), p. 31: "Ita subdiaconi eligunt, qui de mediali ecclesia angelorum sunt et huiusmodi rerum auctoritatem habent, sed et de mulieribus ordo diaconissarum delectus est, et earum quae portas claudunt, quia totum agmen domus Adami unum est, etiamsi fecunditate et naturali copia inter se diversi sint." W. De Vries, *Sakramententheologie bei den Nestorianern*, OCA 133 (Rome: 1947), p. 145, believes that this simply refers to deaconesses: "The anonymous author mentions deaconesses. Their function is to close the doors."

[52] Chapter 2, 2, above.

[53] *Expositio officiorum Ecclesiae* 4:25, ibid., p. 73.

[54] Op. cit., 5:5, ibid., pp. 97–98.

sketchy to enable us to conclude whether or not its author really knew about the unusual discipline described by Ishô'yahb I.[55]

This discipline was known to the author of the *Liber Patrum*, a work probably composed toward the end of the thirteenth or fourteenth century. After having spoken successively about the patriarch, the metropolitan, the bishop, the priests and the deacons, the author went on to add:

> As for deaconesses, they must be wise. Those who have provided a clear witness of purity and fear of God are the ones who should be chosen. They should be chaste and modest and sixty years or older in age. They carry out the sacrament of baptism for women because it is not fitting that the priest should view the nudity of women. That is why the deaconesses should anoint the women and baptize them with water. The priest should introduce his hand through a window or through a veil and sign the candidates, while the deaconess should carry out both the baptism proper and the anointing.

Immediately after this, the author transcribed the passage concerning deacons from the treatise *The Ordinals of Christ*:[56] "Our Lord himself carried out the function of the diaconate in person when he washed the feet of his apostles the night of his Paschal meal." This suggests that, for the author, deacons and deaconesses were one and the same. He went on to treat of subdeacons, lectors, exorcists, sextons, stewards and porters.[57] The pontifical did not sanction this order of enumeration, at least not in the prayer for the ordination of the bishop, where it was stated that the bishop must ordain "priests, deacons, subdeacons, lectors and deaconesses for the ministry of the holy Church".[58]

The reason that so late a date has been assigned to the *Liber Patrum*[59] is that it was apparently unknown to 'Abdisho' (or Ebediesus) bar Berika (d. 1318), metropolitan of Nisibin (modern Nusaybin) and the last authentically learned scholar of the Nestorian church.[60] 'Abdisho' bar Berika made a brief allusion to deaconesses in his *Collectio canonum synodicorum*; actually it was a reference to the rituals of ordination:

> The Synod [of Isaac in 410 A.D.] prescribed that the bishops must carry out the ordination by laying on of hands for all of the different ecclesiastical orders. This should take place not just anywhere but inside the holy church itself and before the altar. Deaconesses, however, because they are women,

---

[55] Chapter 2, 3B.

[56] Cf. R. Reynolds, *The Ordinals of Christ: from Their Origins to the Twelfth Century*, Beiträge zur Geschichte und Quellenkunde des Mittelalters (Berlin: W. de Gruyter, 1978), 7:22–24.

[57] *Liber Patrum*, latine interpretatus est, notis illustravit I. M. Vosté, CCOF ser. 2, fasc. 16 (1940), p. 34.

[58] I. M. Vosté, *Pontificale*, p. 70.

[59] I. M. Vosté, *Liber Patrum*, pp. 8–9.

[60] Baumstark, *Geschichte der syrischen Literatur*, pp. 323–25.

should receive ordination in the church but before the door providing access to the chancel.[61]

Here, again, we are apparently dealing with a simple literary tradition, because in his *Ordo iudiciorum ecclesiasticorum*, 'Abdisho' did not mention deaconesses when he enumerated the various ecclesiastical orders and degrees, nor did he find any occasion even to mention 1 Timothy 3.[62]

There are, finally, five pontificals of the sixteenth century, all copied around the same date, that give the text for the ordination of a deaconess in the Chaldean rite. There is the Vatican Syriac manuscript 45 of the year 1556, already mentioned; the Vatican Borgian Syriac manuscript 21, written between 1555 and 1562;[63] the Cambridge University Addendum 1988, dated 1558;[64] the Library of the Chaldean Patriarch of Mosul manuscript 55, written in 1568;[65] and the Chaldean Archbishopric of Diayrbakir manuscript 59, dated 1569.[66] If we can believe the note that, in several copies of the pontificals, precedes the texts of the various ordinations, the "rituals and canons of all the ecclesiastical orders, that is to say, lectors, subdeacons, deacons, priests and bishops", were established by Mar Cyprian, metropolitan of Nisibin [d. 767 A.D.], the Venerable Mar Ishô'yahb III, Catholicos Patriarch [d. 680 A.D.] and Mar Israel Harip Zau'e.[67]

This announcement thus tells us nothing about the antiquity of the ritual for the ordination of deaconesses. Moreover, this ritual never appears next to that for deacons in the pontificals. In the Cambridge,

---

[61] *Collectio canonum synodicorum* VI, 4, can. 1, in A. Mai, *Scriptorum veterum nova collectio*, vol. 10, pt. 1 (Rome: Typis Collegii Urbani, 1838), pp. 111–12. The synod referred to is the Synod of Isaac, which took place in 410 A.D., but only the first part of the text is to be found in canon 16 of this synod: J. B. Chabot, *Synodicon oriental* (Paris: Imprimerie Nationale, 1902), p. 269.

[62] Mar 'Abdisho', *Ordo iudiciorum ecclesiasticorum latine interpretatus est et notis illustravit* I. M. Vosté, CCOF, ser. 2, fasc. 15 (1940), pp. 109–10.

[63] I. M. Vosté, *Pontificale*, pp. 187–89.

[64] Ibid., pp. 84–89.

[65] Ibid., pp. 81, 89–90.

[66] Ibid., pp. 82, 90. The Pontifical Vatic. Syr. 43 (*olim* Diayrbakir 11), of the year 1701 A.D. does not contain the ritual for the ordination of the deaconess: Vosté, op. cit., p. 92. I have no indications concerning the contents of the mss. 45 (fifteenth century) and 47 (from the year 1702) of the episcopal library of Siirt, which disappeared during the war of 1914–18; I. M. Vosté, op. cit., p. 82; or of the ms. mentioned by Baumstark, *Geschichte der syrischen Literatur*, pp. 213–14, Urmia 26 (of the year 1714). As for Cambridge University mss. Oo I 15 (of the year 1691) and Oo I 29 (seventeenth to eighteenth centuries), they do not deal with the ordination of the deaconess, if we may judge by the description provided by W. Wright, *A Catalogue of the Syriac Manuscripts Preserved in the Library of the University of Cambridge*, vol. 2 (Cambridge University Press, 1901), pp. 1061–63, 1095–1109.

[67] I. M. Vosté, *Pontificale*, p. 9.

Mosul and Diayrbakir documents it appears after those for priests and for
Shahare, blind people exercising a ministry that could be called "para-
diaconal" or "parapresbyteral", since they substituted for deacons and
priests in carrying out some of the minor functions performed by these
sacred ministers.[68] In Vatican Syriac manuscript 45, it appears after the
rituals for deacons, priests and monks and before those for archdeacons
and the hegumenēs; in Vatican Syriac manuscript 21, it comes after the
rituals for the investiture of monks, the tonsure of monks and of nuns and,
again, before those for archdeacons and the hegumenēs.

Finally, if the *Ordo* as a whole is difficult to date, it is also necessary to
ask whether the rubrics that accompany the ritual are contemporaneous
with it or whether they were added later.[69]

If we leave aside the preliminary chants and prayers, the prayers in the
ritual itself number six in all. The first of them immediately indicates the
"monastic" character of the rite:

> Extend, Lord God, the hand of your mercy from the height of heaven down
> upon your maidservant here, who is prepared to receive the habit out of the
> fear of God and to observe all of your divine and life-giving commandments.

The second prayer is one that was common to all ordinations. Although
its beginning was identical to the classic Byzantine formula, Ἡ θεία χάρις,
it did not have the same purpose: "The bishop does not make the sign of
the cross over the ordinands but over himself, because he makes this
prayer for himself":[70]

> May the grace of our Lord Jesus Christ, which at all times has made up for
> what is lacking, be with us through the goodness of God the Father and
> through the power of the Holy Spirit, and may it through our mediocrity
> accomplish this sublime and important ministry for the sake of our salvation,
> now and always, forever and ever.

The following prayer is taken from the ritual for the ordination of
deacons:

[68] On these *Shahare*, see I. M. Vosté, ibid., pp. 156–57; cf. J. S. Assemani, *Bibliotheca
Orientalis Clementino-Vaticana*, vol. 3, pt. 2 (Rome: Typ. Congregationis de Propaganda
Fide, 1730), pp. 820–26.

[69] The Syriac text of Vatican Syr. ms. 45 has only been published in an adequate fashion
by J. A. Assemani, *Codex liturgicus Ecclesiae universae*, vol. 13 (Rome: Bizzarini, 1776;
reprint. Paris-Leipzig, 1902), pp. 219–22, with Latin translation; J. Morin published only the
"classical" orders from lector through patriarch; J. A. Assemani reproduces the Latin
translation of J. S. Assemani, *Bibliotheca Orientalis*, vol. 3, pt. 2, pp. 852–53. We are also
utilizing here the Latin translation of I. M. Vosté, *Pontificale*, pp. 158–61, based on the mss.
of Cambridge and of Mosul.

[70] I. M. Vosté, *Pontificale*, p. 11.

O God, our king, full of mercy, rich in pity, abundant in clemency; you, Lord, who in your ineffable and mysterious goodness have made me the mediator of the divine gifts dispensed through your holy Church, empowering me to give in your name to the ministers of your holy mysteries the benefits of the overarching ministry of the Holy Spirit—according to the tradition that comes down to us from the apostles by means of the laying on of the hands of a minister of the Church—accept the servants [maidservants] that we here present to you so that they [they = feminine] may be deacons chosen out of your holy Church and for whom we all pray. May there descend upon them [them = feminine] the grace of the Holy Spirit to make them perfect for the sake of that ministry for which they are being presented to you, by the grace and the mercy of your holy Son, with whom. . . .

Here, though, is the principal prayer of the ritual, recited while the bishop's hand is resting on the head of the deaconess:

Lord, strong and all-powerful God, you who created everything by the power of your word, and who maintain under your order everything that you created—you who planted your goodness in men and women alike, giving the grace of the Holy Spirit: You, Lord, now through your mercy, choose your servant for the work of the diaconate and give her through your mercy the grace of the Holy Spirit, that she may serve before you without any stain, with a pure heart and with a clear conscience, keeping spotless the cause of good morals. May she instruct women in the Faith. May she teach them chastity and good works. And may she receive from you the consummation and the recompense of all her good works on the glorious day of your coming, through the grace and mercy of your only Son. . . .

Finally, the two concluding prayers:

Strengthen, Lord, by your grace the servant here before you; help her by your mercy that she may always perfectly fulfill the will of your Lordship, you, Lord of all, Father, Son and Holy Spirit. . . .

Make worthy by your grace, Lord, your servant, that she may have a healthy fear of your word and your judgment. May she be attentive to your commandments. May she always be the dwelling place of the glorious Trinity, Father, Son. . . .

In the judgment of Joseph Simon Assemani—a judgment to which Father Vosté subscribed—the prayer quoted above taken from the ritual for the ordination of deacons, which has a parallel in the rituals for ordination of both priests and bishops, was not a part of the essential formula for ordinations; rather, Assemani considered it rather like "a declaration of election".[71] It was the principal prayer that followed this one, which was a

[71] Ibid., p. 288. Cf. J. S. Assemani, *Bibliotheca Orientalis*, vol. 3, pt. 2, p. DCCCLV.

prayer proper to the ordination of deaconesses; it was recited with the bishop's hand resting upon the head of the deaconess being ordained. This, of course, is a fact which must arrest our attention. It is to be noted also that this prayer refers to the plan of God for women as well as men, although it is shorter than that in the *Apostolic Constitutions* or the Byzantine euchology. Also, as in those documents, the deaconess was assigned "the work of the diaconate", and the Holy Spirit was invoked upon her that she might "serve" before God.

What was new here, however, was the affirmation of a mission to instruct other women, to teach them chastity and good works. This was certainly the mission of the hegumenē of a convent; it also corresponded to the role laid out for widows in the *Testament of Our Lord Jesus Christ* and to that of the "older women" in Titus 2:3–5. There is, however, no allusion made either to the example of the Old Testament or to that of Phoebe in Romans 16:1.

But the rubrics that accompany these ordination prayers appear to have taken great pains to exclude any possible confusion between the ordination of a deacon and that of a deaconess:

> There must be designated a sister from the virgins in the convent consecrated to God; she must be of advanced age and exemplary in the practice of the religious life; she must be prudent and gentle, bearing witness to her good works.
>
> On the command of the bishop, she should be introduced into the *Diaconicon* prior to the celebration of the sacred Mysteries.

I do not at all see how J. S. Assemani and, following him, Denzinger could possibly have understood the *Diaconicon* to be: *"id est intra cancellos altaris, ubi ordinari solent presbyteri et diaconi"* (i.e., "inside the chancel of the altar where the priests and deacons are accustomed to be"). Assemani made reference to the ordination of deacons, where, however, we read that the bishop expressly ordered the deacons being ordained to ascend the step: *"ascendere eos iubet ad gradus"*.[72] We have seen that 'Abdisho' situated the ordination of the deaconess inside the church but in front of the door or gate giving access to the chancel.[73]

Now the ordination of Chaldean deacons was permitted in the course of a Mass (this was not obligatory, as it was in all the other churches), but it always took place in the apse, near where the deacons entered by the great door. They advanced up to the altar lamps; once ordained, the archdeacon led them around the altar.[74] The solemnity of this ordination of deacons

---

[72] J. S. Assemani, *Bibliotheca Orientalis*, vol. 3, pt. 2, pp. DCCCLIV, DCCCIX.

[73] On the layout of the Chaldean Church and the *diaconicon*, see the diagram and references given by R. H. Connolly, *Expositio officiorum Ecclesiae*, CSCO 71:196.

[74] I. M. Vosté, *Pontificale*, pp. 15, 16, 28.

was greater than that of deaconesses and included a large number of "canons", or "chants", and prayers by the bishop. There was also the question of whether or not the candidate knelt down.

> The archdeacon presents the deaconess-candidate to the bishop; her hands are joined, and her head is bowed; she bows deeply from the waist, not, however, bending the knee, which would not be fitting.

Here again we encounter the principle inspired by the symbolism of Pseudo-Dionysius and put into practice by the Byzantines: the candidate for the priesthood knelt on both knees; the candidate for the male diaconate knelt on one knee; but the deaconess remained standing.

"Her hands are joined": this practice, again, was a difference from the ritual for the ordination of deacons, for deacon candidates raised up their hands against their heads in a rather curious fashion and according to a rather studied symbolism.[75] At the end of the ritual, moreover, the deaconess did not receive the signing of the Cross from the bishop; this signing, in the Eastern tradition, was considered to be a gesture so important that it was believed by itself to constitute the seal of the ordination of deacons, priests and bishops.[76] Nor did the Chaldean pontifical provide for the wearing of the *orarion* by the deaconess although, among the Chaldeans, it was given even to the subdeacon.

Even though the Chaldean pontifical did provide for a laying on of hands for the deaconess and, of course, employed the term "ordination", it was nevertheless careful to avoid any misunderstanding on this point:

> The bishop prays, putting his hand on her head, not as for an ordination but rather as for a benediction.

At the end of the ceremony, essentially the same instructions were repeated, along with some important details on the functions of deaconesses:

> Then the deaconess raises herself fully erect and the bishop places his hand on her head, but not in the manner of an ordination; rather, he gives her his blessing, recites a silent prayer over her and commands her to avoid pride.
>
> However, the deaconess has no access to the altar because she is a woman. She has access only to the oil of chrism. Her function is to pray from her heart at the head of all the other nuns during liturgical services and, at the end of the prayers, to say aloud: "Amen!" The nuns repeat this along with her. She anoints the women who present themselves for baptism and guides the hand

---

[75] *Et ambas suas manus apponunt auribus suis modo humili et demisso vultu; et erigunt digitos qui sunt iuxta pollicem utriusque manus in altum. Scire debes extensa diaconi manus et digitos super aures, et erecta quidem in altum, significare eum erectum stare in servitium tamquam subditum coram sacerdote et pontifice*, I. M. Vosté, *Pontificale*, p. 25.

[76] For deacons, cf. ibid., p. 27.

of the priest to them, for it is not permitted to men to anoint a woman, although, in our day, some do it anyway—but no priest should let his eyes fall upon a woman.

"Although, in our day, some do it anyway. . . ." This passing remark tells us a very great deal about how much the traditional role of the deaconess in helping at baptisms had fallen into disuse in the Chaldean churches. On the other hand, the *Ordo* in its entirety, including both prayers and rubrics, simply assumes that even in these Eastern regions deaconesses are properly to be found "at the head of all the other nuns". Deaconesses served, in other words, as the hegumenēs of convents, just as they did in the Eastern churches that had grown up inside the Roman Empire.

Another question, though, is whether there were any deaconesses left in the Chaldean church by the second half of the sixteenth century, when the extant manuscripts of the Chaldean pontificals containing the rituals for their institution were recopied. For three of these existing pontificals include an *Ordo* for the *cheirotonia* of convent hegumenēs.[77] Father J. M. Vosté, citing a passage from 'Abdisho', added that henceforth no further mention of deaconesses among the Chaldeans was even made: "*nunquam audivi inter Chaldaeos mentionem fieri de diaconissis*".[78]

---

[77] I. M. Vosté, pp. 397–98, translated it following the manuscript of Mosul, but it is also to be found in the Cambridge manuscript, f. 81v, and in the Diayrbakir manuscript: I. M. Vosté, ibid., pp. 85, 92.

[78] CCOF, ser. I, fasc. 4 (1931), p. 75.

CHAPTER EIGHT

The Disappearance of Deaconesses
And the Memory of Them That Remained

We have been able to verify how difficult it is to rely on liturgical manuscripts to prove the persistence of various rites and Church institutions: *ordines* that perhaps had not actually been used in centuries continued to be recopied. Earlier we found it was even more difficult to rely on collections of canons, in which compilers were as likely as not to include pell-mell documents from entirely different historical eras, sometimes contradicting each other outright or, at the very least, reflecting the usages of different churches. Sometimes, on the occasion of juridical or liturgical consultations, or even as a result of notes inserted into the rubric of a euchology or pontifical, we catch a glimpse of how a usage has fallen into disuse—though it nevertheless continues to be described or recalled in the sources.

We did not search out all the sources in order to try to date, at least approximately, the disappearance of deaconesses from the Chaldean church. The fashion in which the medieval authors generally referred to deaconesses suggests, however, that the institution was no longer a living institution for them. In the case of the other churches, it is a somewhat easier task to arrive at an approximate date for the disappearance of deaconesses.

1. AMONG THE JACOBITES OF TAGRIT

We will recall that for the Jacobite communities of Persia, living as they did among the Chaldean (Nestorian) churches, although they owed obedience to the metropolitan of Tagrit (Tikrit), the presence of deaconesses was, in antiquity, a necessity. It was as important to the Jacobites as it was to the Chaldeans to have deaconesses—for the baptism of women, for their education and also for the direction of the "daughters of the covenant".[1] However, an author from around the middle of the third quarter of the eleventh century bears witness to the fact that, in his time, the institution

---

[1] Chapter 2, 3A, above.

of deaconesses had already been defunct for centuries. In effect, this is what we are told in the following, from *The Book of Guidance* of Yahya ibn Jarir:[2]

> In antiquity deaconesses were ordained; their function was to be concerned with adult women and prevent their being uncovered in the presence of the bishop. However, as the practice of religion became more extensive and the decision was made to begin administering baptism to infants, this function of deaconesses was abolished. But there was another reason as well—namely, that the queens penetrated into the sanctuary, and so permission was abolished.[3]

This reference to "the queens [who] penetrated into the sanctuary" is a most unusual one—all the more so considering that access to the sanctuary had always been forbidden to deaconesses during the liturgy and often outside the liturgy as well. Whatever the facts behind this attestation of Yahya ibn Jarir, it is certainly an important one, both because it originated in Persia and because its author was a Jacobite.

2. AMONG THE WESTERN SYRIANS

We have established that, in the region of Edessa, already in the fifth century but especially in the sixth, deaconesses served as the hegumenēs, or superiors of nuns, and also that they no longer played any role in the baptism of women.[4] The following is what we read in the Syriac pontifical —a work of Michael the Great, who was patriarch from 1166 to 1199,[5] the manuscript of which is dated 1172 (Vatican Syriac manuscript 51):[6]

---

[2] On the subject of Yahya ibn Jarir and his *Book of Guidance*, see: G. Graf, *Geschichte der christlichen arabischen Literatur*, vol. 2, ST 133 (1947), pp. 259–62; G. Khouri-Sarkis, *Le Livre du guide de Yahya ibn Jarir*, OS 12 (1967): 303–18; French trans. of chaps. XXIX (On the Construction of Churches), XXX (On the Resurrection) and XXXI (On the Priesthood), ibid., pp. 319–54, 421–80.

[3] Ibid., p. 461.

[4] Chapter 6, 4, above.

[5] On Michael the Great: Baumstark, *Geschichte der syrischen Literatur*, pp. 298–300.

[6] On this ms.: S. and J. S. Assemani, *Bibliothecae Apostolicae Vaticanae codicum manuscriptorum Catalogus*, vol. II, *Codices syriaci* (Romae: Barbiellini, 1758), pp. 314–28; I. M. Vosté, *Pontificale iuxta ritum Ecclesiae Syrorum occidentalium, id est Antiochiae, Versio latina* (Typis polyglottis Vaticanis, 1941–44), pp. 1–8. Other manuscripts: Baumstark, op. cit., p. 299, n. 2. The Latin version of Vosté is based on Vatican Syriac manuscript 51; the other manuscripts were utilized only when this one proved to be difficult to read. Later, I. M. Vosté published his *Additamenta* (Vatican City, 1944), but this work was concerned mainly with the modern Pontifical compiled by patriarch Ignatius Tappouni, and there is certainly no mention of deaconesses in that one.

20. *Ordination of the Deaconess*

Ordination, or *cheirotonia*, was formerly carried out also for deaconesses, and it is for this reason that a ritual for this was always transcribed in the ancient books. In ancient times there was a need for deaconesses, principally to assist with the baptism of women. When converts from Judaism or paganism became disciples of Christianity and thereby became candidates for holy baptism, it was by the hands of the deaconesses that the priests and bishops anointed the women candidates at the time of their baptism. This was why they performed an ordination or *cheirotonia* on the one chosen to be a deaconess.

But we can plainly see that this practice has long since ceased in the Church. The reason for this is that it is now at birth or during infancy that those who are destined for baptism receive this baptism. There is no longer any need for deaconesses because there are no longer any grown women who are baptized. For this reason and for other reasons besides we have not transcribed the ritual for this here, although in many authentic and carefully copied books it is to be found.

If, however, a bishop, acting under the spur of a passing necessity, finds it necessary to ordain a deaconess, then he should ordain a woman of proven chastity who is getting along in years; for the holy apostles and Fathers decided that these were the requisite qualities for ordination.

What are the functions of the deaconess? James of Edessa described them as follows. . . .[7]

It would be tempting to interrupt this quotation right here, for we have already covered the text of James of Edessa, taken from the twenty-fourth of his *Canonical Resolutions*.[8] However, it is worth repeating here, for some curious variations occur:

She has absolutely no power at the altar, because, even when she is ordained, she merely remains in the church. And this is what her power consists of: she cleans the altar and lights the sanctuary lamps, but she only does that when there is no priest or deacon around. She may take the mysteries from the tabernacle [cabinet] in the absence of the priest or deacon in order to give Communion to women and children. But she may not take these mysteries from the altar, nor may she put them back there; nor in fact may she so much as touch the table of life in any way. When adult women present themselves for baptism, she anoints them as directed by the priest. She visits and anoints women who are ill. These are her powers, and she thus has functions similar to those of a deacon. It is for this reason that she is ordained to serve in the presence of the priests and bishops in the holy Church of God.

[7] I. M. Vosté, *Pontificale*, pp. 201–2. On the subject of this text, see also the references indicated by A. Vööbus, *Syrische Kanonessammlungen*, CSCO 307, pp. 259–60.

[8] Chapter 6, 4.

First of all, this version lacks the indication that the deaconess "is not ordained in the name of the altar". Further, her permission to distribute Communion is not restricted to the situation where "she is in the convent". The care she provides to the sick extends also to anointing them.[9] The last sentence in this version is different as well. We saw already that the twenty-fourth of his *Canonical Resolutions* ended with the sentence: "This is the power of the deaconess in what concerns the work of the priest." Yet in this Syriac pontifical we read instead: "These are her powers, and she thus has functions similar to those of a deacon. It is for this reason that she is ordained to serve in the presence of the priests and bishops in the holy Church of God."

Thus we are manifestly dealing here with an attempt to extend the power and dignity of deaconesses, contrary to the teachings of James of Edessa[10] and the other ancient Syriac authors whom we have cited.[11]

Unfortunately, we no longer possess copies of "the many authentic and carefully copied books" to which Michael the Great referred the bishop who, "under the spur of a passing necessity", needed to ordain a deaconess. If we could believe Joseph Simon Assemani—who never indicated where he derived the information[12]—the bishop merely had to recite over the deaconess-candidate the two prayers for "the election of the choirmaster, the visitor, the abbot or the abbess".[13] This, evidently, is not an ancient formula; it deals with several governing positions all at once.

About a century after Michael the Great, the prolific Syrian author of encyclopedias Gregory Abu il-Farag, known also as Bar Hebraeus (1225–86 A.D.),[14] mentioned deaconesses in three of his compilations: *The Book of the Candelabra of the Sanctuary*, an essay on dogmatics; *The Book of Rays*,

---

[9] This was something noticed by P. Hindo, *Disciplina antiochena antica, Siri*, 3 CCOF, ser. 2, fasc. 27 (1941), p. 63.

[10] However, the text of James of Edessa was accurately transcribed in the *Synodicon* copied in the year 1204 A.D., cf. A. Vööbus, *The Synodicon in the West Syrian Tradition*, CSCO 368 (1975), p. 242.

[11] Chapter 6, 4, above.

[12] J. S. Assemani, *Bibliotheca Orientalis Clementino-Vaticana*, vol. 3, pt. 2 (Rome: Typis Congr. de Propaganda Fide, 1728), p. DCCCXXXII. Vatican Syriac ms. 51, f. 81v, contains, at the end of the ritual for choirmasters, visitors, abbots, abbesses, a marginal rubric: "If it is the superior of a convent". However, the rest of this note has been lost; I. M. Vosté, in *Pontificale*, p. 199, states that "*translata autem prima verba videntur referenda ad sequentem ritum chirotoniae diaconissae*". Perhaps J. S. Assemani's opinion in this regard was based upon this fragmentary rubric.

[13] I. M. Vosté, *Pontificale*, pp. 197–99.

[14] On Bar Hebraeus, see: Baumstark, *Geschichte der Syrischen Literatur*, pp. 312–20; A. Vööbus, *Syrische Kanonessammlungen*, CSCO 317, pp. 499–552.

which is a kind of summary of the previous book; and, especially, the *Nomocanon*, which was a codification of canon law. Bar Hebraeus was only able to bring in deaconesses by transcribing pretty much end to end and without regard to any question of proper sequence or dating many of the texts that we have already encountered in the course of this study. He thus furnished no real testimony with regard to the actual practices of his own age. This should not be surprising. The medieval Latin canonists and liturgists, from Isidore of Seville to Gulielmus Durandus, bishop of Mende, were satisfied with the same methodology.

Here is what Bar Hebraeus wrote in the sixth part of *The Book of the Candelabra of the Sanctuary*:

> Just as widows have been established in the Church, so have deaconesses. As Clement wrote, during the offering of the eucharistic Sacrifice, they were located in the presbyterium, behind the subdeacons. James of Edessa wrote that the deaconess has no permission whatsoever to act within the area of the altar, but that she cleaned the lamps apart from the altar, whenever ordered to do so; she also lighted the lamps. She did not have the right to touch the altar, although she did have the right to remove the Mysteries from the wall tabernacle when no priest or deacon was present. And if there were adult women to be baptized, she anointed them, just as she anointed the sick when they were sick.[15]

The reference to "Clement" here is rather easily recognizable as a reference to the *Testamentum Domini*.[16] The text of the twenty-fourth of the *Canonical Resolutions* of James of Edessa is repeated with the same inexactitudes that we have already encountered in the Syriac pontifical.[17] The alert reader will have noticed, however, that the care of women who were ill has quite clearly become the task of anointing "the sick when they were sick".

In the *Book of Rays* of Bar Hebraeus we find pretty much the same account as that just quoted from *Candelabra*.[18] Finally, section 7 of chapter

---

[15] It is known that *The Book of the Candelabra of the Sanctuary* has been translated and published only in part in the *Patrologie orientale*. Of the *Sixième base*, we have only the German translation of R. Kohlhaas, *Jakobitische Sakramententheologie im 13. Jahrhundert, der Liturgiekommentar des Gregorius Barhebraeus*, LQF 36 (Münster, 1959). The text on deaconesses is to be found on p. 25; commentary on pp. 58–59.

[16] Book I, c. 23:1; I. Rahmani, *Testamentum*, pp. 36–37; P. Ciprotti, *La version syriaque de l'Octateuque de Clément*, p. 36. See Chapter 2, 2, above.

[17] See this chapter's treatment of the Syriac Pontifical, above.

[18] *Livres des rayons* 8:3, quoted in French trans., following the ms. of Sharfe 28/10 by P. Hindo, *Disciplina antiochena, Siri, II, Les personnes*, CCOF, ser. 2, fasc. 26, 1951, p. 334; it seems unlikely that this translation could be entirely correct.

VII of the *Nomocanon* treated of the subject of deaconesses;[19] in the process
it quoted in full "Cephas", that is to say, canon XXI of the *Ecclesiastical
Canons of the Holy Apostles*;[20] "Andrew", or canon XXIV of the same
collection;[21] "Clement", or the passages on widows taken from the
Testament of Our Lord Jesus Christ;[22] the *Didascalia*;[23] canons 11 and 44 of
Laodicea;[24] canon 24 of St. Basil on widows (although logically we would
have expected a citation of canon 44);[25] canon 15 of the Council of
Chalcedon;[26] canons 9 and 11 of the "Replies of the Holy Fathers",
presented as from the hand of Severus of Antioch himself;[27] eight of the
replies of Bishop John bar Qursos of Tella to the "Questions Asked by the
Priest Sargis";[28] and, finally, two of the *Canonical Resolutions* of James of
Edessa.[29] Bar Hebraeus added a gloss following a canon of Patriarch
Qyriakos that was also included: "This means that the subdeacon is
ordained in the sanctuary and not outside the [chancel] gate like the
deaconess [*m^{e}samsonithō*]."[30]

There is no point in trying to expect exactness in quotations included in
Bar Hebraeus; his versions were often very defective. In the case of the
same passage from James of Edessa, quoted differently in the Syriac
pontifical and in two works of Bar Hebraeus, it seems that the very
tradition of the texts handed down by the Syrians was fluid. And the
reader will have noticed that Bar Hebraeus made little distinction between
widows and deaconesses: three different times he applied to deaconesses
texts that actually concerned only widows.[31]

[19] Latin trans. by J. A. Assemani, in A. Mai, *Scriptorum veterum nova collectio*, vol. 10, pt. 2
(Rome: Typis Collegii Urbani, 1838), pp. 50–52.

[20] Chapter 4, 2A, above.

[21] Ibid., especially n. 53. If we are to believe the translation of J. A. Assemani, Bar
Hebraeus read "deaconess" instead of "diaconate" or "ministry".

[22] Bk. I, c. 40:1 (beginning); 41:1; 41:2: I. Rahmani, *Testamentum Domini*, pp. 94–95.

[23] Chap. 16: Chapter 2, 1, above.

[24] For canon 11, see Chapter 5, 1B, above. Canon 44 reads: "Women must not enter the
sanctuary", Joannou, vol. I, pt. 2, p. 148.

[25] Joannou, vol. 2, p. 126.

[26] Chapter 5, 1E, above.

[27] Chapter 6, 4, above.

[28] They are the replies to questions 33, 34, 35, 37–38 (telescoped into one), 40, 42;
Chapter 6, above; but the translation is very unreliable.

[29] Resolutions 23 and 24, Chapter 6, 4, above.

[30] A. Mai, op. cit., p. 53; Syriac text kindly verified for me by Msgr. J. M. Sauget in the
edition by P. Bedjan, *Nomocanon Gregorii Bar Hebraei*, vol. 2 (Lipsiae: Harrasowitz, 1898),
pp. 102–3. This is apropos of canon 3 of the Second Synod held under patriarch of Antioch
Qyriakos (812/813): A. Vööbus, *Syrische Kanonessammlungen*, CSCO, 307, p. 23.

[31] The Synod of Sharfe of 1888 A.D. adopted the text of Severus of Antioch on
deaconesses (Chapter 6, 3A, above): "Duo genera diaconissarum adhibebantur, unum earum
quae in monasteriis feminarum degebant; alterum earum quae in civitatum et oppidorum
ecclesiis constituebantur"; but judged it inopportune to reestablish them: "Sed multa saecula

3. AMONG THE BYZANTINES

Several texts later than the Barberini euchology 336 allow us to verify the existence of deaconesses in Byzantium. One of them is the *Book of Ceremonies* of Emperor Constantine VII Porphyrogenitus (905–959 A.D.). Describing the "Great Sabbath", this book envisaged the emperor, after having offered his gifts, passing out "through the narthex of the part of the church reserved for women, where the deaconesses of the great church habitually find their place".[32] Emperor Alexius I Comnenus (1081–1118 A.D.), according to his daughter Anna Comnena, restored and enlarged a large orphanage in the area of the acropolis in Constantinople, which was located next to a sanctuary dedicated to St. Paul:[33] "Following the example of Solomon, he wanted both male and female cantors for this sanctuary; his concern extended to the work of the deaconesses [ἐπιμελὲς γὰρ καὶ τῶν διακονισσῶν πεποίηκεν ἔργον]; similarly, he was equally concerned with the foreign nuns who had come here from Iberia."[34]

What was this "work of the deaconesses" that seemed to be connected (γάρ) to the orphanage? The terms employed by Anna Comnena should not mislead us. Otherwise there would have had to be a very rapid development taking place within a few decades in the course of the twelfth century.

This was how the Byzantine canonist Theodore Balsamon commented upon canon 15 of the Council of Chalcedon toward the end of that same twelfth century:

The subject matter of this has completely fallen into disuse [ἐσχόλασαν]. Today deaconesses are no longer ordained [οὐ χειροτονεῖται] although certain members of ascetical religious communities [τίνες τῶν ἀσκητεριῶν] are erroneously styled deaconesses. For there is a law that prohibits women from entering the sanctuary.[35] How then could a woman who does not even have the right to approach the altar possibly exercise the office of deacon?[36]

---

transiere ex quo in Ecclesia syriaca institutio et officium diaconissarum propter temporum mutationem cessavit, nec opus est eas hodie revocare". In P. Hindo, *Disciplina antiochena antica*, Siri, vol. 2, CCOF, ser. 2, fasc. 26 (1951), p. 334, n. 1.

[32] *De ceriminoiis aulae byzantinae*, bk. I, chap. 44 (35), PG 112, cols. 425–26; trans. A. Vogt, *Le Livre des cérémonies*, vol. I, *Collection byzantine* (Paris: Belles Lettres, 1935), p. 171.

[33] Cf. R. Janin, *La géographie ecclésiastique de l'Empire byzantin*, 1st pt., *Le Siège de Constantinople et le patriarcat oecuménique*, vol. 3, *Les églises et les monastères*, 2nd ed., *Publications de l'Institut français d'études byzantines* (Paris, 1969), pp. 567–68.

[34] Anna Comnena, *Alexiade*, XV:7, 8, ed. and trans. B. Leib, vol. 3, *Collection byzantine* (Paris: Belles Lettres, 1945), p. 217.

[35] Canon 44 of Laodicea, and it reads θυσιαστήριον, not βῆμα.

[36] *Scholia in Concilium Chalcedonense*, PG 137, col. 441. It should be noted that, at the beginning of the same century, John Zonaras and Alexius Aristhenes, PG 137, cols. 441–44, commented on this canon as if it were still in force; but that was the typical proceeding of that age.

From this passage it is clear that Theodore Balsamon possessed very inexact knowledge about the historical institution of deaconesses. He was not alone in knowing little about the deaconesses of earlier times. Patriarch Mark III of Alexandria (1164–89) wrote to him, as we will recall,[37] asking for information about deaconesses: "The holy canons make mention of deaconesses. We would like to know what their function is." This was how Theodore Balsamon replied:

> Formerly [πάλαι] there were sometimes recognized orders [τάγματα] of deaconesses, and they too had their place in the sanctuary [βαθμὸν ἐν τῷ βήματι]. But the impurity of their menstrual periods dictated their separation from the divine and holy sanctuary. However, in the most holy church of Constantinople, some women are nevertheless designated as deaconesses. Certainly they have thereby no access to the altar but in most respects simply form part of the assembly [ἐκκλησιάζουσαι δὲ τὰ πολλά]; they direct the women's group according to the rules of the Church [τὴν γυναικωνῖτιν ἐκκλησιαστικῶς διορθούμεναι].[38]

Theodore's information is doubly erroneous. At no time did deaconesses in the Byzantine rite ever have access to the sanctuary, nor was this prohibition in any way based upon the views of impurity found in the Book of Leviticus. The only text that made any allusion to this was not even Greek. It was a response of the Syrian bishop, John of Tella, and this question concerned only the competence of the deaconess in the convent in the absence of a priest or deacon.[39] But when Theodore recorded that "today deaconesses are no longer ordained", must we take him quite literally? Or did he, owing to the inexact idea he had of the ancient institution of deaconess, consider the deaconesses present in Constantinople in his time not to be *true* deaconesses?

Ignorance of deaconesses was even more pronounced in 1335, when Matthew Blastares[40] wrote his alphabetical *Syntagma* of the canons, in which he dealt at length with the subject of deaconesses:[41]

> Formerly [ἦν ποτε] there existed an order of women deacons [τὸ τῶν διακόνων γυναικῶν τάγμα] and another order of widows. But what exactly

---

[37] Chapter 6, 3, above.

[38] *Responsa ad interrogationes Marci* 35, PG 138, col. 988.

[39] Chapter 6, 4, above. *Réponse 37 aux Questions posées par le prêtre Sargîs*. A similar prohibition with regard to widows is contained in the *Testament of Our Lord Jesus Christ*, I, 42:2: "If she [the widow] follows the rules, she will remain inside the temple but will not approach the altar, not because she herself is impure but out of respect for the altar", I. Rahmani, op. cit., p. 101; P. Ciprotti, op. cit., p. 54.

[40] On Blastares: A. Van Hove, *Prolegomena*, 2nd ed., *Commentarium Lovaniense in Codicem . . .* I, 1, p. 169, n. 7 (Mechliniae: Dessain, 1945).

[41] *Syntagma, littera Gamma*, PG 144, cols. 1173–76.

the ministry of deacons was in the era of the Fathers is almost universally unknown today [τοῖς πᾶσι σχεδὸν ἠγνόηται νῦν]. There are those who claim that they served at the baptism of women, because it was considered a sacrilege for adult women being baptized to be viewed naked by men. Others claim that they were permitted to approach the altar [θυσιαστήριον] and to share a role with male deacons pretty much on an equal basis with them. Later, however, the holy Fathers forbade them to approach the altar and carry out any service [ὑπηρεσίας] there because of their menstrual periods. That women were once permitted to approach the altar may be concluded from, among numerous other indices, the funeral oration composed by Gregory the Theologian [St. Gregory Nazianzus] for his sister.[42] However, I personally do not believe it plausible that a woman could have been a minister (διάκονον) of the holy and unbloody Sacrifice. It would be contrary to reason to allow this. Women are not allowed to teach in public, nor are they allowed to accede the rank of deacon [εἰς διακόνου βαθμόν]. Deacons are charged with clarifying the teaching for those infidels who decide to accept baptism. . . .

Blastares then described ordination as recorded "in the old books [τὰ παλαιὰ τῶν βιβλίων] that enumerated all the various ordinations". However, the "old books" to which he referred were the euchologies, some of which were contemporaneous with him.[43] Here again we encounter the anachronisms so characteristic of some liturgical books. The ritual for the ordination of a deaconess was still being copied and recopied at the same time that Matthew Blastares was asserting that this ritual had long since fallen into disuse. Indeed, Theodore Balsamon was asserting the same thing around the end of the twelfth century. Both Blastares and Balsamon, in fact, demonstrated how thoroughly ignorant they were of the institution of deaconesses; their knowledge consisted only of a few bits and pieces gathered from here and there.

Not all of the copyists, of course, were slaves to routine to the same degree. The extract from a euchology to be found in Greek manuscript 2509 (formerly 1741) in the Bibliothèque Nationale, for example, does not contain this ritual.[44] Nor, for similar reasons, was it included in the

[42] This assertion of Blastares is not sustainable: it was only at night, without possessing any office, and as a gesture of despair that Gorgonia approached the altar. See Saint Gregory Nazianzus, Oratio 8 (olim 11), n. 18, PG 35, cols. 809–12: gravely ill and "despairing of human remedies she turned toward the universal physician in the middle of the night . . . she prostrated herself in faith before the altar, praying as she cried"; she imitated thereby the woman in the gospel with a hemorrhage: "What did she do? She leaned her head against the altar with tears and cries and declared that she would not go away until she was cured."

[43] Chapter 7, 1B.

[44] J. Morin, Commentarius de sacris Ecclesiae ordinationibus (Parisiis: G. Maturas, 1655), pp. 86–87; Antuerpiae (= Amstelodami), H. Desbordes, 1695, p. 70. H. Omont, Inventaire sommaire des manuscrits grecs de la Bibliothèque Nationale, vol. 2 (Paris: Picard, 1888), pp. 274–75.

euchology of Allatius, Barberini Greek manuscript 390, dating from the sixteenth century.[45]

The great liturgist Simeon, archbishop of Thessalonica (d. 1429), in his *De Sacris Ordinibus*, dealt at length with lectors, subdeacons, deacons, priests, sacred vestments, the bishop and the patriarch.[46] He did not neglect to mention even the office of deputy [τοῦ δεσποτάτου] or that of chandler [κηροφόρου]; he did not understand why these offices had been dropped, considering that they had still been active ministries in the church of Thessalonica not long before [πρὸ ὀλίγου] and were fully "described in the ancient formularies".[47] However, Simeon never so much as mentioned the word "deaconess", nor does it appear in the index prepared by John Molivdos.[48]

4. WERE THERE DEACONESSES
AMONG THE MARONITES?

The Maronite pontifical, tracing its history as far back as possible, that is to say, back to the thirteenth century,[49] has never contained any ritual for the ordination of a deaconess.[50] Nor is there any mention of deaconesses in any of the other rituals. Most of the other rituals distinguish, with regard to the prebaptismal anointing, between the role of priest, who anointed the head only, and the role of the deacon, who anointed the rest

---

[45] A. Jacob, *Les euchologes du fonds Barberini grec de la Bibliothèque Vaticane*, in *Didaskalia* 4 (1974), pp. 169–73.

[46] Simeon of Thessalonica, *Dialogus, De sacris ordinationibus*, cc. 156–238, PG 155, cols. 361–453.

[47] Op. cit., c. 156, PG 155, col. 361.

[48] Reproduced by Migne, PG 155, cols. 977–1004. In order to be complete, we must mention the fifteenth response of Nilus Diasorenus, metropolitan of Rhodes (ca. 1365–76 A.D.), to the hieromonach Jonas: "In casu necessitatis potestne monialis porrigere sacerdoti incensum? *Resp*. Monialis magni habitus, aetate provecta, non prohibetur quominus ob necessitatem sacerdoti porrigat incensum servitii causa, quia et antiquitus ordinabantur quae sexaginta annos attigerunt." In I. Croce, *Textus selecti ex operibus commentatorum byzantinorum iuris ecclesiastici*, CCOF, ser. 2, fasc. 5 (1939), p. 227, following the ed. A. Almazov (Odessa, 1903), p. 73. Finally, let us mention that G. Ferrari, *Le diaconesse nella tradizione orientale*, in *Oriente cristiano* 14 (1974): pp. 46–48, believed that he had found traces of the existence of deaconesses in a Graeco-Albanian community in Sicily; in my opinion, it required considerable imagination to interpret in this sense the necessary citations from a "Treatise against the Greeks" from 1579–1580.

[49] On the history of the Maronite Pontifical, see P. Dib, *Etude sur la liturgie maronite* (Paris: Lethielleux, 1919), pp. 169–74.

[50] Denzinger, pp. 108–226, following J. Morin, De Renaudot and J. A. Assemani, *Codex liturgicus Ecclesiae universae*, vols. 9–10 (Rome: Barbiellini, 1756–1758).

of the body, as in the Jacobite rite. But there is not a single mention of any possible participation by a deaconess in the ritual of baptism, nor of any possible problem posed by female nudity at baptism. In fact, the problem of possible adult candidates for baptism is not raised. It is true, of course, that all of the copies of extant rituals are relatively modern. The oldest of them, Vatican Syriac manuscript 313, probably dates from around the fifteenth century.[51]

The Synod of Mount Lebanon of 1736 nevertheless raised the question of deaconesses and tried to deal with it in an integral fashion. The synod produced a curious text, which consists of a plethora of the formulas that we have already encountered. The origins of these formulas varied considerably, but not a single one of them was Maronite, properly speaking; certainly none of them represented or reflected any real usage among the Maronites. The entire text was artificial and, indeed, "archeological".

With regard to this Maronite synodal text, we should note that the treatment of deaconesses came not in its second part treating *De Sacramento Ordinis*, as we would have expected, but only in the third part, *De Ministris, Presbyteris, et Praelatis*. The second part described ordinations and blessings of the psalmist (*succentor*), the lector (*anagnostes*), the subdeacon, the deacon, the archdeacon, the priest, the visitor, the archpriest, the choir leader, the bishop and the patriarch.[52] The second part also indicated, however, that, as in the Roman rite, the offices of porters, exorcists and acolytes had existed.[53] In the third part, in its second chapter entitled "*De cantore, lectore, subdiacono et diacono deque diaconissa, exorcista, archidiacono et oeconomo*", this paragraph on deaconesses was included:

> Diaconissae apud nos sunt, quae vel perpetua virginitate servata, vel secundis repudiatis nuptiis, castitatem dicant et ministeriis quibusdam ecclesiasticis, episcopi benedictione accedente, devoventur.[54]

Unless I am mistaken, this paragraph is the echo of a canon found in the *Apostolic Constitutions*.[55] In fact, the Synod immediately went on to

---

[51] A. Mouhanna, *Les rites de l'initiation dans l'Eglise maronite*, *Christianismos*, 1 (Rome: P. Institutum Orientale, 1978), analyzed seven rituals, of which several were from the sixteenth century. Cf. also P. Dib, *L'initiation chrétienne dans le rite maronite*, in *Revue de l'Orient chrétien*, 2nd ser., 5 (1910), pp. 73–84.

[52] I. D. Mansi, *Sacrorum conciliorum nova et amplissima collectio* . . . continuata curantibus J. B. Martin and L. Petit, vol. 38 (Parisiis: Welter, 1907), cols. 141–49. On the Synod and its vicissitudes, see P. Dib, *Maronite (Eglise)*, DTC 10 (1927), cols. 79–86.

[53] I. D. Mansi, op. cit., cols. 150–51.

[54] Ibid., col. 163.

[55] VI, 17:4, ed. Funk, p. 341; Chapter 3, 2, above.

explain, expressly citing both the *Apostolic Constitutions* as well as St.
Epiphanius, that there were two types of deaconesses: widows and
virgins. And this is how the functions of deaconesses were then set forth:

> [Diaconissarum] officia sunt, ut mulieri honestati ac pudori in Ecclesia
> consulatur. Nam diaconissarum opera necessaria est:
>
> 1. ut sanctae portae, per quas mulieribus ad ecclesiam patet aditus, ab iis
> custodiantur, et quo unaquaeque sedeat loco, statuatur;
>
> 2. ut baptizandas mulieres exuant vestibus, baptizatasque et ex baptisterio
> eductas suscipiant;
>
> 3. ut chrismate vel oleo nuda earum corpora tam in baptismo et confir-
> matione quam in extrema unctione ungant, defunctas etiam lavent et sepeliant;
>
> 4. ut rusticis et imperitis mulieribus principia fidei vel baptismi ritus
> exponant;
>
> 5. ut negotiis urgentibus mulieres episcopum vel presbyterum vel diaconum
> alloqui volentes, diaconissae tamquam honestatis illarum testes deducant;
>
> 6. Quum de amissa integritate virgo Deo sacrata in suspicionem venit, ut
> diaconissarum examini et sententiae relinquatur explorandum;
>
> 7. Denique ut earum curae moniales in monasteriis et tota sacra coeno-
> biorum virginum suppellex committatur.[56]

"Guardians of the doors". This expression, of course, comes from the
Apostolic Constitutions (II, 57 and VIII, 28). From the archetype of book
VIII, this mention passed over into the Alexandrian *Synodos*.[57] It is also to
be found in the Mesopotamian *"Ordo and the Canons concerning Ordination"*
of Tagrit (Tikrit).[58] The role of women as helpers for baptisms goes all the
way back to the *Didascalia* and, of course, reappears in the works that
derive from or depend upon the *Didascalia*. As for anointings, it might be
considered surprising to see spelled out, alongside the traditional role of
deaconesses in prebaptismal anointings, a mention concerning their participation in the anointings connected with confirmation and the sacrament
of the sick as well. This reference to the sacrament of the sick, or "extreme
unction", is nothing else but the Latin version of the formula of Bar
Hebraeus to the effect that the deaconess "anointed the sick when they
were sick".[59] And Bar Hebraeus had merely adopted and made explicit
the text of the pontifical of Michael the Great: "She visits and anoints
women who are ill."[60] The role of preparing for baptism country women
and women who were illiterate did not come from any Greek or Oriental
text; it was taken from a Latin treatise, which we will be examining later

---

[56] I. D. Mansi, op. cit., col. 163.
[57] Sahidic canon 71, Arabic canon 58, Ethiopic canon 59.
[58] Chapter 2, 3, above.
[59] Part 2 of this chapter, above.
[60] Ibid.

on, the *Statuta Ecclesiae Antiqua*.[61] The duty of accompanying women wishing to speak to the bishop, priest or deacon came from the *Apostolic Constitutions*.[62] The examining of the integrity of a consecrated virgin could refer, at least implicitly, to St. Epiphanius;[63] but it more probably was derived from the Latin canon law. Finally, the supervisory responsibility over nuns and the affairs of their convents was, as we have now abundantly seen, the traditional role for deaconesses in earlier times, in both the Byzantine and Syrian traditions.

But the entire description really reflects a condition of desuetude. The 1736 synod actually prohibited baptism by immersion in any case, for reasons of public decency.[64] Moreover, the synod was quite conscious of the anachronism involved, since it added further:

Quamvis autem diaconissarum officia quoad sacramenta baptismi, confirmationis et extremae unctionis iam diu cessarint, quum non amplius totius corporis unctiones fiant, durant tamen quoad dicatas Deo in sacris coenobiis virgines, quibus abbatissae praeficiuntur. Abbatissae enim diaconissarum benedictionem accipiunt, et munia omnia quae illis in conciliis sunt concessa exsequuntur. Ad altare tamen accedere, aut communionem monialibus praebere, etiam in absentia presbyteri aut diaconi, nullatenus permittuntur.

Si quis vero episcopus, praeter monasteriorum abbatissas, diaconissam propter urgentem necessitatem ordinare voluerit, mulierem ordinet, cuius de castitate et doctrina secundum allegatos canones testimonium habeatur, ut possit mulieribus in ecclesia praeesse, rudioresque feminas in iis, quae ad sacramenta baptismi, confessionis et communionis spectant, instruere.[65]

The second paragraph here echoes the Syriac pontifical of Michael the Great in opening up the possibility of the bishop ordaining a deaconess in exceptional circumstances. This exception would seem to be aimed at carrying out an effective pastoral ministry. On the other hand, the Mount Lebanon synod established the equivalence of deaconess and abbess to such a degree that abbesses are to receive "the blessing of deaconesses".

However, any bishop ever attempting to carry through with this ritual and put it into practice would have found himself embarrassed, for in chapter 3 of the fourth part of the synodal text, *De Monialibus*, the synod also went on the record with a ritual for the blessing of abbesses and another one for the blessing of consecrated virgins.[66] Both of these rituals were very economical and symmetrical; in them there is hardly the

---

[61] Chapter 9, 2B, below.

[62] II, 26:6, ed. Funk, p. 105; Chapter 3, 1, above.

[63] Chapter 5, 2A, above.

[64] Second pt., c. 2, n. 2, I. D. Mansi, op. cit., col. 43.

[65] I. D. Mansi, op. cit., cols. 163–64.

[66] Ibid., cols. 252–53.

slightest hint or memory that abbesses are supposed to receive the blessing of deaconesses; the only reference to this, in fact, comes in a stipulation that this blessing is not to be accorded to either widows or virgins still living in the home of their parents.[67]

5. WERE THERE DEACONESSES AMONG THE ARMENIANS AND GEORGIANS?

We will recall that there were texts that seemed to attest to the presence of deaconesses in Roman Armenia in the fourth century.[68] However, this evidence remains isolated and precarious. Greater Armenia, on the other hand, underwent such frequent and grave persecutions that we have very little information about convents of women there.[69] Dependent at one and the same time both upon Cappadocian usages and Hierosolymitan ones, the Armenian liturgy could hardly have kept a place reserved for women to assist in the baptism of women. The question is whether the successive prohibitions that we find in the canons of the fifth century do not perhaps mirror a reaction against possible Persian or Chaldean infiltrations. For example:

> Baptism must be carried out with the fear of God in mind. Women should not dare to stand beside the priests at the time of baptism, as certain women have boldly done, attempting to baptize along with the priests. Rather, women should remain praying in their proper place.[70]

This canon has been attributed to the Catholicos Sahak (Isaac the Great, d. 438). More likely, however, it appeared in the form of an edict under his successor, Joseph, at the Synod of Sahapivan in 444.[71] The same theme was repeated in 527 by the Council of Dvin in its canon 16. It then appeared in this form, issued by Catholicos Nerses II (548–557):

> Women should not have the boldness to stand near the priests. Rather, the deacons should serve the priests, and the women should pray in their own

---

[67] I. D. Mansi, op. cit., col. 250, can. 20.

[68] Chapter 6, 1, above.

[69] G. Amaduni, *Disciplina armena, II, Monachismo, Studio storico-canonico e fonti canoniche*, CCOF, ser. 2, fasc. 12 (Venice: Mechitaristi, 1940), pp. 138–41.

[70] V. Hakobyan, *Kanonagirk' Hayoc'*, vol. I (Yerevan, 1964), pp. 377–78, reference and translation kindly communicated to me by Dom Athanase Renoux, monk of En-Calcat, who is currently one of the most outstanding specialists on the subject of the Armenian liturgy. I owe to him a knowledge of a number of the points that I have been able to make in this work on the problem of deaconesses in the Armenian Church.

[71] G. Garitte, *La Narratio de rebus Armeniae, édition critique et commentaire*, CSCO 132 (1952), pp. 88–91.

places, not attempting to assist the priests or take the place of the deacons—as we have heard happens.[72]

In these canons the term used for "women" is *kanayk'*—a word that means "married women". In itself, then, this term does not correspond to what was understood by the term "deaconess" in the churches in which deaconesses were accepted. In the ancient canonical literature, the term "woman deacon", *sarkawag kin*, is simply not to be found except in the Armenian translations of the "Canons of Clement" and those of the Council of Nicaea.[73]

It is not until the twelfth century, in the *Liber processualis* of Mxit'ar Gos, a codifier who lived between 1130–1213, that we encounter a real discussion of deaconesses. It appears in connection with the rule concerning strictly cloistered nuns:

Sunt et mulierum diaconissae ordinatae chirotonia ad praedicandum mulieribus et legendum evangelium, ne ingrediatur ibi vir et ne illa extra conventum mulierum egrediatur; et quando sacerdotes baptismum conferunt adultis mulieribus, adveniunt diaconissae piscinam et abluunt aqua mulieres, et sacerdos ungit intra velamen.

Regula diaconissarum eadem est in omnibus cum credentibus (mulieribus); tantum crucem habet ipsa in fronte et scapulas ad dexteram humerorum.

Neque aliquid novi vel inordinati opinemini hoc, o sancti fratres, sed a traditione sanctorum Apostolorum discimus; nam ait quod "commendo vobis Phoebem sororem nostram, quae est diaconissa Ecclesiae".[74]

The adjuration with which this description concludes seems to betray an ambition on the part of Gos to convince the reader that what he was saying was wholly traditional, whereas he must have known that it was not: not only did he go plainly contrary to sixth-century canons on baptism; but also, at the time that he wrote, it had been a long time since there had even been any regular baptisms of adults, and even if there had been adult baptisms, it is not clear how they could have been carried out at cloistered convents. On the other hand, it would have been normal if the preaching for such strictly cloistered nuns had been confided to a deaconess (*sarkawaguhi*). In fact, after Gos, this principle was taken up again by Smbat Aparapet (Constable Sempad), in his *Code* of 1265,[75] and by Stefan

---

[72] V. Hakobyan, op. cit., p. 485 (translation of A. Renoux).

[73] Ibid., pp. 76, 130, to which the tables refer.

[74] Translation by G. Amaduni, op. cit., p. 140, of chap. 113, of *Liber processualis*; the Armenian text given on facing pages is taken from the Pasdamiantz edition (Echmiadzin, 1880), pp. 257–58.

[75] Ed. J. Karst, *Sempadscher Kodex* (Strassburg, 1905), indicated by G. Amaduni, op. cit., p. 140.

Orbelian, in his *History of the Province of Sunik*, which dates from the end of the thirteenth century.[76]

That there were nevertheless deaconesses in the convents seems to have been assumed by a rubric of the Venice *Mastoc'* (ritual), San Lazzaro, manuscript 457, which dates from the ninth or tenth centuries. In the *Ordo* for the creation of an anchorite contained in this document, we find the following: "The same ritual is to be employed when conferring the habit on women, with the only exception to be that deaconesses are the ones who will divest the candidate [of her secular clothes]."[77]

The formulary that the bishop would have employed in conferring "ordination" upon a deaconess in a strictly cloistered convent is not to be found in the current euchology. Perhaps it is to be found in the great *Mastoc'* (pontifical) manuscript, but this document is not accessible. Many of the other ancient sources are silent on the matter.[78] Conybeare has indicated the presence of this ritual in the San Lazzaro manuscript 199 (323), which dates from 1216.[79] Dom Athanasius Renoux found it in the Yerevan *Mastoc'* 907, dating from the seventeenth century, but which was supposed to have been copied from a ninth-century manuscript (folios 309v–310r), as follows:

> *Ordination of Women Deacons (sarkawagkananc') called Deaconesses*: The forty-fourth Psalm is recited. The bishop then says this prayer: "Gracious and most merciful Lord, you who created all things with a word of command, and by the incarnation of your only begotten Son, made equal in holiness both male and female—since it has seemed good to you to grant not only to men but also to [married] women the grace of the Holy Spirit, choose now in the same way your [female] servants to perform the work of service as needed by your holy Church and give them the grace of your Holy Spirit: may he keep her in the pure justice, mercy and compassion of your Christ, to whom

[76] Ed. G. Chanazarian (Paris, 1859): 2:80.

[77] F. Conybeare, *Rituale Armenorum* (Oxford: Clarendon, 1905), p. 156. Translation verified for me by Dom Athanase Renoux by reference to the Armenian text published in the *Grand catalogue des manuscrits arméniens de la Bibliothèque des Mékhitaristes de Venise* (in Armenian), vol. 3 (Venice: San Lazzaro, 1966), col. 32.

[78] It is not in the Venice San Lazzaro manuscript 457 (320), cited above, or in the Aleppo manuscript 26 (eleventh century) or in the Yerevan manuscript 1001 (tenth century). This has been verified for me by Dom A. Renoux, who could find no mention of it in the tables of the catalogues of either Venice or Vienna. The catalogue of Venice, however, notes (vol. 3, col. 74) with respect to manuscript 199 (323): "This canon does not appear in the oldest rituals, that is to say, those of the tenth century. It appeared in the *Mastoc'* in the twelfth or thirteenth centuries. There is a prayer but without a ritual of 'ordination'. It was a question of a 'prayer', or 'blessing', or 'benediction' for the woman who had been chosen [elected?] to be a servant carrying out a work of service in response to the needs of the Church." It will be immediately evident that there were exceptions to this rule.

[79] Folio 49b: F. Conybeare, op. cit., p. 535; *Grand catalogue*, vol. 3, col. 74.

with you, all-powerful Father, and the life-giving and liberating Holy Spirit, is given all glory, power and honor now and forever. . . ."[80]

It is rather well known to what degree the Georgian liturgy was dependent upon the Armenian liturgy. There exists a Georgian pontifical,[81] copied in the last part of the tenth century or around the beginning of the eleventh, which reproduces for the order of Mass a translation from the Greek; this was at a time when Georgia adhered closely to the Jerusalem rite. This pontifical contains three prayers[82] for the blessing of deaconesses, the second of which is the very one we have already encountered according to two Armenian rituals:

> O Lord, God of hosts, who before all the women commanded Miriam, sister to Moses, to invoke his name; who gave the gift of prophecy to Deborah; who so ordered things in the new economy of salvation through your Holy Spirit that deacons should be "serious, not double tongued, not addicted to much wine" (1 Tim 3:8), but should teach with benevolence and give an example of everything that is pleasing—deign now to promote to that same dignity your [female] servant here present so that she may anoint with oil those who come to holy baptism, escort them to the sacred fount and become a "deacon"[83] of your Church according to the order of Phoebe whom the apostle ordained to be a minister at Cenchreae. Give her also the gift of instructing and convincing the young in the fulfilling of their duties. Give her the grace to express everything in your name so that, serving you in a worthy manner and without fault, she may be emboldened to intercede at the hour fixed by your Christ, with whom. . . .

> You who created all things with a word of command and who by the incarnation and passion of your only Son sanctified and made equal man and woman as it pleased you; you who gave the grace of your Holy Spirit not only to men but also to women—establish now officially your [female] servant here present in this service, O all-powerful God. Give her the grace of your spirit that she may walk in pleasing fashion and without reproach in the works of justice and thereby be given the pardon of your Christ, with whom. . . .

> All-powerful Lord, who have embellished your Church with the ministry of the diaconate and filled with the grace of the Holy Spirit the multitude of

---

[80] Translation of Dom A. Renoux of Yerevan manuscript 907; *le Grand catalogue* . . . , ibid., only gives a part of the text of San Lazzaro manuscript 199 (323); it gives enough, however, to enable us to identify it as the same as Yerevan manuscript 907.

[81] Tiflis manuscript 86, which contains an ordination ritual following the liturgy of St. James: C. Conybeare and O. Wardrop. "The Georgian Version of the Liturgy of St. James", in *Revue de l'Orient chrétien* 18 (1913): 396–410; 19 (1914): 155–73.

[82] Op. cit., 19 (1914): 165.

[83] "*Diaconad*, a deacon: there is no gender in the Georgian language", ibid., note 3.

churches, deign now, O Lord, to promote to this same degree of the ministry
of the diaconate your [female] servant N. here present. Give her the grace
to fulfill with respect and sanctity this noble ministry. Accept and ratify her
vow and give her the strength to persevere, for to you. . . .

Such as they are, these three blessings were not simply borrowed from
rituals known to the other churches. They do include, of course, a number
of elements in common with some of the formularies that we have
examined in the preceding chapters. The allusion to Miriam and Deborah
refers to book VIII of the *Apostolic Constitutions*, no doubt by way of the
Octateuch of Clement. It is curious, however, that the other examples from
the Old Testament—Hannah, Huldah and the guardians of the doors—
should have been dropped. The mention of Phoebe is to be found only in
the Byzantine euchology. With the *Apostolic Constitutions*, again, can be
identified the formula "you who gave the grace of your Holy Spirit not
only to men but also to women". We can also perhaps discern here traces
of the Chaldean pontifical, in which we could read such things as: "You
who made all things through the power of your word"; "you who were
equally well pleased with both men and women"; "give her the gift to
instruct the women".

But all these similarities are much too general to allow us to speak of any
outright borrowing or derivation. Are we perhaps dealing with a Hierosolymitan formulary, one based on the Jerusalem rite? I do not think so. I
do not think so because we also find a reference here to the ministry of
deaconesses assisting at baptism in a way that does not occur in any other
ritual. And this was a ministry that seems never to have been practiced in
Jerusalem.[84]

CONCLUSION

In the end, the institution of deaconesses in the Eastern churches appears
to have been much more limited than the abundant references and documentation we possess on the subject might at first have led us to believe.
The institution was geographically limited, since it was not accepted by
the church of Egypt, or among the Maronites or (except very belatedly)
by the Armenians. The institution was quite simply unknown to the
Slavic peoples, who adopted Byzantine practices at a period after the
Byzantines had ceased to accord any role to deaconesses. For the institution
was also very limited in time. Even though it is not always easy to fix the
exact date of its desuetude in the various churches, it does seem pretty

---

[84] Chapter 6, 3Aff., above.

clear that, by the end of the tenth or eleventh centuries, deaconesses had pretty much disappeared in the East, even though the memory of them continued, anachronistically, to be revived in the recopying of liturgical books, and—in a defective and imprecise fashion—in the tradition of the canonists.

Even when the institution was at its height, it assumed somewhat different forms, according to the needs of particular churches. In the extreme Eastern regions of the Roman Empire and, beyond them, in Chaldea and Persia, social mores required the creation of a feminine ministry for the evangelization of women, for assisting at baptisms and for visiting sick. In those regions where the separation of the sexes was not so strict, this particular kind of feminine ministry was not required; nevertheless, the female diaconate was introduced as a degree of honor, either to consecrate with religious solemnity a candidate entering a religious state of life or, especially, to enhance the dignity of the woman religious called upon to provide direction in a convent.

Already limited to certain Eastern regions in any case, the baptismal function of deaconesses ceased when adult women typically ceased to be primary baptismal candidates and infant baptism took over. As we have seen, this was a development that occurred quite early—to such a degree that, almost everywhere, deaconesses quickly became identified with abbesses. Since in the East convents were often located in out-of-the-way places where the regular presence of priests and deacons could hardly be counted upon, the hegumenē-deaconess came to substitute for them in many respects: distribution of Communion, the recitation of the divine office and so on. But even this category of deaconess gradually disappeared. We have to ask why. If any hypothesis may be ventured, I personally believe it came about because of the creation of a liturgical rite of the blessing of the hegumenē that proved to be more appropriate to the actual situation. A ritual for the ordination of the deaconess came to seem more like merely an "archeological" memory or even an outright fiction. However, we still lack too many of the necessary elements that would illuminate the history of some of the rituals in the various Greek and Eastern euchologies and pontificals.

PART TWO

Deaconesses in the Latin Church

CHAPTER NINE

There Were No Deaconesses in the Latin Church During the First Five Centuries

In the eastern extremities of the Roman Empire, the institution of deaconesses appeared during the first decades of the third century and went on to develop in various ways in the Greek-speaking and Semitic-speaking churches. The Latin-speaking churches, however, did not experience the same development of this institution, nor did the church of Egypt. This may have been the result of the fact that, in Rome as in Alexandria, the *Apostolic Tradition* of St. Hippolytus of Rome remained the ideal for ecclesiastical organization. We have observed how this document envisaged no place for any feminine ministry. More than that, doubtlessly, the lack of the institution of deaconesses in the West was also the result of the fact that no such feminine ministry was considered necessary; it even aroused suspicions in some quarters.

However, some historians have nevertheless been so thoroughly convinced of the existence of deaconesses throughout the entire ancient Church that they have diligently searched for any evidence to support their thesis—they have searched even beyond the bounds of probability.

1. NO DEACONESSES IN ROME, AFRICA OR SPAIN

A. In Rome

The situation was absolutely clear so far as Rome was concerned: there was no possible role for deaconesses. We possess two different enumerations of the different categories of ministries to be distinguished within the assembly of the Christian people. About fifty years or so after Hippolytus had published his *Apostolic Tradition*, in the year 251 or 253 A.D., Pope St. Cornelius, writing to Fabius, the bishop of Antioch, on the subject of the Novatian schism, expressed surprise that the dissident Novatian could have been so ignorant of the church that had existed before his time in Rome—a church that was all the more visible in that it possessed a very elaborate organization: "Forty-six priests, seven deacons, seven subdeacons, forty-two acolytes, fifty-two exorcists, lectors and doorkeepers and more than fifteen hundred widows and dependent poor people".[1] Two new ministries had thus been added in the church of Rome since the time of Hippolytus: exorcists and doorkeepers. There was no question of confessors in this list. The numerous widows mentioned were no doubt beneficiaries of assistance, as were orphans. If there had been any deaconesses, Pope Cornelius would surely not have omitted mentioning such a visible constituent element of the local church.

This list of ministries has often been linked with another similar list, preserved in one of the monitions of the universal prayer for Good Friday. Although we possess the text of this latter list only in sacramentaries dating from the seventh to the eighth centuries, it is generally considered to reflect the structure of the Roman church a short time after the end of the persecutions:

> Oremus et pro omnibus episcopis, presbyteris, diaconibus, subdiaconibus, acolythis, exorcistis, lectoribus, ostiariis, confessoribus, virginibus, viduis et pro omni populo sancto Dei.[2]

B. In Africa

We have already taken note of the fact that, in Tertullian's time, there were no deaconesses in North Africa. As Roger Gryson has aptly stated: "The assertion of various authors that, for Tertullian, *vidua* is synonymous with *diaconissa* and *viduatus* synonymous with *diaconatus* is an entirely arbitrary assertion."[3] The same silence on the subject is to be found in the works of St. Cyprian.[4] It is similarly in vain that we seek the slightest mention of deaconesses in the documents of the African councils,[5] in African inscriptions,[6] in the letters of St. Augustine[7] or in any of the anecdotes with which the latter embellished *The City of God*.[8] In spite of this, F. Van der Meer was so convinced that it was impossible for the diocese of Hippo to

---

[1] Eusebius, *Ecclesiastical History*, 6:43:11, Fr. trans. G. Bardy, SC 41, 1955, p. 156.

[2] P. de Clerck, *La prière universelle dans les liturgies latines anciennes*, LQF 62 (Münster: Aschendorff, 1977), pp. 136–39.

[3] R. Gryson, *Ministère des femmes*, p. 48, who listed some of these authors in his notes. See Chapter 1, 2C, above.

[4] Ed. G. Hartel, CSEL 3:3 (1871), *Index nominum et rerum*, pp. 384–85.

[5] C. Munier, *Concilia Africae a. 345–a. 525*, CCL 149 (1974), *Index rerum*, p. 385; *Lexica et notabilia*, p. 402.

[6] There is nothing, for example, in A. L. Delattre, *L'épigraphie funéraire chrétienne à Carthage* (Tunis: Barlier, 1926); similarly, there is nothing in N. Duval and F. Prevot, *Recherches archéologiques à Haïdra, I, Les inscriptions chrétiennes*, Collection de l'Ecole français de Rome, 18 (Rome, 1975). However, there is no complete, comprehensive collection of the Christian inscriptions of North Africa; cf. N. Duval, *Les recherches d'épigraphie chrétienne en Afrique du Nord*, 1962–72, in *Mélanges de l'Ecole française de Rome, Antiquité* 85 (1973), pp. 335–44.

[7] A. Goldbacher, CSEL 58: 192, 360.

[8] F. Van der Meer, *Saint Augustin, pasteur d'âmes* (Colmar, Alsatia, 1955), translated from the Dutch edition published in Utrecht, 1949, and augmented with notes by H. Chirat,

get along without deaconesses that he introduced them twice into his rather fanciful description of the liturgy presided over there by St. Augustine. Needless to say, he could not support this from any text.[9]

C. In Spain

As far as Spain was concerned, the only text usually brought forward[10] did not in fact concern deaconesses at all, not even for the purpose of excluding them. The text in question is canon 1 of the First Council of Saragossa, held in the year 380 A.D.; this canon warned Catholic women against irregular assemblies, no doubt those of the Priscillianists:

Ut feminae fideles a virorum alienorum coetibus separentur.	Women among the faithful should not mingle with groups of aliens [to the Catholic Church].
Ut mulieres omnes ecclesiae catholicae et fideles a virorum alienorum lectione et coetibus separentur, vel ad ipsas legentes aliae studio vel docendi vel discendi conveniant, quoniam hoc Apostolus iubet. Ab universis episcopis dictum est: Anathema futuros qui hanc concilii sententiam non observaverint.[11]	Baptized women members of the Catholic Church should not join themselves to the assemblies or read the writings of aliens [to the Catholic Church], nor should they out of a desire for teaching or learning join themselves to the women reading these writings. Such is the command of the apostle. The judgment of all the bishops must be: Let all who fail to observe this decision of this council be anathema.[12]

2:396. Van der Meer interpreted in a fashion that appears to me to be incorrect the anecdote that appears in *The City of God* 22:8, CCL 48, p. 818: a woman stricken with cancer of the breast "was advised to approach the women in the baptistery at Eastertime, and to go *among the assisting matrons*, and there to ask the first 'reborn' woman emerging from out of the baptismal waters to make the sign of the Cross over her tumor". But Augustine wrote merely: "... *ut in parte feminarum observanti ad baptisterium, quaecumque illi baptizata primitus occurrisset.* ..."

[9] Op. cit., 1:55; 2:140. The only strictly accurate description of the liturgy celebrated at Hippo is that of W. Rötzer, *Des heiligen Augustinus Schriften als liturgie-geschichtliche Quelle* (München: Max Hueber, 1930), pp. 156–69 (for baptism).

[10] I obviously do not believe it necessary to include Prudence, *Peristephanon*, 2, 302–4: "*Miraris intactas anus primique post damnum tori ignis secundi nescias.*" This was cited by J. Pien, *Acta sanctorum* 40, Sept. 1, p. XIII, who commented: "*Fieri posset ut poeta sacer per viduas monogamas intellexerit diaconissas*"!

[11] J. Vives, *Concilios visigóticos e hispano-romanos*, *España cristiana Textos*, 1 (Barcelona-Madrid, 1963), p. 16.

[12] Vives translated *virorum alienorum* "de otros hombres que no sean sus maridos", "of other men who are not their husbands", but it seems to me that *alieni* is properly to be contrasted with "the faithful", as R. Gryson also correctly grasped, op. cit., pp. 162–63. The terms *diacona* or *diaconissa* similarly do not appear in the *Index* of Vives, op. cit., p. 543.

No references to deaconesses are to be found in the Christian inscriptions surveyed by J. Vives.[13] Even when Spain was opened to liturgical influences from the East, deaconesses continued to be unknown there. The *Liber ordinum*, which reflected the practices of the Visigothic church of the seventh century, knew only about widows in addition to consecrated virgins: *Benedictio super viduas mafortem accipientes*. The name *mafors* or *maforte* used here to apply to the veil being taken by these widows does not represent a reference to the Byzantine ceremonial for the ordination of deaconesses; the word is to be found in other authors, notably Cassian, and its use is not limited to the habit of a religious.[14] In any case, the widows who were given this particular blessing were not destined to fill any particular ecclesiastical function; they were merely vowed to an ascetical way of life. They occupied the second rank after the virgins and devoted themselves ceaselessly to prayer.[15]

2. OPPOSITION TO THE INSTITUTION OF DEACONESSES IN ROME AND IN GAUL DURING THE FOURTH AND FIFTH CENTURIES

In Rome as well as in Gaul, from the end of the fourth century on, the fact of the existence of deaconesses in the East was neither unknown nor passed over in silence; deaconesses were mentioned expressly in order to be excluded. The different geographical churches were actually in close contact through the various councils, by means of the exchange of correspondence between bishops and through pilgrimages and banishments. It even came about that the various Greek and Eastern canonical collections were translated into Latin: the *Didascalia* from Syria; the *Ecclesiastical Canons of the Holy Apostles* from Egypt;[16] perhaps even the *Apostolic Constitutions*.[17] We must not, however, exaggerate the influence

---

[13] J. Vives, *Inscripciones cristianas de la España romana y visigoda*, 2nd ed., *Biblioteca histórica de la Biblioteca Balmes*, ser. 2, vol. 18 (Barcelona-Madrid, 1969), *Indices*, pp. 204, 268.

[14] *Thesaurus linguae latinae* 8 (Lipsiae: Teubner, 1936–66), cols. 49–50.

[15] *Liber ordinum*, ed. M. Ferotin, *Monumenta Ecclesiae liturgica* 5 (Paris: Firmin-Didot, 1904), cols. 80–82. Cf. J. F. Alonso, *La cura pastoral en la España romanovisigoda* (Rome: Iglesia Nacional Española, 1955), pp. 474–76.

[16] This is the collection partially preserved by the palimpsest of Verona, Bibl. Capitolare LV (53), published by E. Hauler, *Didascaliae apostolorum fragmenta latina* . . . (Lipsiae: Teubner, 1900), then by E. Tidner, Chapter 4, 2A, n. 38, above. It will be recalled that the author of this Latin version read *diaconissam* wherever the author of "*Ecclesiastical Canons of the Holy Apostles*" wrote διακονίαν; see Chapter 4, 2A, above.

[17] At any rate the author of the *Statuta Ecclesiae antiqua* was often inspired by the *Apostolic Constitutions*, which he read in both Greek and Latin: C. Munier, *Les Statuta Ecclesiae antiqua*, *Bibliothèque de l'Institut de droit canonique de l'Université de Strasbourg* 5 (Paris: Presses Universitaires de France, 1960), p. 125ff.

of these translations, for those who rejected deaconesses quite obviously got their information about them from other sources.

A. *Exegetical Commentaries of Ambrosiaster and Pelagius*

The unknown Roman author known as Ambrosiaster attributed the institution of deaconesses to the Cataphrygians, about whom we will shortly learn more. In his commentary on the First Epistle to Timothy, written during the pontificate of Pope St. Damasus, Ambrosiaster wrote:

> In their audacious folly, on the pretext that Paul addressed himself to women after having done so to deacons, they claim that deaconesses too must be ordained. They are nevertheless well aware of the fact that the apostles chose seven deacons. Is it plausible that at that time there were no women also capable of serving, especially considering that we read of the holy women who were present among the apostles? In the manner of heretics, whom we see trying to base their opinions on words and not on the profound meaning of the law, they employ the words of the apostle in order to go counter to his thought. The apostle commanded women to remain silent in church, but they claim for women the very authority that in the Church is conferred through the diaconate.[18]

Ambrosiaster seems even more strongly unwilling to concede that Phoebe could possibly have been considered a deaconess. In his commentary on the Epistle to the Romans, however, he was content merely to repeat the formulas of St. Paul in Romans 16:1–2, without underlining them: *"Foeben venientem commendat sororem communem, id est de lege, quam ut merito commendet, ait hanc ministram esse ecclesiae Cencris, et quia multis adiutorio fuit, etiam ipsam dicit adiuvandam peregrinationis causa."*[19]

The Briton Pelagius, who was in Rome during the same period as Ambrosiaster and who also prepared a commentary on the Epistle to the Romans, had much more exact information on the institution of deaconesses than did Ambrosiaster. Apropos of Phoebe and of the phrase *"quae est in ministerio ecclesiae quae est Cenchris"*, Pelagius explained: "Even now in the Eastern countries, there are women deacons [*diaconissae mulieres*]

---

[18] *In 1 Tim 3:11*, ed. H. I. Vogels, CSEL 81:3, p. 268: "Sed Catfrygae occasionem erroris captantes, propter quod post diaconos mulieres adloquitur, etiam ipsas diaconissas debere ordinari vana praesumptione defendunt, cum sciant apostolos septem diaconos elegisse: numquid nulla praesumptione defendunt, cum inter undecim apostolos sanctas mulieres fuisse legamus? Sed cum haeretici animum suum verbis, non sensu legis adstruere videantur, apostoli verbis contra sensum nituntur apostoli, ut cum ille mulierem in ecclesia in silentio esse debere praecipiat, illi e contra etiam auctoritatem in ecclesia vindicent ministerii." The reading *"diaconissas"* is that of the most ancient version; in the most recent version, the manuscripts have *"diaconas"*. We have utilized the translation of R. Gryson, op. cit., p. 156, who included a commentary on this text, ibid., pp. 156–57.

[19] *In Rom 16:1–2*, ed. H. I. Vogels, CSEL 81:1, 476. Cf. R. Gryson, op. cit., p. 157.

who serve members of their sex in baptism and in the ministry of the word, for we find women who have taught in private [*privatim*], such as Priscilla, whose husband was called Aquila."[20] And his gloss on 1 Timothy 3:11 reads as follows: "He commands that women should be chosen in the same way as deacons. It should therefore be understood that he was speaking of those women who, even today in the East, are called deaconesses [*quas adhuc hodie in Oriente diaconissas appellant*]."[21] Farther on in his commentary he wrote apropos of the "*vidua eligatur*" of 1 Timothy 5:9: "*Tales voluit eligi diaconissas, quae omnibus essent exempla vivendi.*"[22]

For Pelagius, the Eastern institution of deaconesses seems to have been not a recent creation but rather a survival (*adhuc hodie*) of a practice dating from apostolic times, a testimonial voice, but for him probably without a future in the Church—however that may have been for him, the church of Rome did not in fact have the practice.

There is yet another curious fact to be cited: St. Jerome, a man who traveled widely in the East and knew it well, to my knowledge nowhere ever spoke about deaconesses, not even in his letter 394 to the priest Nepotian, to whom he indicated the proper attitude to adopt toward virgins and widows.[23]

---

[20] *Pelagii Expositio in Rom 16:1*, ed. A. Souter, "Pelagius' Expositions of Thirteen Epistles of St. Paul", vol. 2, TS IX:2 (1926), 121–22. I have slightly modified the French translation of R. Gryson, op. cit., p. 160.

[21] *In 1 Tim 3:11*, ed. A. Souter, op. cit., p. 487. Cf. R. Gryson, op. cit., p. 160.

[22] *In 1 Tim 5:9*, ed. A. Souter, op. cit., p. 494. This commentary of Pelagius was revised and interpolated by Pseudo-Jerome (in reality, John the Deacon around the middle of the sixth century); E. Dekkers, *Clavis Patrum latinorum*, no. 952; PL 30, cols. 714, 880, 883; and also by a disciple of Cassiodorus, Pseudo-Primas: PL 68, cols. 665, 668. Cf. A. Souter, op. cit., vol. 1, TS IX, 1 (1922), pp. 290, 318ff.

[23] Letter 52, ed. and Fr. trans. J. Labourt, *Collection des Universités de France*, vol. 2 (Paris: Belles-Lettres, 1951), p. 179. The sole mention of deaconesses in the correspondence of St. Jerome is in letter 51 addressed by St. Epiphanius to Jerome; see Chapter 5, 2A. It is true that we have no commentary of Jerome either on the Epistle to the Romans or on 1 Tim. Neither the word "*diacona*" nor "*diaconissa*" is to be found in the index of PL 30. A *Passio*, BHL 5587, late and devoid of any historical value, and modeled in any case on a Greek *Passio*, represented as a deaconess a certain St. Martina, a Roman martyr whose existence is not even certain: cf. A. Amore, in *Bibliotheca sanctorum*, vol. 8 (Rome: Instituto Giovanni XXIII, 1967), col. 1221. The lavish encomium of a certain Synclectica by Sedulius in his *Epistola ad Macedonium* has also often been noticed: "*Quis non optet et ambiat eximio Syncletices, sacrae virginis ac ministrae, placere iudicio . . .*," CSEL 10 (1885): 9. The implication would seem to be that she was a deaconess (*ministra*) living a religious life and going about doing works of mercy. But who was Syncletica, and to what country did she belong? J. Huemer, *De Sedulii poetae vita et scriptis commentatio* (Vindobonae [Vienna], 1878), pp. 24–25, believed that she had to be the sister of that Eustathius who translated into Latin the *Hexaemeron* of St. Basil; but we are hardly any better informed about him than we are about her; indeed we are not any better informed about the life of Sedulius himself. And since, according to Sedulius,

B. Decisions of the Bishops of Gaul

In Gaul it was not the scholars and exegetes but rather the bishops themselves who spoke about deaconesses. The bishops at the Council of Nîmes in 396 A.D. thus spoke about the institution of deaconesses in order to reject and reprove it:

Can. 2. Illud etiam a quibusdam suggestum est ut, contra apostolicam disciplinam, incognito usque in hoc tempus, in ministerium feminae, nescio quo loco, leviticum videantur adsumptae: quod quidem, quia indecens est, non admittit ecclesiastica disciplina, et contra rationem facta, talis ordinatio distruatur: providendum est ne quis sibi hoc ultra praesumat.[24]

Equally, it has been reported by some that, contrary to the apostolic discipline —indeed a thing unheard of until now— it has been observed, though it is not known exactly where, that women have been raised to the ministry of deacons. Ecclesiastical discipline does not permit this, for it is unseemly; such an ordination should be annulled, since it is irregular; and vigilance is required lest in the future anyone should have the boldness to act in this fashion again.[25]

The First Council of Orange in 441 A.D. was no less peremptory, even in its brevity:

Can. 25. Diaconae omnimodis non ordinandae: si quae iam sunt, benedictioni quae populo impenditur capita submittant.[26]

In no way whatsoever should deaconesses ever be ordained. If there already are deaconesses, they should bow their heads beneath the blessing which is given to all the people.

It has been pointed out that this canon,[27] in the acts of the Council of Orange, follows the canons concerning deacons and subdeacons and precedes the canon concerning widows. And while the Council of Nîmes seemed to be aiming at a practice proper to somewhere else and not very clearly spelled out, the bishops of the Council of Orange were reproving an abuse much closer to home and perhaps existing within their own

---

Perpetua, the sister of Syncletica, was a married woman, the linking of her with the *Vita Syncleticae* found among the *spuria* of St. Athanasius is no more helpful either (*Bibl. hagiogr. graeca*, nos. 1694, 1694a), for the sister of this Syncletica was blind.

[24] CCL 148 (ed. C. Munier), p. 50.

[25] Fr. trans. J. Gaudemet, SC 241, 1977, pp. 127–29; commentary in Gryson, *Ministère des femmes*, pp. 163–64.

[26] CCL 148, p. 84.

[27] Gryson, op. cit., p. 166.

territory, an abuse, moreover, that involved a member of the hierarchy, since there was an ordination. Which "deaconesses" were involved in all this?

We could certainly imagine that the same need that motivated the creation of deaconesses in Mesopotamia and Chaldea could have manifested itself in Gaul as well. However, it was not in fact deemed necessary there to take precautions with respect to the baptismal nudity of women and to commit to deaconesses the responsibility for administering the oil of exorcism; this question simply never arose anywhere in Gaul. But would there not have been some advantage in turning to deaconesses to give instructions to women being prepared for baptism? The fact is, though, that the author of the *Statuta Ecclesiae antiqua*—without doubt Gennadius of Marseilles—who was concerned precisely with this ministry, proposed that it be entrusted to widows or to women religious. He did not employ the word "deaconesses"—with which he was nevertheless well acquainted from some of the Eastern collections of canons he compiled:

> Canon 100. The widows and nuns who are chosen for service to those women who are to receive baptism must be well prepared for this office; they must be able to teach clearly and with exactitude unlearned women from the country about how at the time of their baptism they must make the responses to the interrogations of the one performing the baptism and also how they must live after they have been baptized.[28]

Nevertheless, as the author of the *Statuta* does not fail to recall, women could neither baptize nor teach in the assembly.[29] Without exaggerating the importance of this source, for the *Statuta* were a merely private collection, we can nevertheless conclude from it that the demands of catechesis in southern Gaul had not given rise to the institution of deaconesses.[30]

---

[28] "Viduae vel sanctimoniales, quae ad ministerium baptizandarum mulierum eliguntur, tam instructae sint ad id officium, ut possint aperto et sano sermone docere imperitas et rusticanas mulieres tempore quo baptizandae sunt, qualiter baptizatoris ad interrogata respondeant et qualiter accepto baptismate vivant," ed. C. Munier, *Les Statuta Ecclesiae antiqua*, Bibliothèque de l'Institut de droit canonique de l'Université de Strasbourg, 5 (Paris: Presses Universitaires de France, 1960), pp. 99–100; commentary, ibid., pp. 136–37. It is well known that the *Statuta* were included in the collection of canons compiled for the Fourth Council of Carthage.

[29] "37. Mulier, quamvis docta et sancta, viros in conventu docere non praesumat"; "41. Mulier baptizare non praesumat", ibid., p. 86, cf. pp. 137, 138. Cf. Gryson, op. cit., pp. 167–68.

[30] I note a minor inexactitude in C. Piétri, *Roma christiana*, Bibliothèque des Ecoles françaises d'Athènes et de Rome, 224 (Rome, 1976), 1:642, n. 1: basing himself on the *Statuta*, he believed that, in Gaul as in the East, "widows and deaconesses assisted in the baptism of women". Not only do the *Statuta* not mention deaconesses; they do not even specify that the "*ministerium baptizandarum mulierum*" that they do mention is a liturgical function. In any

The councils must have been aiming at something else. Indeed, two very different abuses must now be carefully distinguished: one of them was perhaps the survival of an ancient evil; the other was destined to end up with a certain de facto recognition.

We will recall that Ambrosiaster spoke of the Cataphrygians: this was the term originally used to designate those who eventually came to be called Montanists.[31] And it appears that Montanist communities continued to exist, here and there, up to the beginning of the sixth century. The Montanists practiced the ordination of women, at least to the diaconate if not to the priesthood and the episcopate.[32] Moreover, the Montanists conceded to deaconesses a role in the eucharistic liturgy that they were never accorded in the Great Church. So perhaps it was these Montanist communities that provoked the solemn protestation of the Council of Nîmes, which would explain the imprecision of this Council in specifying the locality of the abuses against which it was going on record: *"nescio quo loco"*. As for the expression *"in ministerium leviticum adsumptae"*, it was certainly referring to "women deacons" in the full sense of the word and not merely to deaconesses. However that may be, there is another source, a letter dating from the beginning of the sixth century, that points in the same direction. This letter was addressed to two Breton priests, Lovocatus and Catihernes, and its authors were three bishops of northwestern Gaul, Licinius of Tours, Melanius of Rennes and Eustochius of Angers:

> From a report of the venerable priest Speratus, we have learned that you have not ceased to carry among your compatriots, from house to house, certain tables, upon which you celebrate the holy sacrifice of the Mass with the assistance of women to whom you have given the name of *conhospitae*. While you distribute the Eucharist, they take up the chalice and dare to administer to the people from it the Blood of Christ. This is a novelty; it is an unheard-of superstition. We have been profoundly saddened by this reappearance in our time of an abominable sect that had never been introduced into Gaul. The Eastern Fathers call it "Pepodian", from the name of Pepodius, the author of the schism. And with regard to anyone whosoever who might dare to associate women with the divine sacrifice, they have decided that every partisan of this error must be excluded from eucharistic Communion.[33]

---

case, B. Botte has shown that it is not possible to rely on the *Statuta* for accurate knowledge of the Christian institutions of Gaul: *Le rituel d'ordination des Statuta Ecclesiae antiqua*, in *Recherches de théologie ancienne et médiévale* 11 (1939): 223–41.

[31] P. de Labriolle, *Les sources de l'histoire du Montanisme*, Collectanea Friburgensia 24, Nouv. sér. 15 (Fribourg, Switzerland, 1913), pp. 275–76.

[32] An accusation in this vein was registered by St. Epiphanius, *Haeres.* 49:2, PG 41, col. 881; this has been placed in doubt by P. de Labriolle, *La crise montaniste* (Paris: Leroux, 1913), pp. 510–12; but it has been admitted by G. Bardy, *Montanisme*, in DTC 10 (1929), col. 2368.

[33] Text and Fr. trans. in P. de Labriolle, *Les sources* . . . , pp. 226–30; commentary in de

Along with this text can be quoted a passage from the decretal *Necessaria rerum* of Pope Gelasius, addressed to the bishops of southern Italy and Sicily. It was dated March 11, 494, and was reproduced in the great collections of canons:

26. Nihilominus impatienter audivimus, tantum divinarum rerum subisse despectum, ut feminae sacris altaribus ministrare firmentur, cunctaque non nisi virorum famulatui deputata sexum, cui non competunt, exhibere.[34]

It is with impatience that we learned this: divine things have suffered such a degradation that female ministers serving the sacred altars have been approved. The exercise of roles reserved to men has been given to the sex to which they do not belong.

This ministry of women at the altar, suspected of being a resurgence of Montanism and, as such, vigorously reproved, had nothing in common with the ordination of women, which is what the Council of Orange was condemning in 441 A.D.; this condemnation, however, confirmed the existence of the practice. We shall see the significance of this piece of evidence more clearly when looking at the first half of the following century.

Labriolle, *La crise montaniste* . . . , pp. 499–507.

[34] A. Thiel, *Epistolae Romanorum pontificum genuinae* . . . (Brunsbergae: Peter, 1868), pp. 376–77. Cf. R. Gryson, op. cit., pp. 168–69.

CHAPTER TEN

The Uncertainties and the Various Forms of the Introduction of Deaconesses into the West
(Sixth to Eleventh Centuries)

We have seen how the condemnation of the Council of Orange in 441 A.D. verified the fact that the abuse of ordaining deaconesses had infiltrated into southern Gaul. This occurred in spite of the clear disapproval of the practice proclaimed by the Council of Nîmes fifty years earlier. Henceforth, juridical texts and other documents began to attest to the existence of deaconesses, first for a certain period in Gaul and then in Italy. Under the name of "deaconesses", however, two very different institutions first came into being and then later disappeared. We will trace their main characteristics here.

1. WIDOW–DEACONESSES IN GAUL
IN THE SIXTH CENTURY

There were two successive councils that repeated the condemnation of deaconesses decreed by the Council of Orange in 441. The first of these was the council that met in Epaone in Burgundy in 517, and the second was the Council of Orleans in 533. These additional condemnations included details that enable us better to understand exactly what the condemned practices were. Here, for example, is canon 21 of the Council of Epaone:

> Viduarum consecrationem, quas diaconas vocitant, ab omni regione nostra penitus abrogamus, sola eis paenitentiae benedictione, si converti ambiunt, imponenda.[1]

And here is canon 17 of the Second Council of Orleans of 533:

> Foeminae, quae benedictionem diaconatus hactenus contra interdicta canonum acceperunt, si ad coniugium probantur iterum devolutae, a communione

---

[1] *Concilia Galliae a. 511–695*, ed. C. de Clerq, CCL 148A (1963), p. 29.

pellantur. Quod si huiusmodi contubernium admonitae ab episcopo cognito errore dissolverint, in communionis gratia acta paenitentia reuertantur.[2]

"Those who are called deaconesses" (*quas diaconas vocitant*) were widows who had received a liturgical consecration: "*consecratio viduarum*"; "*benedictio diaconatus*". It is to be noted that both councils avoided the term "*ordinatio*". The phrase "*consecratio viduarum*" leads us to think of the ritual of "*consecratio virginum*", and it suggests that widows formed a group apart in the assembly, as had been the case in Africa in the time of Tertullian. But why did certain bishops or priests insist upon giving widows a *benedictio diaconatus*, which the Gallic councils were equally insistent in periodically condemning? The reason was that the liturgical discipline of the Latin churches was very different from the disciplines of the Greek and Eastern churches.

In the Roman church, at least from the second half of the fourth century, the ritual of the *velatio virginis* was celebrated with great solemnity,[3] like a true wedding. The celebration was presided over by the bishop himself before the entire Christian assembly.[4] Pope Gelasius required that it take place only on major feasts.[5] Yet it was a ritual that was never included in any of the Greek or Eastern euchologies. On the other hand, the ritual for the blessing of a widow, which we found in the *Testamentum Domini*, was expressly rejected by the Latin churches of the sixth century. In this respect, the Gallic councils were no stricter than was Pope Gelasius in Rome. In his decretal that we have mentioned, Pope Gelasius protested against the tendency to repeat for widows the ritual for the consecration of virgins:

> Viduas autem velare pontificum nullus attentet, quoniam quod nec auctoritas divina delegat, nec canonum forma praestituit, non est penitus usurpandum; eisque sic ecclesiastica sunt ferenda praesidia, ut nihil committatur illicitum.[6]

Certainly the bishops recognized that widows could take public vows to practice a state of life aiming at perfection; this was traditional. But this state of life already had its rule. It was that of the *conversi* ("*si converti ambiunt*"). It had its ritual, which was the entry into penitence ("*paenitentiae*

---

[2] Ibid., p. 101.

[3] R. Metz, *La consécration des vierges dans l'Eglise romaine* (Paris: Presses Universitaires de France, 1954), pp. 80, 125ff. To be supplemented by the articles indicated by A. Nocent, in A. G. Martimort, *L'Eglise en prière*, 3rd ed. (Tournai: Desclée, 1965), p. 628.

[4] PL 13, cols. 1182–83, *Canones synodi Romanorum Ad Gallos episcopos*, cap. 1, no. 3; H. T. Bruns, *Canones apostolorum et conciliorum* (Berolini: Reimer, 1839), 2:275.

[5] Gelasius I, Epist. 14 (March 11, 494), no. 12, ed. A. Thiel, *Epistolae Romanorum pontificum genuinae* (Brunsbergae: Peter, 1867), p. 369.

[6] Same letter, no. 13, ibid., pp. 369–70.

benedictione imponenda") and its distinctive habit.[7] The Second Council of Tours added a liturgical argument in 567: "Everybody knows that a blessing of a widow is not found in the liturgical books, for her own decision in the matter is sufficient."[8]

However, the humble state of life here required was no doubt something not easily imposed upon widows of high rank. This was why, in certain regions of Gaul, there arose a desire to imitate the ritual that the Byzantine church had performed for an Olympias and to confer, especially upon women of higher social class, a "diaconal blessing" as an honor accompanying the public profession of intention to embrace a life of Christian perfection. This meant according them a prominent place in the assembly. The Council of Orange of 441 did not want any such thing: *"Si quae iam sunt, benedictioni quae populo impenditur capita submittant."* It is necessary, however, to admit that this abuse occurred anyway. In spite of the canonical prohibition, there were indeed women, some of whom had remarried (*ad coniugium probantur iterum devolutae*), who received a "diaconal blessing" (*benedictionem diaconatus acceperunt*); they therefore had to be excluded from Communion. If they recognized their error, however, they could be received back into Communion after having done penance.[9]

Repeated condemnations, then, attested to the existence and persistence of a practice that the bishops assembled at Orange, Epaone, Orleans and Tours considered to be a pastoral error and an occasion for abuses. However, at the same time that the Council of Orleans of 533 was decreeing that henceforth there would be no further such "diaconal blessings" given to women because of the many defections that occurred among those so blessed,[10] we suddenly encounter the names of two deaconesses: the daughter of St. Remy and the queen, St. Radegunde. It was in the last will and testament of St. Remy, bishop of Rheims (d. 533), that mention was made of his daughter on account of the bequest that he made to her: *"Filiae meae Helariae diaconae"*.[11] However, we know nothing else about her.

The case of St. Radegunde, as described for us by Fortunatus of Poitiers, poses some problems for historians. With the consent of her

---

[7] With regard to the *conversi*, see E. Griffe, *La Gaule chrétienne à l'époque romaine*, vol. 3 (Paris: Letouzey, 1965), pp. 129–39, 153. The Councils of Orleans in 549, canon 19; of Tours in 567, canon 21; and of Paris in 556/573, canon 5, spoke of a *mutare vestem* for nuns, widows and virgins living in the world: ed. C. de Clercq, CCL 148A, pp. 155, 185–86, 207–8.

[8] *"Omnes sciunt quod numquam in canonicis libris legitur benedictio vidualis quia solus propositus illi sufficere debet . . . ,"* canon 21 (20), ibid., p. 187.

[9] Second Council of Orleans of 533, canon 17; see beginning of this chapter.

[10] Canon 18: *"Placuit etiam, ut nulli postmodum feminae diaconalis benedictio pro conditionis huius fragilitate credatur"*, ed. C. de Clercq, CCL 148A, p. 101.

[11] Ed. B. Krusch, CCL 117 (1957), p. 477. Cf. E. Dekkers, *Clavis Patrum latinorum*, no. 1072.

husband, Clothaire I, she traveled to Noyon to visit the bishop, St. Medardus, and implored him to consecrate her to the Lord and bestow the religious habit upon her. While the bishop hesitated, she put on the religious habit herself. Overcome by her insistence, St. Medardus finally gave in and: *"Manu superposita, consecravit diaconam."*[12] Thus, here again, we have the case of a "consecration" conferred upon a woman of distinction who had lived in the married state. The case clearly recalls that of Olympias at Constantinople.

In order to avoid recourse to such "diaconal blessings" of women, it was considered preferable to relax the strictness of the prohibition against any ritual of blessing for widows. Thus it was that the books henceforth copied in France, such as the *Missale Gallicanum Vetus*, the *Missale Francorum* and the Gelasian sacramentary, began to include the text for the blessing of a widow.[13] The editions of the liturgical books utilized by the Fathers of the Second Council of Tours in 567, of course, did not contain such a ritual. Eventually, it was even accepted that the widow could receive a veil, provided she did not receive it from the hand of the bishop, as was the case with consecrated virgins; the widows themselves had to take their veils from the altar and cover their own heads with them.[14] There was henceforth no further pretext to confer any "diaconal blessing" upon them.

---

[12] Fotunatus Pictaviensis, *Vita sanctae Radegundis*, 12, ed. B. Krusch, MGH, *Auctores antiquissimi* 4:2, p. 41. Cf. *Acta sanctorum, Aug.* 3, p. 70. Many objections have been raised regarding this narrative, notably the "diaconal blessing" itself and how it could have occurred at all considering the decision of the Council of Orleans, so recently completed, and, indeed, the rulings of the Council of Chalcedon itself: *Acta Sanctorum, Aug.* 3, p. 54.

[13] Ms. Vatic. Palat. lat. 493, ed. L. K. Mohlberg, *Missale Gallicanum vetus*, REDF 3 (1958), pp. 7–8, nos. 15–16 (without title); Ms. Vatic. Regin. lat. 257, ed. L. K. Mohlberg, *Missale Francorum*, REDF 2 (1957): 16–17, no. 51, *Benedictio uestimentorum uiduae*; no. 52, *Consegratio uestium*; no. 53, *Benedictio uiduae quae fuerit castitate professa*; nos. 54–55; *Item alia*; Ms. Vatic. Regin. lat. 316, ed. L. K. Mohlberg, *Liber sacramentorum Romanae Aeclesiae ordinis anni circuli (Sacramentarium Gelasianum)*, REDF 4 (1960): 124–26, nos. 787–91 (virgins); 792, *Item oracio super ancillas Dei quibus conuersis uestimenta mutantur*; p. 213, no. 1471, *Benedictio uiduae quae fuerit castitate professa*. Is this Gelasian formulary Roman or Gallic? I think it is Gallic in spite of the contrary judgment of A. Chavasse, in *Le sacramentaire gélasien*, *Bibliothèque de théologie*, ser. 4, vol. 1 (Tournai: Desclée, 1958), pp. 507–10. For the persistence of these formularies in Frankish books, see: *Supplément d'Aniane*, nos. 1251–52, ed. J. Deshusses, *Le sacramentaire grégorien*, *Spicilegium Friburgense* 16 (Fribourg: Ed. Universitaires, 1971), p. 419.

[14] E.g., the Romano–Germanic Pontifical, XXV, 2, ed. Vogel-Elze, vol. 1, ST 226, p. 59.

2. WIVES OF DEACONS CALLED DEACONESSES

It continued to be the case that *diaconissae* were spoken about, but the word was used to describe a very different category of persons: the wives of deacons. Henceforth the term *diaconissa* was analogous to the term *presbyterissa*, indeed of *episcopissa*. Thus it was that the Second Council of Tours of 567, mentioned above, decided in its canon 20:

> Nam si inventus fuerit presbiter cum sua presbiteria aut diaconus cum sua diaconissa, aut subdiaconus cum sua subdiaconissa, annum integrum excommunis habeatur et depositus ab omni officio clericali. . . .[15]

It is well known that, according to the ancient Latin discipline, priests and deacons who had previously contracted marriage were required, upon ordination, to practice continence[16] but were not required to separate themselves from their wives. In Gaul, as in Rome, these wives were then called *presbyterissae* or *presbyterae*; *diaconissae* or *diaconae*. In Rome, in the ninth century, they received a special blessing, if we are to believe a rubric of *Ordo 36* (we do not otherwise have any information concerning this particular detail),[17] and a special costume was even conferred upon them.[18] This fact makes it difficult for us to identify deaconesses in the strict sense of the word. It is evident that when the word *"diacona"* is used in a parallel fashion with *"presbytera"*, as in the *Ordo* quoted above, we are dealing with the wives of deacons, not with deaconesses.[19] This is the situation, for example, with regard to the decisions of the Roman councils of 721, under Gregory II, and of 743, under Zacharias.[20] But when this proper context is lacking for the word *"diacona"* in a contract or inscription, we can no longer determine the true meaning of the word.

---

[15] C. de Clercq, CCL 148A, p. 184.

[16] The texts on this assembled by Andrieu, OR 4:140, n. 2: cf. E. Griffe, op. cit., pp. 68–70, 85–88.

[17] *Ordo Romanus* 36, no. 27: *"femine diaconisse et presbiterisse qui eodem die benedicuntur"*, in Andrieu, OR 4:114. This *Ordo* dates from the second half of the ninth century.

[18] This fact emerges from a letter of St. Gregory the Great, *Registrum epistolarum* IX, 197 (July 599), ed. Ewald-Hartmann, vol. 2, MGH *Epist.*, vol. 2 (1893), pp. 185–86: an abbess claims the right to wear, not a nun's habit, but rather the habit of the *presbyterae*. Cf. Andrieu, OR 4:140.

[19] Andrieu, OR 4:140ff. This problem was early identified by C. du Fresne du Cange, *Glossarium ad scriptores mediae et infimae latinitatis*, v. *Diacona*.

[20] Council of 721: *"Si quis presbyteram duxerit in coniugium, anathema sit; si quis diaconam in coniugium duxerit, anathema sit"*; Mansi, vol. 12, col. 263; Council of 743, cap. 5: *"Ut presbyteram, diaconam, nonnam aut monacham vel etiam spiritalem commatrem nullus praesumat nefario coniugio copulari"*, ed. A. Wermingoff, MGH *Legum* III, *Concilia* II, *Concilia aevi karolini 1* (1906): 13.

3. THE FIRST DEACONESSES IN ITALY
(Seventh to Eighth Centuries)

The uncertainty of the actual meaning of the Latin word for "deaconess" renders problematical the interpretation of the rare mention of deaconesses to be found in Latin inscriptions. Diehl's collection includes only two such mentions. One of these, undated but no doubt from the sixth century and found not in Italy but at Doclea in Dalmatia, reads simply: AUSONIA DIAC.[21] The other one is an inscription concerning a certain THEODORA DIACONISSA, who died in Pavia on July 22, 539.[22] To these two inscriptions can be added a votive inscription, judged by De' Rossi also to date from the sixth century, in accordance with which DOMETIVS DIAC. ET ARCARIVS SCAE SED. APOSTOL. ADQVE PP. VNA CVM ANNA DIAC. EIVS GERMANA HOC VOTVM BEATO PAVLO OPTVLERVT.[23] The *titulus* found in the *Museum Veronense* of Scipio Maffei is known to be a forgery.[24] Moving from epigraphy to diplomacy, we will note that such a contract would have entitled a certain Matrona to the title of *religiosa diaconissa*.[25]

From the second half of the seventh century, however, there exist elements that enable us to discern more precisely the existence in Italy of deaconesses, properly speaking—alongside the wives of deacons. Doubtlessly the Gregorian sacramentary of the time of Pope Honorius (625–638 A.D.) still contained only the formulary for the consecration of virgins.[26]

---

[21] E. Diehl, *Inscriptiones latinae christianae veteres*, Berolini, apud Weidmannos (1961), no. 1239 (= CIL 3, 13845): AVSONIA DIAC. (P)ROVOTO SV ET FILIOR(V)M SVOR(V)M F(E)C(IT).

[22] Ibid., no. 1238 (= CIL 5, 6467): HIC IN PACE REQVIESCIT B M THEODORA DIACONISSA QVAE VIXIT IN SECVLO ANNOS P L M XLVIII D XI KAL AVG V P C PAVLINI IVN V C IND II. There is nothing in the *Supplementum* published by J. Moreau and H. I. Marrou (Berlin: Weidmann, 1967). Father A. Ferrua has told me that he has never found any inscription referring to deaconesses in Rome itself.

[23] R. Fabretti, *Inscriptionum antiquarum quae in aedibus paternis asservantur explicatio* (Romae, 1699), p. 758, no. 639. Repeated in A. Silvagni, *Inscriptiones christianae Urbis Romae*, vol. 2 (Rome, 1935), no. 4788.

[24] S. Maffei, *Museum Veronense* (Veronae: typis Seminarii, 1749), p. 179: Daciana Diaconissa. . . . Maffai acquired this inscription from the well-known forger Girolamo Baruffaldi, of Ferrara; G. B. De' Rossi, *Inscriptiones . . .*, vol. I, XXIX: CIL 5, no. 180. I owe this information to the kindness of Father A. Ferrua, the eminent honorary rector of the Pontifical Institute of Archeology.

[25] Text in Fabre-Duchesne, *Le Liber censuum de l'Eglise romaine*, vol. 1 (Paris: Fontemoing, 1905), p. 352, no. 61 (under Gregory II, 715–31); Andrieu, OR 4, p. 143: "There is nothing to prove that this deaconess, provided as she was with sons and nephews, was anything but the widow of a simple layman." This text and several others were quoted by O. Casel, in *Jahrbuch für Liturgiewissenschaft* 11 (1931): 277–78, following notes sent to him by A. Kalsbach.

[26] On the status of the Gregorian sacramentary in the time of Pope Honorius, see: J. Deshusses, *Le sacramentaire grégorien, ses principales formes d'après les plus anciens manuscrits*, vol. I, *Spicilegium Friburgense* 16 (Fribourg, Switzerland, 1971), pp. 50–53.

But the sacramentary of Trent, as well as the one called the *Hadrianum*, already included an *"Orationem ad diaconam faciendam"* in the formularies, which were later to constitute an appendix to the Gregorian sacramentary. Dom Jean Deshusses believed this *Orationem* could be attributed to the pontificate of Leo II (682–683).[27] The formula itself is rather colorless:

> Exaudi domine preces nostras, et super hanc famulam tuam *illam* spiritum tuae benedictionis emitte, ut caelesti munere ditata et tuae gratiam possit maiestatis adquirere, et bene vivendi aliis exemplum prebere.[28]

The compiler of this appendix made no effort at all to be original; all that he did here was to render in the feminine the preparatory prayer for the ordination of a deacon.[29] However, the meaning that this compiler wanted to give to the blessing can be deduced from its location in the appendix, where it was placed among monastic or paramonastic rituals:

211. Orationes ad capillaturam
212. Ad clericum faciendum
213. Oratio ad barbas tondendas
214. Orationem ad diaconam faciendam
215. Orationem ad ancillas Dei velandis
216. Oratio ad abbatem faciendum vel abbatissam[30]

We should take note that the *Hadrianum*, even with this appendix, did not contain any prayer for the blessing of widows; this may have been because the blessing of deaconesses took its place.[31] But we should also note that the prayer *Ad diaconam faciendam* was placed next to the prayer *Ad ancillas Dei velandas*. These *ancillae Dei*, or servants of God, were not consecrated virgins who were to be beneficiaries of a traditional solemn consecration reproduced in the body of the sacramentary; rather, they represented

----

[27] J. Deshusses, op. cit., p. 54: "The papal sacramentary was destined to receive successive additions of various kinds. First there was the Mass of St. George added under Leo II (682–83). The Mass of St. Peter-in-Chains, for August 1, must have been introduced in about the same era. I believe there were two other important additions dating from about the same time: first, the addition of sections 1 to 4. The fact that these sections are lacking in the *Paduense* but are included in the *Tridentinum* suggests that they were introduced around the same time as the Masses for the feasts of St. George and of St. Peter-in-Chains. For the same reason, it seems to me that the appendix itself was augmented about the same time with sections 194 to 200 and 205 to 225, while sections 201 to 204, which were certainly of great antiquity, were surely part of the original text.".

[28] J. Deshusses, op. cit., p. 341, n. 994.

[29] Op. cit., p. 97, n. 31.

[30] Op. cit., pp. 339–42, n. 991–96.

[31] In the Sacramentary of Trent, however, there is a *Benedictio viduae* borrowed from the Gelasian sacramentary: ibid., p. 714, n. 411.

another category of pious women, a kind of third order.[32] In the tenth
century, this kind of third order was in effect headed by a deaconess.
Another fact to be underlined, once and for all, is that whenever the later
Latin liturgical books contain the prayer for the blessing of a deaconess, it
is always to be found in the monastic or paramonastic context. Thus it was
in no sense an ordination, even an ordination to "minor orders". Rather,
it constituted an ecclesiastical recognition of a religious state of life.

In order for any new blessing to be added into a papal sacramentary of
the seventh century, it was necessary that either its need or its utility be
apparent. And now there were deaconesses in the region or regions where
the Gregorian collection was in use. To the extent that this represented an
innovation, it was certainly one that arose out of the current of Byzantine
influence that was very real in the Italy of the seventh century generally,
but particularly with regard to liturgical questions. This fact has been
commented on by historians.[33]

One of the rare known examples of a deaconess in Italy illustrates the
phenomenon of imitating Eastern usages. The case dates from the middle
of the eighth century. Apropos of Sergius, who became archbishop of
Ravenna in 753 A.D., the *Liber Pontificalis* of Father Agnellus specified:
"*Iste laicus fuit et sponsam habuit quam, postquam regimen Ecclesiae suscepit, eam
Euphemiam sponsam suam diaconissam consecravit et in eodem habitu permansit.*"[34]
It can be said, of course, that this merely constituted the application of
Byzantine law, as formulated by the Trullan Synod in 692 A.D.[35]

In Rome, the existence of deaconesses is attested to incidentally from
about the end of the eighth century and the beginning of the ninth. On
November 29, 799, as Leo III was returning to Rome following the
terrible ordeal he had undergone, he was met at the Milvian Bridge by the
clergy, the nobles, the Senate, the army, "*et universo populo Romano cum
sanctimonialibus et diaconissis et nobilissimis matronis*".[36] This was reported in
the *Liber Pontificalis*. Again in 826, a council warned the Roman people

---

[32] Cf. the texts cited by H. Leclercq, *Ancilla Dei*, DACL, 1 (1907), cols. 1992–93;
St. Gregory the Great, *Registrum epistolarum* VII, 23; "*ancillis Dei quae vos graeca lingua
monastrias dicitis*", ed. Ewald-Hartmann, MGH, *Epist.*, vol. I (1887), p. 468. It is to be noted
that, on the occasion of a litigation concerning a priest, Gregory quoted number 123 of
Justinian's *Novellae* (c. 21): "*Si quis contra aliquem clericum aut monachum, aut diaconissam aut
monastriam aut ascitriam habet aliquam actionem . . . , Epist.* XIII, 50, *Iohanni Defensori*, August
603, *Registrum epistolarum*, vol. 2, ed. cit. (1893): 414. This is the only mention of deaconesses
in the entire *Registrum* of St. Gregory the Great.

[33] Kalsbach, *Diakonisse*, col. 924; Gryson, *Ministère des femmes*, p. 150.

[34] Agnelli . . . , *Liber pontificalis ecclesiae Ravennatis*, ed. O. Holder, MGH *Scriptores rerum
Longobardicarum* (Hannoverae: Hahn, 1878), p. 377 (PL 106, col. 725).

[35] Chapter 5, 1E, n. 30, above. This was noted by Andrieu, OR 4:146.

[36] *Liber pontificalis*, ed. L. Duchesne, 2:6; cf. Andrieu, OR 4:143.

against illegitimate unions: *"Cavendum ut nullus ex propria cognatione, aut velatam, diaconam vel raptam uxorem accipiat."*[37] In both of these texts, there can be no question that the wives of deacons could have been the ones being referred to. No: here deaconesses were clearly considered as forming a category similar to but distinct from those of virgins and women religious.

4. DEACONESS–ABBESSES IN ROME AND ELSEWHERE
(Tenth Century)

It is not of the greatest interest that one of the abbesses listed in the necrology of Remiremont possessed both the title "abbess" and the title "deaconess": *"XVIII kal. mai. Ida migravit abbatissa atque diaconissa ex hac luce".*[38] She was, however, the only one on the list with this double title. A more instructive anecdote is to be found in the *Life of St. Nilus the Younger*, a work very likely composed by Barthelemy, abbot of Grottaferrata (d. c. 1050). As St. Nilus (910–1015) was entering Capua, everyone came out to receive his blessing, and "among them there was a deaconess who was the hegumenē of a convent [μία διάκονος ἡγουμένη μοναστηρίου], along with her priest, who was young and bubbling with youth; she led the virgins over whom she presided and thus went forward to meet the saint".[39] This was a region of Italy where Byzantine culture, liturgy and discipline reigned; it was normal to find a convent of religious women with a hegumenē who was a deaconess.

It would have been surprising, in fact, if the institution had not spread as far as Rome. We are too scantily informed, though, about these deaconesses that we have encountered around the end of the eighth and beginning of the ninth centuries; we do not know in what activities they engaged or what responsibilities they had, if any. The accidents of archival research, however, have uncovered several deaconess-abbesses functioning in the tenth century.

A certificate from Pope Sergius III dating from the year 905 is on record; it confirmed to a certain *"Euphemiae ven. diaconae et abbatissae"* the possessions of the convent over which she presided. This convent was attached to the

---

[37] Can. 9, ed. A. Werminghoff, *Concilia aevi karolini*, vol. 1, MGH *Concil.* 2, p. 557; cf. Andrieu, OR 4:142.

[38] This necrology, from the ninth or tenth century, is found in a ms. of the Biblioteca Angelica of Rome: A. Ebner, *Der Liber vitae und die Nekrologien von Remiremont*, in *Neues Archiv* 19 (1894): 66; the mention of Ida has been taken note of by K. H. Schaefer, *Die Kanonissenstifter im deutschen Mittelalter* (Stuttgart: Enke, 1907), p. 53.

[39] AASS, *Septembris VII*, p. 330 (307).

church of St. Mary of the Corsicans. Pope Leo IV had established an *"ancillarum Dei Congregationem"* in this church.[40] It would later be given the name of Sts. Dominic and Sixtus (San Sisto Vecchio).

But it was the publication of the charters of the church of Santa Maria in Via Lata[41] in Rome that first attracted attention to the title *"diacona-abbatissa"*. In a series of successive contracts issued throughout the length of the tenth century, this title was given to Odocia, Alvisida and Euphrosyne, who succeeded each other as abbesses of the Convent of Santa Maria and that of St. Blaise in Nepi, in the province of Viterbo; it was also given to Agatha and Sergia, who were successively abbesses of the Convent of Saints Cyriacus and Nicholas, also on the Via Lata in Rome.[42] The double title was not always consistently given; often the women were referred to merely as *abbatissae*.[43] Nor was this particular custom influenced, as might at first have seemed plausible, by the fact that the Convent of Sts. Cyriacus and Nicholas was located near the diaconate of Santa Maria in Via Lata, for it was not until the fifteenth century that the convent was incorporated into the basilica. As for the convent at Nepi, the presence of its charters in the archives of the basilica arose from the fact that it belonged to the domain of the Convent of Sts. Cyriacus and Nicholas. As was the case with St. Mary of the Corsicans, the religious who were directed by the abbesses of Nepi or the Via Lata were called *ancillae Dei*, and thus they belonged to that category of pious women who were, properly speaking, distinct from nuns. It was a blessing for these pious women that we saw linked to the blessing of a deaconess in the Roman supplement to the Gregorian sacramentary.[44]

---

[40] P. K. Kehr, *Italia pontificia*, vol. 1, *Regesta pontificum Romanorum* (Berolini: apud Weidmannos, 1906), p. 121.

[41] L. M. Hartmann, *Ecclesiae S. Mariae in Via Lata Tabularium* (Vindobonae: C. Gerold, 1895–1913), 3 vols.

[42] Op. cit., 1:1–2, doc. 1 (dec. 921): "Donna Odocia venerabilis diacona et abbatissa venerabilis monasterii sancte Dei Genetricis Marie . . . ancillarum Dei, qui ponitur intro civitate Nepesina ad posterula subterranea . . . pp. 2–3, doc. 2 (juill. 947): "Alvisida venerabilis diacona et abbatissa"; pp. 4–5, doc. 4 (nov. 950): "Donna Eufrosina diacona et abbatissa . . ."; p. 11, doc. 9 (ann. 978–79): "Agathe venerabilis diacona atque abbatissa venerabilis monasterii sancti Christi martyris Cyriacy et confessoris Nicolai quod ponitur in Via Lata . . . congregatione ancillarum Dei eiusdem venerabilis monasterii . . ."; p. 19, doc. 14 (oct. 5, 987): "Domna Sergia venerabilis diacona et abbatissa . . ."; p. 21, doc. 16 (oct. 19, 988), same title.

[43] E.g., signature of Agatha, doc. 9, p. 12; title of Sergia in doc. 17, p. 22; doc. 19, p. 24; doc. 20, p. 25ff.

[44] Part 3 to this chapter, above. For the record, we should recall that in 1053 a certain *Constantia diacona* bequeathed her worldly goods to the clergy of the Church of St. Martin next to the Basilica of St. Peter, but there is no way of telling to which category of deaconesses she belonged; L. Schiapparelli, *Le carte antiche dell'Archivio capitolare di San Pietro*, in *Archivio della R. Società Romana di storia patria* 24 (1901): 466–67; cf. Andrieu, OR 4:143.

5. THE SILENCE OF THE CAROLINGIAN LEGISLATION

We have taken note of the presence of deaconesses in Italy and even in Rome, beginning from some time before the eighth century. However, outside of central and southern Italy no further evidence has been uncovered for the existence of deaconesses even in the midst of the flowering of the Carolingian renaissance.

Certainly when the Sacramentary of Pope Hadrian (*Hadrianum*) was copied in the *scriptoria*, the *Oratio ad diaconam faciendam* was almost always included, but this merely denoted the fidelity of the copyists to the text being copied. Sacramentaries on the Gelasian model did not include this prayer, although they offered an abundance of monastic-type formularies; the rituals for tonsure, for the blessing of abbots and abbesses, for the consecration of virgins and for the blessing of widows were all habitually included.[45] Among the earliest pontificals, the Aurillac pontifical (Albi 34) and, even earlier, the Cologne collection (Köln, Bibl. capit. 138) were just about the only ones to adopt the *Oratio ad diaconam faciendam* from the *Hadrianum*.[46]

The Carolingian discipline was meticulous in fixing ecclesiastical practices. Among the abuses stigmatized were those connected with the intrusion of women into the liturgical service. According to a Council of Paris held in 829, it was possible in a number of provinces to find women approaching the altar, presenting sacerdotal vestments to the priests and, worse yet, distributing Communion to the faithful under one or the other species. These tasks were not even permitted to lay men; it was believed impossible to reprove them severely enough.[47] Was this a resurgence of the same kind of disorder indicated variously by the canons of Laodicea, by Pope Gelasius and by the three bishops Licinius, Melanius and Eustochius? Or was the Council simply repeating traditional warnings as a precautionary measure?

The Roman *Liber Pontificalis* preserved a tradition of papal interventions in the same sense, aimed particularly at monks and nuns. Pope St. Boniface I (418–422) was credited by the *Liber Pontificalis* to be the author of this tradition and, earlier, Pope St. Soter (165?–174) was similarly credited.[48] Thus nobody should be surprised to find in the Pseudo-Isidorian

---

[45] P. de Puniet, *Le sacramentaire romain de Gellone*, in *Ephemerides liturgicae* 51 (1937): 128–33.

[46] For the Cologne Collection (first quarter of ninth century): Andrieu, OR 1:106; for the Aurillac pontifical (end of the ninth or beginning of the tenth centuries): V. Leroquais, *Les Pontificaux manuscrits des Bibliothèques publiques de France*, vol. I (Mâcon: Protat, 1937), p. 12 (text verified for me in the manuscript, 42v–43rff., by Father Robert Cabié).

[47] Cap. 45, ed. A. Werminghoff, *Concilia aevi karolini*, vol. I, p. 639.

[48] *Liber pontificalis*, ed. L. Duchesne, vol. I, pp. 58–59 (Soter, 1st ed.), 135 (Soter, 2nd ed.), 227 (Boniface).

decretals, fabricated around 850, a purported letter from Soter forbidding
women from handling sacred vessels, altars, linens or incense.[49] In none
of these cases, however, was the slightest mention of deaconesses made.

To my knowledge, there are only two juridical texts from the Carolingian
period that even mention deaconesses. There was the Council of Worms
of 868, which, in its canon 73, reproduced the text of canon 15 of the
General Council of Chalcedon.[50] It is impossible to deduce from the
action of this council whether it was aiming at a local usage or not, since
several of the canons enacted by it deal with practices that belonged
exclusively to Eastern discipline. Then there were three collections of
canons dating from the ninth to the tenth centuries, the glosses of which
represented perhaps the first attempt to reflect on the sources of law. All
three of these collections comment on canon 15 of the Council of Chalcedon,
explaining as follows: "*Diaconissa, id est abbatissa*". The authors of these
glosses thus seem to have understood the way that the Eastern churches
understood the ancient institution of deaconesses, which already risked
becoming the Roman practice as well. However, two of the three collections
of canons add:

> Quae, XX annis a Pauli iussu deminutis, per manus impositionem ab
> episcopo ordinatur, non ante XLum annum, ut instruat omnes christianas
> feminas fide et lege Dei, sicut erant in veteri Lege. De qua et Apostolus:
> Vidua eligatur, non minus LX annorum. Et haec erant presbiterisse in
> evangelio, Anna octoagenaria; nunc vero Chalcedonicus canon quadra-
> genarium indulget.[51]

From at least the end of the ninth century, many members of the Latin
Church had fallen into almost complete confusion regarding deaconesses,
abbesses and widows. For example, the Corbie sacramentary (Bibl. Nat.
Lat. 12051), dating from the first half of the ninth century, included the
Hadrianum's prayer for the blessing of a deaconess under the title: "*Oratio
ad abbatissam faciendam*".[52] The commentators did not refer to any existing
institution when commenting on the canons of the great councils or on the
ancient collections that spoke about them. Rather, they attempted to make
reference to biblical examples or to ancient traditions. A typical example
of this occurred in the middle of the tenth century, in the case of the

---

[49] P. Hinschius, *Decretales pseudo-Isidoriane* (Lipsiae: Tauchnitz, 1863), p. 124.

[50] J. D. Mansi, *Sacrorum Conciliorum nova et amplissima collectio*, vol. 15 (Venetiis, 1770),
col. 882.

[51] F. Maassen, *Glossen des canonischen Rechts aus dem karolingischen Zeitalter*, in *Sitzungsberichte
der kaiserlichen Akademie der Wissenschaften* (zu Wien), *Philosophisch-historische Classe* 84
(1876): 235–98 (esp. 274).

[52] PL 78, col. 174 (= H. Ménard, *Divi Gregorii . . . Magni Liber sacramentorum*, 2nd ed.,
in [D. De Sainte-Marthe], *S. Gregorii . . . Opera omnia*, 3 [1705]: 167).

response given by the bishop of Vercelli, Atto (d. 968), to the priest Ambrose, who had asked him *"quid in canonibus presbyteram, quidve diaconam intellegere debeamus?"* He was very embarrassed by the very term *"presbytera"* and fabricated a highly unusual hypothesis, which turned Phoebe into a kind of priestess.[53] At the end of his explanation, however, he added: *"Possumus quoque presbyteras vel diaconas illas existimare quae presbyteris vel diaconis ante ordinationem coniugio copulatae sunt."* This was correct since, as we have seen, these terms were used for the wives of priests and deacons. As for deaconesses, Atto knew that women had been utilized in certain regions of the East to assist at baptisms, *"quod nunc iam minime expedit"*, since only the baptism of children was then carried on. But he added: *"Sunt etiam qui eas priscis temporibus diaconas asseruere appellatas, quas nunc abbatissas nominamus"*—a usage he found quite inadequate. Finally, if it was still necessary to retain the term "deaconess" at all, Atto thought it could most properly be applied to older women enrolled in a religious life and performing duties somewhat similar to those of modern women who assist in the sacristy.[54] In those troubled times, what was happening in Rome itself was unknown in northern Italy.

However, around 950, at the very time that Atto of Vercelli was caught up in the question of deaconesses, a monk at the Abbey of Saint-Alban of Mainz was compiling a monumental liturgical book that was destined to be put into use virtually everywhere. This was the "Romano-Germanic" pontifical, as it was called. It was a book that contained not merely a prayer for the blessing of a deaconess; it contained a complete ceremony *Ad diaconam faciendam*, inserted into the proper of a Mass.

---

[53] "Videtur nobis, quoniam in primitiva Ecclesia, quia secundum dominicam vocem . . . *operarii pauci* videbantur, ad adiumentum virorum etiam religiosae mulieres in sancta Ecclesia cultrices ordinabantur. Quod ostendit beatus Paulus in Epistola ad Romanos: *Commendo vobis Phoebum*. . . . Ubi intelligitur quia tunc non solum viri, sed etiam feminae praeerant ecclesiis, magnae scilicet utilitatis causa. Nam mulieres, diu paganorum ritibus assuetae, philosophicis etiam dogmatibus instructae, bene per has familiarius convertebantur et de religionis cultu liberius edocebantur. Quod Laodicense postmodum prohibet Concilium, cap. 11, cum dicitur: Quod non oportet eas, quae dicuntur, presbyterae vel praesidentes, in ecclesiis ordinari", PL 134, col. 114. On the canon of Laodicea, see Chapter 5, 1B, above.

[54] "Quapropter si huius officii nomen nunc etiam quoquomodo perduraret, in his quae per mulieres adhuc dispensari videntur, illas diaconas putaremus, quae aetate senili devictae, religiosam vitam cum castitate servantes, oblationes sacerdotibus offerendas fideliter praeparant, ad ecclesiarum limina excubant, pavimenta detergunt": PL 134, cols. 114–15.

6. THE PONTIFICAL OF SAINT ALBAN OF MAINZ (950)
AND ITS UTILIZATION IN ROME

The prehistory of the Mainz pontifical remains in large part obscured, in spite of the labors of Michel Andrieu, Cyril Vogel and Reinhard Elze. It was completed only after many trial efforts, about which bits and pieces of evidence have come down to us. The compiler of this work was responding to important spiritual needs of his time; from among the many different liturgical usages of his time, he chose rites and formulas that he amalgamated into rather grandiose wholes. The most remarkable of his syntheses were the rituals for the consecration of virgins and for the dedication of churches.

A. The Ritual "Ad Diaconam Faciendam"
Of the Mainz Pontifical

Right after the great *Ordo* for the consecration of virgins (XX–XXI), the compiler developed the following *ordines*:

> *XXII.* Ordinatio abbatissae canonicam regulam profitentis.
> *XXIII.* Consecratio virginum quae a saeculo conversae in domibus suis susceptum castitatis habitum privatim observare voluerint.
> *XXIV.* Ad diaconam faciendam.
> *XXV.* Consecratio viduae que fuerit castitatem professa.

Following these *ordines*, a series of other rituals concerning states of perfection for males was included:

> *XXVI.* Ordinatio abbatis.
> *XXVII.* Missa pro abbate.
> *XXVIII.* Ordo ad faciendum monachum.
> *XXIX.* Ordinatio monachi.
> *XXX.* Aliae orationes pro monachis.
> *XXXI.* Orationes et preces pro monachis ad missam.

We should also take note of:

> *XXXII.* Ordinatio abbatissae monasticam regulam profitentis.

There was a very clear distinction made in all this, arising no doubt from the utilization of sources of diverse origin, between those rituals that concerned persons professing the Rule of St. Benedict and those rituals pertaining to an otherwise consecrated life, whether out in the world or within a canonical community. The *Ordo ad diaconam faciendam* belonged in this latter rather vague category, and, as we noticed above, it was placed next to the *Consecratio viduae*. We shall see that this was not a fortuitous placement.

As far as the ceremonial *Ad diaconam faciendam* is concerned,[55] the manuscripts exhibit the same divergences in detail that obtain for the pontifical as a whole, namely, that the manuscripts can be classified into two distinct manuscript families, between which it is impossible to reach a conclusion as to which of the two families better represents the Mainz original.[56] This fact, of course, does not have much importance as far as understanding the nature of the ceremonial for deaconesses is concerned. In the "Bamberg" manuscript family, as it is called, there is lacking only one of the formulas found in the second, so-called Cassino-Vallicellian group of manuscripts. The latter group, however, has more developed rubrics.

The initial rubric, evidently inspired by Byzantine books, provides a notification that the deaconess will be receiving the *orarium* from the bishop, and that henceforth, when she comes into the church, she must place the two ends of this *orarium* that hang out on each side underneath her tunic.[57]

The formulary of the Mass corresponds, on the whole, with the one for the religious profession of widowhood. Chapter XXV, *Consecratio viduae que fuerit castitatem professa*, in fact, refers back to the preceding *Ordo* concerning deaconesses: "*Oratio ad missam in natalis (!) viduae: Deus castitatis, Require ut supra, in consecratione diaconissae.*"[58] In fact, the collect, the secret and the post-Communion of the Mass for the deaconesses was taken from the old Gelasian model, where a Mass was fitted out *Item alia eiusdem* for the "*ancillas Dei quibus conversis vestimenta mutantur*".[59] The Epistle for the Mass was taken from 1 Corinthians 6:15ff.: "*Fratres, nescitis quoniam corpora vestra. . .*"; the Gospel from John 3:27ff.: "*Respondit Johannes et dixit: Non potest homo accipere. . . .*" One characteristic particularity is to be noted: the Alleluia verse reads: "*Amavit eam dominus et ornavit [eam, stolam gloriae induit eam]*", thus alluding publicly to the *orarium*.[60]

As is the case with most of the constitutive rituals for individual persons, the actual blessing of the deaconess was located between the

---

[55] C. Vogel–R. Elze, *Le Pontifical romano-germanique du dixième siècle*, vol. I, ST 226 (Vatican City, 1963), pp. 54–59.

[56] Ibid., pp. XIII–XVI.

[57] No. 1, ibid., p. 54, lines 6–9.

[58] Ibid., p. 62, lines 6–7.

[59] L. K. Mohlberg, REDF 4 (Rome: Herder, 1960), 127, nos. 797–99.

[60] Nos. 2–5, 15, Vogel-Elze, pp. 54–55, 57.

Alleluia and the Gospel. This blessing began with a litany of saints, during which the deaconess prostrated herself before the altar. At the end of this litany, the bishop pronounced the prayer *"Exaudi Domine preces nostras"*,[61] which, as we saw in part 3 to this chapter, came from the *Hadrianum* sacramentary but which henceforth was to serve as a simple prelude to the consecratory prayer: *"Sequitur consecratio in modum prephationis."*[62] The prayer itself, which began with *"Deus qui Annam filiam Phanuelis"*, was taken from Gallican books, where it was also used as a blessing for widows.[63]

After this, according to a structure the same as the one used for the consecration of virgins, the bishop gave to the deaconess the signs and marks of her office. He first presented her with the *orarium*: *"Stola iucunditatis induat te Dominus"*, a formula different from that used by the bishop when giving the stole to the deacon.[64] Then the deaconess herself took the veil from the altar and placed it on her own head—we should recall that Pope Gelasius had forbidden the bishop to extend to widows the ritual for *velatio*, which was proper to virgins. The deaconess then chanted the antiphon *Ipsi sum desponsata*, as was the practice after the consecration of virgins.[65] The prayer *Preces famulae tuae*, which then followed, was taken from the Gelasian sacramentary, where it was always found in Masses for *conversae*.[66] After this, the deaconess received the ring and the crown (*torques*), at the same point as did consecrated virgins with the same formulas. All the while the antiphon *Anulo suo* was sung, as was the case at the consecration of virgins.[67] The prayer following in the Cassino-Vallicellian manuscript "family" raises a problem: it appears to be a rather clumsy patchwork of formulas taken from an *Ordo* for penitence

[61] No. 7, ibid., p. 55, lines 11–17; cf. p. 54, lines 11–13, for the Bamberg version.

[62] No. 8, ibid., pp. 55–56.

[63] *Missale Gallicanum vetus* . . . , ed. L. K. Mohlberg, REDF 3 (Rome: Herder, 1958), 7–8, no. 16; *Missale Francorum*, ed. L. K. Mohlberg, REDF 2 (Rome: Herder, 1957), 17, no. 55. The text of the pontifical exhibits, in relation to its sources, several omissions, notably: *"et pro eo quod amisit coniugis solatium temporale, tu* (!) *qui rerum omnium requies es sequantur; et vitae spatium spiritali consolatione compensa."*

[64] There are two of them for the deacon, Vogel-Elze, p. 27, nos. 15–16: "Accipe stolam tuam, imple ministerium tuum; potens est enim Deus ut augeat tibi gratiam suam . . . *Alia.* Accipe stolam candidatam de manu Domini, ad omnibus vitiorum sordibus purificatus in conspectu divine maiestatis ut omnibus vita tuae conversationis praebeatur exemplum plebsque dicata Christi nomine possit, imitando te, imitationem acquirere iustam."

[65] Nos. 9–10, ibid., p. 56; cf. p. 44, no. 19.

[66] E. Mohlberg, REDF 4, p. 127, no. 800.

[67] Ed. Vogel-Elze, p. 57, nos. 12–13. On the subject of these rituals, R. Metz, *La consécration des vierges dans l'Eglise romaine* (Paris: Presses Universitaires de France, 1954), pp. 206–12.

or, at any rate, from a blessing of *conversi*. However that may be, it has the appearance of a distinctly foreign body within this ritual:

> Famulam tuam, quaesumus, Domine, pia devotione [= pia devotio te?] iuvante, perducat ad veniam, quatenus mereatur a cunctis mundari sordibus delictorum et reconciliatam tibi per Christum sereno vultu respicias, et omnia eius peccata dimittas, severitatem quoque iudicii tui ab ea clementer suspendas et miserationis tuae clementiam super eam benignus infundas. Per.[68]

After the offertory and the secret, the manuscripts of the Bamberg "family" include a proper preface, of which the patchwork character is even more manifest; its beginning seems to have been taken from a *super oblata* or from a *Hanc igitur*:

> Te deprecamur, omnipotens Deus, ut haec oblatio quam tibi pro famula tua offero, sit in oculis tuis semper accepta; et sicut sanctis tuis eorum fide recta pervenit ad coronas, ita eam devotio te iuvante. . . .

The rest of this is identical to the prayer *Famulam* cited above.[69] It was in this way that the formula of the Cassino-Vallicellian manuscript family was recouped by those of the Bamberg family. Both "families" agreed in offering a *Hanc igitur* and a benediction. The *Hanc igitur* was as follows:

> Hanc igitur oblationem servitutis nostrae, sed et cunctae familiae tuae, quaesumus, Domine, quam tibi offero pro incolumitate famulae tuae, ob devotionem mentis suae pius ac propitius clementi vultu suscipias, tibi vero supplicantes libens protege, dignanter exaudi, diesque. . . .[70]

As for the benediction, it was already in use as a *benedictio dominicalis* in the Gellone sacramentary and the Augsburg benedictional. In order to adapt it for use in this ritual, all that was required was to change *"familiam"* to *"famulam"*![71]

A final rubric, not found in the manuscripts of the Cassino-Vallicellian group, indicates: *Diacona vero illa inter misteria sacra communicet et post missam episcopus ei pastorali banno pacem confirmet, ut sua cum securitate et quiete possideat*.[72]

It should be noted that the word *"diacona"* itself only appears three times in this Mainz pontifical, and always in the rubrics. In the rituals themselves and in the prayers, only the conferring of the *orarium*, with the formula

---

[68] No. 14, ibid., p. 57.

[69] No. 19, ibid., p. 58.

[70] No. 20, ibid., p. 58.

[71] E. Moeller, *Corpus benedictionum pontificalium*, vol. I, CCL 162 (Turnhout: Brepols, 1971), p. 31, no. 72.

[72] No. 24, Vogel-Elze, op. cit., p. 59. On *bannum*, see R. Metz, op. cit., pp. 213–14.

accompanying it, and the allusion in the Alleluia verse remind us that we are dealing with a deaconess. The ceremony as a whole is nothing more than the consecration of a widow, only more solemn than the formulary of that name, the *Consecratio viduae quae fuerit castitatem professa*, which follows it in the Mainz pontifical. This latter ritual, unlike the former, was not reserved to the bishop and did not include the prayer called *in modum praefationis*, the bestowal of the ring and the crown or the singing of any antiphon.

B. *The Mainz Pontifical in Rome and the Blessing Of Deaconesses (Eleventh Century)*

Copies of the Mainz pontifical found their way all over Europe from the end of the tenth century on. There were copies of it available in Rome and it was used up to the pontificate of Gregory VII.[73] The kind of compilation that it was obviously made impossible the use of its entire content in any single church. Was the *Ordo ad diaconam faciendam* really used, then, and, if so, by and for whom?

It would seem to be eminently possible to reply to this question. Do we not possess the proof that deaconesses were indeed consecrated in Rome in the first half of the eleventh century? And would not the Mainz pontifical quite obviously have provided the ritual for this? In fact, there were four successive decretals including this ceremony, among those in which the popes allowed the suburbicarian bishops to carry out rituals within Rome itself. The bishops of Porto saw confirmed on three occasions the privileges of celebrating in the Trastevere area *"omnem ordinationem episcopalem, tam de presbyteris quam diaconibus vel diaconissis seu subdiaconibus, ecclesiis vel altaribus. . . ."*[74] The bishop of Silva Candida (that is, Santa Rufina) was granted the right to carry out within the Leonine City *"consecrationem ecclesiarum, altarium, sacerdotum, diaconorum, seu diaconissarum totius civitatis Leoninae"*.[75] The place occupied by deaconesses in these enumerations, however, removes us a bit from the perspective of the Romano-Germanic pontifical. For were not these deaconesses the wives of deacons, consecrated at the same time as their husbands?[76] However, there was another decretal,

---

[73] Andrieu, OR 1:511–25.

[74] Benedict VIII, *Quotiens illa* (Aug. 1, 1018), Jaffé, no. 4024; PL 139, col. 1621; P. Kehr, *Italia pontificia*, vol. 2 (Berlin: Weidmann, 1907), p. 20, no. 10; John XIX, *Quoniam semper* (May 1025), Jaffé, no. 4067; PL 141, col. 1121; Kehr, ibid., no. 11; Leo IX, *Supplicantium desideriis* (Apr. 22, 1049), Jaffé, no. 4163; PL 143, col. 602; Kehr, op. cit., p. 21, no. 13.

[75] John XIX, *Convenit apostolico* (Dec. 17, 1026), Jaffé, no. 4076; PL 141, col. 1130; Kehr, op. cit., p. 26, no. 3.

[76] Andrieu asks this question: Andrieu, OR 4:144; at that date, there was no further question of blessing *presbyterissae*, since all priests by then had to pass through the stage of the

also addressed to the bishop of Silva Candida, that confirmed the immunities in favor of *"presbyteri, diaconi, monachi, mansionarii, clerici, cuiuscumque ordinis sint vel dignitatis, sanctimoniales seu diaconissae omnes"*.[77] This time we find deaconesses mentioned alongside nuns, which corresponds much more closely to the image that the Mainz pontifical provided for us.

C. *The Roman Pontifical of Gregory VII*

One of the decretals we have mentioned was issued by Pope St. Leo IX. From the time of one of his near successors, perhaps Stephen IX or Gregory VII, a pontifical was assembled in Rome that maintained some of the features of the Mainz pontifical but pruned out some of the others, since it was deemed important to have a document more in conformity with the traditions of the city of the popes.[78] This Roman pontifical, under the title *Missa ad diaconam consecrandam*, included, although in a different order, practically the entire corresponding Mainz formulary.[79] In fact, the only thing lacking was the prayer *Exaudi*, which was the only one that could have suggested even a remote connection with the male diaconate. Also, the benediction came before Communion. The enigmatic prayer *Famulam* was not presented independently as in the Cassin-Vallicellian group of manuscripts in the Romano-Germanic pontifical. Rather, it was made part of the preface, as in the Bamberg group of manuscripts.[80] The new Roman pontifical included none of the rubrics for the ceremony, and thus we do not know whether or not the deaconess was given the *orarium* to wear, which in any case she did not receive from the hand of the bishop. The Alleluia verse (indicated in error as *Grad.*) remained: *"Amavit eam Dominus et ornavit eam stola. . . ."*

---

diaconate before they could advance to the presbyterate. In the pontifical known as the Egbert of York pontifical, there is a *Benedictio episcopalis in ordinatione diaconissae*, placed after the blessings of the Common of the Saints and just before the blessings styled *in ordinatione diaconi* and *in ordinatione presbyteri*: ed. *Surtees Society*, 27 (1853): 94; if it is the text of the episcopal blessing of virgins found in the *Supplementum Anianense*: J. Deshusse, *Le Sacramentaire grégorien*, p. 593, no. 1776; E. Moeller, *Corpus benedictionum* . . . , vol. [2], CCL 162A (Turnhout: Brepols, 1971), p. 713, no. 1742.

[77] Benedict IX, *Convenit apostolico* (Nov. 1037); Jaffé, no. 4110; PL 141, col. 1352; Kehr, op. cit., p. 26, no. 5.

[78] This pontifical is represented by the manuscripts Vatic. Barberin. lat. 631, Ottobon. lat. 270, London: British Museum, Add. 17005: M. Andrieu, PR 1, ST 86 (Vatican City, 1938), pp. 95–102, 112–14 (initial letters B, C, O).

[79] Andrieu, PR, pp. 168–69. This is the concordance between the items in this pontifical and those of the Romano-Germanic pontifical: 1 = 2; 2 = 3; 3 = 4; 4 = 5a and 6; 5 = 7a or 11; 6 = 8; 6[sic] = 5b; 7 = 15; 8 = 17; 9 = 18; 10 = 19; 11 = 20; 12 = 22; 13 = 23; 14 = 12; 15 = 13a.

[80] In the Romano-Germanic pontifical, Cassino-Vallicellian group, no. 14; Bamberg group, no. 19; in the Roman pontifical of Gregory VII, no. 10.

The inclusion of this ceremony in this Roman pontifical does not prove that the ceremony was actually utilized on any continuing basis. In fact, a number of rituals and ceremonies were simply preserved as a result of rote recopying by scribes. Some of them, quite obviously, could serve no further role in the Rome of Gregorian reforms.[81]

[81] Andrieu, PR, pp. 9–15, 96.

CHAPTER ELEVEN

The Disappearance of Deaconesses
And the Memory of Them That Remained
In the Twelfth and Thirteenth Centuries

Toward the end of the eleventh century, the institution of deaconesses in Latin Christianity was very limited. The Carolingian legislation had been silent on the whole subject. Only in central and southern Italy were deaconesses actually to be found. The use of the Mainz pontifical spread all over Europe, yet did not seem to be the cause of any revival of interest in deaconesses. In Rome itself it is difficult to trace the further history of deaconesses beyond the pontificate of Pope St. Gregory VII. As time went on, the very memory of deaconesses became more and more blurred and deformed—this can be verified in liturgical books as well as in the canonical and theological literature.

1. DISAPPEARANCE OF THE "ORDO AD
DIACONAM FACIENDAM" FROM THE PONTIFICALS

A complete census of medieval pontificals is certainly far from completion. Nevertheless, we have benefited greatly from the detailed descriptions of many of them provided by V. Leroquais and M. Andrieu and from the publications concerning the pontificals of England.[1] These publications permit us to trace the accurate history of the rituals contained in the pontificals with a high degree of approximation.

Within the limits imposed by the sources of information we possess, then, we find that by the twelfth and thirteenth centuries there were few pontificals that continued to transcribe a ritual for the blessing of deaconesses. More than that, there is no evidence that the rituals that were transcribed were actually used.

[1] For England, the relevant bibliography is indicated quite adequately by J. Brückmann, "Latin Manuscript Pontificals and Benedictionals in England and Wales", in *Traditio* 29 (1973): 391–458.

A *Missa ad diaconam faciendam* was included in a pontifical from Troyes dating from the second half of the twelfth century.[2] It was a reproduction of the text of the Roman pontifical described above. A pontifical from Poitiers, not very well preserved, dating from the beginning or the first half of the thirteenth century, reproduced the text of the Romano-Germanic pontifical.[3] In the library of the Abbey of Engelberg, a pontifical of the twelfth century includes an *Ordinatio abbatissae* and a *Consecratio sacrae virginis* followed by a ritual entitled: *Ad diaconissam faciendam, Consecratio viduae*.[4]

The church of Rome quickly eliminated from its pontificals the ritual for the blessing of deaconesses, which it was perhaps alone in using. Nevertheless, the ritual had disappeared from the edition of the pontifical that appeared around the year 1200; the Apamea pontifical provides the most celebrated testimonial to this fact.[5] The ritual was not, of course, found either in the Pontifical of Innocent III or that of Innocent IV.[6]

At the end of the thirteenth century, the bishop of Mende, Gulielmus Durandus, compiled a new pontifical. It was a vast compilation, in which he included numerous formularies and ceremonials from the old Mainz pontifical. He was, in fact, an erudite liturgist, and his going back beyond Roman austerity to the pomp of the ceremonies of the tenth century was very well received, as the large number of copies of his work still to be found in various libraries amply testifies.[7] Did he bring back the ritual for blessing a deaconess? Yes, he did, but purely as a documentary and historical exercise. Following the *De benedictione abbatissae* but before the *De benedictione et consecratione virginum* was his presentation of the *De ordinatione diaconissae*:

> Diaconissa olim, non tamen ante annum quadragesimum, ordinabatur hoc modo. Lecta etenim epistola, ea ad terram ante altare prostrata, dicebat

[2] Troyes, *Trésor de la Cathédrale*, ms. 4, fol. 121v; cf. Leroquais, *Pontificaux*, 2:400.

[3] Poitiers, Bibl. munic., ms. 39, fol. 1 (= 35)–4v. Leroquais erroneously believed that this ms. concerned the consecration of virgins, ibid., p. 257.

[4] Engelberg, Bibliothèque de l'Abbaye, ms. 54, fols. 90v–93; cf. B. Gottwald, *Catalogus codicum manuscriptorum qui asservantur in bibliotheca monasterii osb. Engelbergensis* . . . , 1891 (snl), p. 92.

[5] London: Royal Library, British Museum, ms. *Add.* 57528. M. Andrieu was not acquainted with this manuscript; he did publish, under the initial letter L, the copy of it that Jean Deslions had made, which is now in the municipal library of Lyons, ms. 570, fols. 289–344v; this copy is substantially correct. In addition to the *Missa ad diaconam consecrandam*, this pontifical omitted the *Ordo ad monachum faciendum*, which did not come from the Romano-Germanic pontifical: see Andrieu, PR 1, p. 174.

[6] On these pontificals, see: Andrieu, PR 2, *Le Pontifical de la Curie romaine au XIIIème siècle*, ST 87 (1940).

[7] Andrieu, PR 3, *Le Pontifical de Guillaume Durand*, ST 88 (1940).

episcopus super eam: *Adiutorium nostrum*, etc. *Oremus*. Oratio: *Exaudi, domine, preces nostras et super hanc famulam tuam* et cet., ut supra. Require supra, sub benedictione abbatis. Deinde dabat ei orarium dicens: *Oremus*. Oratio: *Famulam tuam, domine*, ut supra.[8]

"*Olim*", "*ordinabatur*", "*dicebat*", "*dabat*"—all these references in the past tense constitute an evocation of something that clearly belonged to the past by that time. The ritual described by Gulielmus Durandus was not even the one from the Mainz pontifical. I believe he relied on an oral tradition or possessed an older pontifical containing a ritual about which we have no other information. At any rate, with him, the ritual was reduced to the candidate's prostrating herself, the bestowal of the *orarium* upon her and two prayers, the first of which was so completely traditional, as we know, that it was also used even for abbots.[9] As for the second of these two prayers, can we not conclude that Durandus was misled by the *incipit*, or introductory words, *Famulam tuam*? For he referred the celebrant *ut supra*, that is to say, to a prayer in the *In benedictione abbatissae* that was, in fact, quite inappropriate, since it spoke of *virginitatis sanctae propositum*.[10] In the Cassino-Vallicellian group of manuscripts there was a completely different formula introduced by this same *incipit*.

That by this time the institution of deaconesses was simply an "archeological" memory, carefully preserved by a Gulielmus Durandus or, mechanically, by the copyists of earlier pontificals, can be confirmed by the fact that deaconesses were no longer mentioned by contemporary councils and synods and by the distorted, tentative and indecisive way they were referred to in the documents that did mention them.

2. ABELARD AND THE CASE OF HELOISE

The question has been raised whether Heloise received a "diaconal blessing". This question arose because of the description, provided by Peter Abelard, of her entry into the Convent of Argenteuil. According to Abelard, she arrived dressed in "*vestes religionis quae conversioni monasticae convenirent, excepto velo*"; she advanced toward the altar "*et confestim ab episcopo benedictum velum ab altare tulit et se monasticae professioni coram omnibus alligavit*".[11] This was the typical ritual of profession for a widow as

---

[8] Andrieu, PR 3:411. Cf. n. 30 to this chapter, below, on the feeling of Durandus as expressed in his *Rationale*.

[9] Ibid., p. 408.

[10] Ibid., p. 410.

[11] Abelard, *Epist.* 1, PL 178, cols. 134, 136. I must thank Dom Bernard Gaillard of the Charterhouse of Sélignac, who kindly drew my attention to this fact—which had already been

described in the pontificals of that era. In none of its elements, however, did it differ from the blessing of a deaconess. It is true that Abelard, preaching at the Paraclete for the Feast of St. Stephen, invoked the Acts of the Apostles in order to illustrate the place occupied by widows in the primitive Church; it was for the service of them that the apostles had first instituted deacons. Abelard identified these New Testament widows with deaconesses and saw them as linked to deacons by the order of the diaconate ("*quibus pariter et feminas in hoc diaconatus ordine ab Apostolo coniunctas esse. . .*"). Abelard believed this to be in accord with St. Paul and numerous other doctors. He cited on the subject commentaries of Cassidorus, "Claudius the Spaniard" (Claudius of Turin) and Pelagius.[12] In addition, in his *Institutio seu Regula Sanctimonialium*, enumerating the various factors necessary for the smooth functioning of a convent, Abelard put at the head of the list the "*diaconissam, quam nunc abbatissam nominant*". He attributed to the deaconess "*vicem imperatoris cui per omnia obeditur ab omnibus*".[13] This identification of the deaconess with the abbess had already been made, we will recall, by the Carolingian glossarists.

Alongside the memories preserved by the liturgists, then, there were also memories preserved by the *Magistri de sacra pagina*, of whom Abelard was a prime example of the time. There was also a tradition of canonists and scholastics.

---

noted by C. du Fresne du Cange, *Glossarium ad scriptores mediae et infirmae latinitatis*, v. *Diacona*.

[12] Abelard, *Sermo 31, In natali sancti Stephani*, PL 178, cols. 570–72. The text of Cassiodorus was not preserved anywhere else: "*Significat diaconissam fuisse matris Ecclesiae, quod in patribus Graecorum hodie usque peragitur, quibus et baptizandi usus in Ecclesia non negatur*"; this was a part of a commentary on the Epistle to the Romans, which was itself based on a commentary of Pelagius: cf. A. Souter, TS 9:1 (1922), pp. 318–26. The text from Claudius of Turin was in reality a quotation from Origen's commentary *In Rom. lib. 10, no. 7*, in the translation of Rufinus of Aquileia, PG 14, 1278, cited in Chapter 4, 1B, above, n. 26. As for the quotation from Pelagius, which Abelard thought was from St. Jerome: it was taken from Pelagius' *Exposition in 1 Tim 5:11*: "*Adulescentiores autem viduas devita: Devita aliis in ministerio diaconatus proponere, ne malum pro bono detur exemplum*." See A. Souter, "Pelagius' *Expositiones* of Thirteen Epistles of St. Paul", vol. 2, TS IX, 2 (1926), p. 495.

[13] Abelard, *Epist. 8*, PL 178, col. 267, cf. 268; cf. also *Epist. 7*, cols. 238–40. For Abelard, then, the deaconess was a widow presiding over a convent, while an abbess was a virgin fulfilling this same task. Must we therefore conclude that, for him, the diaconal blessing of a widow corresponded to an abbatial blessing of a virgin? Consider: "*In electione vel consecratione diaconissae consilium praecedat Apostoli . . .*" (col. 268). Did Heloise receive this blessing at the Paraclete? The mere fact that the word "deaconess" was applied to her several times does not by any means assure this.

3. GRATIAN AND PETER LOMBARD

Around the middle of the twelfth century, there appeared, almost simultaneously, two works that would serve for centuries to come as the bases for the teaching of both law and theology. Many commentaries were written on them; these commentaries, in turn, became authorities. The two works in question were the *Decretum* of the Bolognese Gratian and the *Libri Quatuor Sententiarum* (or *"Sentences"*) of the Parisian master Peter Lombard. Whatever knowledge about deaconesses remained available to the Latin Middle Ages tended to crystallize around these two works.

First of all, among the canons concerning the clergy, we find in Gratian the false decretal of Pseudo-Soter, *"Sacratas Deo feminas"*. Gratian's version read: *"Vasa sacrata et vestimenta altaris mulieres Deo dedicatae contingere et incensum circa altaria deferre prohibentur."*[14] We also find the prohibition we have seen in the *Statuta Ecclesiae Antiqua*: *"Mulier, quamvis docta et sancta, viros in conventu docere non praesumat"*.[15] In the second part of the *Decretum*, *Caus.* XV, *quaest.* 3, in the summary (*"in textu"*), Gratian himself, or one of his continuers, in order to explain why an accusation made by a woman against a cleric cannot be sustained, advanced the following argument: *"Mulieres autem non solum ad sacerdotium, sed nec etiam ad diaconatum provehi possunt."*[16] The passage in *Caus.* XX, *quaest.* 1, canon 11, *Devotis* and canon 13, *Sanctimoniales*, had nothing whatsoever to do with deaconesses as far as Gratian was concerned.[17] The two canons that mentioned them, however, provided ample pretext for some of the glossarists who came afterward to talk about deaconesses. Finally, in *Caus.* XXVII, *quaest.* 1, canon 23, there was reproduced canon 15 of the Council of Chalcedon:

> *Diaconissam non debere ante annos quadraginta ordinari statuimus, et hoc cum diligenti probatione. Si vero ordinationem susceperit et quantocumque tempore observaverit ministerium, et postea se nuptiis tradiderit, iniuriam faciens gratiae Dei, haec anathema sit cum eo qui in illius nuptiis convenerit.*[18]

These texts add nothing to what we have already learned; they cannot in any way enlighten us about the presence or absence of deaconesses in the Latin church of the middle of the twelfth century. Nor are we enlightened any more by the *Sentences* of Peter Lombard, except insofar as we can

---

[14] *Prima pars*, Dist. 23, c. 25, A. Friedberg, cols. 85–86. See Chapter 10, 5, n. 48, above.

[15] Ibid., c. 29, col. 86. See Chapter 9, 2B, n. 29.

[16] Ed. Friedberg, col. 750. Are these summaries by Gratian himself? This question has been much discussed: see J. Rambaud, in *Histoire du droit et des institutions de l'Eglise en Occident*, vol. 7 (Paris: Sirey, 1965), pp. 69–77.

[17] Ed. Friedberg, col. 846.

[18] Ibid., col. 1055.

conclude something from his complete silence on the subject of deaconesses. The fact is that, in his fourth book, treating of the sacrament of holy
orders and the various states of perfection, he made not the slightest
allusion to deaconesses, not even from any historical standpoint[19]—no
more than did Hugo of Saint-Victor before him.

4. GLOSSARISTS AND THEOLOGIANS

A. The First Commentators on Gratian and Peter Lombard Up to John the Teuton

The *Decretum* of Gratian became the subject of many glosses and
commentaries almost as soon as it appeared. These works were unanimous in rejecting the institution of deaconesses, and considered them
something from an outdated past. Perhaps the first of the commentators,
beginning in the middle of the twelfth century, was Orlando Bandinelli,
the future Pope Alexander III. He commented as follows on the canon
Diaconissam: "*Antiquitus diaconissas . . . in ecclesiis ordinari moris fuisse dubium
non est.*"[20] I am purposely holding back for the moment a portion of this
quotation.

Perhaps a decade later, it was Rufinus—no doubt the same Rufinus who
in 1179 signed the acts of the Third General Council of the Lateran as
bishop of Assisi—who, in his *Summa Decretorum*, manifested his great
embarrassment in the face of the old texts concerning widows and
deaconesses that the Bolognese master Gratian had assembled. The reflections of Rufinus are well worth reproducing, both because they
demonstrate how little knowledge of the institution of deaconesses
remained in the mind of this learned twelfth-century Umbrian canonist
and also because they opened the door to the glossarists who were to come
after him.

> Cap. 11, *Devotis* etc. *Pontificum nullus*, nec etiam alius: sed ipsae per se
> velamen accipient et capitibus suis imponent, ut infra, caus. 27, q. 1, cap.
> *Vidua quidem* 34.
>   Cap. 12, *Iuvenculas* etc. In his tribus subiectis capitulis diversa et quasi
> contraria ponuntur: in primo dicitur de LX, in secundo de XL, in tertio de
> XXV annis. Sed in primo capitulo agit de abbatissa, quae nisi sit virgo et
> sexagenaria, non debet velari, id est, in abbatissam ordinari. Ubi etiam

[19] The commentators on Peter Lombard raised the question of deaconesses, however:
IV Sent., *quaest.* 20 (on penitence), 25 (on ordination abuses) and 38 (on vows).

[20] *Summa magistri Rolandi . . .* , ed. Friedrich Thaner (Innsbruck: Wagner, 1874), p. 121.
J. Rambaud, op. cit., p. 277, dates the work before 1148 and perhaps as early as 1145.

quaedam sollempnitas accedit, sicut fieri solet cum velantur virgines et consecrantur: imponitur enim digito abbatissae anulus, ipsa eadem prosequente: "Anulo suo subarrhavit me", etc. In secundo capitulo dicitur de diaconissa, quae ante annum XL non debet valari, id est, ordinari, ut infra, caus. 27, q. 1, c. *Diaconissam* 23. Nisi forte quis dicat, pro varietate temporis instituta canonum de consecrandis virginibus emissa esse: unde in primo capitulo abbatissae pro quibuslibet sanctimonialibus ponuntur, sicut in quibusdam locis hoc vocabulum pro illo indifferenter ponitur.[21]

Cap. 23, *Diaconissam* etc. Satis mirandum ducimus, quomodo Concilium diaconissas post annos XL statuat ordinandas, cum Ambrosius [= Ambrosiaster] dicat diaconas ordinari esse contra auctoritatem. Ait enim In Epist. ad Timotheum, super illum locum: "Mulieres similiter pudicas", etc.: "Occasione horum verborum Catafrigae dicunt diaconas debere ordinari, quod est contra auctoritatem."[22] Sed aliud est eas ordinari sacramento tenus ad altaris officium, sicut ordinantur diacones: quod quidem prohibetur; aliud, ad aliquod aliud ecclesiae ministerium: quod hic permittitur. Hodie tamen huiusmodi diaconissae in ecclesia non inveniuntur, sed forte loco earum abbatissae ordinantur.[23]

Another author, who wrote the *Glossae super Sententias* between 1167 and 1175, clarified *Distinction* 38 on vows from the fourth book of Peter Lombard by reference to the authorities quoted in Gratian; this led him to distinguish *"septem velorum genera"* which could be given to women; one of these seven kinds of veils, according to him, was the *"velum ordinationis in diaconissis quadragesimo anno, sed abiit in desuetudinem"*.[24]

It was John the Teuton upon whom there developed the honor of bringing together the various commentaries on the *Decretum* into a single gloss, which henceforth was "standard". He accomplished this work between 1215–17. He ensured the celebrity of the list of veils by inserting it as a gloss on the word *Velamen* in the canon on *Devotis* of *Caus.* XX, *quaest.* 1. However, he enumerated only four of the veils himself:

> Est autem quadruplex velum, scilicet velum professionis, consecrationis, ordinationis, praelationis.

[21] Rufinus, *Summa Decretorum*, ed. H. Singer (Paderborn: Schöningh, 1902), pp. 381–82.

[22] Chapter 9, 2A, n. 18, above.

[23] Rufinus, op. cit., p. 437.

[24] It was Jean Morin, in *Commentarius de sacris Ecclesiae ordinationibus*, ed. d'Anvers (1695), 3rd pt., p. 150, who called attention to this gloss. Since the work was, and remains, unpublished, it had to be consulted in the original thirteenth-century manuscript, which was then in the library of the Abbey of Saint-Victor and now is in the Bibliothèque Nationale in Paris: ms. lat. 14423. It is in this ms. that the *Glossae* were attributed to Peter of Poitiers, but today all historians reject the authenticity of that attribution: see P. Moore, *The Works of Peter of Poitiers, Master in Theology and Chancellor of Paris (1193–1205)*, Publications in Medieval Studies (Notre Dame, 1936), pp. 145–64; Moore dated the composition of the *Glossae* between 1165 and 1175.

Velum professionis imponitur tam virgini quam viduae, dum tamen sit XII annorum, ut infra, q. 2, *Puella*.

Velum consecrationis est quod tantum virginibus imponitur in XXV anno, ut infra, eadem q., *Placuit* et 77 dist., *Placuit*.

Velum ordinationis quod olim imponebatur diaconissis in LX anno, ut infra, eadem q., *Sanctimonialis*.

Velum praelationis est quod in LX anno datur abbatissae, ut infra, eadem q. *Iuvenculas*, 31 q. *Quomodo virginibus*, et per hanc distinctionem multa sedantur contraria.[25]

At the same time as the glossarists were attesting to the desuetude of the institution of deaconesses, they were also attempting to imagine of what their "ordination" could possibly have consisted and what their functions had actually been. They did not know the pertinent Eastern sources, which had not been translated into Latin. Of the Carolingian gloss, they knew only the definition "*Diaconissa, id est abbatissa*". John the Teuton included this in his *Caus*. 27, q. 1, c. 23.[26] But the explanation was anachronistic, since a distinction was henceforth made between the "*velum ordinationis*", which was supposed to be that of the deaconess, and the "*velum praelationis*", which was that of the abbess. For some time the pontificals had included a different ritual for each one. Thus, another explanation was sought: if deaconesses had once been ordained, it must have been for the purpose of exercising functions similar to those that, in the twelfth and thirteenth centuries, were exercised by deacons. And, in that particular period, it was the reading of the Gospel that best characterized the function of the deacon. The Romano-Germanic pontifical introduced into the ceremony for the ordination of the deacon a presentation of the evangeliary to him by the bishop, who then said to him: "*Accipe potestatem legendi evangelium in Ecclesia Dei, tam pro vivis, quam pro defunctis. . . .*" After a period of hesitation, this expressive ritual was adopted in the liturgy of Rome itself. The question was: did deaconesses owe their name to the exercise of a similar function?[27]

Was it Orlando Bandinelli who first entertained this supposition? Here,

---

[25] *Decretum Gratiani . . . una cum glossis, Gregorii XIII pont. max. iussu editum* (Romae: in aedibus Populi Romani, 1582; ed. in-fol.), vol. 2, col. 1620.

[26] Ibid., col. 1972.

[27] The presentation of the evangeliary to the deacon with the use of this formula is to be found in the majority of manuscripts of the Romano-Germanic pontifical: see Vogel-Elze, op. cit., vol. I, p. 27. In two Roman pontificals of the eleventh century, the ritual was added later in the margins. On the other hand, it was included in all the pontificals of the Curia. In Rome the ordination was concluded with a *post acceptam stolam* prayer which had already appeared in another pontifical of the Germanic type, Rome, Bibl. Alessandrina, cod. 173. The prayer was *Exaudi: praebere*, which the *Hadrianum* also utilized, as will be recalled: see Andrieu, PR, 1:133, 2:341.

in full, in his gloss on the subject, which was quoted only in part earlier: *"Antiquitus diaconissas*, ID EST EVANGELIORUM LECTRICES, *in ecclesiis ordinari moris fuisse dubium non est."*[28] As stated here, this "indubitable" usage was never part of any Mass. Had Orlando forgotten that other canon of Gratian, *Dist.* 23, c. 29, which had been taken from the *Statuta Ecclesiae Antiqua*? As will be recalled, it read: *"Mulier quamvis docta et sancta viros in conventu docere non praesumat".* However that may be, the gloss of John the Teuton was to go a step farther. Apropos of canon 15 of the Council of Chalcedon, *Diaconissam non debere ante annos quadraginta ordinari*, he tried to resolve the difficulty posed by the use of the term *ordinari*, which seemed to contradict the earlier doctrine taught by Ambrose (= Ambrosiaster) as well as by the authority of Gratian (or his continuers)—the doctrine that had been set forth in the summary of *Caus.* 15, *quaest.* 3. This canon ruled out the ordination of women even to the diaconate:[29]

> Respondeo quod mulieres non recipiunt characterem, impediente sexu et constitutione Ecclesiae: unde nec officium ordinum exercere possunt, 23 dist. *Sacratas*, nec ordinatur haec: sed fundebatur super eam forte aliqua benedictio ex qua consequebatur aliquod officium speciale, forte legendi homilias vel evangelium ad matutinas, quod non licebat alii.[30]

Once again, we are faced with a hypothesis *(forte)* projected upon the past and devoid of any foundation in reality. But this hypothesis, constructed in order to resolve a problem of interpretation of a canon of the Council of Chalcedon of 451 A.D., in fact addressed itself to a difficulty that at times must have arisen in convents of nuns celebrating the divine office according to the rule of St. Benedict: on the vigils of Sundays and holy days, if the chaplain was unavailable, could the required homily and the solemn singing of the Gospel be assured?[31] It is curious that it required nearly two centuries before this suggestion was finally officially accepted.[32] This was

[28] Ed. F. Thaner, op. cit., p. 121.

[29] See pt. 3 to this chapter.

[30] *Decretum Gratiani* . . . , *una cum glossis*, same ed., 2:1972–73. The gloss added: "Alii dicunt quod si monialis ordinetur, bene recipit characterem, quia ordinari facti est; et post baptismum quilibet potest ordinari, Extra *De presbyt. non baptiz.*, c. ult." Gulielmus Durandus, in his *Rationale divinorum officiorum*, was more affirmative: "velum ordinationis olim diaconissae in quadragesimo anno dabatur ut posset legere evangelium in nocturnis", lib. 2, c. 1, no. 48.

[31] Heloise (or Abelard in her name), *Epist.* 6, complained that the rule of St. Benedict had not anticipated a number of difficulties that would arise specifically for women religious, and, among other things, she specified: "Quid ad ipsas [feminas] etiam quod de abbate statuitur [cap. 11] ut ipse lectionem dicat evangelicam et post ipsam hymnum incipiat?" PL 178, cols. 213–14. Abelard did not respond to this in either *Epist.* 8 or in the customary reply, ibid., cols. 313–26.

[32] Perhaps this occurred among the nuns of Old Castille: among the abuses committed by

not because it failed to be noticed. It was accepted by all of the theologians
who commented on the *Sentences* of Peter Lombard. They accepted it at
face value and interpreted it in the light of the glosses; that is, they attested
to the fact that there were no deaconesses exercising this function in their
own day but that this interpretation nevertheless gave them an idea of
what these deaconesses were of whom the canons spoke but about whom
no real and precise recollection had been preserved.

B. *The Great Scholastics*

As a matter of fact, Distinction 25 of the Fourth Book of the *Sentences* led
theologians to raise a question that had not been specifically treated by
Peter Lombard himself, namely, the question of the incapacity of women
to receive any ordination at all. According to Pseudo-Peter of Poitiers,
St. Thomas Aquinas was one of the first to respond to this question and to
study it in the perspective of the texts of Gratian and their glosses:

> Quidam autem dixerunt quod sexus virilis est de necessitate praecepti, sed
> non de necessitate sacramenti, quia etiam in *Decretis* fit mentio de diaconissa
> et presbytera. Sed diaconissa dicitur quae in aliquo actu diaconi participat,
> sive quae legit homiliam in ecclesia. Presbytera autem dicitur vidua, quia
> "presbyter" idem est quod "senior".[33]

In his commentary on the First Epistle to Timothy, St. Thomas was much
less precise, but much more exact from the point of view of history:

> Dixerunt autem Cataphrygae, quod ex quo inter diaconos agitur de mulieribus,
> mulieres possunt ordinari ad sacros ordines. Sed sciendum est quod in iure
> aliquae mulieres aliquando vocantur diaconissae, non quia habeant huiusmodi
> ordinem, sed propter aliquod ministerium Ecclesiae, sicut in graeco dicitur
> diaconus quilibet minister.[34]

---

abbesses to which Pope Innocent III wanted to put a stop was the one he indicated as "*legentes
evangelium praesumunt publice praedicare*", letter of Dec. 11, 1210, reproduced in *Decretal. Lib.
5*, tit. 38 *De paenit.*, c. 10, ed. Friedberg, vol. 2, cols. 886–87. Henry of Susa (Hostiensis)
(d. 1271 A.D.), *Super quinque Decretal.*, glossed as follows: "ver. subaudi in missarum
solemniis, in matutinis enim ipsum forte legere possunt, unde et diaconissae appellantur",
(Venitiis: apud Iuntas 1581), vol. [5], p. 101.

[33] St. Thomas Aquinas, *In IV Sent.*, dist. 25, quaest. 2, art. 1, sol. 1 corp.: ed. Parmae,
P. Fiaccadori, vol. 7b (1858), p. 908. On Pseudo-Peter of Poitiers, see pt. 4A, n. 24 of this
chapter, above.

[34] St. Thomas Aquinas, *In Epist. I ad Timotheum*, cap. III, lect. 2, vol. 13, p. 600. The
words "*diacona*", "*diaconissa*", do not otherwise appear in the works of St. Thomas,
according to the concordance of R. Busa, *Index thomisticus*, vol. 7 (Holzboog: Frommann,
1974). The fact is that the angelic doctor, commenting on the New Testament only in its
Latin version, saw Phoebe in the Epistle to the Romans only as one of those women who
"served" Christ and the apostles, or who carried out works of charity in the manner of the
widows of 1 Tim 5:10: see *In Epist. ad Romanos 16*, lect. 1, 13:152–53.

This was the viewpoint of Saint Bonaventure on the subject:

Et sic omnes consentiunt quod promoveri non debent [mulieres ad ordinem], sed utrum possint, dubium est. Sane quorumdam opinio fuit quod possunt, qui dicti sunt Cataphrygae, qui etiam non solum praemissis auctoritatibus innituntur, sed auctoritatibus adhaerent canonum et pro se adducunt, in quibus ostenditur mulieres antiquitus ordines suscepisse. Dicitur enim, caus. 27, q. 1, *Diaconissam*. . . , et in eadem quaestione: "Si quis rapuerit vel sollicitaverit diaconissam", et similiter dist. 32, mentio fit de presbytera. Sed certe, si attendatur quod dicitur dist. 32, *Presbyteram*, ibi ostenditur quod presbyterae vocantur viduae et seniores et matronae: et ex hoc colligitur, quod diaconissae dicebantur quae communicabant cum diaconibus in legendo homiliam, quibus fiebat aliqua benedictio. Unde nullo modo credendum est, quod unquam secundum canones mulieres fuerint ad sacros ordines promotae. Et secundum saniorem opinionem et prudentiorem doctorum, non solum non debent vel non possunt de iure, verum etiam non possunt de facto.[35]

Peter of Tarentaise, the future Pope Innocent V (d. 1276), was more concise but no less clear:

Diaconissa vocatur non a charactere ordinis, sed a similitudine actus, illa mulier cui in matutinis competebat legere homiliam, non tamen in missa ministrare, vel evangelium cantare.[36]

When we come to Richard of Mediavilla, we have already reached the end of the thirteenth century or the beginning of the fourteenth—for he seems to have died in 1307 or 1308. Within the framework of the same kind of commentary on the *Sentences* of Peter Lombard and with respect to the same objection drawn from Gratian, Richard attempted a solution without reference to any possible usage of his own time:

Per diaconissam autem intelligitur abbatissa secundum gloss., ibidem. Melius est tamen ut dicamus quod diaconissae dicebantur, quibus fiebat aliqua benedictio ad legendum homiliam in matutino, ut dicit alia glossa, ibid.[37]

John Duns Scotus (d. 1308) was more hesitant in interpreting these embarrassing canons or in attempting to discover whatever actual institution lay behind them:

Forte in Graecia uxor presbyteri potest dici presbyterissa, ubi sacerdotes utuntur licite matrimonio prius contracto: sed apud nos Latinos, ubi castitas

---

[35] St. Bonaventure, *In IV Sent.*, dist. 25, art. 2, quest. 1, ed. Quaracchi, 4 (1889): 650.

[36] *In IV Sent.*, dist. 25, q. 3, art. 1: Innocentii V, *In IV libros Sententiarum Commentaria*, 4 (Tolosae: apud A. Colomerium, 1651): 279.

[37] *In IV Sent.*, dist. 25, art. 4, q. 1: Richard de Mediavilla, . . . *Super quatuor libros Sententiarum* 4 (Brixiae: apud V. Sabbium, 1591): 389.

non coniugalis sed simpliciter est ordini annexa, presbyterissa potest dici
aliqua matrona vidua vel perfecta inter alias mulieres; vel forte in collegio illa
quae praeest omnibus aliis, ut abbatissa inter moniales; sed ista non habet per
hoc gradum altiorem ordinis; immo nec praeeminentiam respectu alicuius
viri.

Consimiliter potest dici ad illud de diaconissa, quod illa, cui competit ex
ordinatione abbatissae vel collegii legere homiliam in matutino, potest dici
diaconissa, sed ille non est actus alicuius ordinis.[38]

This text is interesting because it adds a new fact: in convents of nuns the
practice of having one of the nuns read the nocturnal homily for Sunday
Matins had quietly become established. It was not a case of reading the
Gospel itself but only the homily. Apparently the nun designated by the
abbess to do the reading did not receive any special blessing. She was not a
deaconess, although the name could from time to time be applied to her.
Imperceptibly, however, the evolution of this practice had become
crystallized, and what the theologians had once imagined to be a past
ecclesiastical practice in fact became a present liturgical reality. It was
thought that an ancient institution had thereby been reestablished, but, on
the contrary, it was really an entirely new thing that had come about.

---

[38] John Duns Scotus, *Dist. 25, quaest. 2, Scholium*; Ioannis Duns Scotus . . . , *Quastiones in
lib. IV sententiarum* . . . , 9 (Lugduni: L. Durand, 1639): 571.

CHAPTER TWELVE

Reappearance of Deaconesses
Among Women Religious

1. DEACONESSES IN THE CELEBRATION OF THE DIVINE OFFICE

It is difficult to determine when and in which convents the ritual of the blessing of a deaconess was revived for the purpose of enabling some nuns, to the exclusion of others, to play a role in the celebration of the divine office which normally would have been played by someone in holy orders. St. Benedict had assigned the solemn reading of the Gospel, which took place at the end of Sunday Matins, to the abbot, who in those times was doubtlessly not a priest. However, from the time that the ritual for the ordination of a deacon included a presentation of the book to the deacon, symbolizing the conferral upon him of the power to read the Gospels in the assembly of the faithful, it must have been considered necessary always to have a deacon present for this purpose, or, lacking a deacon, a priest. This presence of one or the other of these was no doubt considered necessary even for a divine office celebrated in the cloister.

A. *The Beginnings of This Development (Fourteenth Century)*

The Dominican Peter de la Palud (d. 1342) commented on the *Sentences* of Peter Lombard during the first half of the fourteenth century, and, in the tradition of Pseudo-Peter of Poitiers and John the Teuton, he took up again the inventory of the various kinds of "veils", that is to say, the various states of feminine perfection. This Dominican identified five of these veils: the *velum professionis*, the veil worn by all the professed nuns in the convent; the *velum consecrationis*, the veil that virgins received in the ceremony of their consecration; the "*velum ordinationis, quod datur anno XL, 27 q. 1, Diaconissam*"; the *velum praelationis*, that is, the veil of choice for the blessing of abbesses; and the *velum continentiae et observationis*, the veil for widows.[1] He failed to include from his sources any mention of the

---

[1] *In IV Sent.*, dist. 38, quest. 5, ad tertium, 2 conclusio: Petrus de Palude, *In quartum Sententiarum . . .* (Venetiis: per Bonetum Locatellum, 1493) (= Hain–Copinger 12286), fol. 184 rb.

desuetude of the institution of deaconesses, perhaps out of a simple desire to sum things up.

Another Dominican, Gulielmus Durandus de Sancto Porciano, master of the sacred palace at Avignon before becoming bishop of Le Puy and later of Meaux (d. 1332), in his commentary on the *Sentences* seemed to imply that the development was already an accomplished fact:

> 11. Ad tertium dicendum quod canones vocant diaconissam non ab ordine diaconatus, sed a benedictione, quia competit ei legere homiliam in matutinis, non autem evangelium in missa, vel ministrare circa altare in missa ut diacono convenit: presbyteram vero vocat canon viduam quae habet custodire res Ecclesiae, sicut apparet ex sequenti cap. *Mulieres*.[2]

A pontifical of Arles of the first half of the fourteenth century, almost contemporary with Durandus de Sancto Porciano, included a ritual for the blessing of deaconesses. In fact, it reproduced the *Ordo* of the original Gulielmus Durandus under the title *Ad consecrandum diaconissam*, putting everything in the present tense.[3] Did this present tense mean that the institution of deaconesses had suddenly been revived in Arles? This would be a very slender piece of evidence on which to base such a conclusion. Another Arles pontifical, this one from the second half or the end of the fourteenth century, also recopied the ritual of the same bishop of Mende, Gulielmus Durandus—but this time everything was left in the past tense: *Diaconissa olim*, etc.[4]

On the other hand, it might be possible to find a witness of the actual state of things from the second half or the end of the fourteenth century by examining a pontifical in which the *Ordo* for the blessing of a deaconess was not merely a simple copy of an earlier one: thus the pontifical of the Avignon pope Benedict XIII was included in a manuscript that was preserved in the seventeenth century at the College of Foix:

> De benedictione dyaconisse, require in Ordinario. Oratio in missa: *Deus castitatis amator.* . . .
>
>   . . . Quando vero benedicitur premictitur letania. Ipsaque completa surgens episcopus dicit. *Pater noster. Et ne nos. Sed libera nos. Domine exaudi. Dominus vobiscum. Oratio. Preces quesumus Domine famule tue.* . . .
>
>   Sequitur benedictio. *Deus qui Annam filiam phanuelis.* . . .
>
>   Deinde imponit episcopus ei orarium sicut in Ordinario continetur.
>
>   Postea dat ei anulum dicens *Accipe.*

---

[2] *In IV Sent.*, dist. 25, quaest. 2, ed. (Venetiis: ex typ. Guerraea, 1571), fol. 364v.

[3] Paris, Bibl. Nat., ms. latin 1220, fols. 41v–42r (text revised on the ms). Cf. Leroquais, *Pontificaux*, 2:119.

[4] Paris, Bibl. Nat., ms. latin 9479, fols. 87r–88r (text revised on the ms.). Cf. Leroquais, op. cit., 2:156.

Postea torquem siue coronam dicens *Accipe*. Require in benedictione virginis.

Secreta. *Munera quesumus domine familie tue*. . . .

Infra actionem. Require in benedictione virginum.

Benedictio pontificalis. *Benedic domine*. . . .[5]

This was clearly a supplement—a local or even a personal one, going back to the rituals of the Germanic pontifical. Evidently the aim was to add it to the ceremonies contained in another book, the *Ordinarium*. This work, if we may judge by the rubrics in other manuscripts, must have been not really an ordinary but rather a pontifical.[6] And the pontifical in question could only have been that of Gulielmus Durandus, since the ritual for the blessing of a deaconess was not included in the curial one.

B. Deaconess-Nuns in Italy in the Fifteenth Century

In the fifteenth century, the existence of the blessing of deaconesses was apparently unknown to Denis the Carthusian (d. 1471), who was content to reproduce the text of St. Thomas Aquinas in his own commentary on the *Sentences*.[7] On the other hand, we have three witnesses from Italy who assure us that the new conception, if not of the female diaconate, at least of a special blessing for deaconesses, by then enjoyed a stable existence in certain churches.

The Florentine Dominican, St. Antoninus, who later became archbishop of his native city (d. 1459), provided a description of the ceremony of blessing in his *Summa Theologica* in the course of enumerating the classical list of "veils":

Tertium est velum ordinationis, quod datur anno quadragesimo, ut 27, quest. 1, cap. *Diaconissam*, ubi dicitur diaconissam non debere ordinari ante annum quadragesimum; ubi dicit Glossa quod diaconissa hic appellatur, non ex eo quod conferatur ordo diaconatus, quum mulier non sit capax alicuius characteris seu ordinis, sed quia confertur ei aliqua benedictio, ex qua accipit officium inchoandi Horas in choro et legere homiliam, quod alias non licet. Unde et ab episcopo datur ei breviarium ad tangendum, ubi sunt homeliae de evangeliis in matutinis. Et hoc adhuc servatur, et fit post consecrationem

---

[5] Paris, Bibl. Nat., ms. latin 968, fols. 155v–158 (text revised on the ms.). Cf. J. Morin, op. cit., III pars, p. 148; Leroquais, op. cit., vol. 2, p. 93.

[6] See, for example, Andrieu, PR 3, pp. 40, 677.

[7] *In IV Sent.*, dist. 25, quaest. 4: *Doctoris ecstatici D. Dionysii Cartusiani Opera omnia* . . . , 25 (Tornaci, typis Cartusiae S. M. de Pratis, 1913): 54. He said nothing about "veils" apropos of Dist. 38. As late as the seventeenth century, the majority of canonists reproduced and even elaborated on, with no reference whatsoever to any contemporary usage, the commentaries of the earlier glossarists: A. Barbosa, *Collectanea doctorum* . . . *in ius pontificium*, 5 (Lugduni, 1656): 350–51 (Cap. *Diaconissam*); P. Fagnani, *Commentaria in Illum librum Decretalium, De regularibus*, c. 4, *Vidua* nos. 1–8 (Venetiis, 1709), pp. 342–43 (the first edition dates from 1661).

earum in eodem officio missae; sed non consuevit dari aliquod velum in hoc:
sed nec etiam illa aetas, scilicet ut sit quadragenaria, exspectatur; sed de
communi consuetudine est, ut, quum consecratur, quae consecratio (seu
velatio) etiam fit ante vigesimum quintum annum, communiter post consecrationem ordinetur.[8]

This commentary, then, declared the teaching of the glossarists, which
since Pseudo-Peter of Poitiers had been transmitted by canonists and
theologians, simply to be lapsed. Thus it reflected the change that two
pontificals almost contemporaneous with St. Antoninus of Florence also
reflected. One of these pontificals was from Perugia. It was another work
inspired by the pontifical of Gulielmus Durandus. The copyist had
included in its normal place the *Ordo* from this latter pontifical for the
blessing of a deaconess: *Diaconissa olim.* . . (fol. 35v). Later, however, on a
folio left blank (fol. 45r), another *Ordo* was included:

De ordinatione dyaconisse

Lecta enim epistola, ea ad terram ante altare prostrata, dicat episcopus super eam.
Adiutorium nostrum in nomine Domini. Dominus vobiscum. Oremus. *Exaudi
Domine preces nostras . . . exemplum prebere. Per dominum.* Oremus. *Familiam
tuam . . . custodiat.* Deinde tradat eis episcopus librum evangeliorum et det eis
potestatem legendi evangelium ad vigilias et incipiendi horas in ecclesia.
Dicit communiter omnibus: *Accipite potestatem legendi evangelium ad vigilias et
incipiendi horas in ecclesia in nomine Domini.* R. *Amen.* Tunc deobsculentur
manus episcopi.[9]

It appears that we are dealing here with a case where a female religious
celebrated the divine office according to the rule of St. Benedict (*legendi
evangelium ad vigilias*). Nevertheless, the ritual is not exactly the same as
that described by St. Antoninus: this *Ordo* was entirely distinct from the
one for the consecration of virgins.

A ritual that resembled much more closely the one described by the
Florentine bishop and saint was the one included in the pontifical of John
Barozi, bishop of Bergamo. It was no doubt written in 1451. Although in
general it followed the pontifical of Gulielmus Durandus, its editor

---

[8] St. Antoninus of Florence, *Summa Theologica*, part. 3, tit. 2, cap. 2, no. 2 (ed. Venetiis,
1571), fol. 42v; ed. Veronae, 1740, cols. 143E–144A. We reproduce here the text of the
Verona edition, which seems to be the more exact. Both editions, however, have been
kindly checked for me by Fr. B. G. Guyot, O.P. The text of St. Antoninus was taken up
again almost word for word by Sylvester Mazzolini, O.P., master of the Sacred Palace
(d. 1523 A.D.), also called Sylvester Prierias, *Sylvestrinae Summae* . . . . , *Pars prima* (Lugduni,
apud heredes Iacobi Iuntae, 1551), p. 196. To the by-then-classical enumeration of "veils"
that we have already encountered, he added a sixth veil: the white veil of novices.

[9] Vatican Library, *Chigi C V* 148. Cf. Andrieu, PR 3, p. 253; P. Salmon, *Les manuscrits
liturgiques latins de la Bibliothèque Vaticane*, vol. 3, ST 260 (Vatican City, 1970), pp. 21–22, n. 43.

omitted the *Ordo* of Durandus concerning deaconesses. At the end of the ritual for the consecration of virgins, however, he added:

> Et si aliquam earum fecerit diaconissam, data corona, dat ei librum omeliarum, dicens: *Accipe potestatem legendi evangelium cum omelia in ecclesia Dei, in nomine Pa † tris et Fi † lii et Spiritus † sancti.* R. *Amen.*

He seems to have been perfectly aware that this usage did not obtain everywhere—perhaps not even in Bergamo itself—for he immediately added:

> Hoc tempore non fiunt diaconisse, sed communiter in quocumque loco ebdomadaria legit evangelium, vel alia secundum consuetudinem monasterii sui. [10]

We should make no mistake about the interpretation of this rubric. It cannot mean that the ritual just described was not practiced, for this ritual was not the same one as included in the pontifical of Gulielmus Durandus. The desuetude referred rather to the discrimination implied by a blessing conferred on certain nuns only (*si aliquam*), at the same time that all of them henceforth would be taking turns fulfilling the weekly function and hence would receive the book of homilies at the time they were consecrated as virgins. St. Antoninus quite expressly said the same thing, using the same formula (*communiter*).

The pontifical of John Barozi deserves further study. Several of the particularities in which it differed from the Durandus pontifical were eventually to turn up in the printed Roman pontifical.

C. The Roman Pontificals of 1485, 1497 and 1595

The ritual recalling what was believed to have been a female diaconate was not included in the first edition of the Roman pontifical that came off the presses of Stephen Plannck in 1485. [11] In the second edition, however, which was printed in 1497 in the shop of the same Stephen Plannck, [12] we read the following at the end of the *Consecratio Virginum*, just before the chant of the *Te Deum*, fol. LXXVIv:

> Et quia in nonnullis monasteriis est consuetudo quod loco diaconissatus, qui in quibusdam antiquis pontificalibus habetur, virginibus consecratis datur facultas dicendi officium et incipiendi horas canonicas in ecclesia, convenienter id fit hoc modo.

[10] Vatican Library, *Vatic. lat.* 1145, fol. 59r. Cf. Andrieu, PR 3, p. 223; P. Salmon, op. cit., p. 35, n. 81.

[11] Hain 13285. We consulted the copy *Inc.* II 135 in the Vatican Library.

[12] Hain 13287. We consulted the copy *Barberini* AAA II 18 in the Vatican Library.

Pontifex stans ante faldistorium predictum sine mitra, virginibus consecratis coram eo genuflexis, dicit: *Dominus vobiscum. Et cum spiritu tuo. Oremus. Exaudi, Domine, preces nostras . . . praebere. Per . . . Amen.*

Tum sedet pontifex, accepta mitra, et tradit breviarium illis ambabus manibus ipsum tangentibus et pontificis manum deosculantibus, singulis dicens: *Accipe potestatem legendi officium et incipiendi horas in ecclesia. In nomine Patris et Filii et Spiritus sancti.*

With a few variants, this text was repeated in the edition of the Roman pontifical promulgated in 1595 by Pope Clement VIII.[13] The mention *"qui in quibusdam antiquis pontificalibus habetur"* had disappeared, as had *"pontificis manum deosculantibus"*. Also, the formula used in presenting the breviary was a little different: *"Accipe librum, ut incipiatis horas canonicas et legatis officium in ecclesia. In nomine Pa † tris. . ."*.

Such as they were, this ritual and the rubrics for it thus became fixed for the next four centuries. The various editions of the Roman pontifical continued to reproduce them without any change whatsoever; this was the case up to and including the year 1962.[14] The ritual and its rubrics were indeed faithfully followed, at least in Benedictine religious houses, where the consecration of virgins continued to be greatly honored. A manifestation of the official character of the divine office for nuns, celebrated by them in the name of the Church, could be identified in the actual practice, but only those who actually happened to read the rubrics were aware of the references to deaconesses. In rereading the same texts, the historian can discern a trace of the long liturgical tradition that they represent— summarizing the Latin Church's idea of deaconesses, an idea that extended from the *Hadrianum* through various avatars to the last of these. In the last avatar, with the disappearance of any mention of reading the Gospel or the homily, all resemblance whatsoever to the diaconate, even symbolic, had also disappeared.[15] There was, however, one other liturgical practice that laid claim to a relationship with the institution of deaconesses: this was a ritual in use among Carthusian nuns.

[13] We consulted the copy in the Vatican Library, *Racc. Gen., Liturgia*, I, 96. The ritual is to be found on pp. 222–23.

[14] Typical ed. promulgated by the decree of February 28, 1962, *Pars prima*, pp. 162–63.

[15] There is no need to dwell upon the case of the *vecchioni* (*vetulones*), "old women", who, in Milan, at the Ambrosian conventual Mass of Sundays, came forward to present the bread and the wine, and who, in the seventeenth century, were commonly called deaconesses, according to A. Tamburini, *De iure abbatissarum et monialium . . .* ed. posterior (Lugduni: L. Anisson, 1648), p. 44 (*Disputatio* 7, quaesitum 8, no. 15); cf. D. and C. Magri, *Hierolexicon sive Sacrum Dictionarium . . .* (Romae: sumptibus Pontii Bernardon, 1677), p. 214, which also mentioned a parish in the diocese of Tusculum for mendicant women who were called "*Sanctesae*".

2. THE CASE OF CARTHUSIAN NUNS

The ritual for the consecration of virgins practiced by Carthusian nuns[16] was fixed by Dom Innocent Le Masson, prior of the Grande Chartreuse; it was made public in a book printed in 1699 and was subsequently reprinted several times. The title was: "Practice of Blessing and Consecration of Virgins according to the Roman Pontifical and the Practices of the Order of Carthusians".[17] At the same time, there was included a notice explaining how the supplement proper to Carthusian nuns had to be inserted into the Roman pontifical:

In order to produce a manuscript with a consecration according to our usage, it is . . . necessary to copy the ritual for the consecration of virgins . . . up to the prayer *Da quaesumus* inclusive . . . and after the response "Amen", which concludes this prayer, it is necessary to add what is particular to our ritual as regards the stole, etc., namely, that which follows:

Quae sequuntur non habentur in Pontificali Romano, adhibentur autem a Pontifice in consecratione virginum Cartusianarum ex antiquissimo usu et consuetudine ordinis.

Finita oratione *Da quaesumus*, Pontifex cum mitra stans incipit, schola prosequente hanc antiphonam: *Transite ad me omnes qui concupiscitis me et a generationibus meis implemini*.

Incepta antiphona, sedet Pontifex cum mitra, et ea finita praesentantur ei a paranymphis duae primae virgines, ut prius, coram eo genuflexae. Ipse autem manipulum accipiens, imponit brachio dextro cujuslibet virginis, seriatim singulis dicens: *Expecta Dominum, viriliter age et confortetur cor tuum et sustine Dominum*.

Deinde circumdat stolam collo, dicens: *Tolle jugum Domini super te et disce ab eo quia mitis est et humilis corde*.

Postea dat illis crucem, reclinans eam super humero dextro virginum, dicens: *Abnega temetipsam et tolle crucem tuam cotidie et sequere Dominum*.

Et mox ambae simul decantant hanc antiphonam: *Dexteram meam et collum meum cinxit lapidibus preciosis, tradidit manibus meis inaestimabiles margaritas*.

Qua cantata reducuntur a matronis praedictis ad loca sua, et aliae praesentantur quae simili modo genuflectunt, cantant et manipulo, stola ac cruce donantur.

---

[16] In the drafting of this section, I am deeply obliged to the accommodating kindness of Dom Bernard Gaillard of the Charterhouse of Sélignac, who, on more than one occasion, kindly replied to my inquiries and furnished me a good part of the documentation mentioned here. Naturally, I alone remain responsible for the interpretation of the very complex history surveyed here.

[17] Cf. H. Elie, *Les éditions des Status de l'Ordre des Chartreux* (Lausanne: Libr. de l'Université, 1943), p. 149.

After this addition for the stole, we return to the pontifical, beginning with the following:

Deinde omnibus genua flectentibus, Pontifex stans, ut prius, sine mitra, dicit hanc orationem: *Oremus. Te invocamus.* . . . [18]

This usage, presented by Dom Le Masson as "one of the ancient customs of the Order of Carthusians", was, around the end of the seventeenth century, neither so ancient nor so universal as implied. It was not included in the oldest known Carthusian *Ordo*, which came from the Charterhouse of Bertrand in the diocese of Gap, a branch house to Prébayon in the diocese of Vaison (the latter being the first house of Carthusian nuns). [19] An extract from a pontifical transcribed around 1188 at the time of the foundation of Bertrand no doubt followed as a model another Prébayon manuscript dating from the middle of the twelfth century—that is to say, from the time that nuns first adopted the Carthusian customs. The verification of this fact alone should suffice to put to rest the legend that is still to be found in some recent works; this is a legend to the effect that the sisters of Prébayon were actually the daughters of St. Caesarius of Arles in the fifth century and beneficiaries, as a result of this supposed heritage, of a "virginal and diaconal" consecration. [20]

The fact is that, even in the seventeenth century, out of the five female religious houses of the Carthusian order, this particular ritual was unknown both to the nuns of Mélan in the diocese of Geneva-Annecy[21] and to those of Salettes in the diocese of Lyons. As for the Charterhouse of Prémol, this was the house that had provoked the intervention of Dom Innocent Le Masson. This convent was situated in the diocese of Grenoble. Cardinal Le Camus, the bishop of Grenoble, when visiting the convent in June 1680 in order to perform the ritual of consecration of virgins, refused to confer on the nuns the maniple, stole and cross: he considered this to be an innovation unknown to his predecessors. Dom Le Masson took the case to Rome, where the decision went in his favor. Six years later, when Cardinal Le Camus came to Prémol for a new ceremony, he did agree to

[18] Lyons, Bibl. municipale, ms. 861, pp. 57–63. It was copied toward 1710 at the Charterhouse of Prémol; cf. Avignon, Bibliothèque du Musée Calvet, ms. 205, fols. 31–33; I. Le Masson, *Pratique* . . . , pp. 62–66; E. Martène, *De antiquis Ecclesiae ritibus*, ed. 1702, 3:141; ed. 1736, vol. 2, cols. 551–52 (A. G. Martimort, *La documentation liturgique de Dom Edmond Martène*, ST 279 [Vatican City, 1978], p. 377, no. 754).

[19] Grenoble, Bibl. municipale, ms. 324 (Catal. 120), fols. 105v–116v (the catalogue dates it from the thirteenth century; it could be from the end of the twelfth).

[20] Y. Gourdel, *Chartreux*, in *Dictionnaire de spiritualité* . . . , vol. 2 (1953), col. 721; M. de Fontette, *Recherches sur les origines des moniales chartreuses*, in *Etudes d'histoire et de droit canoniques dediées à Gabriel Le Bras*, vol. 2 (Paris: Sirey, 1965), pp. 1150–51. With as little historical foundation, others trace these nuns back to St. Radegund: L. Ray and P. Mouton, *Chartreuses* (*Règle des moniales*), in *Dictionnaire de droit canonique*, vol. 3 (1942), cols. 630–32.

[21] Grenoble, Bibl. municipale, ms. 705 (Catal. 617), fols. 146v–147r.

confer the signs of the nuns' new status, and, indeed, he did so in the case of other nuns who had not received them previously.[22]

Only in the two religious houses located in Flanders—Bruges and Gosnay—could these particular rituals lay claim to a certain antiquity. In the case of St. Ann of Bruges, their existence is attested to in a collection dating from around 1480.[23] As for Gosnay in the diocese of Arras, the rituals are found in manuals dating from the end of the fifteenth century to the middle of the sixteenth.[24] However, there was an important difference between these rituals and that of Dom Le Masson; after the antiphon "*Dexteram Meam*", the Bruges collection added:

> Qua finita, retrahat episcopus crucem, et stola et manipulus tollantur a virgine. Et ipsa surgens reducatur ad locum suum. Deinde alie per ordinem ducantur ad episcopum et fiat similiter.[25]

In contrast, the new ritual of the end of the seventeenth century left to the nun the signs that had been conferred on her, since it did not include this rubric. In any case, the change did not date from this time. Already in the middle of the sixteenth century corrections had been made in the manual at Gosnay, which read: "This antiphon having been completed, the bishop must remove the cross but leave the stole and the maniple."[26] Nevertheless, the petition of Dom Le Masson to the Congregation of Rites in Rome in 1687 clearly spelled out: "They do not wear the stole and the maniple except on the day of their consecration itself, on the fiftieth anniversary of that consecration and on the day of their death."[27] Something

[22] See on this subject: Grenoble, Bibl. municipale, ms. 4182, pp. 7–8, *Annotatio sive dissertatio de usu conferendae stolae virginibus cartusianis* (also Avignon, Bibl. du Musée Calvet, ms. 205). The text of the petition to Rome of Dom Innocent Le Masson and the arguments of Cardinal Le Camus can be found in *Analecta juris pontificii*, issue 67, vol. 4, 2nd pt. or 8th series (Mar.–Apr. 1865), cols. 1284–86.

[23] Brussels, Bibl. royale Albert I, ms. 8245, fol. 287v (cf. J. Van Den Gheyn, *Catal.*, vol. 5, no. 3116). However, at the beginning of the seventeenth century, the bishop of Malines raised a difficulty about following them, as appeared from a letter of Dom Juste Perrot, prior of Chartreuse, dated Dec. 28, 1630.

[24] Paris, Bibl. Nat., mss. latins 1437 and 1438; Douai, Bibl. municipale, ms. 569 (dated 1559); Valenciennes, Bibl. municipale, ms. 140 (133).

[25] Brussels, Bibl. royale Albert I, ms. 8245, fol. 287v. Cf. [E. Martène and U. Durand], *Voyage littéraire de deux religieux bénédictins* (Paris, 1717), 2nd pt., p. 198.

[26] Valenciennes, Bibl. municipale, ms. 140, fol. 23r.

[27] *Analecta juris pontificii*, ibid., col. 1284. I. Le Masson, *Disciplina ordinis Cartusiensis*, Lib. 2, c. 6, no. 9 (ed. 1894, Monstrolii, p. 355). This was published in 1687 and republished again in 1703; both editions included the same paragraph: "Quibus, stola nempe et manipulo utuntur tantum in die consecrationis, et in caeremonia Jubilaei, post quinquaginta annos expletos professionis, quae in ambabus domibus Belgii celebratur, et tum demum in die mortis: nam cum istis suae consecrationis insigniis sepeliuntur, prout vidi faciens officium sepulturae in domo monialium Gosnay." Thus it seems that Le Masson admitted that he

else that was emphasized to Cardinal Le Camus was the following: "They are not to be utilized for any function in the church." Was this included merely to reassure the Holy See? It seems not. However that may be, nuns would later claim to be able to make more ample use of the stole!

What could the original meaning of this ceremony have been for the nuns of Flanders? It could be that the editor of the *Ordo* had found the presentation of the stole in the *Ordo* for the blessing of deaconesses in the pontifical of Gulielmus Durandus and had wished to restore it to use. But I am not aware of any liturgical or canonical source that called for the simultaneous presentation of the maniple, the stole and the cross. Perhaps one element of such a source can be found in the marginal notes of another *Ordo* for the consecration of virgins, which was copied at the end of the fourteenth century in the Charterhouse of St. Barbara in Cologne. As I have been able to verify by means of photography, the marginal notes were written in the same hand as the *Ordo* itself. Opposite the rubric concerning the imposition of the maniple, we read: "*Hic datur potestas legendi epistolam.*" Opposite the imposition of the stole: "*Hic datur potestas legendi evangelium in omelia matutinali.*"[28] No explanation was written opposite the rubric for the presentation of the cross.

It might be possible to find an explanation for the ceremony elsewhere, within the framework of the *devotio moderna*; in this perspective, the presentation of the maniple, stole and cross would have been intended to express the mission being confided to the nun to intercede on behalf of the various sacred orders. However that may be, the rubrics of the manuscript of Cologne attract our attention to another development in the practices of Carthusian nuns; they were coming to see the presentation of these signs as connected with certain "rights" in connection with the liturgy to which they laid claim.

The most surprising of these "rights" was that of singing the Epistle at convent Masses, even when clerics were present. The memorandum of 1687 had spelled out that "in the order our consecrated nuns sing the Epistle at sung Masses according to immemorial usage, even when the bishop is present".[29] The universality of this practice was somewhat exaggerated, since another *Ordo* at the beginning of the seventeenth

could only make reference to Flemish practice, although he had said only two lines earlier: "In ipsa monialium consecratione retinetur usus antiquus conferendi illis stolam et manipulum in brachio dextro cum verbis ab Episcopo consecrante pronunciatis ad instar eorum quae in Ordinatione proferuntur."

[28] Darmstadt, Hessische Landes- und Hochschulbibliothek, cod. 710, fol. 176r. This manuscript was copied at the Charterhouse of St. Barbara in Cologne: R. M. Marks, "The Medieval Manuscripts Library of the Charterhouse of St. Barbara in Cologne", vol. 2, *Analecta Cartusiana* 22 (Salzburg, 1974), pp. 303–5.

[29] *Analecta juris pontificii*, ibid., col. 1285.

century merely mentioned the existence of the practice "in some convents"; its antiquity was also exaggerated, since the marginal notes on the Cologne manuscript constitute the first documentation we have of the practice itself. As a result of this "privilege", deceased nuns in Bruges at the end of the seventeenth century were described in their death notices as "subdeaconesses".[30]

At the same time another "right" progressively assumed greater importance: that of reciting the twelfth lesson of vigil services and of proclaiming the Gospel, which, according to classic practice, concluded these services. The custom was to reserve the reading of the last lesson to the celebrant of the divine office. However, this custom had resulted only from the accumulation of precedents; no particular solemnity was connected with it. An ordinance of the general chapter of 1337 recalled:

> Nulla priorissa presente vicario *Benedicite* dicere presumat; nec presente monacho aut clerico presbytero duodecimam legere lectionem. De diuino quoque officio ordinando . . . se nullatenus intromittat.[31]

This text was glossed in the following manner at the end of the fifteenth century:

> *Legere lectionem.* Et si absente monacho vel altero presbytero contingat priorissam vel monialem dicere euangelium in matutino, non dicit Dominus vobiscum, ut notatur in Hostiensi, sicut presbyter, nec accipit stolam, nam haec pertinent ad sacerdotem et diaconum, tum cartusiensis priorissa dictura orationem premittit Domine exaudi orationem meam.[32]

However, this substitution does not seem to have found easy acceptance. In 1566, the nuns of Bruges, having taken refuge as a result of the activities of the Dutch "Gueux" ["Beggars"], went six whole months without singing the divine office: "We could not do so because we needed a priest for singing the hours that were to be sung."[33] The publication of the

---

[30] Stanislas d'Ijdewalle, *De Kartuize Sint-Anna ter Woestijne 1350–1792* (Bruges: Desclée De Brouwer, 1945), p. 315 and outside the text between 34–35; S. Rituum Congregatio, *Confirmatio cultus . . . Beatricis ab Ornacieux . . .* (Rome: ex. typ. Bernardi Morini, 1869), p. 23ff.

[31] C. Le Couteulx, *Annales ordinis Cartusiensis*, vol. 5 (Monstrolii, 1889), p. 383; text reproduced in *Nova Statuta* (Guilhelmi Raynaldi), 3rd pt., c. 4, nos. 10–11, that is found in *Statuta et privilegia ordinis Cartusiensis* (Basel: apud J. Amorbach, 1510, not paginated). The *Statuta* of the general Dom Guillaume Raynaud (1367–1402) date from the year 1368; H. Elie, op. cit., p. 64.

[32] Gloss of the Statutes by Dom Jacobus Sauler, professed monk of Buxheim: Library of the Charterhouse of Aula Dei (Spain), ms. N-i-62. I was unable to find in Hostiensis the indication to which allusion was made.

[33] Chronicle of St. Ann of Bruges by Sister Petronella de Grutere; original Flemish in the Archives of the Charterhouse; Fr. trans. in ms. 56 of the Charterhouse of Sélignac, p. 47.

Roman pontifical, with its rubric *Loco Diaconissatus*, served to eliminate any remaining scruples. This was how the rubric was transformed in the ritual of Mélan:

> Since in some convents there exists the custom of giving to consecrated virgins rather than to subdeacons the power to read the Epistle and the divine office and to initiate the canonical hours in the church, this is appropriately carried out in this manner. . . .

There followed the presentation of the book, as in the Roman pontifical.[34]

Dom Le Masson, in the petition cited above, was content to magnify the importance of the singing of the Epistle in order to justify the conferring of the stole:

> Some exterior sign of that power is necessary, for it is an important power, with regard to the virgin nuns. Since the Church never confers ecclesiastical jurisdiction without some exterior sign, it follows as a necessary consequence that, since the singular power of singing the Epistle is given to these consecrated virgins, as appears above, it must be done through some exterior sign, and it appears that this sign cannot more appropriately be expressed than by the presentation of the maniple and stole to them.[35]

But even with that, Dom Le Masson was not content to make only "subdeaconesses" out of his nuns. He based his petition upon what he thought to be the tradition of deaconesses in the Church. If, therefore, the nuns had understood the argumentation of the prior of the Grande Char-treuse, why should they not have expected to receive the conferral of the stole, when in fact they were carrying out the functions associated with it? In spite of assurances to the contrary enunciated in 1687, by the eighteenth century this was considered not only legitimate, but it was even a venerable custom. In the nineteenth century, the practice was expanded to allow the prioress to carry out the same function in other circumstances of life in the cloister. However, the fact is that none of this really has very much to do with the real historical reality of deaconesses in the Church.[36]

---

[34] Grenoble, Bibl. municipale, ms. 705 (Catal. 617), fol. 146v.

[35] *Analecta juris pontificii*, ibid., col. 1285.

[36] Some Benedictine and Cistercian abbesses of Catalonia also laid claim to the privilege of the stole, but it is difficult to establish the historical origin of this claim. The custom of presenting them with the stole has been preserved here and there down to our own time. However, this custom in no way concerns a fixed ceremonial but is merely considered an honorific sign of their office.

Conclusion

Having reached the end of this historical inquiry on the subject of deaconesses, I believe we have reviewed all of the sources known today that could throw any light on the subject. Indeed, I believe that we have enlarged the number of these sources that those who have occupied themselves with the problem before us had progressively identified as pertinent. We have also tried to specify the place and significance of each of the facts and texts that we have examined, and thus it has become very apparent to us that some of the received ideas on the subject of deaconesses are in need of revision, if we are to base our conclusions on a strict scholarly methodology.

Is it possible to move beyond the analysis that we have already conducted and provide conclusions of a more general kind to questions being asked today, sometimes with considerable passion, not only by publicists but by theologians? Some of these questions, in fact, belong to the domain of the historian, and hence I believe I am obliged to try to respond to them. Others go beyond my competence, however, and to those questions I can respond only with some personal opinions formed by my lengthy preoccupation with all the pertinent historical documents.

1. WHO AND WHAT WERE DEACONESSES?

The Christians of antiquity did not have a single, fixed idea of what deaconesses were supposed to be. In the enumeration of the various groups distinct from the Christian people as a whole, they listed them in different places: sometimes they were listed after deacons; sometimes they were listed after all other ministers; sometimes they appeared in the middle of a listing of consecrated states of life. This kind of variation, as we have seen, was characteristic of legal documents, of lists of intercessory prayers or of the rituals concerning deaconesses as they appeared in euchologies and pontificals.

Wishing to relate the institution of deaconesses to the counsels of the pastoral Epistles, the ancient councils as well as the Greek and Eastern commentators of antiquity referred either to chapter 3 of the First Epistle to Timothy, to chapter 5 of the same Epistle or to both at one and the same time. More and more, however, they placed the accent on the scriptural counsels concerning widows, so that deaconesses very soon came to be considered as engaged in a consecrated state of life. This was the case regardless of whether deaconesses were considered to be entering upon such a consecrated state of life at the time of their institution, or whether they were recruited exclusively from among women already engaged in such a consecrated state of life: the "daughters of the covenant", or nuns.

The Greek and Eastern canonists of the Middle Ages were even less able than those of antiquity to know who and what deaconesses were. This arose from the fact that, in their time and place, deaconesses had long since ceased to exist and the ancient documents that spoke about them were available to these medieval canonists only in very defective forms, having been handed down often in ways that were far from faithful to the original text. The same difficulty obtained even more strongly in the case of the Latins, even though their own tradition in the matter provided a much clearer picture. This was the case because with them there had never been any question of anything but a simple benediction or blessing for deaconesses, one that was at first reserved only for certain abbesses and only later extended to some other nuns.

Is it even possible to speak of deaconesses as a single and unique institution? One of the results of our study has been to recognize that the word "deaconess" has been used very differently from one church to another and from one age to another. Perhaps this inevitably had to be the case because the pastoral problems that had to be resolved were so different; perhaps it had to be the case also because too long a time had elapsed between the fugitive allusions contained in the Pauline Epistles and the time when the institution of deaconesses actually emerged.

The continuity of a true ecclesiastical tradition was lacking in the case of deaconesses. The *Didascalia* alone presented the institution of deaconesses to us as a ministry in the true sense of the word; in that document it appeared to embrace both a pastoral and a liturgical function, responding to a need that existed only in the Eastern regions (Mesopotamia, Chaldea, Persia). But the institution of deaconesses lasted only as long as adult baptisms were the norm; the necessity that had brought about its creation was geographically limited and it rapidly became obsolete. It is also necessary to add that, even if such a ministry was necessary, it did not necessarily follow that deaconesses had to be created in order to carry out that ministry. According to the *Didascalia* itself, it could be carried out by a simple matron. According to the *Testament of Our Lord Jesus Christ*, it could equally be confided to those widows who had "precedence".

Everywhere else the blessing or ordination of deaconesses possessed a radically different significance. The patriarch Severus of Antioch found it appropriate to write that "in the case of deaconesses . . . ordination is performed less with regard to the needs of the mysteries than exclusively with regard to doing honor."[1] "Honor" was a blessing conferred with a greater or lesser degree of solemnity—there were efforts to make it more and more solemn. And this blessing was conferred upon different categories of women, also: the wife of a priest or deacon (and here the name did not even have to come from any ritual of consecration); a widow of distinction; the hegumenē or superior of a convent. From the end of the fourth century on, we have been able to verify the existence of these kinds of deaconesses in the great Greek-language churches. There were some outstanding examples, but it is nevertheless difficult to know exactly how the institution actually came to be created. And contrary to what has been asserted on this subject, the *Apostolic Constitutions* do not really throw any light on the problem, for the institution of deaconesses that emerges from that document simply does not correspond to the evidence of what the actual institution of deaconesses was like in both Antioch and Constantinople, and the formulary proposed for the ordination of deaconesses in the *Apostolic Constitutions* had no antecedents and was not retained in the liturgy.

2. WERE THEY DEACONS?

There are certain authors today who are quite happy to assert that deaconesses were really deacons. This is an impression that they derive from the prescriptions of the *Didascalia*, from the formulas found in the *Novellae* of the Emperor Justinian and, especially, from the entire cere- monial that surrounded the ordination of deaconesses in the Byzantine euchologies. Commenting on chapter sixteen of the *Didascalia*, Cipriano Vagaggini came to the conclusion that we have already had occasion to quote: "The diaconal ministry of the Church had two branches: a masculine ministry and a feminine one for ministering to women specifically."[2] Vagaggini did not fail to highlight the curious formula that is to be encountered twice in the *Novellae* of Justinian, namely διακόνους ἄρρενας καὶ θηλείας (masculine and feminine deacons). And with respect to existing rituals, we find Roger Gryson declaring apropos of the *Apostolic Constitutions* that "women deacons received a true ordination that in no way was distinguished formally from that of their masculine colleagues."[3] And

---

[1] See Chapter 6, 3A, above.

[2] See Chapter 2, 1, above. C. Vagaggini, *L'ordinazione delle diaconesse nella tradizione greca e bizantina*, OCP 40 (1974): 151.

[3] Gryson, *Ministère des femmes*, p. 177, cf. p. 164.

both E. D. Theodorou[4] and Vagaggini[5] have analyzed in detail the ceremonials in the Byzantine euchologies in order to underline the striking resemblances between the rituals for the ordinations of deacons and deaconesses.

Let us remind ourselves of these resemblances one more time. First of all, the ordination of the deaconess, like that of the deacon, took place during the eucharistic liturgy (or during the Mass of the catechumens); it took place within the *bema*, or sanctuary, while the ordination of sub-deacons was neither carried out at the altar nor during the Eucharist. Vagaggini thinks it is possible to interpret this in the light of the principle of Simeon of Thessalonica, who, following Theodore of Mopsuestia, said that no ordination was to be carried out at the altar except for the benefit of one who was to serve in a ministry at the altar.[6]

Then there was the use of the formula Ἡ θεία χάρις, which, in the eyes of the ebullient controversialist Pierre Arcudius, constituted such a scandal: he rejected the authenticity of the ritual that had been handed down on account of the use of this phrase. On the other hand, Jacques Goar had no difficulty refuting it when publishing his collection of euchologies.[7] There was also the gesture made by the bishop when presenting the chalice to the deaconess and, finally, there was the conferral of the *orarion*. This last "feature", Vagaggini has commented, "links the deaconess to the deacon, since the diaconal stole is the sign *par excellence* of the deacon and his ministry".[8]

We have already had occasion to see how, closely examined, these re-semblances are actually fallacious.[9] The principle of Simeon of Thessalonica, in whose commentaries the very existence of deaconesses was never mentioned, cannot be invoked here, since all the authors mentioning deaconesses were unanimous in prohibiting to them any ministry at the altar during the liturgy. With respect to the formula Ἡ θεία χάρις, we should note that it was not as exclusively linked to holy orders as has sometimes been believed.[10] Moreover, we really do not know whether it was included in the ritual for the ordination of a deaconess; no euchology

----

[4] E. D. Theodorou, Ἡ χειροτονία ἤ χειροθεσία τῶν διακονισσῶν, in Θεολογία (Athens), 25 (1954): 583–86.

[5] C. Vagaggini, op. cit., pp. 177–85.

[6] Ibid., pp. 181–83; see Chapter 7, 1C, above, n. 32.

[7] P. Arcudius, *Libri VII de concordia Ecclesiae occidentalis et orientalis in septem sacramentorum administratione* (Lutetiae Parisiorum: Cramoisy, 1626), lib. 6, cap. 10, quoted and refuted by J. Goar, *Euchologion* . . . (ed. 1730), pp. 220–22. On the subject of Arcudius himself (1562–1633), see L. Petit, in DTC I, 1923, cols. 1771–73. Cf. Chapter 7, 1C, above.

[8] C. Vagaggini, op. cit., p. 185.

[9] Chapter 7, 1C, above and Chapter 8, 3.

[10] Chapter 7, 1C, above.

has transmitted the phrase. Goar had no trouble reassuring Arcudius on this score.

Similarly, the presentation of the chalice by the bishop was a simple gesture; the deaconess put it right back and did not participate in any way, as did the deacon, in the distribution of Communion under the species of wine. We have also noted how the *orarion* was not reserved exclusively for the deacon; to invoke the canon of Laodicea on this subject, as Vagaggini has done, is totally anachronistic. Subdeacons quickly acquired the habit of wearing the *orarion*, but differently from the way that deacons wore it. And deaconesses, precisely, did not receive it over their shoulders, but rather around their necks with the two ends hanging down in front; in the course of the liturgy they had no occasion whatsoever to make the kinds of proclamations during which a deacon normally held one end of his *orarion* in his hand.

The resemblance between the ordination rituals of the deacon and deaconess, respectively, should not deceive us. As a matter of fact, the various euchologies had already given fair warning that there were significant differences as well as resemblances, and some of them were clearly indicated. Let us remind ourselves of these differences: the deaconess did not genuflect, nor did she rest her head against the altar during her ordination; she did not receive the *rhipidion*. According to Pseudo-Dionysius, as we have indicated, the fact that she was not permitted to genuflect was the sign that her role was not considered to be equivalent to that of the deacon; further, the deacon genuflected on one knee, the priest on two, and these gestures were precisely intended to signify differences of order. If, during her ordination, the deaconess did not rest her head against the altar, it was because, in fact, she received no power pertaining to the altar and, indeed, did not even have access to the altar. The *rhipidion* was conferred in order to enable the deacon to wave it back and forth above the sacred species during the Eucharist; the deaconess did not receive it because she could not serve Mass or even be present at the altar for such a service.

In the Byzantine euchology, there was a yet more profound difference between the ritual for the ordination of a deaconess and that of a deacon. This difference lay in the texts of the prayers that were recited by the bishop at these ordinations. The text for the ordination of a deacon was never used to ordain a deaconess; a very different text was used upon which we have already commented.[11] Finally, we must recall that deaconesses were never given grounds to hope, as were deacons, that they might aspire to a higher degree of ministry. It was not without consider-

[11] Ibid.

able exaggeration, then, that Cipriano Vagaggini brilliantly concluded as follows:

> Everything considered, this is certain, in my opinion: namely, that in the history of the undivided Church, the Byzantine tradition held that the ordination of deaconesses, by its nature and dignity, belonged to the category of bishops, priests and deacons and not to the category of subdeacons and lectors, and even less to that of the other offices and dignities that were ritually instituted outside of the sanctuary.[12]
>
> If what has been said up to now is accepted, the following conclusion must also be admitted: it results theologically, in virtue of the practice of the Church, that women are able to receive a diaconal ordination that, by its nature and dignity, can be assimilated to the order of deacons and not to that of subdeacons or lectors and, even less, to use contemporary terminology, to that of an inferior ministry constituted by means of what today would be styled a simple blessing.[13]

However, this same author added: "It was nevertheless true that in the same Byzantine tradition the liturgical task of deaconesses was much more restricted than was that of male deacons."[14] The fact is, however, that the Byzantine tradition, to the extent that it was a living tradition, did not assign any liturgical role to deaconesses at all, as we have had occasion to verify.

It was precisely in the Eastern regions where deaconesses did exercise a liturgical role in the baptism of women, namely, among the Chaldeans, that the pontificals expressly excluded any ambiguity about the nature of the ordination that deaconesses received: "The bishop prays, putting his hand on her head, but not as for an ordination but rather as for a benediction."[15] We should also remember that, if we can believe the relatively late testimony of Bar Hebraeus, the Syrian Jacobites did not ordain deaconesses in the sanctuary but rather "by the door".[16] Their practice was thus the same as that of the Chaldeans. Finally, if in these Eastern regions certain liturgical roles were confided to a deaconess presiding over a convent of nuns, we have seen that this occurred strictly in cases of substitution caused by the absence of a priest or a deacon, and the role was also limited to celebrating the divine office or distributing Communion apart from Mass.[17]

---

[12] However, the *procheirisis* of the steward or housekeeper was carried out at the altar (Goar, *Euchologion* [1730 edition], p. 232); but it was also true that he was a deacon.

[13] C. Vagaggini, op. cit., p. 188.

[14] Ibid.

[15] Chapter 7, 2, above.

[16] Chapter 8, 2, above.

[17] Chapter 6, 4, above.

We should also recall that only by means of errors in the interpretation of the ancient texts has it been possible to imagine that deaconesses ever fulfilled a role in carrying out the sacramental anointing of the sick.[18] Even where the role of deaconesses in baptisms has been verified, it has also been shown to have been a very limited role: the intervention of a priest was required to effect a laying on of his hand, to begin the baptismal anointing and, especially, to pronounce the baptismal formula itself. Moreover, it must be even more strongly emphasized that deaconesses were never allowed to teach or preach in public. Of course, it is always possible to attribute these kinds of restrictions to some kind of sociological prejudice, but that changes nothing with respect to the facts, and, especially, nothing with respect to the very general nature of the facts: namely, that during all the time when the institution of deaconesses was a living institution, both the discipline and the liturgy of the churches insisted upon a very clear distinction between deacons and deaconesses.

But

3. THE APPRAISAL OF THE THEOLOGIANS

The only theologian in antiquity who treated of deaconesses *ex professo* was St. Epiphanius, and, as we have seen, he did not deal with deaconesses until he had first dealt with subdeacons and lectors.[19] The Greek and Eastern theologians who wrote about the hierarchy and the priesthood in the Middle Ages passed over the subject of deaconesses in silence, since the institution no longer existed. In any case, theologians almost always left to one side the minor orders and concentrated only on the triad of bishops, priests and deacons.[20] The judgments of the Western canonists and theologians, whose texts have been abundantly quoted in this work,[21] might well be rejected, of course, since they had even less direct knowledge of Byzantine and Eastern deaconesses. The same thing is hardly true,

---

[18] Chapter 8, 4, above. C. Vagaggini goes far beyond Bar Hebraeus: "In the ancient Eastern tradition, it appears more than once that among the tasks of the deaconesses was that of administering the sacrament of the sick to women who were ill", op. cit., p. 189.

[19] Chapter 5, 2A, above.

[20] Cf. A. Raes, *Les ordinations dans le Pontifical chaldéen*, OS 5 (1960): 65. On Simeon of Thessalonica and his *De sacris ordinibus*, see Chapter 8, 3, above. Only the *Liber Patrum* (Nestorian) constituted an exception to this. See Chapter 7, 2, above.

[21] Chapter 11, 3 and 4A, above. In the seventeenth century, François Hallier, in *De sacris electionibus et ordinationibus ex antiquo et novo Ecclesiae usu* (1636) (= J. P. Migne, *Theologiae cursus completus*, vol. 24 [1841], cols. 821–54) did not yet have the benefit of sufficient erudition, and hence he remained back in the class of the authors of the Latin Middle Ages when he treated of deaconesses. The same was true of the canonist A. Barbosa, *Collectanea doctorum . . . in ius pontificium*, vol. 5 (Lugduni: Borde, etc. 1656), pp. 350–51.

however, of the scholars of the seventeenth century, for they had studied and commented on the original documents, and they were brought to consider the question of the import and significance of these documents from the point of view of a theology of holy orders. The value of their judgment has a double interest for us. This is true both because it was formulated in serenity (since, in their day, no one dreamed of having deaconesses in actual fact), and because it manifested complete independence from the scholastic tradition.

We may take the case of Jacques Goar, in 1647 editor of the *Euchologion* of the Greeks following the ancient manuscripts. Goar defended the authenticity of the legitimacy of the Byzantine ritual for the ordination of a deaconess against the attacks of Pierre Arcudius, who considered the ritual "heretical" and the practice of it an "abuse". Arcudius stressed the resemblances between this ritual and the ritual for the ordination of a deacon in order to condemn the Greeks. Goar, however, had little trouble pointing out that there were so many differences between the two rituals that there was no possible way of confusing them. He invited Arcudius to examine both rituals more carefully. Then he concluded:

> In illa [ordinatione] diaconum sacramento instructum et promotum, in hac mulierum benedictioni, non autem gratiae vel characteri subiacentem mirabitur: in illa potestas ad sacramentum, saltem ex parte, distribuendum, in hac ad ministeria quaedam solum obeunda facultas traditur; ibi sacramentum conferre, hic caeremonialem tantum consecrationem perficere pontifex intendit; qua igitur ratione eadem est diaconi diaconissaeque creandorum forma, ubi nec somniari potest una et eadem ministri intentio, et ubi verbis diversum ordinationis subiectum, immutatusque etiam ordinationis eiusdem effectus et finis exprimitur?[22]

In 1655, several years after the publication of the *Euchologion* of Goar, Jean Morin dedicated an entire *Exercitatio* of his *Commentarius de sacris Ecclesiae ordinationibus secundum antiquos et recentiores* to the study "*De diaconissis, earum ordinatione et ministeriis secundum Ecclesiae Graecae et Latinae praxim*".[23] After having underlined the resemblances between the Byzantine rituals of the ordination of deacons and deaconesses, respectively, Morin nevertheless concluded: "*Verum non existimant Graeci ista caeremoniarum communicatione ullam mulieribus proprie dictam χειροτονίαν infundi*." He was satisfied on this score, in fact, by the witness of St. Epiphanius and by some remarks of Blastares, and he did not linger further on the subject because,

---

[22] J. Goar, *Euchologion* . . . (1730), pp. 220–21. See also n. 7 to this chapter, above.

[23] J. Morin, *Commentarius de sacris Ecclesiae ordinationibus secundum antiquos et recentiores* (Parisiis: G. Maturas, 1655; 2nd ed. Antuerpiae [= Amstelodami], H. Desbordes, 1695).

as he wrote, "for the last five hundred years" there had not been any deaconesses, either among the Greeks or among the Latins.[24]

In the eighteenth century, Jean Pien (*Pinius*), a Bollandist, prefaced the first volume for September of the *Acta Sanctorum*[25] with a treatise entitled *Tractatus praeliminaris de Ecclesiae diaconissis*. Nothing in this treatise added the slightest detail to the authentic history of deaconesses in the Church except on the subject of the practices of the Carthusian nuns. And Pien reached exactly the same conclusion as had Goar and Morin before him: "*Ex iam dictis sequitur, ut diaconissae ordinem quendam in Ecclesia constituerint, non quidem stricti nominis, seu sacramentalem, sed mere caeremonialem.*"[26]

Certainly we could judge the expression "*consecratio mere caeremonialis*", which we find in the judgments of these three theologians, to be quite inadequate. I myself would not use it, in fact, even to characterize the consecration of virgins in the Latin church, for this kind of ritual was indeed constitutive and did initiate someone into a state of life upon which the Church invoked the Grace of God. We must therefore bear in mind the motive and convictions that have inspired these learned theologians. They believed it imperative to eliminate all confusion that might have arisen owing to the similarity of the rituals between the ordination of a deacon and that of a deaconess.

In the end, in my opinion, the conclusion that must impose itself at the termination of a historical study such as ours, conducted in accordance with the requirements of modern scholarship, is that theologians must strictly guard against trying to prove hypotheses dependent upon only a part of the documentation available, a part taken out of context at that. The complexity of the facts about deaconesses and the proper context of these facts prove to be quite extraordinary. There exists a significant danger of distorting both the facts and the texts whenever one is dealing with them secondhand.[27] It is also very difficult to avoid falling into

---

[24] 1695 edition, pars III, pp. 143–51.

[25] AASS, *Septembris*, vol. I, Anvers (1746; repr., Paris, Palmé, 1868), pp. i–xxviii.

[26] Ibid., p. v, no. 20. For the record, we should note in Vatic. lat. ms. 9029, fols. 304–55, a dossier of lecture notes on the subject of deaconesses, put together by Giuseppe Antonio Reggi, a former librarian of the Conti, who from 1783 to 1800 was the "custodian" of the Vatican Library and who died in 1802. I thank Msgr. Victor Saxer for having called my attention to this dossier. On the subject of G. A. Reggi, see J. Bignami-Odier, *La Bibliothèque Vaticane de Sixte IV a Pie XI*, ST 272 (1973), pp. 190–91.

[27] Thus it was that Philippe Delhaye, for example, in *Rétrospective et prospective des ministères féminins dans l'Eglise, Réflexions à propos d'un livre de M. Gryson*, in *Revue théologique de Louvain* 3 (1972): 55–75, affirmed, among other approximations, with regard to the *Testamentum Domini*: "There is to be found here important feminine ministries as well as an ordination carried out by the laying on of hands" (p. 64). Yet Roger Gryson did not speak

anachronisms when trying to resolve the problems of the present by
reference to the solutions appropriate to a past that is long gone.

For the fact is that the ancient institution of deaconesses, even in its own
time, was encumbered with not a few ambiguities, as we have seen. In my
opinion, if the restoration of the institution of deaconesses were indeed to
be sought after so many centuries, such a restoration itself could only be
fraught with ambiguity. The real importance and efficaciousness of the
role of women in the Church has always been vividly perceived in the
consciousness of the hierarchy and of the faithful as much more broad
than the historical role that deaconesses in fact played. And perhaps a
proposal based on an "archeological" institution might even obscure the
fact that the call to serve the Church is urgently addressed today to *all*
women, especially in the area of the transmission of Faith and works of
charity.

---

about a "laying on of hands", although he did underline the use of the term *"mqimonuto"*,
which he translated as "ordination", following Rahmani and Nau, cf. *Ministère des femmes*, p. 111.

Indices

I. INDEX OF MANUSCRIPTS CITED

2. INDEX OF BIBLICAL REFERENCES

3. INDEX OF ARABIC WORDS

4. INDEX OF ARMENIAN WORDS

5. INDEX OF SYRIAN WORDS

6. INDEX OF GREEK WORDS (partial)

7. INDEX OF SUBJECTS AND PROPER NAMES